BATTLE *of* BRITAIN
THE
FINAL
CURTAIN

BATTLE *of* BRITAIN

THE
FINAL
CURTAIN

1 OCTOBER 1940–31 OCTOBER 1940

DILIP SARKAR
MBE, FRHistS, FRAeS

AIR WORLD

BATTLE OF BRITAIN THE FINAL CURTAIN
1 October 1940–31 October 1940

First published in Great Britain in 2025 by
Air World
An imprint of
Pen & Sword Books Ltd
Yorkshire – Philadelphia

ISBN 978 1 39905 806 3

Typeset by SJmagic DESIGN SERVICES, India.
Printed and bound in the UK by CPI Group (UK) Ltd.

The Publisher's authorised representative in the EU for product safety is Authorised Rep Compliance Ltd., Ground Floor, 71 Lower Baggot Street, Dublin D02 P593, Ireland.
www.arccompliance.com

For a complete list of Pen & Sword titles please contact:

PEN & SWORD BOOKS LTD
George House, Units 12 & 13, Beevor Street, Off Pontefract Road, Barnsley, South Yorkshire, S71 1HN, England
E-mail: enquiries@pen-and-sword.co.uk
Website: www.pen-and-sword.co.uk

or

PEN AND SWORD BOOKS,
1950 Lawrence Road, Havertown, PA 19083, USA
E-mail: uspen-and-sword@casematepublishers.com
Website: www.penandswordbooks.com

MIX
Paper | Supporting
responsible forestry
FSC® C013604

Contents

Foreword

The very presence of my grandfather Hugh Dowding held us siblings in awe when we were young. As family stepped forward to help him out of a London cab, he brushed them off with 'Quite capable of doing it myself!' I remember his displeasure when my younger brother and I left muddy boot tracks across the hall carpet. His wife, Lady Muriel (our 'Auntie Muriel'), told me years later how silly I had been, as he was 'the sweetest thing'.

His son, my father Derek Dowding, was a Battle of Britain Spitfire pilot with 74 Squadron, but as his father Hugh before him, he rarely talked about those tense wartime years. The occasional utterance helped me glimpse his time in the RAF. Through such comments though, and from reading books, I encountered names like Lord Beaverbrook, Adolf Galland, Robert Stanford Tuck, Douglas Bader etc., later having the privilege to meet some of them. I was born after World War Two, but at school in Great Malvern, on our way to the playing fields we walked past a yellowing, flat-tyred Spitfire, parked in an allotment by the railway overpass.

It was with great interest that I first heard about this new Memorial Trust project and Dilip Sarkar's scholarly volumes. It does now seem that in the 2020s, finally, after eighty plus years, emotions have washed thin enough for underlying facts to surface, to be seen with a clearer eye. Indeed, through these present volumes we can now more dispassionately observe both sides of the old arguments and realize that ultimately most people involved were working primarily towards a common aim, that of blocking the tide of fanatical Nazism. Asked nowadays about my grandfather, I sense that history is judging him on his own merits. Both Sir Winston Churchill and King George VI expressed in writing their hopes for his promotion.

My mother called me the family diplomat, but the story of the rivalries around the way Keith Park conducted 11 Group operations still affects me. Our family understanding is that Hugh Dowding strongly believed that all of his group commanders should work and breathe together; he respected in particular the flexibility, skill and judgement of Sir Keith Park. With no political ambition, they put their heads together to hammer out the best way forward, to fashion these British Isles into a resilient, multi-dimensional fortress, able to absorb and respond to the dreadful upcoming German onslaught. Spread your wings, but a wise hawk will hide its talons.

FOREWORD

Presented in Volume 7 with increasingly accurate facts and figures, we can refine our internal vision of that time, even questioning the validity of some of our long-held concepts. The author lays out newly discovered records in vivid and relentless detail, bringing alive the grinding, seemingly endless battles of attrition in, above, and around the Britain of autumn 1940.

Piers Dowding, 3rd Baron of Bentley Priory, BA LTCL,
Professor Emeritus, Patron of RAF Fighter Control Association

Author's Note and Glossary

The aviation-minded reader will notice that I have referred to German Messerschmitt fighters by the abbreviation 'Me' (not 'Bf', which is more technically correct), or simply by their numeric designation, such as '109' or '110'. This not only reads better but is authentic: during the Battle of Britain, Keith Lawrence, a New Zealander, flew Spitfires and once said to me 'To us they were just "Me's", "109s" or "110s", simple, never "Bf".'

In another attempt to preserve accuracy, I have also used the original German, wherever possible, regarding terms associated with the Luftwaffe, such as:

Abwehrkreis	Essentially a defensive circle formation, each aircraft protecting the tail of the other, but which also had an offensive function, because any enemy fighter entering the circle could be attacked.
Bordfunker	Air force radio operator.
Corpo Aereo Italiano	Italian Air Corps.
Eichenlaub	The Oak Leaves, essentially being a Bar to the *Ritterkreuz* (the Knight's Cross of the Iron Cross).
Erprobungsgruppe	Experimental group, in the case of *Erprobungsgruppe* 210, a skilled precision bombing unit.
Experte/Experten	A fighter 'ace'. Ace status, on both sides, was achieved by destroying five enemy aircraft.
Flieger	Pilot.
Fliegerkorps	Air corps.
Freie Hunt	A fighter sweep.
Freie Jagd	Literally 'free hunting'.
Führer	Leader.
General der Jagdflieger	General of Fighter Pilots.
Geschwader	The whole group, usually of three *Gruppen*.
Geschwaderkommodore	The group leader.
Gruppe	A wing, usually of three squadrons.
Gruppen	Wings.
Gruppenkommandeur	Wing commander.
Jagdbomber ('*Jabo*')	Fighter bomber.
Jagdflieger	Fighter pilot.
Jagdgeschwader	Fighter group, abbreviated to JG.

Jagdwaffe	The fighter force.
Jäger	Hunter, in this context a fighter pilot or aircraft.
Jagdfliegerführer ('Jafü')	Chief of fighter aviation of the *Luftflotte* (air fleet).
Kampfflieger	Bomber aircrew.
Kampfgeschwader/	
Kampfgeschwadern	Bomber group, abbreviated to KG.
Kampfgruppe	Combat format.
Kanal	English Channel.
Kanalfront	Front of the English Channel.
Kommandeur	Commander.
Kommando	Commando.
Kommodore	Commodore.
Kriegsmarine	German war navy.
Luftflotte	Air fleet.
Nachtjäger	Night fighter.
Oberkommando der	
Luftwaffe (OKL)	German air force high command.
Oberkommando der	
Marine (OKM)	German naval high command.
Oberkommando der	
Wehrmacht (OKW)	German armed forces high command.
Reich	German Empire.
Reichsluftfahrtministerium	
(RLM)	The German Air Ministry.
Ritterkreuz	The Knight's Cross of the Iron Cross.
Rotte	A pair of fighters, comprising leader and wingman, into which the *Schwarm* broke once battle was joined.
Schwarm	A section of four fighters.
Seelöwe	Sealion, the codename for Adolf Hitler's proposed seaborne invasion of England.
Seenotdienst	Sea rescue service.
Seenotflugkommando	Luftwaffe air sea rescue organisation.
Stab	Staff.
Stabschwarm	Unit of fighters.
Staffel	Squadron.
Staffeln	Squadrons.
Staffelkapitän	Squadron leader.
Stormi	An Italian Air Force wing.
Stuka	The Ju 87 dive bomber.
Wehrmacht	Armed forces.
Zerstörer	Literally 'destroyer', the term used for the Me 110.
Zerstörergeschwader	Destroyer group, abbreviated to ZG.

Each *Geschwader* generally comprised three *Gruppen*, each of three *Staffeln*. Each *Gruppe* is designated by Roman numerals, i.e. III/JG 26 refers to the third *Gruppe* of

Fighter Group (abbreviated 'JG') 26. *Staffeln* are identified by numbers, so 7/JG 26 is the 7th *Staffel* and belongs to III/JG 26.

Rank comparisons may also be useful:

Adjutant	Adjutant
Feldwebel	Sergeant
Gefreiter	Private 1st Class
General	General
Generalfeldmarschall	General Field Marshal
Generaloberst	Colonel General
Grossadmiral	Admiral
Hauptmann	Squadron Leader
Leutnant	Pilot Officer
Major	Wing Commander
Major General	Major General
Oberfeldwebel	Flight Sergeant
Obergefreiter	Aircraftman 1st Class
Oberleutnant	Flight Lieutenant
Oberst	Group Captain
Reichsmarschall	Marshal of the *Reich* (German Empire)
Unteroffizier	Corporal, no aircrew equivalent in Fighter Command

RAF abbreviations:

AA	Anti-aircraft
AAF	Auxiliary Air Force
AASF	Advance Air Striking Force
A&AEE	Aeroplane and Armament Experimental Establishment
AC1	Aircraftman 1st Class
AC2	Aircraftman 2nd Class
AFC	Air Force Cross
AFDU	Air Fighting Development Unit
AHB	Air Historical Branch
AI	Airborne Interception radar
AOC	Air Officer Commanding
AOC-in-C	Air Officer Commanding-in-Chief
ARP	Air Raid Precautions
ASR	Air Sea Rescue
ATA	Air Transport Auxiliary
ATS	Armament Training School
BEF	British Expeditionary Force
CAS	Chief of the Air Staff
CFS	Central Flying School
CGS	Central Gunnery School

CO	Commanding Officer
C-in-C	Commander-in-Chief
DAF	Desert Air Force
DCAS	Deputy Chief Air of the Air Staff
DES	Direct Entry Scheme
DFC	Distinguished Flying Cross
DFM	Distinguished Flying Medal
DSO	Distinguished Service Order
E/A	Enemy Aircraft
EFTS	Elementary Flying Training School
ENSA	Entertainments National Service Association
FAA	Fleet Air Arm
FIU	Fighter Interception Unit
FTS	Flying Training School
GPC	Guinea Pig Club
HE	High Explosive
HF	High Frequency
HQ	Headquarters
ITW	Initial Training Wing
LAC	Leading Aircraftman
LDV	Local Defence Volunteers (Home Guard)
LFB	London Fire Brigade
LFS	London Fire Service
MC	Military Cross
MG	Machine Gun
MO	Medical Officer
MOD	Ministry of Defence
MOI	Ministry of Information
MRAF	Marshal of the Royal Air Force
MSFU	Merchant Ship Fighter Unit
MT	Motor Transport
MTB	Motor Torpedo Boat
NCO	Non-Commissioned Officer
OR	Other Ranks
ORB	Operations Record Book
OTC	Officer Training Corps
OTU	Operational Training Unit
PDC	Personnel Distribution Centre
PDU	Photographic Development Unit
POW	Prisoner of War
PRU	Photographic Reconnaissance Unit
RAAF	Royal Australian Air Force
RAE	Royal Aircraft Establishment
RAF	Royal Air Force
RAFVR	Royal Air Force Volunteer Reserve

RCAF	Royal Canadian Air Force
RDF	Radio Direction Finding
RFS	Reserve Flying School
RN	Royal Navy
RNAS	Royal Navy Air Service
R/T	Radio Telephone
SASO	Senior Air Staff Officer
SHAEF	Supreme Headquarters Allied Expeditionary Force
SMO	Station Medical Officer
SOO	Senior Operations Officer
SSC	Short Service Commission
SSQ	Station Sick Quarters
TAF	Tactical Air Force
UXB	Unexploded Bomb
VC	Victoria Cross
VHF	Very High Frequency
WAAF	Women's Auxiliary Air Force
UAS	University Air Squadron
U/S	Unserviceable
UXB	Unexploded Bomb
WDAF	Western Desert Air Force

Also, 'Angels' refers to height measured in thousands of feet; hence 'Angles 15' means 15,000ft. A 'vector' is a compass course, measured in degrees, a 'bandit' is a confirmed enemy aircraft whilst a 'bogey' and an 'X-Raid' are, as yet, unidentified but potentially hostile radar plots. 'Tally Ho!' was shouted when the enemy were sighted and the leader was ordering an attack. To the Germans, hostile aircraft were 'Indians' and the German fighter pilot's victory cry was 'Horrido'.

Prologue

'The *Führer* still wishes to carry out a landing in England, even in October,
if the air war and weather conditions develop favourably.'

Oberkommando der Marine,
17 September 1940

As that tumultuous year of 1940 advanced towards winter, German bombers ranged widely over England by night – bombarding London in particular and enjoying such mastery of the air that eluded them in daylight. Indeed, by 30 September 1940, the German daylight bombing offensive against Britain had been defeated, although the day fighting, especially between the opposing fighter forces, continued into October – and, indeed, beyond.

Before our daily investigation of this final, official, month of battle continues, we need to review the situation to date.

Firstly, it is important to appreciate that Germany's lightning advance to the Channel coast and the Fall of France in the spring of 1940 was a shock to all involved – not least Hitler and his generals. Suddenly, a unique and unanticipated opportunity in modern history had arisen: the prospect of invading southern England by sea and defeating Britain quickly – and a swift end to the war in Europe was what Hitler needed. The *Führer* respected the British Empire, which he had no wish to dismantle, the war with Britain being a distraction from his avowed intent to invade Russia and expand the Third Reich eastwards. Moreover, Hitler knew full-well what a hazardous undertaking a sea crossing would be, for various reasons, and he did not wish to be committed with a drawn-out war against the British. Moreover, German generals were cautious of a landing and campaign in Britain, whereas, given their shocking success on land and in the air against the arguably unprepared West in May and June 1940, the *Oberkommando der Wehrmacht* (OKW, German high command) was confident of an equally swift victory against Stalin's Russia. On 23 August 1939, however, Nazi Germany and the Soviet Union had entered into a somewhat unholy alliance, namely the Treaty of Non-Aggression between the two politically bipolar states. This diplomatic move, however, gave Hitler a free hand in the West and time to decide how best to eventually deal with Russia – but first the focus had to be on defeating Britain, especially with this unexpected opportunity.

Having come to power in 1933, and after re-building and modernising the *Wehrmacht*, which had been substantially depleted by the Treaty of Versailles of 1919, Hitler's foreign policy had been aggressive – safe in the knowledge that the Western democracies wanted to avoid another war at virtually any cost, for which they were unprepared. Hitler, therefore, played 'brinkmanship', culminating in the Munich Crisis over the Sudetenland in September 1938, to which British Prime Minister Neville Chamberlain, pursuing his policy of appeasing the Nazi dictator, and France's Prime Minister, Édouard Daladier, gave in. This experience would influence Hitler's strategy during the Battle of Britain.

After the evacuation of the BEF from the Continent following the Fall of France, Dover stood just 22 tantalising miles away from German-held Calais. A seaborne invasion, though, was a complex undertaking, for which the *Wehrmacht* was neither equipped or trained, and neither the three services' general staffs or the high command had any experience of such a vast combined operation. Furthermore, the Channel ports, from which such an operation would sail, had all been badly damaged during the fighting to date, and this first needed repairing. Then, barges and other vessels needed converting for troop-carrying purposes and assembled in those ports. All of this would take time, and with the summer advancing, given the unpredictable temperate climate, the clock was already ticking.

So far as the air war over Britain was concerned, after the Dunkirk evacuation there was a lull, whilst both sides re-grouped. Then, on the night of 18/19 June 1940, some seventy He 111 bombers raided targets in eastern England. By day, however, things remained quiet until 2 July 1940, when fighting broke out over British shipping in the Channel. On that day, the OKW informed the *Wehrmacht* that an invasion of Britain would proceed providing certain essential conditions were achieved – foremost amongst these objectives being control of the air. Arguably, then, it was on that date, not 10 July 1940, which was later 'arbitarily' chosen by Air Chief Marshal Sir Hugh C.T. Dowding as the official start date, that the Battle of Britain began. This is because on 2 July 1940 there was a formally stated intention to invade Britain, focussed upon the importance of aerial superiority and thereby aligning air operations with an intention to invade.

Having so far conquered all before them, the Germans were naturally confident of success, Luftwaffe chief *Reichsmarschall* Hermann Göring boasting that with just four or five days of unbroken weather his air force could destroy the RAF. One reason for Göring's over-confidence was not just, though, the Luftwaffe's success to date and his natural arrogance – Luftwaffe air intelligence had failed to understand how Fighter Command and Britain's aerial defences were organised, especially underestimating the advantage of radar, and so the *Reichsmarschall*'s confidence was as misinformed as it was delusional. Whilst at this time Göring, Hitler's deputy, enjoyed his *Führer*'s confidence, Hitler was nonetheless reluctant to order an all-out aerial offensive against Britain. Instead, Hitler preferred defeating Britain through blockade and, better still, forcing new British Prime Minister Winston Churchill to accept surrender terms – preferably without barely a shot being fired, thereby preserving Germany's resources ready for the inevitable assault on Russia. This was why Hitler's default position was to instinctively first explore what had been so successful for him in his previous dealings with Britain: brinkmanship.

The first bombs had fallen from aeroplanes during the First World War, including on Britain, and the Spanish Civil War of the mid-1930s had seen the Basque town of Guernica devasted by Hitler's re-built and modernised Luftwaffe. The bomber, they said, 'would always get through' to deliver 'a knockout blow', and air power doctrine, inspired by the writings of the Italian *General* Giulio Douhet, invested in his theory that bombing civilian populations would cause panic and so reduce the enemy nation's morale as to provoke uprisings, forcing their governments to surrender. Guernica's fate had provided the world a terrifying example of how devastating aerial bombardment could be, giving credence to Douhet's beliefs. Given this backdrop and fear, the subject of bombing attracted the attention of film makers in Britain, including Alexander Korda who, in 1936, the year before Guernica, produced the foreboding and sinister *Things to Come*, based upon a script by H.G. Wells, in which 'Everytown' – which deliberately resembled London – was flattened by hordes of enemy bombers. In 1937, E.V.H. Emmett's *The Gap* was hardly any more optimistic, and June 1939's *The Warning*, intended as an antidote to these doom-laden films and an attempt to increase public confidence in Britain's defences, failed. Then, the world watched the real-time suffering of Warsaw in 1939, and Rotterdam in 1940 – and the Danes surrendered at the very threat of such an air attack.

Another major consideration for the *Führer* was that whilst the United States remained isolated from European events, despite Churchill's best efforts to persuade the Americans to enter the war against Germany, the unrestricted bombing of Britain's civilian population could, Hitler feared, turn American public opinion against Germany and, at worst, bring America into the war on Britain's side. With such palpable fear of bombing to work with, coupled with concerns regarding America, little wonder, then, that Hitler's first option was defeating Britain not through an all-out air war and a seaborne invasion but the brinkmanship of 'air fleet diplomacy'.

On 4 July 1940, *Oberst* Johannes Fink, *Kommodore* of the Do 17 equipped KG 2 *Holzhammer*, based at Cambrai-Épinoy, was appointed *Kanalkampfführer* (Channel battle leader). It was not so much the destruction of shipping and ports involved that were the Luftwaffe's primary objective, though – these targets were more a means to an end, to draw Fighter Command to battle over the sea. The Germans would dictate the time and place of battle, and have the height advantage. It was impossible for Fighter Command to mount standing patrols from dawn to dusk, there simply being insufficient resources to do so, and, even with radar, warning of such attacks was short. The enemy's intention, therefore, was to overwhelm any small formations of fighters patrolling over convoys, then annihilate reinforcing RAF squadrons, which would be met by German fighters sweeping in strength. The adoption of this strategy represented progress, but *Generalfeldmarschall* Albert Kesselring, whose *Luftlotte* 2 would bear the brunt of this fighting, considered that 'The preliminaries to Operation *Seelöwe* [author's note: 'Sealion'], which was to have as its objective the invasion of England, reveal the planlessness of our conduct of the war.' According to Kesselring, the German army was 'reluctant to tackle an operation against Britain', 'the navy flatly opposed to it', whilst Luftwaffe generals, however, 'were more positively minded'.

On 10 July 1940, the most intense aerial fighting to date was seen over the Channel, involving over 100 aircraft – but, importantly, these skirmishes did not represent an all-out aerial offensive against Britain. Certainly the number of RAF fighters destroyed contributed to a longer-term aim, but, given the ever-advancing clock, there is no question that it was now that the bombardment of key inland targets should have begun. Instead, this was a show of strength by Hitler, intended to frighten the British that this mighty air force could and would be unleashed against mainland Britain unless Germany's terms were accepted. Three days later Hitler approved the army's invasion plan. Then, on 16 July 1940, Hitler infamously issued his *'Führer* Directive No. 16', confirming his intention to 'prepare and if necessary to carry out a landing operation' against Britain to 'eliminate the English motherland as a base from which war against Germany can be continued, and, if necessary, occupy her completely.' Many uphold this statement as irrefutable evidence that Hitler now fully intended invasion – he did not; this was escalating brinkmanship, backed up by the 'air fleet diplomacy' of the Channel air fighting.

What all this was building up to, in fact, was Hitler's great speech and gesture of 19 July 1940, his much promoted and publicised 'last appeal to reason'. Hitler, the supreme warlord and victor of the hour, hoped that, as a result of this 'appeal', the world would see him as reasonable for offering the beleaguered British terms in order to end the bloodshed peacefully, whilst concurrently the air operations over the Channel played on the British public's fear of air attack. Winston Churchill, however, was no appeaser, and was also an historian who knew full-well that states that meekly surrender disappear – whilst the spirit of those that go down fighting lives on to see them one day re-born. There was never any chance, therefore, of Churchill accepting Germany's terms, and the British prime minister refused to respond to *Herr* Hitler, so as not to dignify this 'last appeal to reason'. The War Cabinet, however, decided that there should be a response – and that this should be given by Foreign Secretary Lord Halifax. The choice of speaker was significant – and in itself sent a strong message to Hitler. Halifax had previously been an appeaser, but now left Hitler in no doubt that Britain would never accept terms or back down. On 22 July 1940, Halifax made a radio broadcast from London: 'Great Britain Shall Go Forward: We Remain Unmoved by Threats.' Hitler's 'air fleet diplomacy' had failed.

After Halifax's broadcast, Hitler still refused to give the order for an all-out assault on Britain. Still he prevaricated and wasted further precious time. By 31 July 1940, however, it was clear that Hitler now had no choice but to either back down – or put his faith in Göring's Luftwaffe and escalate the air war with a view to launching Operation *Seelöwe*, the proposed seaborne invasion of southern England. On that day, the *Führer* was at the Berghof, his mountain retreat, and conferred with *Generalfeldmarschall* Walther von Brauchitsch, his army chief, and Admiral Erich Raeder, head of the *Kriegsmarine*, informing both of his plan to invade Britain. On the same day, *Reichsmarschall* Göring conferred with his principle air fleet commanders, *Generalfeldmarschall* Albert Kesselring (*Luftflotte* 2) and *Generalfeldmarschall* Hugo Sperrle (*Luftflotte* 3), who were also informed of Hitler's decision. The Luftwaffe was tasked, Göring explained, with destroying the RAF, in two stages: firstly destroying Fighter Command south of the Gloucester – London line, then extending the air offensive northwards until all RAF airfields were under attack. As a prelude to the *Adler Angriff* – 'Attack of the Eagles' – attacks on Channel shipping and targets on Britain's south coast were to substantially increase. The big attack was planned for

12 August 1940, and, given predictions of weather and tides, Hitler gave Göring until 15 September 1940 to achieve his objective.

So the Battle of Britain continued with renewed vigour on the Germans' part, with attacks by day on a broad front, from the Thames Estuary to Portland. Indeed, during this early period the later maligned twin-engined Me 110 heavy fighter performed well, particularly over the 10 Group area of Portland and Weymouth Bay, and, further east, raids on Dover denied the RN's destroyers of the harbours as an important anti-invasion base. Indeed, Fighter Command lost twenty-five pilots killed on 11 August 1940, the highest number in a single day throughout the entire Battle of Britain (the second being nineteen on 27 September 1940). The *Adler Angriff*, however, was delayed owing to unfavourable weather until 13 August 1940, and it was then that the enemy's primary focus became Fighter Command's airfields in south-east England, especially those of 11 Group's defensive ring around London.

On 15 August 1940, *Generalfeldmarschall* Hans-Jürgen Stumpff's *Luftflotte* 5, based in Norway, participated in the greatest Luftwaffe attack of the entire Battle of Britain, along a front from Sunderland in the North East to Portland in the South West. Escorted only by Me 110s, Stumpff's bombers were decimated by 12 and 13 Groups of Fighter Command – astonishing the Germans that Spitfires and Hurricanes could appear in such strength apparently everywhere. Indeed, *Luftflotte* 5 was defeated in that single day, playing no further part in the Battle of Britain.

Much effort, though, was wasted attacking airfields unconnected with Fighter Command, and although some important sector stations, including Kenley, Biggin Hill and Hornchurch, were badly knocked about, all remained operational. All of this, and the failure to prioritise attacks on radar installations, is further demonstrable proof of how poor Luftwaffe air intelligence was. Still, even these successful attacks failed to achieve the required result, which Göring found incomprehensible. Blaming his fighter pilots for heavy bomber losses, the *Reichsmarschall* shackled the Me 109s and 110s closely to the bombers – instead of allowing them the freedom to seek and destroy the defending fighters. The phase also saw the much-vaunted Ju 87 *Stuka* dive-bomber defeated and withdrawn from the battle, and, instead of sticking to the plan and continuing the attack on 11 Group's airfields, Göring changed tack once more. On the RAF side, both squadrons equipped with the Boulton Paul Defiant single-engined, two-man, turret fighter had been decimated and withdrawn from the daylight battle – but thanks to the dynamic Lord Beaverbrook, the minister for aircraft production and the civilian factory workers toiling day and night, the supply of replacement Spitfires and Hurricanes never faltered.

Still reluctant to bomb London, Hitler had reserved the right to order attacks on the British capital for himself – but on the night of 24 August 1940, a navigational error saw German bombs fall on Central London. This was another turning point, because Göring, frustrated with the Luftwaffe's failure to date then decided that the only sure means of provoking Air Chief Marshal Hugh Dowding, Fighter Command's C-in-C, to commit all of his fighters to battle, where they could be destroyed en masse, was to order a massive assault on London. The heavy attacks on the airfields, therefore, ceased. It was not, however, that 11 Group's airfields were so badly hurt that this latest change of tack saved Fighter Command, as the popular narrative speaks to us – all were actually operational – but had the bombardment continued the sector stations may well have been destroyed. The change of strategy, therefore, was undoubtedly significant, giving the airfields respite from continuous attack.

The round the clock bombing of London began on 7 September 1940, and caused great death and destruction, but these attacks were not maintained by day, the Luftwaffe simply lacking the necessary resources. Then, on 15 September 1940, forever celebrated as 'Battle of Britain Day', Luftwaffe aircrews, told that Fighter Command was down to its last handful of fighters, were met by hundreds of Spitfires and Hurricanes over London, shattering their morale. Already, *Luftflotte* 3's bombers had shifted almost exclusively to nocturnal raids, and now it was clear that the skies of south-east England in daylight would continue taking too great a toll of *Luftflotte* 2's *Kampfgeschwadern*. This was, of course, the date by which Hitler had ordered Göring to defeat the RAF, and on which the *Führer* had to make the decision as to whether *Seelöwe* sailed – or not. Yet again, Hitler was indecisive, delaying his decision by a further two days.

Hitler knew, of course, that his *Kriegsmarine* was no match for the RN, and hoped that superior German air power would compensate for this – but owing to faulty intelligence, the OKW and OKL lacked accurate information concerning the RAF's strength and disposition. Consequently, the situation appeared more optimistic for Germany than it actually was, Luftwaffe intelligence reporting what were exaggerated RAF losses. The OKM, however, was under no illusion, and on 17 September 1940, reported that the RAF was 'by no means defeated; on the contrary they are showing increasing activity in their attacks on the Channel ports and in their mounting interference with assembly movements.' On the same day, Hitler finally made his decision: '*Bis auf weitres*' ('until further notice') – *Seelöwe* was 'postponed until further notice'. The OKM, though, made clear that this postponement did 'not mean the final renunciation of *Seelöwe* … The threat to England is to continue. The *Führer* still wishes to carry out a landing in England, even in October, if the air war and weather conditions develop favourably.' It was agreed, therefore, that the last potential date for a landing, given tides and weather, was 8 October 1940. This further push back evidences the fact that Hitler was reluctant to completely abandon the prospect of invading Britain – which is, of course, significant.

The RN, though, remained a great threat: on 18 September 1940 the OKM reported that the British were

> increasingly taking countermeasures … the main units of the Home Fleet are being held in readiness to repel the landing, though the majority of units are still in Western bases. Already a large number of destroyers have been located by air reconnaissance in the southern and southeastern harbours. All available information indicates that the enemy's naval forces are solely occupied with this theatre of operations.

That was not entirely the case, although clearly the Italians' efforts to tie down British naval forces in the Mediterranean theatre was having little effect.

An important, negative, factor from the German air perspective in the ongoing aerial battle was the Me 109 force being disadvantaged due to the single-engined fighter's limited range, constraining freedom of action, given the need to escort slower and more vulnerable bombers – which consumed more precious fuel. By the end of September 1940, the 109 force was also significantly weakened numerically. By 28 September 1940, for example, JG 53 only had 93 aircraft, only 72 of which were serviceable – just 60 per cent of the *Geschwader*'s authorised strength of 124 Me 109s. The German aircraft factories were simply unable to keep pace with the demand for replacement machines – in September 1940, for example, Germany produced 218 single-engined fighters; Britain, on the other hand, whose aircraft industry was under attack and had suffered the virtual destruction of Supermarine on 26 September 1940, manufactured 467 – only 29 less Spitfires and Hurricanes than in July 1940.

Inadequate German provision for the supply of replacement aircraft meant, in simple terms, the level of superiority required to defeat such an opponent as Fighter Command was impossible to achieve. This was partly because such an intense and drawn-out aerial campaign was as unprecedented as it was unanticipated and, therefore, the number of replacement machines now required, and the production facilities required, had not previously been considered. Quite simply, the Luftwaffe lacked the means, in every respect, to destroy the British aircraft industry – in fact, British production figures confirm that the greater the attacks and danger of invasion, the workers' output actually increased. Suffice it to say that on 1 October 1940, the Germans had 275 operational Me 109s – compared to the RAF's 732 serviceable single-engined fighters recorded on 28 September 1940.

In terms of pilots, by 30 September 1940, taking JG 53 as an example, this *Jagdgeschwader* had suffered twenty-four killed or missing; eighteen more were POWs and six had been wounded. In sum, at the start of the battle, in July 1940, JG 53's establishment was 113 pilots, of which 48 (40 per cent) were now out of action. The *Jagdwaffe* had now reached the point whereby it was unable to replace casualties with experienced pilots, these places being filled by increasingly young and inexperienced officer candidates and junior NCOs fresh from flying training schools. Indeed, 30 September 1940 was one of the worst-ever days for the highly successful JG 26: four pilots lost offset against only seven combat claims (and those were inflated as only two can be confirmed).

German flying training programmes lacked urgency, and the majority of pilots trained and available were bomber pilots who could not be swiftly re-trained as fighter pilots. Conversely, RAF Training Command was now working at full stretch, prioritising producing fighter pilots, given the current need – and replacement pilots, although lacking in combat experience, were made available. A great contribution, of course, was made by the influx of free Poles and Czechs, whose English had sufficiently improved for there to be two Polish fighter squadrons and one such Czech squadron operational, in addition to pilots from those two and other occupied nations to be embedded throughout Fighter Command. Of course, RAF pilots enjoyed one advantage over the Luftwaffe, in that if they survived being shot down over Britain, they would soon fight again – whereas Luftwaffe airmen brought down over England faced long years in a prison camp. The flew of replacement pilots, therefore, was an issue for the Luftwaffe, and whilst new RAF pilots, like their German counterparts lacked combat experience, at least long-term, there was no shortage of them.

It is interesting to review the days during the battle to date on which the numbers of RAF fighter pilots killed reached double-figures, many experienced pilots and leaders perishing amongst them:

    8 August 1940: 15
    11 August 1940: 25
    12 August 1940: 10
    15 August 1940: 13
    18 August 1940: 10

    7 September 1940: 13
    11 September 1940: 11
    15 September 1940: 11
    27 September 1940: 19

Traditionally, thanks to the British historian Dr Alfred Price writing in 1979, 18 August 1940 will forevermore be popularly known as 'The Hardest Day', because both sides lost more aircraft than on any other day during the Battle of Britain: '100 aircraft put out of action, 69 of them wrecked or damaged beyond repair. Fighter Command had 73 fighters put out of action, 39 of them wrecked or damaged beyond repair.' From Fighter Command's perspective, however, it was replacement pilots, at that time, which was the issue, not aircraft. That being so, surely 11 August 1940 (see Volume 2, *Battle of Britain: The Breaking Storm, 10 July 1940–12 August 1940*) was the 'Worst Day', and 27 September 1940 (see Volume 6, *Battle of Britain: Daylight Defeat, 18 September 1940–30 September 1940*), a close second in lost pilots, whist 15 August 1940 (see Volume 3, *Battle of Britain: Attack of the Eagles, 13 August 1940–18 August 1940*), not 15 September 1940, saw the greatest number of sorties, by both sides, and fighting on the broadest front throughout the entire battle. The 15 September 1940, however, deserves its place in history as 'Battle of Britain Day', nonetheless, because the events of that day convinced Hitler that Fighter Command was far from beaten and that the Luftwaffe was incapable of achieving control of the air – leading to the postponement of *Seelöwe* two days later.

Despite deficiencies in manpower and aircraft, and even a lack of aircraft suitable for the job in hand, though, there were occasions between 18 September 1940 and 30 September 1940 that the Me 109 pilots demonstrated how lethal they could still be when left free to roam, with the immeasurable advantages of height, sun and surprise. A primary case in point is 27 September 1940, when in the battles over southern England, twenty-six RAF fighters were destroyed and nineteen pilots killed – a day considered by Churchill to be the Battle of Britain's third greatest day. The defending fighters, of course, had the advantage of early warning from RDF, but often that was short, squadrons having insufficient time to reach 20,000ft or more in good time to intercept the enemy on equal terms. 'Spotters' were being used, single Spitfires at high altitude, watching the enemy forming up and able to report back more accurately than radar regarding the size and composition of assembling and approaching raids, but even this could not fundamentally alter the situation. What is enormously significant, however, is that when the Battle of Britain began, Air Vice-Marshal Sir Keith Park responded using small formations of sections, flights or lone squadrons – but as the battle progressed and enemy formations both increased in size and penetrated deeper inland, providing greater opportunities to intercept, he had no qualms about scrambling squadrons in pairs or threes, as wings, to operate together, meeting the enemy in strength. Considering the row that broke in October 1940 over the 12 Group Wing, the long-accepted narrative that Park only ever met the Germans in small formations is yet another myth of the Battle of Britain. Indeed, this will be explored in great detail in this book.

Another thing Air Vice-Marshal Keith Park did was use Spitfire squadrons in pairs, at high altitude, the Spitfire having a far superior performance to the Hurricane at the great heights the Me 109s intruded at. This provided a high-altitude umbrella, up to 30,000ft and sometimes higher still, allowing the Hurricanes to operate lower down and tackle the bombers, which generally approached between 15,000 and 19,000ft. It was a perfect arrangement – and without the Spitfire's high-altitude performance, things could have turned out very differently, because the Me 109s would then always have had the height advantage over Hurricanes. Indeed, *Generalfeldmarschall* Albert Kesselring wrote that 'Only the Spitfires really bothered us', although, as Group Captain Peter Townsend charged, 'The Luftwaffe seemed to be suffering from "Spitfire Snobbery".' There was certainly more kudos attached to shooting down a Spitfire, as evidenced by *Leutnant* Heinz Knocke of I/JG 52:

> The Supermarine Spitfire, because of its manoeuvrability and technical performance, has given the German formations plenty of trouble. '*Achtung* Spitfire!' German pilots have learned to pay particular attention when they hear this warning in their earphones. We consider shooting don a Spitfire to be an outstanding achievement, which is most certainly is.

Suffice it to say, after the events of 15 September 1940, confused and confounded, but still convinced that his Luftwaffe alone could still defeat Britain, Göring turned away from attacking London, by day at least, instead ordering, primarily, attacks on the British aircraft industry. There were successes in this endeavour for the Luftwaffe, notably the great raid on the Bristol Aeroplane Company at Filton on 25 September 1940, and devastation of the Spitfire producing Supermarine factory at Woolston the following day, but this was all too much too late. Moreover, there were heavy losses too; 27 September 1940, for example, saw the Me 110 force suffer particularly losses in fighting over both the south-east and south-west, after which the type played no further significant part in the Battle of Britain. Indeed, by 30 September 1940, the OKL knew that the heavy losses to the bomber force suffered to date by day were unsustainable. This, though, did not end the day fighting, which now moved into yet another phase – that covered by this book, 1 October 1940–31 October 1940. Arguably, though, at the start of the month the daylight Battle of Britain technically remained ongoing – because *Seelöwe* had been postponed but not yet cancelled. The German air operations involved, however, were never going to achieve the necessary conditions for *Seelöwe* to ever sail.

In order to lure Fighter Command to battle with superior numbers of German fighters, Göring had already ordered that one *Staffel* of every *Gruppe*'s three should be converted to fighter-bombers, which would be used at high altitude. This was another decision unpopular with Luftwaffe field commanders, who already lacked insufficient aircraft. There was, though, logic in this. Radar, at the time, could detected the build-up of an approaching enemy formations but was unable to identify the types of aircraft involved. If information from other sources, such as the Observer Corps or 'spotters', being high-flying solo Spitfires, indicated a raid to be a fighter sweep, RAF controllers were content to leave these single-engined aircraft well alone and simply permit the enemy to harmlessly waste fuel. By including bomb-carrying machines in formations of Me 109s, therefore, no enemy incursion could be ignored. Indeed, the first such raid, on 20 September 1940, assumed to be a sweep by Me 109 fighters, had surprised 11 Group when bombs fell in central London, dropped by Me 109s fighter bombers. Such bombing, from high-altitude, was indiscriminate, the objective of which was not the destruction wrought but the extra pressure these operations put Fighter Command under; unable to ignore these incursions, the idea was to lure RAF fighters up to be met by large numbers of Me 109s fighters, which, as ever, held the keys of surprise, height and sun. Throughout October 1940, the number of these fighter-bomber raids, supported by large numbers of high-flying fighters, mainly aimed at London and the south-east, would stretch Fighter Command to the limit. Such high-altitude sorties in unheated and unpressurised cockpits was also physically exhausting, and, as Squadron Leader Geoffrey Wellum DFC remembered, who was an 18-year-old Spitfire pilot in the autumn of 1940, '"Snappers" [author's note: Me 109s] were always active in the Biggin Hill Sector and caused problems.'

Although the main German bombing offensive was now after dark – which was safer for the enemy bomber crews but less accurate than in daylight – at the beginning of October 1940 the OKL ordered that, going forward, daylight bombing operations, in addition to the fighter-bomber attacks, would involve only lone Ju 88s, on occasions when cloud cover permitted, or Ju 88s of up to *Gruppe* strength escorted by many fighters. Such bombing was obviously too light to pave the way for an invasion, but was considered by the enemy as a long-term investment, yielding increasing damage over time to both industrial and domestic property, hamper production and distribution, and lower public morale – and attacks on London by single bombers or formations of fighter bombers would give the capital's inhabitants – already bombed by night – no rest. The aircraft industry too remained an important target: during October 1940, thirty hits would be recorded on aircraft factories against just eight between 7 September 1940 and 30 September 1940.

In sum, the enemy daylight bombers, the Ju 87 *Stuka* dive bomber and Me 110 had been defeated by 30 September 1940. Shifting the main weight of attack to the hours of darkness, then, conserved the enemy bomber force's strength, whilst the day fighters, released from the close-escort role, and fighter bombers, would impose great pressure on Fighter Command by day, which, it was hoped, would substantially reduce Air Chief Marshal Hugh Dowding's resources. Although Operation *Seelöwe* had been postponed on 17 September 1940, as we have seen the project had not yet been abandoned, and an invasion in October had not been ruled out. The Battle of Britain, therefore, remained ongoing.

This, then, is where we are on 1 October 1940, and, in simple terms, how we got here. What follows is the detailed story of the Battle of Britain's 'final curtain'.

The Final Curtain
1 October 1940–31 October 1940

Tuesday, 1 October 1940

October 1940, so far as the Air Ministry would be concerned, would go down in history as the last month of the sixteen-week long Battle of Britain. It was also the month in which the conniving of the 12 Group 'Big Wing' supporters would manifest itself in a completely unnecessary argument and controversy between senior commanders – with far-reaching consequences.

On 1 October 1940, Air Vice-Marshal Keith Park, AOC 11 Group, sent a comprehensive memorandum to all his sector commanders, setting out the conditions when he considered it appropriate to operate wings of three squadrons, and when it was not, and making clear the differences between the Dunkirk air fighting and the Battle of Britain:

1. There is a feeling among pilots in some squadrons that the only way to defeat the enemy raids against this country is to employ our fighter squadrons in wings of three squadrons. The object of this note is to explain why such formations have been used off and on during the past five months, yet have not been made the standard method of grouping our fighter squadrons in home defence fighting.

2. During the operations by 11 Group over France and Belgium, squadrons were originally employed singly. When the enemy opposition strengthened, squadrons were employed in pairs. Moreover, when squadrons could only raise three sections each, they were employed in wings of three squadrons. The conditions were that our squadrons were being operated on a pre-arranged programme and could be allotted to their tasks some hours in advance and were normally collected and despatched from forward aerodromes on the coast. This gave ample time for squadrons to be arranged into pairs of wings, under conditions which do not obtain the defence of this country, when the enemy can and has made four heavy attacks in one day, giving only the minimum warning on each occasion.

3. In spite of the favourable conditions during the operations over France, for the employment of wings of three squadrons, the best

results during the whole week of this operation were obtained by squadrons working in pairs. Whenever possible, two pairs of squadrons patrolled the same restricted area; two at high altitude to engage enemy fighter patrols, and two about 5,000 to 8,000 feet lower to engage the enemy bombers, which in those days did not normally employ close escorts as they were operating over their own territory.

4. Experience in home defence during the last two months' intensive operations has shown that there are many occasions in which the use of wings of three squadrons is quite unsuitable, because of cloud conditions and lack of time, due to short warning of approaching attack.

5. Experience over many weeks has shown that when there are two or more layers of clouds, the squadrons of a wing have great difficulty in assembling above the clouds at a rendezvous, also in maintaining touch after passing through clouds when on patrol. Instead of devoting their time to searching for the enemy, squadrons have frequently had to devote much of their attention to maintaining contact with other squadrons of than a wing of three. Unless the sky is relatively clear of clouds, pairs of squadrons have been more effective in intercepting the enemy.

6. Quite apart from cloud interference, the lack of time due to short warning of the approach of raids frequently renders it inadvisable to detail wings of three squadrons. Experience has shown that it takes much longer to despatch, assemble and climb to operating height a wing of three squadrons than one or even two pairs of squadrons. Frequently wings of three squadrons have been attacked by enemy fighters while still climbing up over their sector aerodromes. It has been found better to have even one strong squadron of our fighters over the enemy than a wing of three climbing up below them, in which attitude they are peculiarly vulnerable to attacks from above.

7. In clear weather when the enemy attack develops in two or three waves, there is often time for the squadrons or sectors in the flank of the attack, e.g. Debden, Northolt, Tangmere, to be despatched as wings of three squadrons to meet the third incoming wave or to sweep across and mop up the retreating enemy bombers and close escort. There is rarely time for London sectors to get wing formations up to the desired height before the enemy reaches important bombing targets, e.g. factories, docks, sector aerodromes.

8. Until we have VHF in all squadrons, it is not practicable for three squadrons of a wing to work on a common R/T frequency; at least that is the considered opinion of the majority of squadron and sector commanders. Pairs of squadrons can and do work

successfully on a common frequency whenever the State of Preparedness in a sector permits. Here again some squadron commanders prefer to be on a separate R/T frequency in order to have better intercommunication with their squadrons.

CONCLUSION

9. As a result of five months' intensive fighting in 11 Group, it is clear that wings of three squadrons are not the most suitable formations under many conditions of TIME and WEATHER. On the whole, squadrons working in pairs have obtained better results in home defence, especially as our practice since July has been to detail two or more pairs of squadrons to intercept raids in massed formation. However, when conditions are favourable, squadrons will continue to be despatched in wings of three, but the only person to decide whether wings or pairs of squadrons should be the Group Controller. He has the complete picture of the enemy's movements on a wide front from Lowestoft to Bournemouth, and must quickly decide whether the time and cloud conditions are suitable for pairs of wing formations. Squadrons must, therefore, continue to study and develop fighting tactics in wings of three squadrons, which will probably become more common in the spring of 1941.

10. Two copies of this note are to be distributed to each fighter squadron, and one copy is to be read by each sector controller.

Three copies of Park's 'note' were also sent to Fighter Command HQ at Bentley Priory. It is a significant document, confirming that Park was willing to use large formations when appropriate, and knew when it was not. For 11 Group, such large formations were unwieldy and took too long to gain height cohesively, and when battle was joined were split up anyway, with inter-squadron communication impossible. Interestingly, however, Park was already looking ahead to 1941, and had identified the three-squadron-strong wing as a useful offensive formation. Again, the note emphasises tactical flexibility – whereas 'Big Wing' exponents Air Vice-Marshal Trafford Leigh-Mallory DSO and Bar, AOC 12 Group, and Air Vice-Marshal Sholto Douglas DFC, the DCAS, argued that three-squadron wings should be standard practice in both defence and offence. As this narrative continues, we will see how this argument developed and ultimately concluded.

During the day, on 1 October 1940, at least sixteen lone German bombers were active from the Thames Estuary to Beachy Head, one of which penetrated as far inland as Croydon, raking the town with machine-gun fire at 06.13 hrs. There were no casualties or any serious damage caused by these nuisance raids. Thus the curtain was raised on the final month of the Battle of Britain.

Although the Me 110s of both *Luftflotten* 2 and 3 had suffered catastrophic losses on 27 September 1940, leading to the type playing little further part in the Battle of Britain, the final curtain had yet to completely fall on Me 110 daylight operations over southern England. On the morning of this day, *Jafü* 3 ordered a fighter sweep of Swanage, for example, comprising, according to *Luftflotte Kommando* 3 intelligence officer *Hauptmann* Genst, forty Me 109s of all three *Gruppen* of JG 2, eight of II/JG 53, and thirty-two Me 110 *Zerstörer*'s of all three *Gruppen* of ZG 26. From the reports of intercepting 10 Group fighter pilots, it also appears, strangely, that at least two FW200 'Condor' four-engined long-range bombers were involved in this operation, although there is no mention of this in Luftwaffe records. The Condors were almost certainly from KG 40, based at Bordeaux-Mérignac and under the control of the *Fliegerführer Atlantik*, which were used for long-range reconnaissance of the North Sea and Atlantic, seeking Allied convoys and reporting their positions to U-boats. What their purpose was on this operation is unknown, but there is no doubt that Condors were involved. Whilst aircraft identification in the heat of battle was frequently incorrect, there can be no mistaking a four-engined Condor.

Flying Officer Bob Doe, Red Leader and commanding 'A' Flight of 238 Squadron, based at Chilbolton in Hampshire, scrambled at 10.39 hrs with orders to meet with 609 Squadron over base, the Spitfires having taken-off from nearby Middle Wallop at 10.35 hrs. Doe reported that 'We patrolled Southampton and intercepted raid over Poole, heading South', the interception occurring at 11.00 hrs and at Angels 17:

> Made beam attack on Me 110s. As we closed I saw two four-engined bombers 1,000 feet below, guarded by about fifteen Me 109s. Fired a one-second burst vertically from 200 yards and saw bullets go into both four-engined aircraft. Broke away to starboard, attacking one of the guarding fighters. E/A broke away and dived. I gave him a five-second burst in dive from astern at 300 yards range and it dived into cloud. I dived after and found E/A flying underneath. Gave another five-second burst from below and behind at 150 yards. Both engines on fire and rear-gunner U/S. E/A turned back towards coast, gave him remainder of ammunition from port beam and it crashed into the sea. No survivors seen. Confirmed by Red 2. Returned to base and landed at 1130 hrs.

Doe claimed a Me 109 destroyed (although no corresponding casualty appears in Luftwaffe records, again casting doubt on the supposed accuracy of the Teutonic reports).

Doe's Red 2 was Pilot Officer Aubrey Covington:

> I attacked, breaking away to left of Me 110, firing full deflection shot, very short burst from full deflection into cockpit at 100 yards, closing. Flames started in cockpit and he started to go down. I followed and saw E/A go straight into the sea. I climbed up into the sun and out to sea and attacked again on a Me 110, firing from almost quarter, short one-second burst from 100–150 yards; broke away and made another quarter attack, firing another short two-second burst from 80–100 yards. Saw also this time flames in cockpit and E/A started to glide down. Did not see anyone

get out. E/A went into dive into sea and on way down gave it another one-second burst from 100 yards ... I climbed again, got fairly high and saw Me 109 coming head-on. Went straight for him and fired several two-second bursts from head-on, and he gave way and his cannon hit my tail and I also had several bullets in front, and aircraft started to spin. It spun right round and as I got out of the spin I was facing him and gave another burst of two-seconds ... from 50–100 yards, head-on and E/A was seen to be going down very slowly. Could not follow him down as there were other E/A about but he must have been considerably damaged by the head-on attacks. Returned to Chilbolton and landed 1130 hrs.

(According to 238 Squadron's ORB and various secondary sources, Covington was shot-up in this engagement, baling out near Sherborne – but that is clearly not actually the case, the bale-out actually occurring on 7 October 1940.)

After this action Covington was credited with the destruction of two Me 110s and a damaged Me 109. According to Luftwaffe records, only one Me 110 was lost, a machine of 3/ZG 26: the pilot, *Leutnant* Artur Scharnhorst, was captured but died of wounds the following day, and his *Bordfunker*, *Obergefreiter* Martin Stephan, was killed in the action.

For some unrecorded reason the Spitfires of 609 Squadron were not involved in this combat, during which 238 Squadron lost a pilot: Sergeant Frederick Sibley, who was shot down over Poole harbour at 11.10 hrs. Having only joined 238 Squadron on 19 August 1940, straight from 6 OTU, the missing man was described as being 'Of stocky build and solid character, Sergeant Sibley was lost before he had found opportunity to show his mettle.' [ORB]. The 26-year-old remains missing.

At 10.25 hrs, Sergeant Peter Burnell-Phillips, a five victory 'ace', had led Yellow Section of 607 Squadron up from Tangmere to patrol base, his numbers two and three being the recently arrived Flying Officer Maurice Kinder, a New Zealander, and the similarly inexperienced Sergeant Leslie Barnes. Yellow Section were then ordered to Swanage, thence to orbit Cowes, and took no part in the subsequent combat.

With RDF indicating the enemy approaching from the south-east, at 10.40 hrs Flight Lieutenant Francis Blackadder DSO scrambled with seven more 607 Squadron Hurricanes with orders to patrol Swanage at 20,000ft. Before Yellow Section could join the rest of the squadron, Blackadder's pilots sighted three German formations approaching, each numbering some twenty aircraft apiece, stepped up from 18,000ft and on the Hurricanes' starboard side. Blackadder put 607 Squadron into

sections line astern and turned to met the lowest enemy formation head-on and from slightly above them. This lower formation of Me 10s, which did not maintain their formation, returned Hurricanes' attacks. Both the enemies and Hurricane formation then broke up and a dogfight ensued, the general enemy formation turning out to sea. [ORB]

At 10.45 hrs, west of The Needles, Pilot Officer Cecil Young, Red 2, set the port engine of a Me 110 alight before having to break away himself upon being attacked by another

110. Young reported having watched the 110 he had hit 'dive down towards the sea, but could not observe final outcome'; he was credited with a 'damaged'.

During Blackadder's head-on charge, however, two of 607 Squadron's pilots were lost: Flight Lieutenant Charles 'Chatty' Bowen, a veteran of the Fall of France, was shot down by a 110 off the Isle of Wight and never seen again, and Sergeant Norman Brumby was similarly killed.

In this action over Poole and off the Isle of Wight, three Hurricane pilots were killed: Sibley of 238 Squadron, and Bowen and Barnes of 607 Squadron. On this occasion, however, the German fighter pilots substantially overclaimed: *Hauptmann* Helmut Wick, *Gruppenkommandeur* of I/JG 2, claimed and was credited with two 'Spitfires' south of Swanage, these being his thirty-fifth and thirty-sixth aerial victories; Spitfires were also claimed in the same area by both *Leutnant* Franz Filby of *Stab* I/JG 2, and *Oberfeldwebel* Rudolf Täschner of 1/JG 2. The Spitfires concerned were those of 602 Squadron, which had scrambled from Westhampnett at 10.41 hrs, to reinforce 607 Squadron and patrol Portsmouth and the Isle of Wight. At 11.00 hrs, when at 23,000ft over St Catherine's Point, 'Blue Section was attacked by eight-ten Me 109s. No casualties were inflicted and fortunately none suffered.' [ORB]. The JG 2 pilots, therefore, had substantially overclaimed.

Hauptmann Karl-Heinz Greisert of *Stab* II/JG 2 and *Unteroffizier* Kurt Bühligen of 6/JG 2 each claimed a Hurricane south of Bournemouth, and *Hauptmann* Johann Schalk, *Kommandeur* of III/ZG 26, also claimed a Hurricane. The eight Me 109 pilots of II/JG 53 who flew this mission made no claims – but back in France there was a portent of things to come: bomb shackles were being fitted to the Me 109s of 8/JG 53, the *Geschwader*'s designated the *Jabo-Staffel* (fighter-bomber squadron), which was strengthened by the arrival of four new but very junior and inexperienced pilots.

The next engagement involved Pilot Officer Harbourne Mackay Stephen DFC of 12 Group's 74 Squadron, which was still repairing at Coltishall prior to another tour in 11 Group. There, the 'Tigers' legendary South African CO, Squadron Leader A.G. 'Sailor' Malan DSO DFC, received replacement pilots and provided further training, in addition to patrolling convoys off the east coast and intercepting prowling enemy bombers and reconnaissance machines. On this occasion, Stephen had been patrolling over the North Sea for over an hour, leading Green Section, when at 13.30 hrs, 15,000ft south-south-east of Cromer, the Spitfire pilot sighted a lone He 111 due north of him and at the same height – obviously seeking British shipping. Perfectly positioned up-sun, Stephen attacked immediately, head on, achieving complete surprise. The enemy bomber then reared up and fell onto its side in a stall turn, briefly returning fire. Stephen saw 'pieces of fuselage break away' and was sure that he had damaged 'if not completely wrecking his port engine as I shot away the port cowling'. The Heinkel then made for cloud 2,000ft below, but the Spitfires were unable to pursue the bomber owing to lack of fuel: upon returning to Coltishall, Stephen had just 10 gallons left, his Green 2 only 9 gallons, and Green 3 only 5 gallons. The He 111 was claimed as damaged.

At 13.05 hrs, in response to RDF warning of an approaching raid, Flight Lieutenant Norman Ryder DFC, Blue 1, led the Spitfires of 41 Squadron up from Hornchurch to patrol the Hornchurch to Rochford line at 28,000ft, the squadron commander and former Olympian Squadron Leader Donald 'Don' Finlay flying Blue 2. Seven minutes later, a fighter sweep by *Jafü* 2, comprising fifty Me 109s, crossed in over Dover, and at 13.10 hrs the 11 Group controller scrambled the Hurricanes of Northolt's 303 (Polish) and 1 (Canadian) Squadrons, which took-off between 13.10 and 13.15 hrs, rendezvousing over the airfield before proceeding to jointly patrol the Kenley – Brooklands line at 20,000ft. Of the Northolt pilots, only Canadian Flight Lieutenant John Kent managed to engage the enemy, at 14.00 hrs over the North Foreland:

> We saw several formations of Me 109s, and several trails in the sky left by them. After being vectored around, we were eventually told that there was a large formation of bombers and fighters to the East of us. We met many E/A, Me 109s, above, on a level, and below us. I saw E/A a long way below us in vics of three, and assumed they were the bombers. Expecting No 1 (Canadian) Squadron to engage the higher fighters, I dived down. On the way I got my sights on some Me 109s in front of me. I saw some tracer pass me, so I turned quickly and found I was all alone. I was being attacked by several Me 109s; I immediately went into a tight circle, and when I straightened out I found about eight Me 109s across my bows at 200 yards, so I opened fire from the beam, and the nearest one went down smoking furiously. I was again attacked, so I did not see what happened to it. I manouvered the enemy off my tail and got to within 300 yards of another Me 109 and raked it from ¾ astern. It went down with the engine in flames.
>
> I was then attacked from behind by two Me's. I rolled and came up underneath them. I fired a burst at one, and he half-rolled away and joined his companions. They then left me alone, and flew off above me in a southerly direction. I followed below them, hoping to entice one or two to come down. I counted thirty-eight of them, which would mean there had been forty at the outset.
>
> After some time I descended below cloud, flying westerly, and came out near Dungeness. I flew along the coast under the cloud in the hope that I might pick up a straggler, but I was unfortunate, so climbed back over cloud and saw one Me 109 flying towards France just over the top of the cloud. I fired two bursts at it but it took cover. I again descended below cloud but saw no more of it.
>
> As I climbed to 12,000 feet on my way back to base, twenty-eight Me 109s passed over me, flying South at 20,000 feet.

Kent was accredited with one Me 109 destroyed and a probable, both over the North Foreland, although there are no corresponding enemy losses to be found.

Thirty of the Me 109s involved on this incursion had flown to Maidstone and Biggin Hill, but no bombs were dropped. Then, at 14.05 hrs, fifty more penetrated to Biggin Hill, followed by another fifty, although the latter formation quickly turned about and withdrew; bombs fell at Lyminge and New Romney. *Major* Adolf Galland, *Kommodore* of JG 26, was leading his Me 109s, escorting the fighter bombers, two of his pilots, namely *Oberleutnant* Walter Schneider, *Staffelkapitän* of 6/JG 26, and

Feldwebel Harry Koch of 5/JG 26, both claiming Hurricanes destroyed at Horsham and Brighton respectively; there were, however, no RAF losses at all arising from this raid. During the withdrawal, 4/JG 26, though, was intercepted by the Spitfires of 41 Squadron; Squadron Leader Donald Finlay engaging at 14.15 hrs, 30,000ft over 'Epsom':

> An Me 109 attacked from below. It dived steeply with smoke pouring out. I still dived after it. During dive I momentarily broke off attack as Green 2 almost collided with me. I continued the attack, firing bursts in the dive until the Me 109 dived into cloud at 4,000 feet, with black smoke pouring out.

Flying Officer Denis Adams, Green 2:

> I saw Blue 2 (Squadron Leader [Donald] Finlay) attacking an Me 109, and being in a position of advantage I attacked also. The enemy dived away and Blue 2 and I followed and fired in my dive. The E/A started to emit black smoke and what looked like glycol. Smoke from the sides and glycol underneath.

This time, there was no mistake: *Unteroffizier* Hans Blunder went in vertically and was killed at Balmer Down, when his machine exploded at Falmer, just inland of Brighton, with such violence that no trace of the pilot was ever found.

For a while, all went quiet, then, at 16.10 hrs, another enemy fighter sweep, comprising seventy Me 109s in three waves, crossed the Kentish coast and flew towards Kenley. Nine Spitfires of 41 Squadron, however, had left Hornchurch at 15.50 hrs to patrol Maidstone, and were vectored to intercept 'Raid 15'. At 16.45 hrs, the Spitfires were at 30,000ft, south of Canterbury, when, according to Flying Officer Tony Lovell, 'about twenty Me 109s and five Me 110s' were sighted:

> Being 500 feet above them, we attacked. I chose a 109 and fired all my ammunition in short bursts into it, starting at 250 yards and closing to fifty yards. At my first burst, white vapour came out from the wing roots on both sides. The 109 continued down into the cloud and home, and having no more ammunition I flew in line astern of this aircraft and noted the following:
>
> a) it had a large 9 on the starboard side.
> b) its fuselage had many bullet holes in it.
>
> It had a cannon in each wing.

'Incidentally, the pilot had his head as far back against the armour plating as possible.'

Although Lovell only claimed the 109 as 'damaged', beyond doubt he was responsible for the destruction of '9+' of 2/JG 51, which crashed at Shadoxhurst, at 16.50 hrs; the pilot, *Unteroffizier* Eduard Gerneth, baled out and was captured unhurt.

Pilot Officer George 'Ben' Bennions of 41 Squadron also claimed a 109 destroyed in this action (having also possibly attacked Gerneth) – but was himself shot down, probably by *Unteroffizier* Josef Keil of 8/JG 3, who claimed a 'Hurricane' south of London, this being the only German combat claim arising from this sweep. A cannon shell exploded in Bennions's cockpit, seriously wounding his right arm and leg, and blinding him in the left eye. Although in shock and bleeding profusely, Bennions baled out, landing safely by parachute, although unconscious, his Spitfire crashing nearby at Alborne. Unfortunately the 27-year-old ace pilot permanently lost the sight in his injured eye, and would spend many months under the care of Sir Archibald McIndoe at the famous burns unit at East Grinstead's Queen Victoria Hospital – where 'Ben' became a founder member of the famed 'Guinea Pig Club'. Unable to resume operational flying, Bennions later served as a fighter controller – and his optical disability did not prevent him becoming, amongst other things, a skilled silversmith post-war. An exceptional fighter pilot with twelve enemy aircraft destroyed to his credit, in addition to others probably destroyed or damaged, perhaps appropriately Bennions's DFC was gazetted the very day he was wounded. The citation read, 'Pilot Officer Bennions has led his section with great distinction. He has destroyed seven enemy aircraft and possibly several others. His determination and coolness have had a splendid influence on his squadron as a whole.'

This skirmish concluded the day fighting on this first day of October 1940.

With the Luftwaffe's switch to high-altitude fighter and fighter-bomber sweeps, using Me 109s, this meant that RDF warning was short, because these raids moved faster than those involving twin-engined bombers. Moreover, RDF was unable to differentiate between a single or twin-engined fighter or fighter-bomber, meaning that every such threat required a reaction. RDF, being only outward looking, was of no help once a raid crossed over the British coast, and these high-flying raids presented difficulties for the Observer Corps, owing the height and cloud, in accurately tracking them. Consequently, towards the end of September 1940, Air Vice-Marshal Keith Park, AOC 11 Group, started using lone Spitfires as 'spotters', flying at high-altitude, in order to provide more accurate information regarding an assembling or approaching raid's composition.

During the day on 1 October 1940, Coastal Command had dropped mines into Lorient harbour, covered naval units operating off Texel, and attacked Cherbourg. Swordfish and Ansons of 812 FAA Squadron swept the Channel and North Sea, and the usual anti-submarine patrols, on one of which a Sunderland of 10 RAAF Squadron inconclusively engaged several Me 110s off Land's End. One coastal aircraft failed to return, a Blenheim of Sumburgh's 248 Squadron, which disappeared whilst on a Norwegian sortie. Poor weather, however, saw Bomber Command scrub all operations except a North Sea sweep by seven Blenheims, which proved uneventful. By night, eighty-eight of Bomber Command's night bombers attacked various targets, including the invasion ports, and industrial targets and marshalling yards in the Netherlands and Germany, Wellingtons successfully bombing both a munitions factory and a power station in Berlin. A 44 Squadron Hampden crashed into the North Sea on its return flight, the crew all reported missing, as was a 9 Squadron Wellington up from Honington, which came down off Lowestoft; Dishforth's 78 Squadron lost a Whitley on the Sterkrade Holten raid, shot down near Arnhem by *Leutnant* Hans-Georg Mangelsdorf of 2/NJG 1, who was cooperating with radar-controlled searchlights – the five-man RAF crew were all killed.

For 504 Squadron at Filton, which had routed the Yate raid over Bristol on 27 September 1940, the day saw quite a result:

> A section of the Bristol Aeroplane Company have collected £39 as a gift to the Squadron in appreciation of their efforts, also another section has sent 2,000 cigarettes. This overwhelming generosity on us is embarrassing as we are all in this, each doing their part. The £39 is to be sent to the RAF Benevolent Fund. [ORB]

Clearly, the RAF's efforts were much appreciated by the public, and on the Home Front, Daily Home Intelligence Reports and Weekly Summaries, kept the Ministry of Information informed of the people's mood and morale. Of 'General Morale', for example, on 1 October 1940, the Daily Summary commented,

> Public confidence in our ability to win the war by hitting Germany harder in the air and repelling invasion stimulated by Bernard Newman's tour (R.I.O. Belfast).
>
> Some jumpiness reported in Exeter but morale not weakened and no direct or indirect sign of defeatism (R.I.O. Bristol).
>
> The more timorous people having gone away, the general attitude seems to have stiffened (Bethnal Green Housing contact).
>
> Book sales have increased lately. The public are on the whole reading light literature or books dealing with such subjects as air warfare, etc. On the other hand, sales of magazines have decreased (Lord Hambleden in a letter).
>
> Of 'reactions to War Experiences': Morale continues excellent, though office workers still go to shelters the moment sirens are sounded (Birmingham).
>
> Public disturbed at Luton over bombing without AA retaliation (Cambridge).
>
> Evacuees in Bath talk of unbelievable destructiveness of bombs in London. Barnstaple is reported to have taken its first bombs very well. Thousands watched routing of enemy planes by British fighters over Bristol. Demand for reprisals growing in Devon; there is said to be a prevalent idea that we refrain from bombing Berlin owing to vested interests in that capital. (Bristol).
>
> Public who have lost their clothes through bombing express anger at their having to rely on charity (WVS. Contact in Marylebone).
>
> Horror at torpedoing of children's evacuee ship appears to be healing breach between England and Eire (South Wales).
>
> Following quotations stated to sum up effect of air raids: 'We are quite unconcerned about it; in fact it would feel quite lonesome if we didn't hear the drone of a plane overhead.'
>
> 'I've sent my forms in for the RAF. I've got a job and we are doing our bit, but I feel I can do more.' (South Wales).

Wednesday, 2 October 1940

By now, after weeks of hard fighting, which included the Battle of France, even *Major* Adolf Galland's highly successful JG 26 was showing signs of exhaustion. The previous day, Galland had led a *Geschwader*-strength mission escorting *Jabos*, and only the day before, 30 September 1940, JG 26 had suffered its worst day, losing four pilots, two being killed, two captured and another wounded. The constant pressure was beginning to tell, not least owing to the Me 109's limited range: some pilots, short of fuel, failed to even reach the French coast, let alone their Pas-de-Calais bases, ending up in the Channel or, at best, forced-landing short of their airfields. For the first time, morale began to suffer – and it was clear that the RAF was still nowhere near defeated. Indeed, in 1996, *Hauptmann* Gerhard Schöpfel, *Kommandeur* of III/JG 26, remarked to this author that 'The objective was beyond our means to accomplish, given the aircraft at our disposal and the changing season, but everything, of course, becomes clear with hindsight.' On the subject of morale, *Oberleutnant* Ulrich Steinhilper of 3/JG 52 commented, 'we began to openly discuss the subject of *Kanalkrankheit* – "Channel Sickness" – ... some court-martials had been instituted for pilots who had returned too frequently with mechanical faults which could not be found by the ground-crews.'

Another problem for the *Jagdwaffe* was *Reichsmarschall* Hermann Göring's insistence that one *Staffel* in every *Jagdgeschwader* become a *Jabo* unit, fitted out to carry a single SC250KG bomb. As previously explained, there was some merit in this, because the fighter bombers meant that fighter sweeps could no longer be ignored, and no longer shackled to closely escorting ponderous bombers, the Me 109s were free to seek and destroy RAF fighters. Nonetheless, the initiative was unpopular with the *Jagdflieger*, and Galland felt especially strongly that lacking sufficient strength to achieve the set task, the loss of a *Staffel* in each *Jagdgeschwader* was an unnecessary drain on already stretched resources – and Galland knew full well that the damage likely to be inflicted by the *Jabos*, with their single bomb, could never affect the outcome of the battle. Galland wrote,

> The fighter-bombers were put into action in so great a hurry that there was hardly any time to give the pilots bombing training, and most of them dropped their first bomb in a raid on London or on other targets in England. We had a total of 250 fighter-bombers. The Me 109 carried a 500lb High Explosive bomb ... No great effect could be achieved with that ... the fighter pilots were 'browned off' with carrying cargo and glad to get rid of their bombs anywhere.
>
> The fighter-bomber raids were carried out in the following way: each *Gruppe* escorted its own bombers. The approach altitude was about 18,000 feet. At the start, we let the fighter-bombers fly in bomber formation, but it was soon apparent that the enemy fighters could concentrate fully on the bombers, so we distributed them in small units throughout the entire formation and thus brought them fairly safe over their target area. This type of raid had no more than nuisance value. The passive behaviour towards enemy fighters, the feeling of inferiority

when we attacked, because of loss of speed, manoeuvrability and rate of climb, added to the unconvincing effect of single bombs scattered over wide areas, combined to ruin the morale of the German fighter pilot, already low because of the type of escorting that had previously had to be undertaken.

On 2 October 1940, Galland's exhausted JG 26 was rested – but clear skies dictated that *Jafü* 2's other *Jagdgeschwader* had a busy day ahead. The previous day, 8/JG 53's Me 109s had been fitted with bomb shackles and designated the 'Pik As' *Geschwader*'s *Jabo* unit. On this day, the *Jabo-Staffel* would fly its first mission, against Biggin Hill. Amongst 8/JG 53's pilot now preparing for this raid was *Oberleutnant* Lothar Siegfried Stronk, a married man and 'Spaniard' who had flown He 111 reconnaissance bombers during the Spanish Civil War. At some future juncture, Stronk, known as 'Siegfried', transferred to fighters, joining 8/JG 53, recording his first aerial victory, a Spitfire, on 7 September 1940, and his second, an Albacore, four days later. Towards the end of September 1940, Stronk had run out of fuel and ditched in the Channel, fortunately being rescued by a *Seenotdienst* floatplane (and regarding which he wrote to a friend on 29 September 1940, see Volume 6, *Battle of Britain: Daylight Defeat, 18 September 1940–30 September 1940*). Now, Stronk was about to cross the '*Kanal*' yet again – this time carrying a 500lb bomb.

As the *Jafü* 2 units busied themselves in readiness for the day's missions, Luftwaffe reconnaissance bombers were active from dawn onwards, and not uncommonly the day's first action involved one of these snoopers. At 08.51 hrs, Blue Section of Westhampnett's 602 Squadron, comprising Flight Lieutenant Robert Findlay Boyd DSO DFC and Bar and Pilot Officer Patrick 'Paddy' Barthropp, scrambled 'to intercept a single raider off Shoreham' [ORB]. Later, Boyd reported that at 09.15 hrs, 10 miles south-east of Selsey Bill, a Ju 88 was sighted at 10,000ft, which both Spitfire pilots attacked, resulting 'in enemy crashing into sea. No survivors.' Both RAF pilots were experienced and clearly saw their quarry crash into the Channel – but, yet again, no such casualty appears in Luftwaffe records, once more calling into question this supposed irrebuttable presumption apparently promoted by Luftwaffe enthusiasts that these records are complete; the evidence, however, proves otherwise.

The morning saw three raids by formations of up to fifty Me 109s, all of these reaching London's Inner Artillery Zone, bombs being dropped on Woolwich, Camberwell, Beckenham and Lewisham, and the coastal locations of Margate, Lympne and Hastings. At 09.10 hrs (BST), all three *Gruppen* of JG 53 took-off, bound for London. The mission would be uneventful for I and II/JG 53 – but III/JG 53 was intercepted by Spitfires.

At 08.55 hrs, 66 Squadron had taken off from Gravesend, patrolling south of London. Amongst the 'Clickety-Click' pilots was Pilot Officer John 'Durex' Kendall, a replacement pilot fresh from OTU who had joined the squadron just two days previously and was now making only his second operational flight. The day before, he had been 'allowed to go up and "have a crack"', but was dismayed 'not to see a thing'.

Of 2 October 1940, however, Kendall wrote that having scrambled,

> [No. 66 Squadron] climbed North to gain height. They informed us from the ground that there were quite a lot of Huns about. As we went up, I clearly remember setting my sights and setting my gun-button to 'Fire'.
>
> We had gained height and were flying South towards the coast when I saw above us some pairs of Me 109s. I was flying 'tail-end Charlie' at the time and was surprised to see the Squadron go into line-astern, as if going into the attack, and turn to starboard and downwards. I then did a very silly thing, as I learned afterwards. I left the Squadron and climbed towards the nearest 109.
>
> As I did so, I kept a keen look-out on all sides for any others who may take a pot at me. They were painted a brown colour on top and all white underneath – I noticed this as I closed on them. As I reached about 32,000 feet I got into range on one chap who was flying across my nose and above me. My sights were not working but I allowed as far as I could for deflection and opened fire. My shots were a bit wide at first, but using my tracer carefully, I could bring the shots to bear on him. After two or three bursts, he suddenly half-rolled to the left and dived. I was, of course, below him, so I throttled back and did the same. As I did so, I was amazed to see that instead of continuing to dive he levelled out, presenting himself as an excellent target: I could see my incendiary bullets hitting all round the cockpit. It gave me a great thrill at the time. Then, suddenly, things began to happen to the Jerry. I couldn't make them out at first, but when the hood flew open and I saw the pilot leave the plane with a stream of white trailing behind, I knew I had got my first Hun – was I thrilled, or was I? I can remember shouting at the top of my voice and feeling very pleased with myself. Then, and not until then, I began to think of looking around for the rest of the chaps, and also to see if there were any other Huns about. The sky was clear, so I dived down to where I hoped I should find the wreckage of my Hun. I came through cloud at about 2,000 feet and saw a column of smoke rising from a hillside, so I went over and investigated.
>
> Yes, it was the wreckage of some machine or other: I hoped it was mine. Anyway, I then flew home very content and full of hat I was going to tell my young brother and the folks at home.

Kendall was the only 66 Squadron pilot to contact the enemy, his combat having occurred at 09.30 hrs, 21,000ft above and 5 miles west of Merstham. The Me 109 pilot concerned was *Oberleutnant* Walter Radlick, *Staffelkapitän* of 9/JG 53, whose parachute failed to open, his body being found at Hookwood Park, and whose fighter crashed at Limpsfield Common.

At 09.20 hrs that morning, 603 Squadron had scrambled from Hornchurch on a 'Defensive Patrol' [ORB]. An hour later, the Spitfires ran into III/JG 53, as the combat reports of Squadron Leader 'Uncle' George Denholm's pilots' described.

Flying Officer John Haig, 'A' Flight, 10.20 hrs, 'Above 8/10 cloud, Croydon area':

> When at about 29,000 feet we sighted about ten Me 109s below. We dived on them and I fired a good burst at one Me 109 as it dived away to port. I saw a white glycol stream just starting to issue from it, and I then broke away and did not see it again. On landing I discovered that Pilot Officer Goldsmith, who was my Number 2 in my Section and just behind me in the attack, saw the Me 109 streaming with glycol and also clouds of black smoke started and it went down out of control.

This 109 was claimed as damaged.

Pilot Officer Henry Matthews, 'A' Flight, 10.20 hrs, 'West of Croydon':

> When patrolling at 28,000 feet, the Squadron was ordered into line astern and dived to the right after enemy, but owing to the difficulty of getting into line astern in the rear section, I climbed to lose speed and sighted for Me 109s to the left. The last one I attacked from close astern. The Me 109 was hit and dived down with smoke and glycol issuing from it. No evasive action was taken or was any attempt made to get away. Height 25,000 feet.

This 109 was claimed as a 'probable'.

Sergeant George Bailey, 'A' Flight, 10.20 hrs, 'five miles south-west of West Malling':

> After meeting E/A at 26,000 feet, I lost height and saw E/A in cloud; after coming through cloud I saw AA fire and the sighted enemy again and opened fire on it from astern, he then began to lose height with a stream of glycol coming from the machine. I followed it to about fifty feet, when I lost sight of it ...

This Me 109 was claimed destroyed at 4,000ft, but although leaking glycol and unlikely to get home, the outcome of the combat actually appears inconclusive.

Flight Lieutenant John Boulter, 'B' Flight, 10.05 hrs (this time is incorrect, it should be 10.20 hrs), 'Above cloud, approximately over Biggin Hill':

> The Squadron went into line astern and dived on a formation of Me 109s. I attacked the rear aircraft of a pair which had become separated from their formation and were climbing. I fired two bursts of approximately two seconds, closing my range. On the second burst it slowed suddenly, pieces flew off both wings, the port wheel dropped down, and white vapour came from underneath the aircraft. I left it to engage the leading aircraft and saw the one I had fired at turn over and go into an inverted dive.

This 109 was claimed as damaged.

Flying Officer Peter Hartas, 'B' Flight, 10.20 hrs, 'Over Biggin Hill':

> When I was on patrol with 603 Squadron, flying at 30,000 feet, we saw two Me 109s about 2,000 feet below us. The CO dived and attacked one of them to my port. I attacked the other, which immediately turned to starboard and dived steeply. I followed it down and fired three bursts of three seconds, and after the second a thin spiral of white smoke started trailing from the enemy aircraft. This grew thicker and was pouring out when I finished my third burst. Almost immediately after the third burst the enemy aircraft turned slowly on its back and dived vertically into the cloud, which was then only about 1,000 feet below. I then broke off, but was through the cloud before recovering from the dive. I came below the clouds immediately over an aerodrome which I assumed to be Biggin Hill. Having circled this once, I saw a fire burning to the south-west. On examination this turned out to be an aircraft on a road.

Again, this Me 109 was claimed as destroyed.

Pilot Officer Ludwik Martel, a Pole, 'B' Flight, 10.20 hrs, 'Over Biggin Hill':

> When on patrol with 603 Squadron I saw an Me 109 coming underneath from the starboard quarter, the Squadron being 1,000 feet below me. I dived and made a stern attack and saw glycol smoke come out of the Me 109, which took evasive action. I then saw two Me 109s in my rear-view mirror, so I half-rolled and dived away.

This Me 109 was claimed as damaged.

In addition to the foregoing, Me 109s were also claimed destroyed by Pilot Officer Brian Carbury DFC, a New Zealander, ('Near Croydon') and Pilot Officer Peter Dexter ('South of Croydon', but unfortunately neither combat report is preserved at The National Archives). Dexter was then shot down himself over Croydon at 10.30 hrs, baling out with a badly wounded leg and receiving treatment at Croydon Hospital. Two pilots of 9/JG 53, *Leutnant* Erich Schmidt and *Unteroffizier* Robert Wolfgarten, claimed two Spitfires destroyed each, although Dexter's was actually the only Spitfire lost in this action, so either German pilot, or even both, could have shot him down.

The *Jabos* of 8/JG 53, however, suffered at the hands of 603 Squadron. It appears fairly certain that Sergeant George Bailey was responsible for shooting down *Oberleutnant* Walter Fiel, whose 109 crash-landed at Addelsted Farm, East Peckham; *Gefreiter* Heinz Zag was also captured having forced landing at Forge Farm, near Goudhurst. The final 8/JG 53 *Jabo* pilot not returning home was *Oberleutnant* Lothar Siegfried Stronk – who was killed, his aircraft crashing at Sutherland Avenue, Biggin Hill. From the incomplete evidence available, with the exception of Fiel, it is impossible to say who shot down who. It is quite possible, however, that Stronk was shot down by either Flight Lieutenant John Boulter or Flying Officer Peter Hartas – or probably both, their combat reports suggesting that they actually attacked the same 109, unaware of the other's presence (as so often happened).

At the time, John Nelson was a pupil at Biggin Hill School:

The day began much the same as most others since the summer holidays had ended. No sooner than we arrived at school than the siren on top of the hose-drying tower behind the Fire Station sounded the warning of an impending air raid. We all filed down the steps to the shelters below what is now a supermarket car park. Afterwards, when the danger had passed, we emerged into the bright afternoon light and our Headmaster, Mr Frank Hicks, indicated to several of us 'usual suspects' to stand over to one side. 'Earlier this morning', he said, 'after being attacked by a Spitfire, a German *Messerschmitt* blew up in the air overhead and pieces have fallen in gardens mostly along the other side of Sutherland Avenue. I'm telling you now that you're not to touch any of it.' A wry smile flickered across his face – some hope!

Dismissed, we all stampeded towards the back gate of the school and out into Sutherland Avenue. My brother, Peter, and I went home, which was immediately opposite the school gate, to get something to eat. Our mother knew what had happened. As she had been alone, she had been very kindly invited to share our neighbours' Anderson Shelter. When a large piece of fuselage crashed down into our Bramley apple tree, the boy of the family, who had left school, asked if he could have it – and she gave it to him. But it was ours. It fell in our garden but he refused to give it back, and never did. It lay in long grass in his garden for years afterwards.

Later on, we joined other boys in Sutherland Avenue on the usual hunt for souvenirs. The pilot, who had almost certainly been killed in the mid-air explosion, had plummeted down into the front garden of 'Lindenwood', where Miss Chew had previously run a small private school. His body, which had been covered over, was taken away on a truck sent out from Biggin Hill airfield. Mrs Win Aldridge, a nurse at the local First Aid Post returning home from duty, had checked and confirmed that the unfortunate pilot was indeed dead, and noted that on his belt was an empty leather holster – perhaps a Luger was not very far away, but we never found it.

Further along was a bungalow called 'Hainault', the temporary residence of the Pastor of Biggin Hill Baptist Chapel, Mr Felmingham. Fortunately, he was not at home when the main part of the aeroplane crashed through the roof of his front bedroom. By the time we got there a soldier, standing on guard at the gate with a rifle and fixed bayonet, told us to keep away. With trees and shrubs in full leaf in the front garden there was not much to see, so we went off searching for bits elsewhere.

That evening a truck load of RAF personnel arrived in Sutherland Avenue and manhandled the tailplane, which had landed in one of the back gardens where the land begins to slope steeply towards The Grove, onto the road. They then cut out the swastikas on both sides, loaded everything onto the truck and drove away.

A day or so later the security situation at 'Hainault' was more relaxed. The guard on duty was a member of the Pioneer Corps, enjoying every minute of it. Someone living close-by had found him an old kitchen chair and, with rifle propped up against the hedge, he sat with a regular supply of tea and biscuits. He still asked us to keep out, but whilst a couple of lads diverted his attention with sweets, Woodbines and an exchange of family photos, the rest of us managed to get to the wreckage from Mr Foxlow's garden next door.

The nose of the aircraft was embedded into the floor of the front bedroom with the remains of a double bed around it. The engine and cockpit rose up at an angle of about 45° towards the rear right-hand corner of the room. Still hanging at a crazy angle on the left-hand side wall was a framed biblical text, closely missed by a thick black streak of engine oil. Overall there was an unusual, sickly-sweet, smell, possibly coming from spilt engine coolant.

There was no time to stand around, the object of the exercise was to get away with as much as possible. There were live machine-gun bullets everywhere and these were quickly harvested, and together with any other loose bits of aeroplane crammed into jacket and trouser pockets. The position of other parts, attached by electrical wiring, were noted and removed on a subsequent visit with wire cutters.

With access to most of the gardens between Sutherland Avenue and The Grove, we were able to find various other bits and pieces. Notable amongst these were the discovery by Colin Martins of the complete instrument panel and the control column lying close together in a wooded area. John Aldridge found the aircraft's First Aid kit, containing phials of morphine which were promptly confiscated by our GP, Dr Mary Pease. The kit also contained a large triangular bandage on which were printed various instructions as to its various uses. John De'ath somehow acquired the cockpit canopy and my own collection, apart from an armoury of bullets, included the radio aerial with porcelain insulator in an aluminium cone, a badly damaged bank of electrical circuit breakers, which I had cut away from the cockpit, and several rectangular black magnets, probably from the generator.

One weekend, all of the souvenirs were collected together and exhibited in John Aldridge's garage. A modest entrance fee was charged and a grand total of nine shillings was collected and donated to the St John's Ambulance.

Whilst Stronk's Me 109's wreckage provided a source of great excitement for Biggin Hill's schoolboys, news of the airman's death was devastating when received in Germany: his wife, Maria, was pregnant and daughter, Erika, would be born on 8 January 1941, never knowing her father.

Returning to the action on 2 October 1940, at 08.40 hrs the Hurricanes of 17 Squadron had scrambled from Debden, joining up with those of 73 Squadron over base to patrol Hornchurch. Ninety minutes later, when returning to base after an uneventful sortie, 17 Squadron was vectored to intercept a lone Do 17. Unfortunately the Hurricanes were already running low on fuel, and Green 2 and Green 3 had no option but to break off the chase: Flying Officer Peter 'Cowboy' Blatchford, a Canadian, forced-landed at Bacton, and Pilot Officer František Fajtl, came down safely near Pulham, both out of fuel. Jack Ross, Green 1, continued, following Blue Section, the leading Hurricanes engaging the Dornier at 10.20 hrs at 1,500ft near Cretingham. Tagging along behind, his fuel stakes critical, Ross saw Flight Lieutenant Alfred Bayne, Blue 1, attack but decided to return to base. En-route, the Do 17 suddenly appeared out of cloud 200 yards in front of Ross, who fired and set the port engine alight. Another Hurricane, which Ross believed to be Pilot Officer Leonard Stevens, Blue 3, then followed the bomber out of the clouds. Ross saw the Do 17 forced-land in a field at Cretingham, and then landed himself, out of petrol, in an adjacent field. This raider, of *Stab* KG 2, which had previously bombed and strafed Colchester, was another expensive loss for the enemy: the crew of four were captured, which included *Oberleutnant* Hans Langer, another *Staffelkapitän*.

There were further fighter-bomber sweeps during the afternoon, bombs falling on Camberwell and Aylesford, and in coastal areas Margate, Dover, Hastings, Eastbourne and Worthing, but there were no interceptions. Despite the losses of III/JG 53, the evening's report on operations by *Fliegerkorps* II reported favourably on the day's events:

> Today, fast, surprise bombing raids were undertaken by fighters. This new offensive tactic presented the enemy with a completely new situation. His reaction was helplessness. The first attack waves were attacked by about thirty Spitfires just short of the target. Then the enemy fighter squadrons were for the most part recalled by ground control. The success was convincing. The last attack wave met no defending fighters after clear signs of exhaustion and lack of will to attack were observed in the previous attacks. Committed as fighter-bombers were fifty-three Me 109s of I/LG 2, eleven of JG 51, two of JG 53, eleven Me 110s of *Erprobungsgruppe* 210.

Much of this, however, was complete nonsense, again evidencing how Luftwaffe intelligence officers told their chief what he wanted to hear, rather than the unpalatable actual facts: and the *Jabo Staffeln*, of course, was Hermann Göring's personal idea. The reality of this first day of what was a new offensive tactic was that four Me 109s had been destroyed against the loss of one Spitfire, the pilot of which was wounded but safe. After the last *Jabos* retired, lone raiders continued prowling about.

At 18.20 hrs, Pilot Officer Irving Smith, a New Zealander, was leading Red Section (two Hurricanes) of 151 Squadron up from Digby, to which 12 Group station the unit had been withdrawn at the end of August 1940 to re-fit, on local flying practice. Being a fully operational pilot, Smith was alerted by the sector controller to the presence of a bandit and ordered to intercept, whilst his Red 2, a replacement pilot, was ordered to 'pancake'. At 5,000ft, 15 miles south-west of Skegness, Smith contacted and attacked a He 111 of 1/KG 53, stopping the bomber's port engine. Some 20 miles out over the North Sea the German began losing height, and the pilot turned back towards England, eventually ditching just 200 yards off Chapel St Leonards. Smith watched the crew climb out and swim ashore, where they were captured by the army.

The final daylight action occurred an hour later, at 19.20 hrs and off the Scottish coast, when Belgian Pilot Officer Baudouin Marie Ghislain de Hemptinne, Sergeant John McConnell and Sergeant Peter Dunning-White, of Dyce's 145 Squadron's 'B' Flight, intercepted a 1/506 He 115 attacking shipping in the Firth of Forth. The Hurricanes promptly shot-up the seaplane, which landed on the water 5 miles south-east of St Kinnaird Head, where the enemy crew swiftly took to their dinghy before being picked up by the RN.

For Coastal Command, it had been another typical day of the usual round of sorties, including photographic reconnaissance sorties to various ports along enemy-held coastlines in Norway and north-west Europe; a night strike was also made against Rotterdam, and the Ems Estuary was mined; a Blackburn Skua of 801 Squadron FAA was lost with its two-man crew off Norway. By day, Bomber Command Blenheims uneventfully swept the North Sea, but by dark the weather was seriously closing in, negatively affecting nocturnal operations. Nonetheless, seventy-four night bombers attacked German shipping, the invasion ports, oil refineries, aerodromes and the docks at Hamburg and Wilhelmshaven, and more mines were dropped. A Blenheim of 105 Squadron failed to return from a raid on Calais, and a Whitley of 58 Squadron was also lost.

On this day, *Oberst* Walter Warlimont, deputy chief of the operations department of the OKW, informed his boss, *Generaloberst* Alfred Jodl, that RAF attacks on the invasion ports were producing 'serious results'. Since 19 September 1940, the invasion fleet had started to disperse for this reason, but this took over a fortnight to implement in practice – and in the meantime the 'Battle of the Barges' continued. The effect of these offensive operations by Bomber Command and Coastal Command were successful, and deserved of due credit. That so much shipping was assembled was indicative of German over-confidence – Hitler would later admit that this 'excessive concentration' was a mistake – and the repeated attacks, by day and night, on the invasion ports was an ever-constant reminder of the Luftwaffe's ongoing failure to achieve aerial superiority.

Weekly Report by Home Intelligence:

Speculation about the future (including peace aims)

Discussion of invasion is receding. It was only mentioned twice in 300 reports on prominent topics of conversation over bookstalls. What talk there is follows the line that 'we are scotching the invasion threat'.

It is a notable fact that 'wherever air raids have intensified, people's attitude to the future has become a short term one.' This applies not only to peace aims, which for the past week have hardly been mentioned at all, but also to the ultimate road to victory. There is still speculation about the unpleasantness, boredom and danger of the coming winter's black-out and bombing, but people seem now to be living from day to day.

One future event is widely desired – reprisals . 'The desire is much stronger than anything shown in the newspapers.' It is the third commonest subject discussed at bookstalls, the only commoner subjects being the London raids and RAF exploits. This feeling also comes out strongly in the postal censorship: 'against the Germans is strongly expressed, and there are many demands for either indiscriminate bombing or invasion of that country'. At the same time, Regional Information Officers record little on the subject – suggesting that the feeling is common mainly among the lower levels of the people, while thinking people are satisfied with the official policy. The strength of the feeling must however be recognised.

Thursday, 3 October 1940

During the night, the weather over England significantly deteriorated, substantially reducing the daylight operations of both sides.

At 07.00 hrs, the Meteorological Office recorded at Birmingham a light north-north-east wind, and a low layer of stratus cloud at 5,700ft. The weather generally was 'dull, rainy and rather cold'. The base of 10/10ths cloud sank to just 500ft, visibility out of it was just 500 yards. Such conditions were completely unsuitable for the high-altitude fighter sweeps and fighter bomber raids of the previous day, but were conducive to nuisance raids by lone Ju 88s targeting airfields and the British aircraft manufacturing industry. Such harassing attacks had been ordered by Hermann Göring himself, and were only to take place in suitable weather, namely cloud, enabling these solo raiders to conceal themselves whilst approaching and withdrawing, and were only to be undertaken by experienced crews having made a detailed study of their intended target. Such incursions, therefore, were the day's main event, and between 06.30 and 12.30 hrs, nine single enemy aircraft crossed the east coast between Yorkshire and Harwich.

According to the War Room Daily Summary, at 09.40 hrs 'ten HE fell near the premises of Shell Mex BP Ltd on the Isle of Gray [sic‚Grain]. The premises are intact but slight damage was done to the railway.' Then, at 10.18 hrs, a single Do 17 dropped eighteen bombs in a low-level attack on Rushden in Northamptonshire, hitting Alfred Street School, a boot factory and the electricity sub-station; the railway was also damaged and traffic suspended. Four adults and six children, including three evacuees, were killed. According to an eyewitness report in the *Rushden Echo & Argus* the following day, 'some British fighters were above the bomber and he thought that it might have dropped its load to make its escape. After the bombs fell the Nazi made off in a London direction with the fighters in pursuit and it seemed certain that he would be brought down.' This, however, was pure propaganda: the Dornier was not intercepted and returned safely to France.

Oberleutnant Siegward Fiebig and his crew of *Stab* I/KG 77, based at Laon, were briefed to attack, according to Luftwaffe intelligence officer *Oberleutnant* Schambak, the 'Hawker assembly plant at Langley'. For *Oberfeldwebel* Erich Goebel, Fiebig's

Bordfunker, it was his first operational flight, but due to the poor visibility over England the Ju 88 crew failed to find their intended target, so sought a suitable alternative. Near St Albans they found the de Havilland works, adjacent to Hatfield aerodrome, Fiebig's subsequent attack scoring direct hits on both a large assembly shed and the technical school, and a sheet metal shop was completely destroyed. The defences were alert, though, and both machine-guns and heavier Bofors anti-aircraft guns opened up on 'Raid 30', hitting both of the bomber's engines, which caught fire. At 11.26 hrs, Fiebig skilfully forced-landed his aircraft at Eastend Green Farm, Hertingfordbury, the crew climbing out of their wrecked Ju 88 just before it burst into flame. Fiebig, Goebel, *Feldwebel* Ruthof and *Unteroffizier* Seifert were all then captured. Navigation for such missions, flying blind in cloud, was a matter of dead reckoning, which was prone to an element of human error and the weather often affecting the practical outcome of theoretical calculations. Indeed, as we will see, Fiebig's was not the only navigational error made by the enemy on this day.

After midday, a succession of raids crossed the coast, the enemy flying between 1,000 and 1,800ft. Amongst these was the Ju 88 of *Leutnant* Otto Bischoff II/KG 77 (6th *Staffel*), which took-off from Laon at 11.10 hrs (continental time), again according to Schambak, tasked with attacking Coventry's Daimler factory, which produced parts for aero-engines. Fourteen Ju 88s of I/LG 1 headed for London between 12.28 and 15.45 hrs (continental time), but cloud obscured the target so not hits were noted.

According to Fighter Command's Daily Intelligence Summary,

> In two cases aircraft penetrated far inland, one flying to Worcester, where bombs were dropped, to Birmingham and Wellingborough which were also bombed. The second crossed the coast at Bawdsey, flying to North Weald and Debden. Bombs were dropped near North Weald from 1,000 feet.

The provincial south-west Midlands city of Worcester, situated some 35 miles south-west of Birmingham, 40 miles south-south-west of Coventry, would have little direct experience of war – but that it was bombed on 3 October 1940 emphasises how the reach of air power had made the Home Front, everywhere, the front line. Straddled across the River Severn, Worcester's primary industries were pottery, light engineering and clothing manufacture. Nonetheless, like everywhere else, Worcester had been scrutinized by Luftwaffe reconnaissance aircraft, and possible targets were coded accordingly: the Worcestershire Regimental barracks at Norton, petrol storage tanks at East Diglis, government buildings at Whittington, and Worcester's *Zivilflugplatz*, or civilian airfield, at Perdiswell – the wartime home of 2 EFTS.

On the west bank of the Severn lies the Worcester suburb of St John's, where, in Bromyard Road, adjacent to the main western railway line, were the premises of the Mining and Engineering Company Limited, commonly known as the MECO. The busy factory manufactured various equipment for the mining industry, and in 1940 was subcontracted by the Air Ministry to produce surge drums for barrage balloons. Early precautions against air attack had been taken, shelters for workers being constructed, and in conjunction with Worcester Corporation the establishment of an auxiliary fire station, and direct landline communication with the city's Guildhall in respect of air raid warnings. At a cost of £800.00, the works had also been camouflaged.

In Worcester, 3 October 1940, had started like any other day. The MECO's office staff had left for lunch at 12.15 hrs, a few men clocking out early, although the main workforce's mealtime was not scheduled until 12.30 hrs – just before which a lone Ju 88 descended from cloud over Worcester and circled above the Cinderella Works and Alley & MacLellan factory in Bromyard Road. Aviation enthusiast and local historian Maurice Jones was in Castle Street, in the city centre and across the river from St John's. As a German bomber passed over low, he recalled, 'People started to get excited and nurses came out of the infirmary to stare. My mother hurried us on down Castle Street and up Loves Grove. We got into the entrance of my grandmother's garden and I saw the bomber flying East over Moor Street.'

Margaret Woodward was 16 and working at her first job as a shorthand typist in the office of the Quality Cleaners, in Bromwich Road, St John's. Hearing the aircraft passing very low overhead, the typists ran out of the office where they heard gunfire. Only a few yards from where they stood, bullets spattered into the ground: 'The markings of the plane were visible and it was very frightening – we rushed back indoors!'

Aviation mad Frank Appleford was playing hide and seek in Swinton Lane woods, St John's, with his friend, Len Appleby, when the Ju 88 suddenly flew over: 'There was a "whoosh", and then it was gone'.

Terry Hulme, aged 12, was playing with school friends in hop fields towards Bransford:

> We heard aero engines, very low, looked up and saw a Ju 88 approaching at 300 feet from a direction of Malvern. It whizzed over us, pooping off a few rounds of machine-gun bullets, so we ran like hell for home, passing an old gent who was walking his dog; when told that the aircraft was German he didn't believe us until he looked up at the bomber and saw the plainly visible black crosses. He then took off at a right rate of knots and left his dog standing! The aircraft was actually so low that the crew were clearly visible in the nose. On reaching home I yelled to mother to take to the Anderson shelter at the bottom of our garden in the Broadway. We were halfway there when a stick of bombs dropped onto the MECO works causing an explosion and a sheet of yellow flame shot up. We were nearly blown over by the blast.

Fred Beechey was standing in Bromyard Road opposite the Garibaldi pub when he suddenly saw the Ju 88

> roar over at about 300 feet with its bomb doors wide open. Members of the Home Guard started shooting small arms fire at the raider, but two bombs tumbled out of the aircraft, hitting the ground in a horizontal attitude. There was a tremendous explosion and windows smashed all around.

Anne Smith had walked her younger brother and a friend along Winchester Avenue to the corner shop in Pitmaston Road. As the Ju 88 passed overheard, Anne thought 'Funny looking plane, funny markings'. She went into the shop and said, 'Can I have a packet of gravy salts, please?', when 'There was a terrific bang and the ground shook'. As Anne Smith ran home with her young charges, the enemy aircraft machine-gunned St John's.

Bessie Cook was standing in the kitchen of her house, the last in Bransford Road, opposite the junction with Watery Lane, and was stirring some custard:

> Suddenly I heard the plane, very low, as it came right over an apple tree outside the window. Although I saw it clearly, it was actually quite a foggy day. Within seconds it had dropped its load. The lock flew off my front door the length of the hall, and a window blew out across a bed in which someone was lying but she was unhurt.

Gordon Doran was at the Royal Albert Orphanage in Henwick Road, and when out in the playground saw

> the aircraft come over very low. It went away then returned. We watched it circle round, then saw the bomb doors open and a bomb fall out of the plane. The plane then came straight at the school, in fact, it may even have clipped the top of some trees in front of the building.

Jessie Wood:

> I was talking to my friend around the back of the house when that plane came over the roof tops in Broadway Grove, flying towards the MECO. I remember it was 1215 hrs and my husband was soon due home for lunch. I'd just gone into the house and put the oven on when there was this almighty bang. I fell to the floor thinking that my house had been hit as we were so close to the back of the factory. I don't think we had any dinner that day!

Lesley Adams was actually working in the MECO's riveting shop:

> Someone shouted 'Jerry gone over!' but we all laughed as we thought it was a leg-pull. He said 'It's true, I've seen the crosses!', so we all went out, and out of the gloom came this aircraft, and true enough there were the big black crosses. Looking up I saw a bomb drop and fall towards us. I shouted 'God, strewth!' and ran. The bomb went through the roof of the assembly shop, bounced through a brick wall and exploded adjacent to MECO Lane and near houses in Happy Land West. There was another which skidded and hit some houses. Then it was absolute chaos. I ran across the railway line and up the embankment. The bomber then opened fire at the factory as it flew on towards Laugherne Brook. Shaken, I then made my way back to the chaos.

23

Having been lofted from such a low altitude, the bombs ricocheted, one SC250KG bomb had crashed into the machine shop, carving its way out through the factory's east wall. Mr Sadler was working in there at the time, and remembers that 'The bomb hit a girder, bounced and shot outside before exploding'. The canteen was demolished and there seven men were killed; three were seriously injured, amongst them the canteen attendant, Doris Tindall, who lost an eye; sixty other civilians suffered minor wounds. Had the attack occurred a few minutes later when the factory en bloc were queuing to clock out, or taking lunch in the canteen, the death toll would have been far greater. Sadly, amongst the seven MECO dead was young Terry Hulme's father, William, a foreman blacksmith and old servant of the company, having moved down from Sheffield during the late 1920s to help start the Worcester firm. Another fatality was Albert Williams, 42 years old, who had lost both legs above the knees when fighting with the Worcestershire Regiment at the Battle of Gheluvelt in 1914. Nevertheless, he became mobile on prosthetic limbs, and even rode a motorcycle, and when the Second World War broke out he was employed at the Austin works in Longbridge; ironically, being unable to get about quickly during air raids, he decided to move to Worcester, where such attacks were less likely.

The second SC250KG bomb narrowly missed the factory, bounced off a concrete base, across Happy Land West, a suburban street, and exploded in adjacent Lambert Road: some 300 houses were damaged in total.

A child, Margaret Wainwright, also tragically lost an eye, standing in the window awaiting her father's arrival home for lunch at the time.

Margaret Woodward, who lived in Bromyard Road, remembers that 'Our window frames were never quite the same fit afterwards, although the criss-crossed sticky tape with which we all covered our windows had saved the glass.'

Sam Beard had been mobilised with the Worcestershire Regiment's 8th Battalion at Upton, and at the time of the Worcester raid was R Company's runner, making daily trips to Worcester:

> On the day in question, I was making my way along Bath Road, back to barracks at Norton, on an army issue bicycle, when at the top of the bank a plane appeared flying low over the river from a direction of Worcester bridge, flying in fact towards the petrol tanks and Aston's timber yard at Digits. I was higher than the plane. Though I could not make out the individual codes under the wing, I most definitely saw what appeared to be the French tricolour on the rudder of that plane. There was a clear view over the Diglis Dock area from some railings in those days, and I tried to get a better look from there as I was confused as to the plane's identity. It next banked further down the river, and headed for Norton. We had a Bren gun put on the keep's tower, another on Whittington Tump, and one on the Cathedral tower. That at the 'Tump' was manned by the Home Guard during the day, and our chaps by night. I heard small arms fire come from a direction of the barracks, and on arrival was told that the plane had machine-gunned the barracks as it passed over.

Another who saw the raider's withdrawal was Wally Brooks, standing in Mill Lane, between Malvern and Guarlford village, and who was stunned to see the Ju 88 flying fast over Guarlford church in a southerly direction: 'It was at about 200 feet and I clearly saw the German markings. I told my dad but he wouldn't believe me!'

Mary Hayton was a ward sister at the Worcester Royal Infirmary (WRI) in Castle Street:

> We saw the plane going over part of the WRI just as I was dishing out the patients' mid-day meal, then soon afterwards 'Bang' and 'Boom!'. Before long, patients were being brought in from St John's. Poor Matron thought more was to come, so had the top floor patients brought down to ground level; it was bedlam! Blast was the biggest trouble, most injuries being to face and eyes, medical and ophthalmic attention being given on admission.

Local resident Bessie Cook remembered, 'Worcester was asleep at the time, but I can tell you it woke us up!'

The *Worcester News & Times* was soon on the scene to report events, in the resulting article Worcester became an unspecified 'Midlands town', the account recorded in a propagandised style typical of the period:

> Women and children machine-gunned.
>
> A few persons were killed and others injured. ARP services were quickly on the scene. The plane is reported to have flown low, estimated by one eye-witness to have been little higher than 300 feet. The Nazi airman followed his bombs with machine-gun bullets spattered near a children's recreation ground where youngsters and women were. A Mrs Cram and a Miss Binns spoke indignantly of German inhumanity. They said they were next to the recreation ground and had to dive into a patch of nettles. Other women also experienced the machine-gunning, some while they were standing in their back gardens. A woman returning home to lunch from the office heard the plane swoop, a man grabbed her arm and flung her beneath a hedge. She had just got down when she heard machine-gun bullets. The forewoman of the business premises hit said a bomb crashed through the roof of her department where nine girls and more than 100 men were working. 'We ran for shelter; there was not the least panic', she said. All the girls were simply marvellous and followed ARP instructions which had been in operation since the war began.

The report also related that ambulances were quickly on the scene, and how a Mr J.R. Hadley, of the Automobile Association patrol, had immediately begun directing traffic until the police took over, the Home Guard and Special Constabulary placing a cordon around the area. Mrs Alice Smith, aged 71, remarked that 'if Hitler thinks he is going to break our spirit this way, he is very much mistaken'. A female eyewitness reported having seen the black crosses and swastika as the plane passed overhead, before she dived into a ditch from where she heard bombs explode and then saw the raider circle the stricken factory before making off.

Ronald Roberts, 16, was a night worker sleeping in a nearby house: the bomb blast threw him out of bed, but he was unhurt. As Roberts delivered his account to the *Worcester News & Times* reporter, a rescue worker shouted, 'Look out!', as tiles fell from the roof above.

Mr Falls helped to remove casualties but stated that there was no panic: 'Everyone was simply marvellous; cool and quite steady.' A boy of 10 was delighted to tell his father that he had actually seen a German plane drop some bombs! Incorrectly, however, the *Worcester News & Times* report describes the raider as a He 111.

Ironically, it had been intended to make the forthcoming weekend one of rest, as all the MECO factory workers and office staff were very tired owing to working long hours. Instead, the weekend ahead became one of the busiest, clearing up debris and covering roofs, to make them waterproof and restore the all-important blackout. Upon learning of the raid, Minister of Aircraft Production Lord Beaverbrook telegrammed the MECO:

WIRE BACK FULL PARTICULARS DEATHS AND INJURIES MAXIMUM EXTENT OF DAMAGE AND ESTIMATED EARLIEST DATE OF CONTINUATION AND PRODUCTION.

To the great credit of all involved, full production resumed at the damaged Worcester site a week later.

Who was responsible for the MECO raid? The answer lies in page three of *Oberleutnant* Schambak's report:

The Ju 88 of I/KG 77 (start at 1110 hrs) under the command of *Leutnant* Bischoff flew to the Coventry factory twice in order to get a good location for the bombs from a height of 50m. During the third approach to the target fire effects were detected in two assembly halls in the northern part of the facility. Attempted photographic confirmation of the attack with a robot camera failed due to fogged-up lens and haze.

Leutnant Otto Bischoff, however, had not attacked 'the Coventry factory' but mistakenly bombed the MECO – such a navigational error being not uncommon, especially given the bad weather. Although mistaken regarding the target, Bischoff's attack was audacious, orbiting Worcester several times in broad daylight, at low level, before successfully attacking the MECO and returning safely to France. As the only time loss of life was caused by bombing in the so-called 'Faithful City', the incident would be well-remembered by survivors and remains indelibly etched into Worcester history and folklore.

Born in Essen on 24 September 1915, Otto Bischoff was an experienced *Kampfflieger*, and would go on to fight in Russia and in the Mediterranean theatre. Having first received both the Iron Cross first and second class, on 15 December

1941 Bischoff was awarded the German Cross in Gold. By 1 April 1942, promoted to *Oberleutnant*, Bischoff was *Staffelkapitän* of 4/KG 77, based at Comiso, Italy, which was heavily engaged in the siege of Malta. At 21.45 hrs that night, however, whilst on a mission to attack Allied shipping in Valletta's Grand Harbour, Bischoff's Ju 88 was intercepted and shot down into the sea by Pilot Officer Oakes and Sergeant Walsh in their 89 Squadron Beaufighter. Bischoff and his crew, namely *Oberfeldwebel* Karl Eppensteiner (navigator/observer), *Unteroffizier* Wilhelm Kruse (*Bordfunker*) and *Oberfeldwebel* Josef Schmidt (air gunner), all remain missing (whether this was the same crew with whom Bischoff attacked Worcester on 3 October 1940 cannot be ascertained). By the time of his death, the 26-year-old *Oberleutnant* Bischoff had flown over 225 combat missions – for which august feat he was posthumously awarded the coveted *Ritterkreuz* on 3 May 1942.

Returning to 3 October 1940, the War Room Daily Summary records that at 14.40 hrs 'The Gas Light and Coke Company was bombed at Banbury ... and production was suspended for four days.' Again according to *Oberleutnant* Schambak, a lone Do 17 was responsible for this raid on 'a gasworks situated 60km NNW of London – most likely at Leighton Buzzard – with ten SC250 bombs. The same crew also attacked an army depot with remaining ten SC250 bombs. The gas works were set alight.' Again, the German crew was incorrect regarding the location attacked, which was actually in Banbury, 35 miles north-west of Leighton Buzzard.

None of these lone raiders were intercepted by Fighter Command, however, owing to the bad weather. No. 10 Group, though, flew thirty-two patrols, in response to thirty-two individual enemy aircraft operating over the Group area, without a glimpse of even one bandit. No. 12 Group HQ recorded the following:

> By day, enemy activity was on a larger scale than usual although for the most part the raids consisted of single aircraft. Weather conditions were ideal for the 'hit and run' raids as there was very low cloud throughout the Group area. After 1330 hrs the weather became worse and no more fighter action was taken.

A rare day, 3 October 1940, one on which there were no interceptions, or aerial combat claims by either side – one of only three such days throughout the entire Battle of Britain (the others being 17 August 1940 and 31 October 1940).

Up in 12 Group, 19 Squadron, based at Duxford's nearby satellite, Fowlmere, received a 'Visit from AOC discussing new tactics, principally against fighter formations and night interception. Many solutions discussed and information of the new devices and ideas being put forward and being developed for night interception.' [ORB].

At that time, H.E. 'Teddy' Morton was a pilot officer working on 'Ops "B"' at Duxford, and remembered,

> The AOC 12 Group and the Duxford Station Commander, Wing Commander [Alfred Basil] 'Woody' Woodhall, were very close, and on the former's many visits to Duxford the pair of them would walk the Station's hangars talking 'shop'. The same loyal and close relationship

existed between 'LM', 'Woody' (the 'Boss Controller'), and [Squadron Leader] Douglas Bader. I know. I was there.

So far as the development of what would soon become known as the 'Big Wing Controversy' was concerned, this triangular relationship between an AOC, a station and a squadron commander would prove significant.

The weather on 3 October 1940 also dictated a quieter day for Coastal Command, fifty-five aircraft of which flew thirty-seven patrols and offensive operations, during which a Hudson inconclusively engaged two He 115s off Great Yarmouth, and the pilot and observer of a Blenheim were both wounded in combat with a Do 215 off Sumburgh, forcing them to break away. Bomber Command despatched six Blenheims to sweep the North Sea, but most reconnaissance sorties were abandoned because of the weather. Shipping was attacked off Dunkirk, without result, and four Blenheims, unable to locate their intended oil targets, bombed Rotterdam, Heusen and a factory at Wesel. All night operations were scrubbed, and neither Coastal Command or Bomber Command suffered any casualties.

Weekly Report by Home Intelligence:

> The presence or absence of an AA barrage and obvious fighter defences contributes much to the attitude to bombing adopted by the public. A report from Luton says, 'It is the dropping of bombs without any retaliation by gunfire which is getting on people's nerves; one woman down from London told me she felt far safer in London with the guns going off than she does here "hearing German planes come and go as they please".'
>
> Again from Bristol: 'A large scale air-battle over Bristol had a remarkably stimulating effect on the thousands who watched the enemy planes being routed by our fighters.'
>
> From Edinburgh comes the following report: 'Edinburgh has had raids by single bombers during the last two nights, and many are still unaware of the difficulties in dealing with night raiders. The absence of AA fire is commented on with indignation. Parents are alarmed at what they consider to be a failure to sound warnings in time (the night before last there was no warning, and last night the warning followed a few minutes after a bomb). It might be wise to make a special explanatory statement on the comparative absence of AA fire and fighters to the Scottish public, which has so far suffered comparatively little.'

The increasing barrage in London is universally welcomed, and some actually complained of insomnia on Sunday night when both barrage and bombs were missing.

Friday, 4 October 1940

With the weather only a little improved, dawn saw the day ahead featuring continued nuisance raids by lone aircraft or small formations. Most sorties involved reconnoitring convoys, although London was under a red warning for five hours, though fortunately little damage arose.

The first action of daylight occurred at 09.40 hrs and involved Yellow Section of Biggin Hill's 92 Squadron, the two unknown Spitfire pilots having taken off at 09.05 hrs to patrol Deal. There, a Do 17 was intercepted and damaged before it, no doubt, slipped away into the still prevalent cloud.

The Hurricanes of 257 Squadron were scrambled to patrol their Martlesham Heath base at 08.00 hrs, but after nothing was seen ordered to land forty minutes later. Then, at 09.48 hrs, the squadron commander, Flight Lieutenant Robert 'Bob' Stanford Tuck DFC took-off alone to intercept an X-Raid:

> After being given various vectors was in the vicinity of Southwold at 5,000 feet, heading North. I was then informed by the ground station that one bandit was North of me, heading East. I then climbed through cloud, and just as I was clear of it, at 7,000 feet I sighted one Ju 88, about 100 yards in front of me and 200 feet higher. I got in a good surprise attack from below and on the beam and think I killed most of the crew. The E/A continued East but in a steady dive. I expended the rest of my ammunition on it and not one shot was fired at me. I then formated on his starboard side and could see no sign of life left inside it. I broke away from him at 500 feet and the E/A continued on down and hit the water and exploded. I circled around for about five minutes but none of the crew appeared on the surface of the water so I returned and landed Martlesham.

It was a good day for 'Lucky' Tuck: back at base the news awaited that he was 'appointed to the paid rank of squadron leader' [ORB]. The Ju 88 Tuck had destroyed was from I/KG 77, based at Laon and which had lost an aircraft attacking Hatfield the previous day. Tuck was right: the crew were all killed.

At Kenley, 501 Squadron noted that the weather consisted of '10/10ths cloud at 3,000 feet. Rain.' [ORB]. Two aircraft were ordered off to intercept a bandit over Kenley at 07.05 hrs, then vectored to the East Kent area and one of these aircraft patrolled a convoy off Deal; after an uneventful sortie both Hurricanes landed at 08.50 hrs. At 11.08 hrs, Flight Lieutenant Eustace 'Gus' Holden DFC and Pilot Officer Kenneth 'Ken' ('Mac') MacKenzie DFC scrambled to patrol base below cloud; at 11.30 hrs, south of Kenley the pair intercepted and damaged a Ju 88 which also escaped into the gloom.

From RAF Croydon, 605 Squadron also flew patrols in pairs. At 12.15 hrs, Flight Lieutenant Christopher 'Bunny' Currant and Pilot Officer John Milne, a Canadian, caught one of the lone Ju 88 intruders, a machine of 6/LG 1, off Dungeness, which they promptly shot down into the Channel; the enemy crew were all lost.

By 13.45 hrs, however, the weather was once more closing in and would worsen as dusk approached. No. 605 Squadron's Flight Lieutenant Ian James Muirhead DFC and Sergeant Leslie Ralls 'met a He 111 near Rye with a huge bomb twelve feet long and two feet in diameter strung about one foot below the centre of its undercarriage.

The bomb was dropped near Rye, in a cloud.' [ORB]. By then, the low-lying cloud and fog prevented the final patrolling pair returning to Croydon, Sergeant Eric Wright forced-landing at Gatwick whilst Pilot Officer Charles English landed in a field near Oxted, slightly damaging his Hurricane, but was unhurt. Similarly, Flying Officer Denys Jones and Sergeant James 'Ginger' Lacey DFM of Kenley's 501 Squadron also damaged their aircraft in forced-landings owing to the weather preventing them regaining Kenley.

Further west, off Beachy Head, at 12.45 hrs Sergeant Peter Burnell-Phillips and Sergeant Leslie Barnes of Tangmere's 607 Squadron were at 18,000ft when a 'He 111 [sic]' was sighted breaking cloud, above and to starboard. Following the raider into thinnish cloud, the Hurricanes attacked, both pilots hitting the bomber, which went into a steep spiral dive, disappearing into thick cloud; it was shared as probably destroyed. Forty-five minutes later, Flight Lieutenant Francis Blackadder, commanding 'A' Flight of 607 Squadron, was patrolling off Beachy Head with Pilot Officer Michael Ingle-Finch at 15,000ft when informed that a bandit was crossing the coast at 10,000ft. Blackadder, Red 1, sighted a 'He 111 [sic]' flying south through a gap in the cloud; the Hurricanes went into line astern and attacked, after white smoke streamed from the bomber's starboard engine as it disappeared into cloud – when RDF plots ceased. Neither raider intercepted by 607 Squadron's pilots were 'He 111s' – both were Ju 88s, several of which returned to France with combat damage.

So far, Fighter Command had fared well, managing to intercept some of the lone raiders without loss. Unfortunately, the final daylight combat would result in a sad loss for 66 Squadron.

At 15.00 hrs, Flight Lieutenant Kenneth Gillies, commanding 'A' Flight of 'Clickety-Click', took-off from Gravesend with Pilot Officer Hugh Heron in search of a bandit. Climbing above cloud to 13,000ft, a He 111 was sighted in the area of Hastings/Dungeness, which the Spitfires chased into cloud and attacked. Gillies then shouted up on the R/T that he had to land; no reason was given but this was presumably due to having been hit by the bomber's return fire or perhaps a technical malfunction. Either way, nothing was heard of Gillies until 21 October 1940 when his body washed ashore at Covehithe. From Great Crosby in Lancashire, Gillies worked in the insurance business before taking a Short Service Commission in the RAF during 1936. By the year's end he had successfully completed flying training and joined 66 Squadron at Duxford, flying Gloster Gauntlets. Later flying Blenheims with 245 Squadron, on 7 May 1940, by which time 66 Squadron was Spitfire-equipped, Gillies returned to 'Clickety-Click' and made his first combat claims just days later when in action over the French coast. On 7 September 1940, Gillies took over 'A' Flight, continuing to record combat successes, his final score standing at two and seven shared destroyed, two and one shared probable, four and one shared damaged. This was exactly the kind of experienced fighter pilot and leader that Fighter Command could still ill-afford to lose. As Pilot Officer John Kendall wrote of his missing Flight Commander, 'a very fine chap he was too, and one of the best shots in the RAF, also. If he had lived, he would most probably be a DSO, DFC "type".'

During the day, Coastal Command flew its usual round of route patrols, an Anson of 500 Squadron escorting a convoy off Southwold seeing off a Ju 88. At 12.35 hrs, two

42 Squadron Beauforts, detached to Thorney Island, took-off, carrying torpedoes, to patrol Ostend-Ijmuiden, seeking enemy shipping. Flying Officer A.C. Triptree and crew returned at 15.45 hrs, reporting,

> Owing to lack of cloud cover at low altitude, started to climb towards higher layer. At 9,000 feet was attacked by four Me 109s. AA opposition from shore. Dived to the sea, and shook off E/A. Returned to base with hydraulics shot away. Jettisoned torpedo in Thorney Creek, and forced-landed without undercarriage on aerodrome.

The other Beaufort, flown by Pilot Officer F.D. Flinn, failed to return, however – shot down by *Oberleutnant* Ulrich Steinhilper of 3/JG 52. The following day, the victorious young German pilot described the action in a letter to his mother:

> Yesterday was more luck than anything else. We just returned home from an escort when a multi-engined aircraft was reported over Calais. Everybody started searching and apparently I saw him first. He had already turned back towards Dover when I pushed Yellow 2 to her limit but I soon closed on him. Right away he unloaded his bombs into the sea and then waggled his wings ... Normally, only our bombers did this and it meant 'Don't shoot – I'm one of yours!'
>
> 'Well,' I thought, 'I can see for myself that you're not one of ours, so why waggle your wings?' To resolve this I fired a long burst from right to left, the tracer making it apparent to the pilot that the bomber was being fired upon. At this time I realised that in spite of the fact that I'd slowed down he was still slowing, almost gliding. Now it dawned on me: he planned to ditch without a fight. Therefore, I stayed with him in case he changed his mind.
>
> Unfortunately my *Rottenflieger* hadn't read the situation in the same way and fired once more, but without causing significant damage. The pilot put his Blenheim [*sic*] nicely into the water and we watched as one of the crew immediately appeared on the wing with the yellow dinghy and inflated it as the other two appeared and stepped into it as the aircraft sank. All of this happened just 10km from our coast and I called up the *Seenotfleugzeug* and summoned help. I felt really sorry for these boys, sitting down there, waving. In just twenty minutes they were sat in a rescue boat and were prisoners. One of them is badly wounded and is in hospital somewhere close-by. If I get the opportunity I am going to visit him.

Pilot Officer F.D. Flinn and his three-man crew would see the war out in captivity; it was Steinhilper's fifth aerial victory, making him officially an ace.

Despite the bad weather, thirty 2 Group Blenheims were sent, unescorted, to hit targets in Germany. Most were forced to abort the operation but one managed to bomb its intended target whilst other bombed secondary targets of opportunity. Six more

Blenheims uneventfully swept the North Sea; there were no casualties and all nocturnal operations were scrubbed once more.

Daily Home Intelligence Report:

> Public seeing land mines dropped by parachute mistake them for parachutists and rush towards them with dire results. Immediate announcement asked for.
>
> Army fretting against inaction; all praise and glory going to RAF. Air raid near Belfast welcomed by troops as a diversion. Complaints about food at Carrickfergus and Victoria Barracks. Great appreciation of efforts of YMCA. Much praise of camps at Tenby and St. Athan. One gets impression Irish do not get on as well with English as with Scotch and Welsh. New aerodrome building at Magheragall and balloon barrage at Belfast are commented on.

Saturday, 5 October 1940

On this day, Air Vice-Marshal Keith Park circulated an interesting note to all fighter squadrons in 11 Group, with instructions that this memorandum also be shared with incoming units:

1. The opinion has recently been expressed that a wing formation should not be led out of parachute dropping distance from land. It would appear that this attitude of mind, which is quite new, regarding flying by aircraft of Fighter Command over the sea may have been induced by the fact that during recent months we have been forced to fight a defensive battle over our own territory.

2. This is, however, quite a passing phase, during which the enemy has attempted to obtain aerial superiority over this country and to carry out mass bombing attacks by day, in the course of which he has been severely handled and has suffered very heavy losses. We must now look forward, perhaps quite soon, to such improvement in the air situation that we shall once more take the offensive in the air and put strong formations over the Channel and later over the enemy's coastal aerodromes to shoot him down as he assembles and climbs up, in the same way as he has recently done over SE England.

3. It is, therefore, most important that all squadrons and pilots should realise that their duties will occasionally take them over the sea, even though at present we do not normally pursue the enemy more than fifteen miles to sea. Moreover, the improved arrangements for the rescue of pilots who have fallen into the water should enable a much higher percentage of rescues to be made than was the case during the Dunkirk and subsequent operations – such as those over Cherbourg.

4. Finally, it is pointed out that were the practice to be followed of only flying so as to be out of parachute dropping distance of the sea, a north-westerly wind of 30 mph would prevent our aircraft at 21,000 feet from flying much further south-east than Ashford, for example; a parachutist from that height takes about seventeen minutes to descend to earth.

This note is also significant because it confirms that, with the invasion crisis having passed, Park was looking ahead, aggressively, keen to take the war across the Channel to the Germans and recognising that to do so 'strong formations' were required. Indeed, Park had already done this during Operation Dynamo, when sending five squadrons together, in convoy, to operate over the French coast. Again, this indicates flexibility in thought – not the rejection of wing tactics many previous commentators have wrongly assumed; indeed, as previously evidenced, 11 Group was already using wings. During the time of crisis, however, these were simply impractical, owing to the number of incoming raids, requiring a rapid and flexible response. During this current phase of the Battle of Britain, though, the enemy's tactics of high-altitude fighter sweeps and unpredictable fighter-bomber attacks dictated a different response. Because these fast-moving German formations meant less warning was given by RDF, it became necessary for 11 Group to introduce standing patrols of a pair of squadrons over the Maidstone line. Immediately an incoming raid was detected, these airborne squadrons would climb to 30,000ft, there to engage the enemy's high-flying fighter screen and thereby cover additional friendly squadrons scrambling to meet the threat. This required a much higher state of daytime preparedness throughout 11 Group, the standing patrols increasing the amount of operational flying by Park's squadrons to forty-five to sixty hours per day.

With the slightly improved, 5 October 1940 would see a resumption of the enemy's fighter sweeps and nuisance raids directed at London, the aircraft industry, and Southampton. Once more, the *Luftflotte* 2 daily operational plan involved *Erprobungsgruppe* 210, so roughly handled over the West Country on 27 September 1940, two *Staffeln* of which flew to operate from Calais-Marck airfield, landing at 09.45 hrs (continental time). The day ahead would prove another significant day in the unit's history – but again for the wrong reasons.

Throughout the morning, enemy aircraft active over southern England included six Ju 88s of KG 77, which headed for London, Dungeness, Bexhill, Tunbridge Wells, Brighton and Hastings (although the sixth raider aborted owing to a cloudless sky). Similarly, a II/KG 76 Ju 88 briefed to attack the Hawker factory at Brooklands also abandoned that mission due to unfavourable weather, instead also attacking the coastal town of Bexhill. By the afternoon, however, 10/10ths cloud over Cornwall prevented a Ju 88 of 3/(F)121 photographing the airfield at St Eval, so Plymouth was visited instead, where a battleship and two cruisers were noted at anchor. A 2/(F) 123 Ju 88 returned with details of a small convoy off Plymouth, heading west, but a Me 110 of the same unit found no shipping in the Channel to report. Typically, the day's first combats involved interceptions of these marauders.

The first of these combats involved Yellow Section of 253 Squadron, Pilot Officer Alan Corkett, Yellow 1, and Sergeant Ernest Kee, Yellow 2, having taken-off to patrol base at 07.30 hrs. When at 5,000ft and whilst climbing to their allotted patrol altitude of Angels 13, the Hurricane pilots were advised by Kenley control of a bandit approaching the aerodrome from the east. Immediately, Yellow 1 sighted a white vapour trail at 15,000ft over Biggin Hill, climbing the section to Angels 15. This unidentified machine then turned towards the mouth of the Thames, followed by the RAF fighters, until it was lost over Sheerness. Having returned to and orbited Kenley at 15,000ft for ten minutes, another bandit was plotted by RDF so the Hurricanes were sent to patrol the Hastings to Beachy Head line. At 12,000ft over Hastings the 253 Squadron pair separated, Yellow 1 climbing up through cloud to 16,000ft when he saw, at 08.45 hrs, a vapour trail caused by a Ju 88 flying in a thin layer of cloud below. Corkett attacked, hitting the bomber before breaking away. Green Section of Tangmere's 213 Squadron, comprising Flying Officer Wilfred Sizer and Pilot Officer George Westlake, was also searching for the bandit over Beachy Head, and Corkett watched both pilots approach before the latter, in Hurricane AK-U, attacked from astern. Then, Corkett, also from astern, emptied his remaining ammunition into the Ju 88, which was 'last seen at 300 feet over sea, five miles East of Newhaven, having lost height and speed with starboard engine apparently damaged. Newhaven report hostile aircraft down in sea South of Beachy Head at approximate time of engagement.' [No. 213 Squadron ORB]. The Ju 88 belonged to II/LG 1, the crew of which were all killed.

Further east, the two Spitfires of 66 Squadron's Red Section, Pilot Officer Crelin 'Bogle' Bodie DFC and Sergeant Peter Willcocks, were patrolling Dungeness at 15,000ft when at 09.45 hrs AA fire over Dover drew their attention to a Ju 88 incoming over the coast, flying north in a clear sky. The Spitfires gave chase, attacked, silencing the rear gunner, the enemy pilot immediately turning about and heading back towards France in a shallow dive. Having fired several more bursts, Bodie last saw the Ju 88 at 10,000ft over mid-Channel 'with one engine smoking (not the usual full-throttle stuff)'. The bomber was claimed as damaged, and shared equally between the two pilots, who suffered just 'one negligible hole' in Bodie's Spitfire during the combat.

The Spitfires of Westhampnett's 602 Squadron were also patrolling in successive pairs, this enabling a standing aerial presence to be maintained for longer, through thinly spreading resources. At 10.15 hrs, Red Section, namely Flight Lieutenant Christopher Mount, commanding 'A' Flight, and Pilot Officer Osgood 'Pedro' Hanbury, were orbiting Beachy Head when a Ju 88 was sighted flying east, over the Channel. Whilst closing the positively identify the bomber, the Spitfires were sighted by the raider, losing the advantage of surprise. Mount attacked from astern before losing his target in cloud, which was subsequently re-located after a search, heading back to France. Hanbury also attacked, stopping the Ju 88's starboard engine near the French coast, but then three Me 109s appeared, climbing towards the Spitfires. Firing off his remaining ammunition at the approaching fighters, Hanbury then made off into cloud, returning safely to base with Mount, the damaged Ju 88 being shared between them.

At 09.35 hrs, twelve Spitfires of 72 Squadron left Biggin Hill with orders to patrol Maidstone at 15,000ft, swiftly changed to 30,000ft. Unfortunately disaster struck a few minutes after take-off, when Pilot Officer Norman Sutton was killed in a collision with Sergeant Robert Staples, the latter safely returning his damaged fighter to base.

The remaining ten Spitfires then 'intercepted more than thirty Me 109s at about 24,000 feet over Tunbridge and chased them across the Channel. They were, in turn, attacked by more than twenty Me 109s.' [ORB]. Flight Sergeant Jack Steere was weaving behind 72 Squadron and shot-up, returning to Biggin Hill slightly wounded; 72 Squadron inflicted no damage on the enemy.

Biggin Hill's 92 Squadron also fielded twelve Spitfires, which scrambled at 10.20 hrs and rendezvoused with 72 Squadron over Maidstone at Angels 20. For some reason, Flying Officer John Drummond took-off ten minutes after his fellow 'Ganics', which I tried to find. At 11.00 hrs, the lone Spitfire pilot ran into twelve Me 109s at 22,000ft over Dungeness:

> I did a beam attack on the rear two. They turned away from the formation and dived towards the coast. I followed and fired a burst at the rear 109. White smoke came from the 109 and it did a half-roll and a long shallow dive towards the sea. I followed and saw it hit the water.

Very likely, this was a machine of 9/JG 3, based at Desvres, the unknown pilot of which was rescued by the *Seenotdienst*. Drummond continued,

> As I was following the 109 down I saw a Henschel 126 flying low over the water. I followed it and fired a burst as it turned towards the French coast. I followed it, firing short bursts to about two miles off the French coast where it forced-landed on the sea. A He 111 flew past and watched the Henschel forced-land. I also saw a Do 215 flying low across the water but I could not fire at either of these as I was out of ammunition.

The He 126 communications aircraft, of 4(H)/31, had stood no chance against the eight-gun Spitfire.

The main body of 92 Squadron sighted Me 109s above, but were unable to catch them and so investigated bursts of AA fire to the north. There, Pilot Officer John Lund, Red 3, saw 'large numbers of E/A circling round with our fighters after them'.

Squadron Leader Rupert Leigh had scrambled with his 66 Squadron from Gravesend at 11.00 hrs, climbing the Spitfires to 20,000ft over the Tenterden area, the pilots of 'Clickety-Click' also investigating the AA fire. Finding the Me 109s, the squadron broke up, individual dogfights occurring. Sergeant Rufus Ward subsequently reporting shooting a 109 through the cockpit hood, which fell away, then hitting another, which entered a steep dive (according to Ward this was over Tenterden at 11.40 hrs, but more likely ten minutes earlier).

Flight Lieutenant Bob 'Bobby' ('Oxo') Oxspring DFC remembered,

> One yellow-nosed Me 109 broke left to right across my front and I got a nice three-second burst on it from behind and beneath. He turned through the hazy sun as I repeated the dose which resulted in a stream of grey glycol smoke. The aircraft dived down and I followed, firing

from close range. The rudder flew off and almost instantaneously the aircraft burst into flames. Our hurtling descent carried us dangerously close to a squadron of Hurricanes concentrating on a climb-out. I had to giggle when our sudden, spectacular, arrival from aloft split the Hurries' formation, which cascaded in all directions. In trying to avoid ramming one of my startled friends I managed to glimpse the 109 spinning down near Lympne. There was no sign of a parachute.

Pilot Officer John Kendall saw Oxspring's dramatic dive after the 109:

I vividly remember seeing on this particular trip an Me streaking for the ground with black smoke pouring from its yellow-nosed engine, hotly pursued by a Spitfire. Boy! What a thrilling sight. I think I shouted 'Att'her boy, give him hell, chum', or words to that effect. Machines split up and went in all directions – the fight was on. I followed one of the boys down until I spotted a 109 going for home. I immediately got on his tail and was after him like a dig for its dinner.

Closing to about 300 or 400 yards, I opened fire, the bullets roared out over the noise of the engine. They don't rattle like an ordinary Army Vickers gun. No sir! When the eight Brownings open fire – what a thrill! The smoke whips back in the cockpit and sends a thrill running down your spine.

The Jerry seemed to jump in the air and start a gradual descent. I followed, giving short bursts. As I closed upon him, I saw that we were overtaking another 109 at a slightly greater height than we were.

I didn't fancy being shot in the back by this one, so I left my Jerry to his fate, and opened fire upon the second. Nothing much happened to him and by this time we were overtaking a third, this one being also higher and to the right. I held my fire after breaking away from No. 2 and put a burst into No. 3. He semi-half-rolled and dived for the coast. Opening my throttle, I was after him, also giving a short burst. This one then suddenly climbed for the sun. As he did so I pulled my nose up and had him cold. I pressed the button … nothing happened. I had run out of ammunition. Did I swear? I'll say!

Things then went wrong for the defenceless Spitfire pilot:

There was, all of a sudden, a terrific explosion in the cockpit, and smoke seemed to be coming from the engine – not the smell of my guns, but an acrid stench. 'What the hell was that?', I thought, and checked my instruments. At that moment I knew all right what it was when a shower of bullets hit my aircraft and something banged my leg with a sickening thud. I didn't wait to see 'who threw that' but did a complete half-roll to the left and went down in a tight spiral turn, craning my neck to see if there was anything on my tail.

Flattening out at 10,000ft, Kendall checked over his machine and discovered that his hydraulic system had been damaged, rendering his flaps inoperable and only providing sufficient pressure for his undercarriage to lower half-way. Moreover, the pilot had been hit in his left leg, which was covered in oil and glycol, and bleeding, requiring him to set the ruder bias so his right leg took the strain. Back at base he prepared to land with an oil-covered windscreen and at a high ground speed owing to lack of flaps – but fortunately a burst tyre flapping about slowed things down and Kendall survived. Taken to the MO, it was discovered that a bullet had entered his Spitfire from astern and passed through his leg and left flying boot – luckily a flesh wound only.

No. 66 Squadron's Pilot Officer Crelin Bodie and Sergeant Kenneth Wright both also returned to Gravesend with damaged Spitfires, but were fortunately unhurt.

At 10.00 hrs (BST), ten Me 110s of *Erprobungsgruppe* 210 had taken-off from Calais-Marck, 1st *Staffel* tasked with hitting Beckton Gasworks on London's North Bank, whilst 2nd *Staffel* was to attack West Malling airfield. The latter unit successfully bombed their target, although damage was slight – and it was these Me 110s Pilot Officer John Lund saw, formed up into an *Abwehrkreis*:

> I approached them and attacked a Me 110 from 30° astern, firing a long burst from 250–80 yards. I saw the hood fly off as the E/A turned in an attempt to escape. I broke away and attacked again from underneath. Clouds of white smoke and flashes were visible from both engines. When last seen the E/A was losing height. Having fired all my rounds I spiralled to 1,000 feet and returned to base. The combat took place over Maidstone at 1130 hrs.

Lund had hit the Me 110 of *Unteroffizier* Balthasar Aretz, who was wounded and almost passed out, jettisoning his bombs and firing off all his nose-mounted weapons. Aretz put the damaged machine into a shallow dive towards France, crash-landing back at Calais-Marck; Aretz's *Bordfunker*, *Gefreiter* Rolf Schilleng, was unhurt.

At 11.18 hrs, Squadron Leader Harry Hogan DFC took-off from Kenley with his 501 Squadron, which was in company with and leading 253 Squadron, and at 11.30 hrs were vectored towards the Me 110s of 1/*Erprobungsgruppe* 210 and the Me 109s of their fighter escort, which were at 16,000ft, south of the Thames Estuary. Climbing toward the action, 501 Squadron was split in half by an attack by Me 109s, although fortunately without loss. Hogan's Red Section remained together, however, and at 11.48 hrs the CO attacked a 110, 'which went into a steep diving turn, I gave him one long burst and he rolled onto his back and went in, crashing two miles due South of Ashford.' Hogan had shot down *Feldwebel* Fritz Duensing and *Feldwebel* Helmut Krappatsch of 1/*Erprobungsgruppe* 210, who were killed when their aircraft exploded at the Industrial School, Millbank Place, Ashford.

No. 501 Squadron's Pilot Officer Kenneth MacKenzie DFC had ineffectively fired at a Me 110 before hitting a Me 109 with a four second burst. The German fighter dived towards the sea, pursued by the Hurricane pilot who eventually overtook his quarry 6 miles off Margate and

> gave him a final burst from dead astern and above from 250 yards, closing to 100 yards. The E/A immediately went out of control and flew

into the sea at 350–360 mph, disappearing with a large splash. I flew round the spot but saw no trace whatever of the machine or pilot.

Flight Lieutenant Eustace Holden of 501 Squadron claimed a damaged 109, but 253 neither made any claims or suffered losses.

At 11.10 hrs, Squadron Leader Ronald G. Kellett led the Poles of his 303 (Polish) Squadron up from Northolt to rendezvous with 1 (RCAF) Squadron, which led the Hurricanes southward. When Northolt Wing was at 18,000ft, in scattered cloud of between 5/10 and 10/10ths, Me 109s could be seen to the east, over Rochester, flying north. The wing, was led by Canadian Flight Lieutenant Gordon McGregor, who attacked the seven Me 109s, which, he reported, were 'flying in a loose line-astern formation north-west of Folkestone'. Other Me 109s and Me 110s then joining in the melee, which occupied the strata 16,000–22,000ft. McGregor hit a 109 from 'very close range. [The] 109 smoked and pilot baled out', this being either 1/JG 3's *Feldwebel* Franz von Herwerth-Bittenfeld who was captured badly burned, his aircraft crashing at Bethersden, or *Leutnant* Alfred Zeis, a ten-victory ace of 1/JG 53, who was captured unhurt at Pluckley, near Hawkinge. Zeis was also hit by another Canadian, Flying Officer Beverley Christmas, who 'let a final burst go into the cockpit. The E/A dived vertically towards the ground, smoking. E/A should have crashed on landing near Hawkinge.' No. 1 (RCAF)'s Pilot Officer Eric Beardmore damaged a 109 south of Canterbury, and Flying Officer Paul Pitcher claimed one 109 destroyed south of Maidstone, and another damaged.

As the combat drifted towards the coast, over Lympne, the Poles and Canadians caught the rest of 1/*Erprobungsgruppe* 210's Me 110s flying in an *Abwehrkreis* at 20,000ft and heading back to France,

> and there were great number of Me 109s above them, and in the high clouds. Our aircraft attacked the circle singly from head-on and below, and broke it up, inflicting heavy casualties in spite of attacks by Me 109s … Squadron Leader [Ronald] Kellett damaged one Me 109, seeing pieces fly off the engine and wing, and the E/A disappeared in a steep dive. [ORB]

Flying Officer Zdzisław Henneberg chased a 109 to the coast without getting within range, so attacked a Me 110 but forced to break away when a Me 109 intervened. Shaking off his pursuer, Henneberg then went after a Me 110 making for the coast, at which he fired two bursts: 'E/A burst into flames and dived straight for the sea.' Flying Officer Marian Pisarek also described hitting a 110, which 'fell into the sea', as did Pilot Officer Mirosław Ferić, who 'fired a burst from about twenty yards into his cockpit. E/A immediately dived into the sea.' All three pilots were independently credited with Me 110s destroyed – but the fact is only one was actually lost in such circumstances. Nonetheless, it was an expensive loss, being *Erprobungsgruppe* 210's acting *Gruppenkommandeur*, *Oberleutnant* Werner Weyman and his *Bordfunker*, *Unteroffizier* Erwin Hübner, who were both killed. Weyman was the unit's fourth *Gruppenkommandeur* killed in the Battle of Britain, this mission a failure for 1st *Staffel*, which was unable to reach its target owing to such stiff defensive opposition.

Sergeant Stanislaw Karubin 'destroyed one Me 109, which exploded' [ORB], this being either *Feldwebel* Franz von Herwerth-Bittenfeld or *Leutnant* Alfred Zeis. Sergeant Anton Siudak claimed a 109 destroyed near Ashford, and another in the sea off Littlestone, and attacked a 110 in company with a Spitfire, 'which was destroyed', this actually being the same 110 claimed by both Pilot Officer Lund of 92 Squadron and Squadron Leader Hogan of 501 Squadron. Near Lympne, Sergeant Jan Palak shot down 1/JG 53's *Unteroffizier* Wilhelm Ghesla, who forced-landed and was captured at Aldington. Sergeant Marian Belc claimed a Me 110 destroyed near Lympne, from which he saw an airman bale out, the only candidate being Weyman's aircraft, which went into the sea. (According to 1 (RCAF) Squadron's ORB, the Canadians damaged two Me 110s, but no other details are given; Flying Officer Peter Lochnan was possibly responsible, but no personal combat report appears to have survived.)

Although only two Me 110s were lost, 303 (Polish) Squadron claimed four destroyed – but *Oberfeldwebel* Robert Schulze of 1/*Erprobungsgruppe* 210 did crash-land back at Calais-Marck, wounded and his aircraft damaged in combat. No. 303 (Polish) Squadron's records, however, are confused in respect of this combat, Flying Officer Marian Pisarek, for example, being accredited in the ORB with having 'destroyed a 109 on land and damaged another', whilst no mention is made of the 110 he shot down into the sea. As we have seen, however, and not uncommonly, it was not the Poles alone who were responsible for 1/*Erprobungsgruppe* 210's losses on this particular afternoon. Yet again this is further evidence, as if any were needed, of now a single aircraft loss could be multiplied on the balance sheet.

Unfortunately, however, 303 (Polish) Squadron's success was not without loss: Flying Officer Wojciech Januszewicz was shot down in flames and killed, his Hurricane crashing at Stowting. Neither did 1 (RCAF) Squadron return to Northolt without loss: Flying Officer Hartland Molson was shot down by a 109 over Canterbury and baled out, 'doing a delayed jump' [ORB], his Hurricane crashing at Smarden; wounded, the Canadian was admitted to Chartham Hospital, although the squadron diarist considered that 'he was amply revenged'.

Having scrambled from Hornchurch at 11.05 hrs, the Spitfires of 41 Squadron also entered the fray north-west of Folkestone, at 11.50 hrs. Pilot Officer Denys Mileham, Green 3, saw three yellow-nosed Me 109s passing his port side, so engaged one of these. Smoke emitted from the enemy fighter's engine, the aircraft falling away, out of control. This was witnessed by Pilot Officer Denis Adams, who confirmed having seen Green 3's attack and the 109 going 'down with black smoke pouring from around the cockpit'. The first 109 was claimed as destroyed, the second damaged. At noon, Sergeant Cyril Bamberger, Yellow 3, reported hitting a 109 over Canterbury, firing from close range: 'smoke and flames appeared about the cockpit and engine' – very possibly being the same 109 hit by Mileham. Pilot Officer John Lecky Jr and Pilot Officer Robert Boret claimed 109s damaged in the clash, during which Flight Lieutenant Tony Lovell's Spitfire was hit in a wing, although the pilot returned to base unhurt.

Five minutes after 41 Squadron scrambled from Hornchurch, so too had Squadron Leader George Denholm DFC, leading eleven other 603 Squadron Spitfires. Amongst

Denholm's men was Pilot Officer Ludwik Martel, who reported that at 11.45 hrs, at 15,000ft west of Dover:

> I saw a circle of Me 109s, and one Me 109 left the circle and started to climb and I dived on him and made a beam attack, firing for about three seconds. The Me 109 took evasive action by skidding and I attacked again with slight deflection, firing the remainder of my ammunition from 200 yards. The Me went up and then dived gently into the sea. I saw him crash into the sea about six miles East of Dover.

Sergeant Andrew Darling reported descending from Angels 25 to 15 over Maidstone to attack 'a formation of He 111s [*sic*] and Me 109s' between 11.45 and 12.00 hrs. Darling engaged a 109, which he last saw 'almost over coastline, going South at approximately 200 feet, with white smoke pouring out and losing height'. Surrounded by Me 109s, the Spitfire pilot was unable to press home his attack but broke away, returning to base. Flying Officer Brian Carbury, Green 1, described how 603 Squadron went into line-astern to attack, Me 109s being seen above and 110s below, west of Dover and at 11.45 hrs. Carbury 'saw two 109s, so gave chase and Green 2 followed me – he chased me. I climbed after the other and he had one wheel down. A short burst and the other came down and white smoke streamed out. I broke off down, as Me 109s were coming from above.'

Almost certainly Carbury had shot down *Feldwebel* E. Pankratz of 6/LG 2, who forced-landed at Pelsham Farm, Peasmarsh, where he was captured, wounded. In response, 603 Squadron's James Morton was shot down over Dover, baling out and suffering from burns and landing at Chilham.

So far, three fighter and *Jabo* attacks had been launched against south-east England, in such quick succession that these are difficult to dissect from a Luftwaffe perspective. The first wave had come in over Dover at 09.30 hrs, thirty Me 109s which were intercepted at Maidstone. The second, heavier raid, at 10.45 hrs, saw 150 enemy aircraft incoming over Lympne, 100 Me 109s sweeping towards London but only ten breaching the Inner Artillery Zone. The third attack involved 120 aircraft which came in between Eastbourne and Folkestone, fifty of which penetrated the Inner Artillery Zone whilst twenty more only reached South London.

Luftwaffe intelligence documents indicate that all of these attacks were aimed at London, making a busy day for the Me 109s of LG 2, I *Gruppe* contributing nineteen aircraft, II *Gruppe* twenty-three, and II/LG 1 twenty; 5/JG 51, that *Jagdgeschwader*'s *Jabostaffel*, made its first fighter-bomber attack that day, and three such missions in total, and ten Me 110s of *Erprobungsgruppe* 210 were sent against London and West Malling airfield. During the fighting covered so far, on this day the pilots of 2(J)/LG 2, JG 3, JG 51, JG 53, JG 54 and JG 77 claimed the destruction of six Spitfires and as many Hurricanes in addition, strangely, two 'Curtiss' fighters. In reality, Fighter Command's combat losses amounted to one Spitfire destroyed and five damaged; two Hurricanes were destroyed, one pilot killed and three wounded. Considering the number of German aircraft unleashed against south-east England, this hardly seems a worthwhile return.

The fighter combats had so far exclusively involved 11 Group's pilots, who had filed the following combat claims: fifteen Me 109s destroyed, three probables and thirteen damaged; six Me 110s destroyed, two damaged, and an unfortunate Hs 126 destroyed, which is confirmed. Only six Me 109s were, in fact, lost: two were shot down into the sea, one was abandoned over the Channel by the pilot due to combat damage, and three more crashed in England, their pilots all captured. Just two Me 110s were destroyed, and two damaged. What cannot possibly escape the reader's attention is just how similar various pilots' combat reports are: clearly, they are describing the same incident, whilst attacking independently and unaware of the other – owing simply to the speed of aerial combat deceiving the human eye. It is also a demonstrable fact from the evidence available that certain squadrons commonly overclaimed, not least amongst them, it must be said, the 303 (Polish) Squadron – which on this occasion claimed, according to victory claim records held by the MOD AHB, five Me 110s destroyed and two damaged, four Me 109s destroyed and two damaged. Although evidence has previously been provided and it argued that Luftwaffe loss records are perhaps not as complete as most historians believe, there is no reason to doubt their accuracy on this particular day. The simple fact is that the statistics speak for themselves. The practical issue arising from these inaccurate figures and analysis by both sides in 1940 is that the Luftwaffe and Fighter Command were unable to actually gauge what damage was really being done to the enemy – and this was certainly a problem for the Luftwaffe, because such inflated figures misinformed strategic decisions.

Returning directly to the events of 5 October 1940, although the fighting over the south-east was not quite over, the main attacks on London and Kent had been made.

At 14.05 hrs, Green Section of 74 Squadron, up from Coltishall and namely Pilot Officer Harbourne Stephen and Flying Officer Roger Boulding, and Polish Pilot Officer Henryk Szczeny, were patrolling off Harwich when they sighted a prowling Do 215 below them, at 15,000ft. Stephen, Green 1, ordered line-astern and the three Spitfires attacked. Boulding, Green 2, noted 'very wild' return fire 'at first, but ceased firing before I broke away'. Afterwards Boulding was unable to locate the bandit and so returned to base. Unfortunately the other two pilots' reports do not appear to have survived, but although there is no corresponding Luftwaffe loss, the Dornier was accredited as destroyed, shared between the three 'Tigers' involved. The combat was 12 Group's only action of the day.

The next major attack was made across the central Channel area, a *Frei Jagd* over the Isle of Wight and Swanage area. On this operation, *Jafü* 3 despatched forty Me 109s of JG 2, seven of JG 53, and thirty-eight Me 110s of ZG 26 – a dangerous force indeed which advanced towards the Dorset coast at 13.00 hrs (BST).

At 13.20 hrs, Flight Lieutenant Jim Bazin led 607 Squadron up from Tangmere with orders to patrol St Catherine's Point, the southernmost tip of the Isle of Wight, at Angels 20. Whilst proceeding there, however, the ten Hurricanes were vectored to patrol Swanage, also at 20,000ft. When Bazin's formation was over the sea between The Needles, on the Isle of Wight's western coast, and Swanage, Flight Lieutenant Francis Blackadder reported to Bazin that he could see a gaggle of enemy aircraft at 23,000ft – but this warning of bandits above went unheard. Then, the inevitable happened: Pilot Officer John Sulman, Green 1, 607 Squadron's weaver, shouted a warning of Me 109s diving onto the squadron's rear, from above and behind.

Under attack, the Hurricanes immediately broke up – but four aircraft were hit: Pilot Officer David Evans baled out, landing unhurt near Fareham, whilst Flight Lieutenant Bazin and Flight Lieutenant Blackadder, and Sergeant Richard Spyer, were all shot-up and made forced-landings. Also, 'The six other Hurricanes took successful evasive action, and returned to base with minor damage to certain of their aircraft.' [ORB]. No. 607 Squadron made no combat claims. *Stab* I/JG 2 and 1 and 3/JG 2 were responsible for what was a completely successful ambush.

Similarly, the Hurricanes of 238 Squadron, based at Middle Wallop, were also bounced by the marauding Me 109s, of 3/JG 2. At 13.30 hrs twelve of the squadron's Hurricanes scrambled from Chilbolton to patrol Middle Wallop but 'while heading North they were surprised by fifteen Me 109s attacking from astern. No member of the Squadron had an opportunity to fire.' [ORB]. Sergeant John McLaughlin was shot down over Shaftesbury, baling out badly burned; Polish Pilot Officer Władysław Różycki ran out of petrol, so put down and re-fuelled at Fareham; the remaining ten Hurricanes returned safely to base.

Entirely successful though this *Freie Jagd* was for JG 2, which suffered no loss, the combat claims arising do not stand scrutiny. Ten Hurricanes were claimed destroyed south of Bournemouth, relating to 607 Squadron's losses, which were one Hurricane destroyed, the pilot of which baled out, three being shot-up and forced to land, and an unknown number of the remaining six fighters returned to base with minor damage. Unlike the RAF system of classifying claims as 'destroyed', 'probably destroyed' or 'damaged', however, the Luftwaffe only awarded victories for aircraft considered destroyed. Ten Hurricanes may well have been hit in this ambush, but only one of 607 Squadron, in fact, was destroyed. North of Bournemouth, 3/JG 2 claimed one Hurricane and a Spitfire destroyed – but no Spitfires were either involved or lost, just the sole 238 Squadron Hurricane.

Of particular interest regarding the German claims is that *Hauptmann* Helmut Wick, *Gruppenkommandeur* of I/JG 2 and a leading *Jagdwaffe* ace, personally claimed the destruction of three Hurricanes in the attack on 607 Squadron. Wick may well have hit three of 607 Squadron, but he certainly did not destroy the three, and nor can it be said, given the claims for Hurricanes destroyed in this action by five other JG 2 pilots (one of whom claimed two Hurricanes) that he alone was responsible for shooting down Pilot Officer Evans, and shooting-up Flight Lieutenant Bazin and Flight Lieutenant Blackadder, and Sergeant Richard Spyer, all three of whom forced-landed. These three victories awarded Wick were, as recorded in *Hauptmann* Genst's after action report for *Jafü* 3 (*Einzelmeldung* Nr 5 vom 5.10.40), increased his score to thirty-nine. On 25 August 1940, Wick had achieved his twentieth aerial victory, as a result of which, two days later, he was awarded the *Ritterkreuz* by *Reichsmarschall* Hermann Göring at the Nazi chiefs Karinhall estate. This made Wick a national war hero, many articles and features concerning his explours appearing in the press, including the popular *Berliner Illustrite Zeitung*, a mass-market illustrated magazine, and *Der Adler*, the Luftwaffe magazine. What happened next defies belief.

The first *Jagdflieger* awarded the *Ritterkreuz* was *Major* Werner Mölders, who achieved his twentieth victory on 27 May 1940. On 1 August 1940, *Major* Adolf Galland followed suit. On 20 September 1940, Mölders recorded his fortieth victory, for which he became only the second German serviceman to receive the coveted *Eichenlaub*, the silver oak leaves indicating a double award of the *Ritterkreuz* (the first was awarded to *Generalleutnant* Eduard Wohlrat Christian Dietl, 'The Hero of Narvik'). On 25 September 1940, Galland became the third recipient of the *Eichenlaub*, having scored his fortieth kill the previous day. These exceptional decorations jet-propelled Mölders and Galland into the stratosphere, so far as fame was concerned – they were both household names, adored by the public, and well beyond Germany. Who, though, would be the third of the *Experten* to receive the *Eichenlaub*?

At 16.51 hrs, eleven Hurricanes of 238 Squadron again left Chilbolton to patrol Middle Wallop:

> Subsequently, fifty E/A were seen five miles out to sea between Southampton and Portland Bill. No attack was made by our aircraft, although other friendly squadrons were in the vicinity, as a trap was suspected. The E/A made no attempt to offer battle. [ORB]

No other 10 Group Hurricane or Spitfire squadrons (79, 87, 152, 234, 504, 601 and 609) were patrolling in The Solent – Portland area at that time or later in the evening. The only sorties from the adjacent 11 Group Tangmere sector were as follows: 607 Squadron made its fifth sortie of the day between 15.20 and 15.40 hrs, a 'Patrol' [ORB], and a patrol of base, Tangmere, between 17.05 and 18.25 hrs; on both occasions, the result was 'Nothing seen' [ORB]. Between 16.00 and 17.50 hrs, Tangmere's 213 Squadron patrolled base uneventfully, and between 16.55 and 17.50 hrs similarly patrolled 'Base and Portsmouth, 15,000 feet' [ORB]. Likewise, the Spitfires of Westhampnett's 602 Squadron patrolled without event 14.00–15.10 hrs, 16.00–16.20 hrs, and 16.55–17.50 hrs. None of these 11 Group squadrons either saw or contacted the enemy.

Nonetheless, eager for his fortieth victory, the *Eichenlaub*, accolades and attention that went with the prestigious award, *Hauptmann* Wick was up again that afternoon, sweeping the area from Portland to east of the Isle of Wight. It was undoubtedly Wick's formation that 238 Squadron sighted and which 'made no attempt to offer battle'. No RAF fighters, therefore, were lost in this area after JG 2's previous *Freie Jagd*; (the only Spitfire down was further north, at 18.15 hrs, when 609 Squadron's Polish Flying Officer Tadeusz 'Novi' Nowierski abandoned N3223 over Salisbury Plain due to a technical problem).

That being so, why, then, did *Hauptmann* Wick claim Spitfires destroyed at 18.35 hrs (continental time) and 18.40 hrs, in the Isle of Wight area? And, more to the point, considering that Luftwaffe claims supposedly had to be witnessed and subjected to stringent vetting before the OKL would accredit a victory, why were these 'victories' – numbers forty and forty-one – awarded? These were, of course, significant numbers: firstly, because the first Spitfire claimed meant that Wick would receive the *Eichenlaub*, being the third ever and final airman to do so in 1940, the second Spitfire, being his fifth victory of 5 October 1940, making him, uniquely for a German fighter pilot in the Battle of Britain, an ace in a day. The problem is, these two victorious did not happen – there was no combat and no Spitfires, or Hurricanes, therefore lost. The only It is inconceivable that a fighter ace of Wick's obvious skill should crave fame and attention so much that he would lie – but the evidence, sad to say, suggests no other explanation.

The following day, 25-year-old Wick was summonsed to Berlin, where he was to report to Hermann Göring on the afternoon of 7 October 1940, from where the pair travelled in the *Reichsmarschall*'s personal train, *Asia*, to Berchtesgaden. There, on 8 October 1940, Wick received his *Eichenlaub* from the *Führer*, after which investiture he was presented to an international press audience at a reception held by Dr Otto Dietrich, as a German war hero. This did not go well. The *American Life* magazine later headlined that 'Nazi Flier Laughs at British Airmen; Says Best of Foe's Aviators Have Been Shot Down ... Thinks Others Scared. Claims Full Air Mastery. Decorated Fighter Ridicules Anti-Aircraft Fire and Use of Barrage Balloons.' Such arrogance was not well received – and provides a clear indication of Wick's vain character.

Returning to the events of 5 October 1940, whilst JG 2 was enjoying success off Bournemouth, there was more action further east. More Me 109s of *Jafü* 2 were sweeping the Channel in the Dover area, where 41 Squadron was patrolling. At 14.30 hrs, Flying Officer John MacKenzie, a New Zealander, sighted two Me 109s beneath him and dived towards them. One broke starboard, the other dived towards the sea. The Spitfire pilot overtook the latter, his first burst causing smoke to emit from the engine, and a second, closer, burst saw flames issue from the 109's starboard side. MacKenzie watched,

> Another three Me 109s ... patrolling above, or were returning to France, and I watched them. As I was short of ammunition I decided to return to the coast. Then I saw Me 109 pilot discard his hood, with the obvious intention of baling out. A few seconds later, I turned round again and could see no sign of pilot or machine.

The 109 was credited as destroyed.

Having landed at 14.40 hrs, exactly one hour later 41 Squadron was off again from Hornchurch to patrol the Channel off the south-east Kent coast. At 16.00 hrs the Spitfires were at 27,000ft south of Dungeness when twelve to fifteen Me 109s were sighted below. 'Mitor Squadron' dived on the German fighters.

Pilot Officer Eric 'Sawn-off' Lock:

> I singled one Me 109 out. I attacked him slightly astern and above. I fired one burst of about one second. He climbed nearly vertically and the aircraft fell forward into a vertical dive with glycol leaking from under right wing. I watched it down to 7,000 feet, where I left it. It did not make any attempt to recover. He would crash somewhere in the Tonbridge – Maidstone – Sevenoaks area.

This 109 was also credited as destroyed, but it would appear to have returned home, because no German fighters crashed in Kent that afternoon. These skirmishes concluded the day fighting.

For Coastal Command it had been an unremarkable day, seventy-two aircraft carrying out forty-two patrols, during which Hudsons attacked enemy shipping off Norway. At night, before the weather closed in again, strikes were also made against shipping at Brest and Gravelines. One aircraft was lost, a 233 Squadron Hudson based at Leuchars, the crew of which baled out over the North Sea but were lost in bad weather. No. 2 Group's Blenheims aborted proposed raids on Germany due to a lack of cloud cover, and the worsening nocturnal weather reduced Bomber Command's subsequent operations. Wellingtons attacked shipping at Rotterdam and bombed Flushing, whilst Hampdens attacked Gelsenkirchen and sowed mines in the Elbe. The Hampden force lost four aircraft: a 50 Squadron machine and crew disappeared on a sortie to Cologne; a 61 Squadron bomber crashed in Yorkshire, killing its crew, having mined the Elbe; an 83 Squadron bomber returned early from Gelsenkirchen due to icing but crashed near Scampton, one crewman being killed, and a 144 Squadron Hampden vanished on the Elbe trip. No. 53 Squadron lost a Blenheim returning from a patrol of the Dutch coast, which crashed near Manston, killing its crew.

Weekly Report by Home Intelligence:

Shelters
A detailed study on shelters has been made by Mass Observation. A few of the main points which emerge are as follows:

In early days of intensive bombing of London, the number of people going to outside shelters or Anderson shelters increased. It has now decreased again, and on September 26th, 71% slept in their own homes, 25% in their own shelters, and 4% in public shelters. The majority of those who stayed at home slept either on their ground floors or in their basements. (A repeat investigation on September 26th gave a similar result.) Anderson shelters were popular mainly because of their nearness to home, and their homeliness. Brick shelters are still much the most unpopular type, though in the East End their popularity is on the increase – perhaps because they are relatively substantial compared with the homes of the people themselves. The objections to brick shelters are mainly on the grounds that they are no better than ordinary houses. Trench shelters are popular, mainly because they are 'underground' and therefore, people think, safer. Tubes are considered completely safe. The absence of sound is welcomed. Those who do not use them give as their reasons, fear of panic and fear of being buried. The most popular reason for staying at home was that 'you were not safe anywhere.' People who use shelters at night tend to do so regularly and to use the same one. They take some bedding with them, but little food, and little to occupy their time.

Sunday 6 October 1940

So that there could be no ambiguity, Air Vice-Marshal Keith Park issued extensive instructions to 11 Group regarding how wings were to be used:

1. When the sky is mainly clear of clouds and the Group Controller receives ample warning by RDF of the forming up and approach of mass attacks over the French coast or from the South, some squadrons will be despatched in wings of three units. Moreover, this type of formation will continue to be used to bring sectors in the North and South of London in to meet the third wave of a prolonged attack or to 'mop' up raids that are retreating after having been engaged by other squadrons around London.
2. As a result of practical experience during the last five months by squadrons, sectors and Group Headquarters, the following brief instructions are issued. As further experience is gained by squadrons working in wing formations, fresh and more detailed instructions will be issued for the benefit of all concerned. Much of that which follows applies to squadrons working in pairs; the normal formation for reasons already stated in my letter 11G/486, dated 1 October.

Leadership
3. The squadron and leader of the wing must be decided by the sector commander before the beginning of daylight operations each day. After a heavy engagement it may be necessary to change the leadership, when the strongest squadron should be appointed to lead the wing.

Take-off
4. Squadrons should take-off separately and not form up in a wing on the ground.

Assembly
5. The Group Controller will order the place and height of rendezvous, according to the cloud conditions and proximity of enemy raids. The rendezvous will, whenever possible, be well inland in order to enable squadrons to join up at the height ordered before engaging the enemy. The wing leader must report immediately the wing assembles, and Sector Controller is to report to Group Controller, who will then detail wing to a raid or a patrol line above the enemy raids.

Failure to Assemble
6. If slow take-off or unexpected cloud conditions unduly delay the assembly of the wing when enemy raids are approaching targets, the Group Controller may be compelled to detail one or more

squadrons of the intended wing to intercept approaching raids to break up or harass bombers before they reach the target. In this event, it will be necessary for squadrons having VHF to revert from common frequency to their own R/T channel.

Rendezvous

7. Group Controller will normally select an aerodrome or other good landmark well back from the approaching enemy raids.

R/T Frequencies

8. Until all squadrons have VHF it is not considered practical for all units in a wing to work on a common R/T frequency. This ruling is based on the experience of many squadrons in several sectors over a long period. On the introduction of VHF, squadrons will work on a common R/T frequency as soon as they assemble as a wing. If the wing becomes broken, squadrons should revert to their own R/T frequency to facilitate communication with the Sector Controller.

Formation

9. The leading squadron will normally be lower than the two following squadrons. Sectors, however, are to try out stepping down one or more of the following squadrons.

Tactics

10. Before leaving the ground it is essential that the three squadrons shall know which unit is to take on the bombers, which to attack the escort, and lastly which squadron is to act as above-guard or screen to hold off enemy high fighter screen. As the enemy close escort may be above the bombers, in rear, or on a flank or even ahead, and on other occasions may fly weaving between the bomber sub-formations, it is not always possible to lay down rigidly beforehand which squadrons in the wing will attack bombers or their escort. This makes it all the more necessary for the general tactics of the wing to be discussed and decided on the ground before a patrol.

Look-out Guards

11. Each squadron should provide its own look-out guards, especially for the period prior to assembly, and after the wing has become split up by an engagement with the enemy. The wing should normally have one squadron slightly in the rear and above, to act as cover to the whole wing against very high enemy fighters.

Pip-squeak

12. Each squadron is to provide one aircraft with pip-squeak to enable fixing at Sector Operations Room.

The Sun

13. The wing formation should whenever possible patrol across the direction of the sun. Enemy fighters attacking out of the sun will then be offered only deflection shots at our fighters.

Section Formation

14. When in wing formations, sections should normally be composed of four aircraft, consisting of two pairs of fighters. Each squadron should, therefore, have three sections of four aircraft.

Assembly After Combat

15. It is not considered necessary or advisable for squadrons to try to reform wing after a general engagement takes place over enemy territory or over the sea, then it may be advisable to lay down beforehand the wing rendezvous.

Breaking Off from Wing

16. If squadrons are detailed to be detached from the wing formation, Sector Controller should give the order 'X Squadron break away, Vector ...', and then inform the Wing Leader that X Squadron has been ordered to break away.

It is noteworthy that Park had rejected the prescribed vic of three fighters as the standard section formation, replacing this with the section of four, sub-divided into two pairs – similar to the enemy's *Schwarm* and *Rotte*. The difference, however, was that the German formation was in line abreast, stepped up, each aircraft at least 200m from its neighbour, occupying the positions of an outstretched hand's four fingers, whilst the RAF had moved towards sections of aircraft in line astern. The German formation was more flexible, enabling the two pairs to break, leader and wingman together, the former's job being to take the shot, the latter to protect his leader's tail. In time, the RAF would copy the *Schwarm*, and call it the 'Finger Four' or 'Crossover Four', but that would not be until May 1941 – so in the meantime experiments continued.

Regarding the use of wings by 11 Group, Park reported having 'learned the following lessons':

a) There are relatively few days in autumn when cloud conditions are suitable for formations of wings.

b) A much longer time is required to despatch, assemble and climb wing formations.

c) The employment of wing formations considerably reduced the duration of fighter patrols.

d) Mass formations of even three squadrons are slow and cumbersome, and likely to be out-flanked, so fail to intercept the faster German fighter formations.

e) Better results can be obtained by two pairs of squadrons than by four squadrons operating in a wing.

f) The delay caused by the use of wing formations would on many occasions allow enemy fighter-bomber raids to attack vital objectives and escape without interception.

g) All squadrons must be trained to fight and fend for themselves as squadrons before attempting to work in mass formations.

With regard to the assembly of wing formations, it is often written that the 12 Group Duxford Wing lost time in forming up, and was therefore too slow and impractical for that reason alone. This, however, is not the case, as Wing Commander Douglas Blackwood, in 1940 CO of Duxford's 310 (Czech) Squadron, explained:

> There was never really time to get three or four squadrons off the ground and into some shape and form to attack the usual mass of enemy aircraft effectively. On one or two occasions I, as deputy senior squadron commander, was detailed by Bader and the AOC to lead the formation, so I know a little about this difficulty. Of course, Douglas Bader was at the front and so he never saw the 'Tail End Charlies' – it was chaos at the back with chaps being left behind and all sorts. Remember too that the Hurricane had not the power of a Spitfire.

So far as the fighting was concerned on 6 October 1940, during the previous night, the weather closed in again, the day dawning cold, cloudy and with heavy rain. Consequently, the weather kept the German fighters grounded whilst lone bombers intruded, continuing harassing attacks.

At 10.35 hrs, Flight Lieutenant Myles Duke-Woolley and Pilot Officer Leonard Murch of 'A' Flight, 253 Squadron, made up Red Section and left Kenley to patrol Beachy Head at Angels 10. At 11.00 hrs, 'Raid 34' was sighted by the Hurricane pilots at 7,000ft – a lone Do 17 which immediately turned south, heading for cloud. Both pilots attacked, setting the raider's port engine alight before their target jettisoned bombs just south of Tunbridge Wells and disappeared into cloud. Murch, Red 2, dived below the cloud layer but was unable to see the Dornier, and upon climbing to re-join Red 1 saw a Do 215 2,000ft above, flying north. As Murch climbed to attack this bomber also turned south and dived for cloud cover. With only twenty rounds remaining Murch opened fire from 300 yards, without effect. The two Hurricanes then returned to base where operations informed them that an aircraft had crashed at 'Butcher's Wood near Hayfield at the time of engagement' [ORB]. This was a 7/KG 76 Do 17 engaged on a reconnaissance of southern England, which collided with a tree when crash-landing at Snape Wood Reservoir, near Wadhurst, at 11.05 hrs – and exploded; the crew were all wounded and captured.

One of the raiders prowling about over Kent attacked Biggin Hill from low level, seriously damaging a 72 Squadron Spitfire on the ground and slightly damaging the runway. Interestingly, the airfield's defences included No. 1 Parachute And Cable Post, 'which came into action and hit E/A but failed to bring it down' [ORB]. This was a fearsome contraption: a 480ft length of steel cable was fired vertically by a rocket to a height of 600ft, at which point the cable was released and a parachute at the top of the cable opened, thereby suspending the cable in mid-air – hopefully so that a low-flying aircraft would fly into it. If so, a second parachute opened at the bottom of the cable, the collective drag produced sufficient to send an aircraft out of control. The PAC had first been used in anger at Kenley on 18 August 1940; on this occasion the raider had a lucky escape. According to the 72 Squadron ORB, there were no personnel casualties, but actually there was: 23-year-old LAC Alan Mackley, from Lockton in the North Riding and a member of 72 Squadron, was killed in the attack.

There was also high drama at RAF Northolt, as described by the 229 Squadron ORB, timed at 12.10 hrs:

> A Ju 88 appeared to the North of the aerodrome, out of the clouds, and came in on a dive from North to South, machine-gunning the outer buildings. At 200 feet it dropped a large and a small bomb over 'C' Hangar, which missed and landed on the tarmac some fifty feet away. The E/A turned slightly, coming lower, and dropped two oil bombs on the aerodrome, machine-gunning towards 229 Squadron Dispersal point.

The blast from the bomb aimed at 'C' Hangar, however, destroyed a taxiing 303 (Polish) Squadron Hurricane killing 31-year-old pilot Sergeant Antoni Siudak and AC2 Henry Stennert, who had the misfortune to be lookout on Hangar 5's roof.

At 11.30 hrs, 229 Squadron's Pilot Officer Victor Verity, a New Zealander, and Sergeant John Hyde, had taken off on patrol and encountered the Northolt raider:

> Pilot Officer [Victor] Verity on patrol attacked the Ju 88 from above and astern, and saw his ammunition entering the fuselage. Several explosions in the air about 100 yards behind the E/A were noticed, as if something had been thrown out. Sergeant Hyde was astern and turned South to intercept E/A on its run across the aerodrome. He closed from 400 to 100 yards, using all his ammunition, which was striking the E/A but without apparent result. The E/A climbed and escaped into the clouds with smoke coming from its port engine. [ORB]

According to the 'Success Report' filed at 00.45 hrs (BST) on 7 October 1940 by *Oberleutnant* Schambak of *Luftflotte Kommando* 3, *Gruppe* Ic, the Northolt attack was carried out by *Hauptmann* Walter Storp, *Gruppenkommandeur* of II/KG 76. A Spanish War veteran, Storp had previously served as the personal pilot of Luftwaffe Chief of Staff *General* Hans Jeschonnek, and temporarily commanded III/KG 4 before taking over II/KG 76 on 12 September 1940. On 12 October 1940, Storp would become the 149th member of the *Wehrmacht* to receive the Knight's Cross, and the following year received the Oak Leaves whilst commanding *Schnellkampfgeschwader* 210, a fighter-bomber unit he led on the Eastern Front. Storp would end the war as commander of the 5th *Flieger*-Division, and died peacefully in Goslar in 1981.

At 12.20 hrs, Flight Lieutenant Robert Smith, a Canadian, led a section of 229 Squadron Hurricanes up on a fruitless search for Storp's Ju 88, culminating in Smith crash-landing near Leatherhead, out of fuel, writing off his aircraft; the pilot was unhurt.

According to 249 Squadron at North Weald, it was a day of

> very bad weather. Two aircraft took off on an interception of bandit over aerodrome. Pilot Officer Neil DFC intercepted a Do 17 in bad weather to the north-east of the aerodrome and got in a three second burst. Starboard engine appeared to catch fire as this aeroplane disappeared into the clouds. Pilot Officer Neil subsequently saw two other E/A which disappeared into cloud before he could get at them. Intelligence later revealed that the Dornier which Pilot Officer Neil first attacked was finished off by 17 Squadron. [ORB]

That end result, however, was optimistic:

> At 1230 hrs Pilot Officer Ross and Sergeant Steward took-off [author's note: from Martlesham Heath] to patrol below cloud. They were vectored to intercept a Do 17, which they saw and attacked, but did not see the result owing to weather conditions and therefore claim no enemy casualty. They landed at 1310 hrs. Two aircraft took-off at 1325 hrs, but did not intercept and landed at 1440 hrs. [ORB]

These were the last interceptions of the day, as the weather deteriorated as the afternoon wore on. Although Fighter Command suffered no casualties it is clear that the sheer volume of these lone raiders, although unable to achieve anything in a strategic bombing sense, did generate damage, disruption, and maintained pressure on the defenders even when bad weather prevented wider operations. *Oberleutnant* Schambak's report provides details of a relentless succession of lone or small formations of Ju 88s launched against London, Portsmouth and various aircraft factories throughout the day. The majority of these aircraft either aborted due to a lack of cloud cover, bombed without being able to observe results because of cloud, hit secondary targets such as Brighton and Reigate, or returned early owing to technical faults. London's AA defences were described as 'weak', but strong AA fire was reported from ships at Portsmouth.

The bad weather substantially reduced even Coastal Command's operations, although thirty aircraft patrolled and fourteen convoys were escorted. Unfortunately, a 229 Squadron Hudson was shot down attacked armed vessels off Horns Reef and went into the North Sea, the crew never to be seen again. No. 2 Group sent twenty-one Blenheims to targets in Germany, but ten aborted owing to the weather, attacking secondary targets, including Diepholtz aerodrome, on which hits were recorded. The weather also led to all Bomber Command's night raids being scrubbed.

Weekly Report by Home Intelligence:

Alarmist and despondent talk

The alarmist stories of damage to London spread by refugees are declining. 'At first, they were led to do this so as to excuse and justify their flight from London, as the papers were speaking each day of their marvellous courage in staying put. But as the number of refugees swelled – it is now practically impossible to get a room anywhere within 70 miles of London – the need for self-justification vanished, and alarmist stories have become much less conspicuous.' Wild talk of devastation by refugees is still reported from Yeovil and Leeds.

Monday, 7 October 1940

In the Hornchurch sector, 41 Squadron reported that the weather was 'Wind westerly, becoming calm, partly cloudy, visibility moderate to good, becoming poor', although at Croydon 605 Squadron was more positive, recorded the day as 'very fine'. This improvement on the previous few days heralded increased fighting, permitting *Luftflotte* 2 to launch successive waves of heavily escorted fighter-bombers against London – *Major* Adolf Galland's rested JG 26 now back in action and foremost amongst them. Further west, *Luftflotte* 3 would make what was the last major daylight raid of the Battle of Britain, so the fighting over the south-east and West Country will be dealt with separately in the following narrative (all times BST).

At 09.35 hrs, 605 Squadron left Croydon to patrol the Biggin Hill area in company with 501 Squadron, which left nearby Kenley two minutes later. The Glaswegian Squadron Leader Archie McKellar DSO DFC was leading the former, 'Turkey Squadron', at 27,000ft, 2,000ft above and behind 501 Squadron, and 'after various vectors' was informed by 'Runic' (Kenley control) of bandits to the north-east, by this time, 10.20 hrs, the Croydon Hurricanes being north-west of Maidstone. No. 501 Squadron then turned west, flying in that direction north of the Thames, their approach preceded by 'friendly' AA fire, whilst McKellar maintained 605 Squadron south of the river, 'in the sun', also searching westwards. In the distance, over Northolt area, McKellar saw aircraft, which he was unable to identify, warning both his pilots and Runic accordingly. Within seconds, the distant machines were confirmed as seven or eight Me 109s, which were approaching, heading south-east, 1,000ft below and between the two Hurricane squadrons, in McKellar's opinion 'trying to steal out between and slightly below the two squadrons'. Having immediately put 605 Squadron into line astern, McKellar ordered individual attacks:

> so stall-turned and attacked one Me 109, watching in my mirror all the time to see there was none on my tail. I opened fire from a slight dive at 300 yards and could see my De Wilde [author's note: incendiary ammunition] hitting and then dense white vapour coming from his

radiator. I continued to attack, but without any further noticeable result; the E/A then started to climb and draw away from me and was last seen at 15,000 feet over Dungeness, flying south-east, with black smoke coming from it. I therefore returned to base as I could not keep up with the E/A and there did not appears to be any use in maintaining chase over the Channel. Landed [at RAF] Croydon at 1100 hrs.

It is possible that this was a machine of 2/JG 51, which crash-landed at Calais with combat damage.

Sergeant Eric Wright was leading 605 Squadron's Yellow Section, and also dived to attack the retreating *Schwarm* of Me 109s, turning left after three of them and firing at the second machine. The 109 dived away, pursued by Wright, who cleverly positioned himself in the German pilot's blind spot, behind and below:

after he had made a few turns, and deciding that he was not followed, he throttled back. I got to within 150 yards before opening fire with a seven second burst. He immediately put out some smoke from the top of the engine cowling (obviously a blind) and started to climb. I held position and, as the smoke stopped, I used the rest of my ammunition from astern and observed glycol pouring from his radiator. I left him about five miles SE of Maidstone, losing height.

Alone over south-east England and streaming coolant, the *Staffelkapitän* of 2/JG 51, the *Geschwader*'s *Jabostaffel*, *Oberleutnant* Viktor Mölders, brother of JG 51's famous *Kommodore*, was only going one place: down. After a forced-landing at Doleham Farm, Guestling, north-east of Hastings, Mölders was captured unhurt.

When 605 Squadron had first sighted the enemy, Flight Lieutenant Ian Muirhead, commanding 'B' Flight, was Blue 1, his section weaving behind the squadron. Muirhead attacked and hit the leading 109, from which 'pieces came adrift', but then there was

a loud explosion occurred behind and my aircraft straight away went into a spin. The rudder controls had apparently been severed and I was unable to get the machine out of the spin. I then undid my telephone and waited until I was low enough to undo my oxygen tube. I left the aircraft at cloud level, 4,000 feet, and landed in a wood near Dartford. My aircraft was burnt out.

The Hurricane crashed west of Dartford, at Bexley, Muirhead returning to Croydon, unhurt, two hours later. The 109 attacked was claimed as damaged.

North-west of Ashford, 501 Squadron joined the action, Flight Lieutenant Eustace Holden turning onto five Me 109s at 24,000ft, all of which were already under attack by 605 Squadron. Holden, in the slower Hurricane, thinking he could not catch the faster 109, fired a long eight second burst from long range, 400 yards, but without effect. Holden then 'steamed after him with all haste and after juggling various controls, appeared to be catching him'. Having closed to 300 yards whilst approaching the coast,

Holden delivered a four second burst, 'which appeared to have some effect, and smoke belched out. At 2,000ft he passed through cloud over the coast, I closed and gave him the rest of my rounds and saw him dive to the sea, some four miles, approximately, off Dungeness.' This 109 was claimed as destroyed, but had not been seen to crash into the sea, and no corresponding casualty appears in Luftwaffe records.

Unfortunately, whereas 605 Squadron's Flight Lieutenant Ian Muirhead was shot down and baled out unhurt, 501 Squadron lost a pilot: Pilot Officer Nathanial Barry, a 22-year-old South African, was shot down by a 109 over Wrotham, between Sevenoaks and Aylesford; although he safely abandoned his Hurricane, Barry was found dead at Wilmington. At 10.35 hrs (BST), *Leutnant* Friedrich Eberle of 1/JG 51, and *Oberleutnant* Josef 'Pips' Priller, *Staffelkapitän* of 6/JG 51, both claimed 'Spitfires [*sic*]' destroyed, over the Thames Estuary and '20km North of Canterbury' respectively; they were not Spitfires, but the Hurricanes of Muirhead and Barry.

Although 603 Squadron's records are poorly recorded and incomplete, it is known that these Hornchurch Spitfires were also up on patrol at 09.35 hrs, but were bounced over Tenterden by elements of JG 26, Galland's men providing escort for fighter bombers attacking London. Pilot Officer Henry Matthews (in Spitfire K9807, not N3109 as often stated) was shot down and killed, his Spitfire crashing at Godmersham. Sergeant John Strawson was also hit by an unseen opponent (in Spitfire N3109), ditching in the Thames Estuary, just offshore. Not uncommonly in such circumstances, considering that the gunsight is situated immediately in front of the pilot's face, Strawson banged his head on the instrument, injuring his face, and after a struggle, as the Spitfire turned over and sank, managed to break free, regaining the surface. Unsurprisingly, he ingested an unhealthy amount of sea water but was picked up, still conscious, by a rescue launch. No. 603 Squadron made no claims in this action, and only one Spitfire was claimed destroyed, by *Feldwebel* Willi Roth of 4/JG 26.

Hornchurch's 41 Squadron was operating from the forward base at Rochford, and scrambled to patrol overhead at 10.40 hrs. At 11.10 hrs, Squadron Leader Donald Finlay, commanding, sighted a lone bomber, described as a 'Do 215', 10 miles south-west of Maidstone at 25,000ft, travelling east. Puzzled as to why Green Section failed to obey his order to attack, 'Mitor Squadron's' CO did so himself, from astern, before breaking away. When [Donald] Finlay re-contacted the raider off Dover, its port engine was 'smoking badly', but he was unable to press home another attack as another 41 Squadron Spitfire 'slid over me'. According to the 41 Squadron ORB, Flying Officer John MacKenzie also damaged the Dornier – but it is now that our narrative goes awry.

According to the 41 Squadron ORB, having been damaged by Squadron Leader Donald Finlay and Flying Officer John MacKenzie, the Do 215 was 'attacked and shot down by Pilot Officer [John] Lecky [Jr] ... Pilot Officer Adams had to bale out and landed at Douglas Farm, Postling, near Folkestone, uninjured. The aircraft was wrecked.'

Pilot Officer John Lecky Jr was a Cranwellian and still only 19. Having first been posted to an army cooperation squadron, the teenage pilot answered Fighter Command's call for volunteers and joined 610 Squadron at Biggin Hill in August 1940. Lecky made no operational flights with 610 Squadron, and on 1 October 1940 was posted as a replacement pilot to 41 Squadron at Hornchurch; his first operational sortie came on four days later, and on 5 October 1940 he damaged a Me 109. On 9 October 1940, Lecky wrote to his parents, Lieutenant-Colonel John Lecky Sr and his wife, Dorothy, of the action occurring on 7 October 1940:

> it was what we dream for. We sighted a lone bomber ... As I had plenty of ammunition I broke my principles and followed him out over the Channel, with one other Spitfire, and aimed a deflection shot at the starboard engine. He descended steeply towards the sea.

The other Spitfire pilot, he wrote, had seen the bomber crash, continuing 'Oh boy, oh boy! My first confirmed victory on the second day, which seemed all right.' Again, no corresponding loss appears in Luftwaffe records, although in 1988, Denis Adams, who left the RAF as a squadron leader and had emigrated to South Africa, wrote to me about the incident:

> I let the chaps think that I had been a clot and let the Dornier's rear gunner get me. In fact we had a new boy flying as my number three, and he was trying to get himself a squirt. As I turned to attack he let fly and took out my controls plus half the instruments, and also put bullets into my fuel tank! When I got back to Hornchurch in a commandeered car I was just sobering up, having met a very friendly farmer who insisted that I share a bottle of brandy with him. Oh boy, Kentish hospitality! Needless to say, I had quite a chat with the young man responsible next morning!

As ever, this first-hand testimony confirms that official records do not always tell the whole story.

At 12.50 hrs, another fast raid of escorted fighter bombers was incoming, which crossed the coast between North Foreland and Beachy Head. Numbering 130 Me 109s, these penetrated as far as Biggin Hill and South London. During the earlier attack, all three *Gruppen* of JG 5 had escorted the *Jabos* of 3 and 8 *Staffel*, and now flew this second escort mission to London, along with Me 109s from JG 27 and JG 51.

At 12.45 hrs, Squadron Leader Archie McKellar and 605 Squadron scrambled from Croydon once more, again with orders to link up with Kenley's 501 Squadron, which left at 12.50 hrs, made haste towards northern Kent. McKellar reported,

> I was leading Turkey Squadron and following 501 Squadron and told to patrol Sevenoaks line, and after various vectors we were brought round in a sweep by Dungeness and Dover. About here, several Spitfires came down as if to attack us. As they were coming up in a most unnecessarily threatening manner, I broke the Squadron up to do evasive tactics. This flight of Spitfires was most troublesome and I would like to register a strong protest (the lettering of one machine was LZ). It was quite unnecessary and I would suggest that they be taken to a Hurricane squadron and shown over and about Hurricane aircraft, if they are so completely unable to identify friendly aircraft.

The Spitfires belonged to 66 Squadron, which noted that 'Some Me 109s seen but no combat reports compiled' [ORB]. Squadron Leader Archie McKellar was justifiably angry – but it could have been worse: the Spitfires did not open fire.

Despite this exasperating start, it would be a memorable sortie for McKellar – for all the right reasons:

> I asked Control to tell all Turkey Squadron aircraft to join up with me, and seven of them did so. We were then told to come back at patrol base. Shortly after this Control informed me that there were bandits approaching from the south-east, and from the East, and that they were very near us at Angels 15 to 25. I therefore kept my Squadron into the sun as much as possible.
>
> Shortly after this I noticed fifteen Me 109s at approximately Angels 18, near Biggin Hill, followed by about fifty at various heights, and I ordered the Squadron into line astern and to follow me. I dived down on the fifteen Me 109s at 18,000 feet and, as they were going rather fast, I had to do a No 1 Attack. I saw a bomb being dropped from this machine, pieces fly off his wings, and dense white smoke or vapour pour from him, and he went into a most violent outside spin. This E/A was seen by Yellow 3 (Sergeant Lawrence Sones), to crash in flames in a field North of the railway station between Brasted and Westerham.

Sones, however, was mistaken: he had not seen the *Jabo* crash which his CO had attacked, but the Hurricane of 605 Squadron's Pilot Officer Charles English, who was shot down by either *Oberleutnant* Ernst Düllberg or *Unteroffizier* Paul Legge, both of 5/JG 27 and who claimed Hurricanes destroyed at the material time in the 'London' area. Indeed, English was the only RAF fighter destroyed in this action, and no German fighter crashed near the given location.

Squadron Leader Archie McKellar continued,

> I could see another Me 109 coming up to attack me; I therefore turned sharply to the right and found myself just behind and slightly below a Me 109. I opened fire and could see my De Wilde hitting this machine. It burst into flames almost at once and went diving down over the inverted somewhere East of Biggin Hill.
>
> As again I had a Me 109 trying to come on my tail, I spiralled down to about 15,000 feet, and by now there appeared to be Me 109s straggling all over the sky and heading SE. I followed one, pulled my boost control, and speedily made up on him. I gave him a burst from dead astern, and at once his radiator appeared to be hit as dense white vapour came back on me and, as I was rather close, my windscreen was all fogged up. This speedily cleared and I gave him another burst. This machine burst into flames and fell in a wood with a quarry near it, West of Maidstone.

The speed of combat, however, must have deceived the eye, because there is no record of such a crash.

Finally, Squadron Leader Archie McKellar reported,

> I then noticed another Me 109 nipping in and out of the clouds, which were broken and scattered. I followed him, still with the boost pulled, and attacked him from astern, and saw his machine catch alight and the pilot bale out. This E/A crashed slightly North of the Ashford railway line, between Ashford and Tonbridge. My ammunition was then expended, so I returned to base at 1410 hrs.

There was no mistaking this victory: the Me 109 of 9/JG 27, which crashed at Oak Farm, Headcorn, south of Maidstone. Pilot *Unteroffizier* L. Bartsch baled out and was captured, unhurt. This enemy aircraft was also claimed by 605 Squadron's Pilot Officer Bob Foster, and Pilot Officer Derek Forde damaged a 109 over Sevenoaks. McKellar was credited with a total of four Me 109s destroyed, although we know today that only one actually was, at least over land, but several damaged machines did make it back to crash-land in France, and one pilot was forced to bale out off Boulogne, so badly damaged was his 109. Either way, it was good shooting, described by 605 Squadron's diarist as 'remarkable' – which it was.

At 13.15 hrs, 501 Squadron intercepted a pair of Me 109s north-west of Ashford, five more German fighters engaging the Hurricanes from astern.

Pilot Officer Kenneth MacKenzie:

> I followed Red 1 (Squadron Leader Harry Hogan) in attacking an Me 109. Red 1 emptied his guns and damaged the E/A, hitting its glycol tank. Red 1 broke away to the right as the E/A entered low cloud at 4,000 feet. I flew above Red 1, below the bank, and saw the E/A come out above it at right angles at about 5,000 feet. I was above him at 6,000 feet to 6,500 feet and attacked from astern. He was losing height fast and went into the sea off Hythe from 3,000 feet. The E/A sank slowly, the tail being visible for some time. I circled twice and saw the machine sink, and then flew back to the coast at 23,000 feet.

The Me 109 pilot concerned survived: *Leutnant* Erich Meyer of 2/JG 51 took to his dinghy, and was captured by a coastal patrol vessel off Sandgate.

Having returned to the coast, MacKenzie found no sign of 501 Squadron and so patrolled alone between Dover and Folkestone, 8 to 10 miles inland,

> At about 1334 hrs I saw eight Me 109s coming across the coast from the East, about 1,800 feet above me. I attacked the three rearmost machines in vic formation from beneath and a fourth E/A doing rear-guard flew across the line of fire, and he developed a leak in his glycol tank. He half-rolled and dived towards the coast. I followed him and his aircraft was only about 200 yards and so was easy to catch. I emptied the rest of

my ammunition into him from 200 yards, but he still flew on and came down to eighty – 100 feet off the sea. I flew around him and signalled him to go down, which had no result. I therefore attempted to ram his tail with my undercarriage but it reduced my speed too low to hit him. So, flying alongside I dipped my starboard wing-tip onto his port tailplane. The tailplane came off and I lost the top of my starboard wing. The E/A spun into the sea and partially sank. I did not wait to see the final plunge as two Me 109s were attacking me from above and behind. I flew back to Folkestone at twenty to thirty feet above sea-level and weaving up and down. They emptied a lot of machine-gun and cannon fire into my machine and damaged the engine, which belched oil and smoke into the cockpit. They broke off the engagement about one mile from the coast. I managed to make the coast and forced-landed between Folkestone and Hawkinge. My aircraft was pretty badly damaged and shot-up.

MacKenzie's courage and tenacity is almost inconceivable: the stuff of Victoria Crosses, for sure – except, commonly with fighter combat, the incident went unseen by anyone else; no-one, however, could argue that such a high award was not deserved. 'Mac' crash-landed at Hope Farm, near Hawkinge, at 14.05 hrs, suffering facial injuries. Two Me 109s went into the Channel on this day, an unknown pilot of 9/JG 27 who ditched and was rescued by the *Seenotdienst*, and a *Jabo* pilot, *Unteroffizier* Heinrich Bley of 4/LG 2, who crashed in the sea 2 miles off Greatstone, near New Romney, at 14.00 hrs. Given the timing of Bley's ditching and MacKenzie's forced-landing, these would appear a match for the combat which forever more became known as 'MacKenzie's Knock'.

Elsewhere, 501 Squadron's Sergeant James Lacey claimed a 109 probably destroyed between Ashford and West Malling, at 13.15 hrs; apart from the damage to MacKenzie's Hurricane, the squadron suffered no loss.

The Northolt Wing of 1 (RCAF) and 303 (Polish) Squadrons were also up, defending London against the *Jabo* attacks, having taken-off at 13.15 hrs, 303 (Polish) Squadron leading, to patrol the Kenley-Brooklands line at Angels 20.

No. 303 (Polish) Squadron ORB:

Over London were about fifty Me 109s and four He 113 [*sic*] flying NE at 25,000–30,000 feet. They dived down in groups of five, and two groups attacked No 1 Canadian Squadron, and others followed them, then dived away southwards. The Squadron tried to overtake them, unsuccessfully. The Squadron then shadowed another formation of Me 109s flying westwards, and these came down to attack and were chased South, over the Channel. The Hurricanes could not catch the Me's in level flight. All the Me's had yellow noses.

Flying Officer Marian Pisarek dived on four Me 109s, which made off into cloud, then 'noticed a Me 109 flying below the clouds to the sea. I attacked it from beneath, firing a burst of about forty rounds from a distance of fifty yards. E/A dived into the sea, smoking from the port wing and engine.'

Given that only two Me 109s can be confirmed as having gone into the sea, it is impossible to reconcile this claim as no location is recorded.

Sergeant Marian Belc hit a Me 109, which 'began to smoke and right side of the engine burst into flames. E/A dived straight towards the earth, and disappeared beneath the clouds. The place of its crash would be south-west of Redhill.' There was no Me 109 crash near 'Redhill' – but *Unteroffizier* G. Mörschal of 4/LG 2 crash-landed at the Spa Golf Club at Tunbridge Wells, some 20 miles to the east; the German was captured, wounded.

Sergeant Eugeniusz Szaposznikow claimed a Me 109 damaged over South London at 13.50 hrs, which 'began to smoke but evaded me', then attacked another over the coast, at which he fired from 150 yards: 'there was no sign of smoke or flame, although the E/A fell into the sea just off Brighton'. There were no 109s in the sea 'off Brighton', so far as can be established, so it is likely that Szaposznikow was further east, although that too is difficult to reconcile. The Poles returned to Northolt unscathed.

According to Flying Officer Peter Lochnan of 1 (RCAF) Squadron, the Canadians met the Me 109s at 13.48 hrs over Rochester, going west, before splitting up, some flying north. Lochnan pursued them, and attacked me travelling south, a 'long burst raking his aircraft and bits flew off, then I attacked slightly to the right and astern. He burst into flame and went down in a gentle dive, due South.'

Although there was no confirmation that this aircraft crashed, it was claimed and awarded as destroyed; it was possibly the same 109 hit by Sergeant Marian Belc. Lochnan's was 1 (RCAF) Squadron's only claim, the squadron's sole casualty being Flying Officer Dean Nesbitt, who, 'had his aircraft severely damaged and landed at Biggin Hill' [ORB], fortunately unhurt. The Germans claimed two 'Spitfires' destroyed, *Leutnant* Erich Schmidt of 9/JG 53 at 13.20 hrs, over Mayfield, and *Oberfeldwebel* Werner Hübner of 4/JG 51, south-west of Dover at 13.50 hrs; no Spitfires were, in fact, lost.

At 15.30 hrs, fifty plus bandits crossed the Kentish coast and again headed for Biggin Hill and London – but the next Fighter Command casualties were not combat related. As the Germans crossed the coast over Romney, 607 Squadron scrambled from Tangmere ad headed north-east. Unfortunately, shortly after take-off, two Hurricanes collided near Arundel: South African Pilot Officer Ivor Difford crashed at Eartham Farm, Slindon, and was killed, whilst Pilot Officer Alex Scott baled out safely.

At 15.40 hrs, 249 Squadron took-off from North Weald with orders to join with Stapleford's 46 Squadron and patrol Rochford at Angels 20. Four minutes later, Squadron Leader George Denholm scrambled with his 603 Squadron Spitfires from Hornchurch, and by 16.15 hrs, all of these fighters were over the Ashford area at Angels 20.

Flying Officer Brian Carbury was leading Green Section of 603 Squadron and sighted Me 109s 5,000ft above. The Spitfires went into line astern and Carbury made to attack three Me 109s flying in a circle,

> but I could not press home my attack as Hurricanes were diving on my tail. I broke away and found two E/A, gave a short burst from 250 yards. He wobbled a bit and following another burst from quarter beam he

went straight down into the ground. I broke away as more Hurricanes were coming at me.

The enemy aircraft, however, does not appear to have actually crashed, although it was accredited to Carbury as destroyed. The Hurricanes belonged to 249 Squadron, Green 1, Australian Pilot Officer William Millington DFC reported,

> [No.] 46 Squadron, with 249 escorting, joined a dogfight between Spitfires and Me 109s at 21,000 feet. Formation broke up and I chased a Me 109 which dived steeply down. I left him to a Spitfire and climbed back to about 22,000 feet into the sun and dived onto a Me 109 which was on the tail of a Spitfire. The Me 109 broke off his attack and turned steeply in front of me, offering a plan view of the underside of the fuselage at point blank range. I gave him a short burst and he turned on his back and dived steeply, emitting black smoke. I was then tackled by two Spitfires, so broke off engagement ... The battle, in my opinion, broke up due to Spitfires mistaking Hurricanes for Me 109s and attacking them.

Millington claimed a probable. In the confusion of battle such chaotic circumstances were not uncommon, as we have seen, but, strangely, according to 46 Squadron, 'No enemy aircraft were sighted' [ORB] on any of the three patrols flown this day.

Having already had a busy day, at 15.35 hrs Squadron Leader Archie McKellar scrambled from Croydon and climbed his Hurricanes to 27,000ft. Five minutes later, 253 Squadron left Kenley to rendezvous with 605 Squadron over base, the latter leading a patrol of the Dungeness – Hawkinge area. Ordered to intercept Raid 11–12, 253 Squadron then patrolled Dungeness – Margate for thirty minutes, but no enemy aircraft were seen. According to the 253 Squadron ORB, 'Later, seven – nine Me 109s were encountered at 25,000 feet near base and 605 Squadron attacked this formation. [No.] 253 Squadron chasing individual aircraft.'

Sergeant Eric Wright, Yellow 1 of 605 Squadron, reported seeing a *Schwarm* of for Me 109s approaching from ahead, below and to port. 'In a position to jump the Me 109s' [ORB], both Wright and Polish Sergeant Jan Budzinski, Red 2, fired at a 109, which dived away, 'apparently undamaged'. Budzinski, together. With Flying Officer Cyril Passey, Red 3, fired at the same enemy fighter from astern, the windscreen of Passey's Hurricane being covered in glycol leaking from the damaged 109. As the German dived, all three 605 Squadron pilots fired again, as a result of which the 109 'lost height and speed and crashed into a large plantation with a lake two miles North of it, thought to be near Cranbrook.' The victory was shared between all three pilots. *Unteroffizier* P. Lederer of 5/JG 27, who had been escorting II/LG 2 *Jabos* to London, forced-landed at Bedgebury Wood, Cranbrook, where he was captured, slightly wounded.

A few miles to the west, Squadron Leader Archie McKellar also claimed a 109 destroyed (although no personal combat report appears to have survived). *Unteroffizier* Paul Legge of 5/JG 27 was killed, his fighter crashing at Mayfield Flats, Hadlow Down, near Heathfield, south of Mayfield. This, of course, was McKellar's fifth claim for an enemy aircraft destroyed on 7 October 1940, making him a rare ace in a day. Indeed, only four other RAF fighter pilots achieved this distinction during the Battle of Britain, namely Polish Sergeant Antoni Głowacki of 501 Squadron and Sergeant Ron Hamlyn of 610 Squadron on 24 August 1940, Flying Officer Brian Carbury of 603 Squadron on 31 August 1940, and 85 Squadron's South African Pilot Officer Albert Lewis on 27 September 1940. McKellar was the fifth and last of 'The Few' to claim five enemy aircraft destroyed in a single day during the Battle of Britain.

For Westhampnett's 602 Squadron it was a much quieter day – although a sad one. At 15.30 hrs, the Spitfires were scrambled to patrol Southampton when at 16.19 hrs, Blue Section, Flying Officer Donald Jack, Blue 1, and Sergeant Basil Whall DFM, Blue 2, were detached to intercept a bandit identified by RDF north-east of Worthing. Blue Section orbited over Beachy Head at 22,000ft when Jack sighted a Do 17, 2 miles away at 20,000ft, flying west. The Spitfires went into line astern and attacked the bomber head on, after which both made several attacks from astern and abeam. Jack eventually broke off the pursuit in mid-Channel, but which time the Do 17 was at 3,000ft, travelling east, 'diving and swerving', as Jack reported, adding that 'after my second attack it made no attempt to escape to France. Its behaviour suggested that pilot had decided he had got to alight on water and was doing his best to avoid further damage before alighting. In my opinion the E/A was probably destroyed.' Jack reportedly last saw Whall, a veteran of the Norwegian campaign, 'still attacking, but he crashed near Seaford and was killed'. It can only be assumed that Whall was hit by return fire in the exchange, because his Spitfire span in whilst the pilot was attempting to make a forced-landing near Lullington; this courageous and successful fighter pilot was fatally injured in the crash and subsequently died at Princess Alice Hospital in Eastbourne.

Further east, the enemy maintained the pressure: at 16.30 hrs, thirty plus bandits swept over Dungeness, penetrating to Central and North East London. At 15.35 hrs, thirteen Spitfires of 222 Squadron had left Hornchurch to patrol base at 25,000ft before being ordered to intercept the incoming raid over Maidstone. Whilst in that vicinity, according to casualty records, Pilot Officer John Broadhurst 'was seen to leave the formation and twelve Spitfires returned to Hornchurch at 1700 hrs.' Enemy aircraft were not encountered, but it was confirmed by ground observers that Pilot Officer Broadhurst had dived on a formation of enemy bombers and was shot down during the attack. The aircraft crashed at Hawkhurst, Kent.

Broadhurst, a 23-year-old married man, baled out but was killed, falling to earth at Longhurst, north of Maidstone. At the material time, *Oberleutnant* Josef 'Pips' Priller, *Staffelkapitän* of 6/JG 51, claimed a Spitfire destroyed in the Thames Estuary area, as did *Feldwebel* Walter Krieger of the same unit, north of Dungeness; Broadhurst's was the only RAF fighter lost at this time.

No. 253 Squadron's Green 2, Pilot Officer Guy Marsland was at 24,000ft over Hawkinge when he 'saw Yellow 2 break formation. I watched him going down. At the same time, I saw one unidentified aircraft following him. I covered him and aircraft turned away. I could not find my own formation, so I patrolled South of Biggin Hill at 23,000 feet.' At 17.00 hrs, Marsland alone barred the way back to France for twenty Me 109s approaching him from a direction of London. Undeterred by the unfavourable odds, Marsland attacked three 109s from abeam, raking one of these with a burst of eight to nine seconds. Pieces broke off the 109, but Marsland broke away without observing any further result. Yellow 1, it was later established, was one of two 253 Squadron Hurricanes which returned to base early with engine trouble, their windscreens covered in oil, and two others landed at 17.00 hrs, having lost the squadron in the sun during a steep turn. By this time, the weather conditions were 'practically no cloud, visibility very good' [ORB].

Although *Feldwebel* Josef Gärtner of 8/JG 26 claimed a Hurricane destroyed somewhere over south-east England late on the afternoon of 7 October 1940, none were in fact lost. Marsland's inconclusive combat marked an end to the day fighting over the 11 Group area. The fighter-bomber raids on London had all been intercepted, and at least seven Me 109s destroyed against the loss of five Hurricanes, two of which collided, three damaged, with three pilots killed (one from the collision). Four Spitfires had been shot down, one allegedly as the result of 'friendly fire' and another by return fire from a Do 17; two more were damaged, and three pilots killed (one as the result of engaging the Do 17 off Beachy Head and so unconnected with the fighter sweeps and *Jabo* raids). As the result of these raids, however, some eleven Londoners were killed and seventy injured, and beyond the capital nine more civilians were killed and forty-two injured, twenty-two seriously. There was no damage of any military significance.

Whilst 11 Group fought off the afternoon's raids on London, trouble was heading for 10 Group – the heaviest raid of the day, directed at Westland Aircraft at Yeovil. In the offensive against the British aircraft manufacturing industry, *Generalfeldmarschall* Hugo Sperrle's *Luftflotte* 3 had so far scored the greatest success, KG 55 flattening Bristol Aircraft at Filton on 25 September 1940, and the following day gutting the all-important Supermarine factory at Woolston. There had been failures too: on 27 September 1940, *Erprobungsgruppe* 210 and ZG 26 had been routed by 504 Squadron over Bristol whilst en route to attack Parnall Aircraft at Yate, suffering heavy losses; three days later KG 55 headed for Westland Aircraft but, finding the area covered by cloud, mistakenly bombed nearby Sherborne in error, virtually obliterating the town centre. Now, the Germans were once more bent upon the destruction of Westland Aircraft – on this occasion the mission was entrusted to *Major* Friedrich Winkler's II/KG 51, based at Paris-Orly. Equipped with the Ju 88, KG 51 was an experienced group, having participated in numerous raids throughout the Battle of Britain, by day and night, and Winkler's II *Gruppe* was no stranger to targets in the West Country. *Luftflotte* 3, *Fliegerkorps* V, intelligence documents record that the Yeovil raid was to be made by twenty Ju 88s of II/KG 51, which were to be escorted by thirty-nine Me 110s of the one-legged *Oberstleutnant* Joachim-Friedrich Huth's ZG 26, fifty-two Me 109s of *Major* Wolfgang Schellman's JG 2, and seven more of *Oberst* Günther Freiherr von Maltzahn's JG 53 – a formidable force indeed.

At 13.00 hrs, the British Meteorological Office recorded a ridge of high pressure moving eastwards across the country, the weather set fair in the Midlands, East Anglia and southern England. At Portland Bill, a force 4 WSW wind was reported, the sky being 'partly cloudy with a layer of 4/10ths stratus at 4,000 feet'.

Between 13.46 and 13.47 hrs (BST), II/KG 51 took-off from Paris-Orly, the twenty Ju 88s carrying a total of forty-four SC250 HE bombs and twenty-four Flamm SC250s. Flying on a flank of the formation was *Oberleutnant* Sigurd Hey, who recalled that when the bombers rendezvoused with their Me 109 escorts over Cherbourg, the single-engined fighters

> had already been airborne half an hour, so could only escort our *Gruppe* as far as the British coast, after which time, because of fuel shortage, they had to return to their bases. Thus, our only fighter escort from there on consisted solely of twin-engined Me 110s, hardly sufficient protection against the many Spitfires and Hurricanes that would soon be attacking from all sides.

The Dorset coast lay some 70 miles north of Cherbourg – a much longer flight for the escorting Me 109s than for those based around the Pas-de-Calais, just 22 miles from Dover. For II/KG 51, therefore, the mission had not started well. At 15.42 hrs, the approaching raid was detected by RDF and designated 'Raid 139', the Ju 88s flying at 17,000 feet, Me 110s behind and above, in line astern, occasionally forming up into an *Abwehrkreis* as the armada progressed across the Channel.

At 15.30 hrs, Squadron Leader Michael Robinson, who had succeeded Squadron Leader George Darley in command of 609 Squadron three days previously, had taken-off from Middle Wallop with eleven Spitfires to patrol base at Angels 20. At the same time, Squadron Leader Harold Fenton led 'A' Flight of his 238 Squadron up from the same airfield with identical orders. Overhead, the two squadrons rendezvoused, the Hurricanes taking up position on the Spitfires' left flank. That morning, the Boscombe Down based 56 Squadron sent ten Hurricanes to operate from Warmwell, the Middle Wallop forward base just inland of Weymouth, from where these aircraft also scrambled at 15.30 hrs, led, in the absence of the CO, Squadron Leader Herbert Moreton 'Pinners' Pinfold, who was in conference at Exeter, by Flight Lieutenant Richard Brooker, commander of 'A' Flight; the Hurricanes hastened towards the coast and incoming raid. Finally, twelve Spitfires of Squadron Leader Peter Devitt's 152 Squadron also scrambled from Warmwell, at 15.37 hrs, and climbed rapidly to combat height.

Pilot Officer David Crook DFC was flying in the 609 Squadron formation, and wrote,

> I don't think I have ever seen such a clear day in my life. From 15,000 feet I could see Plymouth and far beyond into Cornwall; up in the North the whole coast of South Wales was clearly visible, from the Severn at Gloucester and way beyond Swansea in the West ... on our left, to the South, the Channel glistened and sparkled in the sun, and the French coast and the Channel Islands, although seventy-five miles away, seemed to lie just under my wing-tip. But I can't say that I appreciated this superb view very much under the circumstances, because I was busily engaged behind the Squadron, anxiously scanning the sky for the Messerschmitts we knew would soon be arriving.

And in due course, arrive they would.

Although 152 Squadron's records are deficient, it appears that these Spitfires were the first to sight and engage the enemy, according to Polish Sergeant Zygmunt Klein, Blue 2, at 15.45 hrs, 5 miles west of Swanage, flying north-west and, according to the ORB, flying 'in straggling vics of three'. The Spitfires, however, had the advantage, being 3,000ft higher, went into line astern – and attacked. Pilot Officer Fred Holmes, Red 1, led the charge against the Ju 88s, from above and abeam, and after an inconclusive first volley fired again and saw white smoke streaming from two bombers. The Me 109s, however, were still present, and having climbed to 23,000ft over Dorchester, Holmes saw Me 109s above, which he managed to lose whilst climbing into the sun.

Pilot Officer Ian Norman Bayles, Red 2, and Sergeant Ralph Wolton, Red 3, also broke away after the first attack, noting no results, after which both failed to resume contact. As Sergeant Klein prepared to attack the Ju 88s, he sighted three Me 110 escorts 3 miles behind them, and so climbed into the sun and attacked the starboard *Zerstörer*: 'I fired three bursts at close range, then climbed back into the sun. White smoke was issuing from both engines and E/A was losing height. I attacked again but had to break away before opening fire as there were 110s on my tail.'

Five minutes after take-off, 609 and 238 Squadrons were vectored to proceed to Portland, to intercept the advancing enemy, Squadron Leader Michael Robinson of the former later reporting that his Spitfires flew on the Hurricanes' left flank, and when at 19,000ft sighted the bandits 15 miles to the south, over Portland. No. 238 Squadron's Squadron Leader Fenton ordered a No 1 Attack, with Flying Officer Bob Doe's Red Section leading, Fenton's Yellow following – but then, according to Robinson,

> [No.] 238 Squadron suddenly appeared to break-up and turn to the East, and at the same time I saw Me 109s above us and in the sun. It was extremely bright, and as we were heading into the sun it was very difficult to pick out E/A, which were now ahead of us, and we were rather embarrassed by the Me 109s still above us. I ordered the Squadron into sections line astern and turned underneath the 109s…

No. 238 Squadron had been attacked by Me 109s, from out of the sun, the Hurricanes breaking up and taking evasive action. Afterwards, Pilot Officer John Urwin-Mann, a Canadian, reported that afterwards the enemy formation was seen at 16,000ft, 4 miles ahead and flying towards Bristol. Meanwhile, 152 Squadron's Sergeant Edmund Shepperd, Yellow 1, was closing on a vic of three Ju 88s, firing from 50 yards; one of these then streamed white smoke, jettisoned its bombs and dropped back. At 4,000ft, it went into a spin, four of the crew baling out. Nos. 238 and 609 Squadrons on the scene, and other pilots also engaged this Ju 88.

Pilot Officer Richard Covington of 238 Squadron recalled, 'I followed Flying Officer Bob Doe into attack, and was going to have a go at this daisy chain of Me 110s that were milling about when an Me 109 got me from behind. I baled out – quickly!'

Covington, it seems likely, was shot down by 3/JG 2's *Leutnant* Egon Mayer, who claimed a Hurricane destroyed north-west of Portland at 16.00 hrs (BST). The Hurricane pilot landed safely by parachute but was slightly wounded and admitted to Blandford

Cottage Hospital; his Hurricane crashed at 16.00 hrs, at Meriden Wood, Winterbourne Houghton, near Blandford Forum.

Flying Officer Bob Doe continued his attack on the Ju 88:

> My first burst stopped the starboard engine. Overtaking speed was very high so I half-rolled upwards and attacked the enemy aircraft from above with a short burst from about 100 yards. I broke away and carried out a beam attack from the port side, from 300 yards. I broke away and started diving. As it dived a burst of fire appeared in front of the tail, which flew off. Three people baled out. The aircraft crashed in flames.

Pilot Officer John Bisdee of 609 Squadron also attacked the same bomber: 'My most vivid memory of the entire Battle of Britain is coming right down to see that Ju 88 burning on the Downs with a crowd of yokels waving pitchforks and dancing around it! I did a victory roll over them and went back upstairs to see what was happening'.

Squadron Leader Fenton of 238 Squadron also hit the same 'Do 17 [*sic*]', which 'dived through the clouds and was finished off by Yellow 3, Sergeant Gordon Batt, and seen to crash and was burning when left'.

The Ju 88 concerned was that flown by *Oberleutnant* Sigurd Hey of 5/KG 51:

> My starboard engine's radiator was hit. Though I dropped my bombs at once and switched the damaged motor to a feathered position, I could not hold my position in the *Gruppe* formation and fell behind. I then turned southwards, diving a couple of thousand feet, and tried to make the French coast on one engine. This time three fighters came up attacking from all different directions. First the controls were hit and I was only able to hold the aircraft horizontally by using the trimming system. Next the fuselage tank was hit which set the aircraft on fire. Then I gave the order to bale out, but received no reply as my crew had already left the aircraft unseen by me in the dense smoke. When the aircraft turned into a flat spin I was lucky to get out, but landed safely by parachute when I was taken prisoner by two old men armed with shotguns.

No. 152 Squadron's Pilot Officer Graham Cox, Yellow 3, also damaged a Ju 88, and Pilot Officer Eric 'Boy' Marrs, Blue 1, first damaged a Me 110, which streamed glycol, then attacked a lone 110, the crew of which baled out and their machine dived vertically into Ringstead Bay; both enemy airmen, of 4/ZG 26, were rescued from the water and captured. Pilot Officer Dudley Williams, Green 1, attacked the Ju 88s but made no claim; Polish Sergeant Józef Augustyn Szlagowski, Green 2, was about to attack the bombers when he saw three Me 110s several miles behind him:

> He climbed into the sun and attacked the Me 110s, firing three bursts at close range and broke away. He climbed back into the sun and saw white smoke issuing from both engines of E/A, which was losing height. He attacked again and broke away when two Me 110s were on his tail. [ORB]

Green 3, Sergeant Albert Kearsey, climbed after the initial attack but was fired upon by AA guns and after taking evasive action was unable to re-find the action.

Pilot Officer Roger Hall:

> I became separated from 152 Squadron, but saw what I thought were He 111s [*sic*] and got ahead of them near the Bristol Channel at a point which I think may have been Foreland Point. I did a head-on attack on the leader of the vic, opening at 1,000 yards – one long burst – and broke away above – half rolled and saw the left-hand E/A drop from the formation with glycol pouring from him. He was going down fairly steeply. I then saw what I took to be two other He 111s flying NE. I chased them but caught up a Blenheim well inland past Yatesbury. Came down to 500 feet to pinpoint. Found five gallons in one tank only so put down in a field with wheels down, the engine having cut before I had completed my last turn in to approach the field. Forced landed at Barton Stacey, but the Spitfire was a write-off.

Having taken evasive action upon being bounced by the Me 109s, Pilot Officer Urwin-Mann of 238 Squadron attacked two Ju 88s, but was then fired upon by two Me 110s, and broke away. He then sighted another 'Ju 88 [*sic*]', which he attacked and watched enter a 'spiral dive, pulled out and went into the sea 7 miles south-west of Portland. No-one was seen to get out'. This was actually a Me 110 of II/ZG 26, the crew of which, *Oberfeldwebel* Fritz Stahl and *Unteroffizier* Ernst Mauer, remain missing. Afterwards, Urwin-Mann turned towards base when he 'was attacked by six Me 109s, which I took to be Spitfires, and took sharp evasive action and landed at Warmwell.' This same Me 110 was also claimed by 238 Squadron's Czech pilot, Sergeant Józef Jeka, who 'saw it crash ten miles due South of Bridport. I flew low, then straight for Portland, and over Weymouth Bay I saw a lifeboat going SE, where I saw a big patch of substance in the water' – one of three Me 110s shot down into the sea south-east of Weymouth.

As the enemy approached their target, the Hurricanes of 56 Squadron, being led by Flight Lieutenant Richard Brooker, Red 1, entered the fray, 6 miles south-east of Yeovil. Brooker had climbed the squadron to 19,000ft, and attacked from the sun. By now, the Germans, Brooker reported, 'were in a wide formation, apparently split up. They appeared to be a mixed formation of Do 17 [*sic*] and Ju 88'. Brooker attacked a 'Do 17' without observing any effect, then climbed to 20,000ft to select another target. Polish Sergeant Zbigniew Nosowicz was Brooker's Red 3, and also attacked a 'Do 17 [*sic*]', which he hit and last saw 'gliding towards the sea' before breaking away and taking evasive action upon being engaged himself by Me 110s. Sergeant Clifford Whitehead also attacked the bombers inconclusively before breaking away, after which he 'did not succeed in re-engaging', and Sergeant Peter Hillwood left a 'Do 17 [*sic*]' streaming glycol from both engines.

Sergeant Dennis 'Nick Nichols had joined 56 Squadron as an OTU-fresh replacement pilot at Boscombe Down on 15 September 1940, together with his friend and contemporary, Sergeant Peter Fox:

Like my friend Peter Fox, who had been shot down on the last big show, on 30 September 1940, I was nineteen-years old and this was my first engagement. We took off from Warmwell being on detachment from our base at Boscombe Down. We took off in formation with me on the left of the leader, Flight Lieutenant Brooker, and I was 'Pip-squeak' man, the radio being blocked every 15 seconds to send out a homing signal to ground control. I can't remember hearing any R/T transmissions so perhaps the wireless was on the blink. I did not hear the ' Ho'. Flying in tight formation, the first I saw was tracer coming from one of our leader's guns. Quick glimpse and I saw a Ju 88 and fired my guns, still in formation, but had to break away to avoid collision with Flight Lieutenant Brooker. I then lost the Squadron and pulled up, searching for the enemy. No sign of the bombers but some 110s in a defensive spiral, well above. I pulled the 'tit' for maximum power and went to intercept. A Spitfire was attacking the top of the spiral so I went head-on for the bottom. I fired but, perhaps not surprisingly in view of their heavy forward-firing armament which I must have overlooked, was hit. Flames started coming from the nose of my aircraft and the windscreen was black with oil, so I broke away as I could not see out. I turned the aircraft on its back to bale out at 25,000 feet, first attempt a slow roll but I remained seated. Second time I tumbled out, spinning. I told myself not to panic and gave the ripcord a steady pull. When the parachute deployed, the lanyards on one side were twisted. I tried to untangle them without success but relaxed as at about 15,000 feet appeared to be coming down reasonably slowly. I did not see the ground coming up and crumpled in a heap upon landing. The Home Guard then appeared on the scene and told me to stick my hands up. They thought I was German but I just laughed at them between groans as I had actually broken my back. There was a Jerry parachutist stuck up a nearby tree, from the Ju 88, but the locals would not get him down until they had seen to me.

Contrary to his perception, Sergeant Nichols had not been shot down by a 110, but hit by an unseen Me 109: *Oberleutnant* Anton Mader of 1/JG 2 claimed a 'Spitfire [*sic*]' destroyed 20km North of Portland at 15.57 hrs (BST) – which is exactly where 'Nick's' Hurricane crashed, and he landed heavily by parachute at Austral Farm, near the village of Alton Pancras. At about 16.00 hrs, Charlie Callaway was ploughing in the Vernall field when he saw a parachute drifting towards Buckland Newton. He then saw the Hurricane 'coming down hard and well on fire!' His younger brother, Sam, was rabbiting nearby and he too saw the doomed British fighter 'descending at a shallow angle but all ablaze and travelling sharpish, like. It was so close that I could have reached out and touched it. There were several parachutes in the sky at the same time.' Villagers also recall cartridge cases from the combat overhead raining down on the cobbled streets.

At 15.45 hrs, Yeovil's air raid sirens wailed for the thirty-third time since the Second World War began – and after Sherborne's battering a week previously, the townsfolk hurried to their shelters. At 15.55 hrs, the first bombs fell – like Sherborne, all would hit the town centre. Damage and loss of life was caused at Montague Burton's store in Middle Street, St Andrew's Road, and Summerleaze Park. Direct hits were also recorded on shelters at the Methodist Church in Vicarage Street and at 45 Grove Avenue. An engineering firm, Ricketts Ltd in Belmont Street, and nearby dwellings were also seriously damaged. Sixteen people lost their lives, with nine more seriously injured, twenty less so – and as the German bombers turned for home, they noted 'two large fires burning'. Down below, Yeovilians were enduring a terrifying ordeal.

Margaret Hewlett:

> My husband and I were in Woolworth's at the time, next to Burton's menswear shop, where there was a direct hit. Eight people were killed there. The whole front of Woolworth's was blown in, but, fortunately, we had both moved back from the front of the store. There were several people injured and a lot of panic as a gas main had burst. We all tried to get out by the back exit and as quickly as possible. The emergency services did a good job, though, and the fire was soon under control.

Fred Denham:

> The bombs on Burton's and the billiard hall fell just 150 yards from my First Aid Post. A bomb exploded on the steps between there and Woolworth's, where many were sheltering. I ran there, carrying a stretcher, with another chap. We got two women out from the top of the stairs, but the others were all dead. We did what we could for various people but swiftly moved on to the Methodist Church where a shelter had been hit.

Mr John Chesterman: 'I remember seeing tremendous fighter escort flying around the bombers overhead.'

Henry Smith:

> My elder brother, Albert, was employed at the Southern Railway Station in Yeovil and was in bed following a night shift. My mother and I were in the farm cottage where we lived at Brympton d'Evercy. Suddenly, we heard the siren, followed by explosions from falling bombs. My brother got up and the three of us took shelter in a ditch at the bottom of the garden. In an adjacent field a barrage balloon was sited with two huts housing the crew, I suppose about three miles from the airfield. It would appear that one of the aircraft had overshot the target and dropped its bombs near us. An oil bomb was dropped in the ditch where we sheltered. Fortunately the ditch was dog-legged, which sheltered us from the blast. Another bomb, HE, fell in front of the barrage balloon hut. Following the bombing the NCO in charge came running to look

for us at our damaged cottage and said that one of his men was missing. Then the displaced earth at the edge of the crater moved, and out stepped the 'missing' man – shaken but otherwise unhurt!

As the enemy retreated back to France, the RAF fighters continued to harass them. At 15.45 hrs, Blue and Red Sections of 601 Squadron's Hurricanes had scrambled from Exeter, and this fresh squadron headed for Yeovil. At 16.03 hrs, Flight Lieutenant William Clyde, Blue 1, reported having requested the enemy's current position from 'Ops', the reply being 'Bandits still twelve miles out to sea'. Two minutes later, 'Red 1 [author's note: Pilot Officer Howard Mayers, an Australian] said that bandits were ahead. We were then at Angels 9, just approaching Yeovil. I saw about twenty bombers ... going South, just West of Portland'. The fighter escorts, Clyde explained, stretched from Portland to Yeovil, all travelling south. Chasing the enemy back to the coast, Clyde was half-way between Yeovil and Portland when he was attacked head on by 'twelve Me 110s' from slightly below – fortunately the Germans were out of range, so Clyde dived and opened fire at a 110, which Blue 2 saw 'hit the ground and burst into flame' – which could only have been the machine of 6/ZG 26 which crashed at Brickhills Field, Kingston Russell House, Long Bredy, Dorset; *Obergefreiter* Herbert Schilling and *Oberfeldwebel* Karl Herzog were both killed (this 110, as we will see, was also attacked by at least one other RAF pilot). Afterwards, Clyde 'climbed up and had another crack at some more Me 110s', but after only a short burst he 'was heavily attacked and had to break-away'.

Polish Pilot Officer Jerzy Jankiewicz, Blue 2, claimed a Me 110 damaged over Bridport at 16.10 hrs, and at the same time, Pilot Officer Aylmer Aldwinckle a 'Do 17 [*sic*]' probable over Lyme Bay.

No. 601 Squadron's Red Section, having not seen the fighters, pursued the bombers but only caught the Ju 88s 20 miles out to sea. At that point the Me 110s interfered, Mayers's Hurricane being hit in the glycol tank, forcing him to break away and crash-land in a field south of Axminster, surviving with only minor injuries.

Squadron Leader Robinson and 609 Squadron also became embroiled with the withdrawing Me 110s. Robinson engaged a lone Me 110 from astern, which was also attacked by Flight Lieutenant Brooker of 56 Squadron. According to Robinson,

> The Me 110 dived vertically down with his port engine smoking. I then climbed up and asked 'Bandy' [author's note: Middle Wallop control] for the position of any E/A. He told me of one E/A plotted at 15,000 feet over Lyme Regis. I proceeded to the latter place and found a circle of Me 110s about ten miles NW of Portland. I attacked one from dead astern and it dived vertically onto the ground about five miles North of the coast (Little Bredy).

The first Me 110 involved, of 9/ZG 26, forced-landed at Corfe Castle; the pilot, *Gefreiter* Bernhardt Denmig was captured but his *Bordfunker*, *Obergefreiter* Josef Bachmann was killed. The second was the 110 down at Long Bredy, also attacked by Flight Lieutenant Clyde of 601 Squadron.

Mrs Vestry, on whose land the latter Me 110 crashed, later recalled the somewhat dramatic incident:

> My husband and I were watching the battle from the hill beside our house. There were quite a lot of planes involved but they were very high up so it was impossible to identify friend from foe. Presently, however, a German plane was hit and it nose-dived into a field from about 18,000 feet, and had literally flown into the ground.
>
> We were all very thankful as we thought that it was going to fall on our house. In the event it couldn't have fallen in a better place as it did no damage. There wasn't much of it left above the ground, but what there was burned furiously. It was impossible to get near it for some time, due to exploding bullets.

In the fierce battle ongoing high above, 609 Squadron's Flight Lieutenant Frank Howell, Yellow 1, also hit a 110, 10 miles north-west of Portland, which 'burst into flames from the fuselage to the starboard motor and went down', but, a few minutes later Howell's engine seized, forcing him down in a field 4 miles south of Shaftesbury.

Flying Officer John Dundas, Blue 1 of 609 Squadron, engaged a Me 110 at 16.30 hrs, 6 miles north of Warmwell, causing both engines to 'stream smoke and glycol', but as Dundas tried to 'finish him off', the Spitfire pilot was

> hit by an explosive cannon shell from astern. My aircraft spun and I was obliged to forced-land at Warmwell. I did not see the E/A which attacked me. The Me 110 which I claim was last seen by me gliding at a fast tick-over at 14,000 feet, about five miles North of Weymouth. With both motors out of action I am sure he would not have reached France.

Dundas, however, was wounded by shrapnel splinters in both legs.

At 16.00 hrs, 609 Squadron's Pilot Officer Michael Staples was shot down and baled out, his Spitfire crashing at Shillingstone; the pilot suffered a leg wound and was also admitted to Blandford Cottage Hospital. At the same time, the squadron suffered a fatal casualty: Sergeant Alan Fearey was shot down and killed, his Spitfire crashing at Watercombe Farm, just south of Warmwell; the pilot's body fell nearby, having baled out too low. Of the popular Fearey, the squadron diarist wrote,

> He was a steady, painstaking pilot who, from becoming operational at Northolt on 26 June 1940, had disposed of five and a third E/A destroyed, two probables and two damaged. He seemed to regard his Spitfire with the kind of jealous care and affection that some others bestow upon animals, and the notion has been advanced by those who knew him well that this trait may have contributed to his loss of life, causing reluctance to bale out from a spin which he was unable to control.

It was a sad loss for 609 Squadron.

At 16.30 hours, 609 Squadron's Flying Officer Terence Forshaw claimed a Me 110 damaged, and Sergeant over Portland, and Sergeant Hughes-Rees damaged a Me 109, both being pilots of 609 Squadron, their combats occurring over Portland. At the same time, Pilot Officer Harold Ackroyd of 152 Squadron was shot down over Lyme Regis, crashing at Shatcombe Farm, Wynford Eagle, near Dorchester – he baled out, but was horrendously burnt. Tragically, Mrs Irene Akroyd, a WAAF at Warmwell, had actually watched her young husband's flaming Spitfire's death-dive – not knowing, of course, the identity of the young pilot involved; Harold Akroyd died of his wounds the next day.

By 17.00 hrs, the West Country and Channel off Portland was clear of the enemy. Over the Channel, at 17.15 hrs (BST), however, 2/JG 2 happened across Pilot Officer L.W. Wenman's 59 Squadron Blenheim, engaged on a 'Moon Patrol' reconnaissance off the French coast; in the ensuing combat, Sergeant Eric Neal and Sergeant Gordon Wood were both wounded, Wenman claiming a 109 shot down in flames before beating it back to Detling. *Oberleutnant* Siegfried Bethke and *Unteroffizier* Wolfgang Liedig both claimed Blenheims destroyed – all involved were mistaken, though, as neither side actually lost an aircraft in what was the final sideshow to the day's main event.

During the 'main event', Fighter Command lost two Hurricanes destroyed and one damaged, three of their pilots wounded, and three Spitfires destroyed, two damaged, one pilot killed and three wounded, including poor Pilot Officer Akroyd who subsequently died of his wounds. According to *Hauptmann* Genst's after action report, I/ZG 26 claimed a Spitfire and two Hurricanes, and II/ZG 26 two Hurricanes; I/JG 2 claimed three Spitfires and two Blenheims; II/JG 2 four Hurricanes, and III/JG 2 one Spitfire. Exaggerated though these claims were, there can be no doubting that the German fighter escorts did their job well, as II/KG 51 only lost a single Ju 88. This, however, was at a cost: although the Me 109s returned to France unscathed, ZG 26 lost seven Me 110s in what was also the types last significant showing during the Battle of Britain. In military terms, once more, the raid had achieved nothing of military value, just the devastation of another provincial town centre.

Coastal Command flew its usual patrols throughout the day, five aircraft attacking the port of Le Havre and another Trouville, and PRU Spitfires returned with photographs of the invasion ports. By night, Coastal Command despatched aircraft to attack shipping at Rotterdam, Le Havre and Cherbourg, and mined the Maas Estuary. Pilot Officer L.W. Wenman of 59 Squadron fortunately returned safely to Detling with two wounded crewmen aboard after their brush with 2/JG 2, representing 'Coastal's' only casualties. In daylight, 2 Group sent twelve Blenheims to attack specific targets in Germany and elsewhere in enemy occupied Europe, but owing to a lack of cloud cover all but two crews aborted; the remaining two attacked barges in Dutch ports, and six other Blenheims uneventfully swept the North Sea. That night, Bomber Command raided targets in Germany, including Berlin, Amsterdam's Fokker factory and aerodromes, various harbours, and the heavy gun battery at Cap-Gris-Nez. A Wellington of Marham's 38 Squadron failed to return from Berlin, the crew all killed; a 99 Squadron Wellington from Mildenhall was damaged by a night fighter, returning to crash-land at Honnington, the crew only just escaping before the wreck caught fire; a Blenheim of Wattisham's

110 Squadron crashed returning from attacking the invasion ports, injuring the crew, and a 102 Squadron Whitley from Linton-on-Ouse ditched in the Atlantic due to engine failure, the crew only being rescued after nearly twenty-four cold and miserable hours in their dinghy.

Weekly Report by Home Intelligence:

Evacuation and the return of evacuees

A preliminary report of a detailed study by Mass Observation made in fifty towns and hamlets around London, with special reference to Oxford and Burford reveals the following points:

The evacuees have been much more warmly received this time (as compared with a year ago). Not only were the hosts more sympathetic, but the evacuees were glad to be out of the heavily raided areas. Nevertheless there is friction between adults. There is much profiteering, especially in hotels and boarding houses. There is much less talk of the dirtiness of the evacuees. Indeed, in some places, they are very favourably compared with the last lot (though in fact there is little difference). The Billeting Officers are much less criticised this time than last time. The present relatively satisfactory situation needs watching, and above all careful arrangements are needed in each home as that the evacuees and hosts do not 'get on each others' nerves' as time goes on. There is a steady trickle of people returning to London, including the East End. The reasons given are: dislike of being away from home and familiar surroundings; the decline in raids in London; the barrage makes it easier to stick London; difficulty in getting good billets, and difficulties with hosts. Those returning are mostly young people, but not children.

A study by the Social Survey shows that the elderly and infirm need (and want) special consideration in raids and evacuation.

Tuesday, 8 October 1940

The day dawned clear, heralding a busy day ahead for photographic reconnaissance Spitfires. Before the war, MI6 had formed the so called 'Heston Flight', based at Heston airfield, the Northolt satellite west of London, under the command of Australian inventor and aviation photography pioneer Sidney Cotton, the purpose of which was to undertake clandestine photographic reconnaissance of Europe, flying the Lockheed 12A. By 17 January 1940, the unit had been absorbed by the RAF and became known as the PDU, changing on 19 June 1940 to the PRU, operating various modified aircraft, including the Spitfire. Stripped of armament to save weight, enabling these machines to fly higher and faster, deep into enemy occupied territory, the PRU's unofficial motto was 'Unarmed and unafraid'. After the Battle of France, 'A' Flight remained based at Heston, concentrating on reconnoitring the *Luftflotte* 2 area, and 'B' Flight at St Eval, focussing on *Luftflotte* 3 and the Atlantic ports. Two of the day's actions would involve these unarmed pilots – and the first combat of the day was fought not by Fighter Command but by Coastal Command.

At 06.10 hrs, three Coastal Command Blenheims left Bircham Newton, the three 235 Squadron crews searching for a missing aircraft in the Isle of Wight area. At 08.00 hrs, the Blenheims were off Cherbourg and engaged two He 59 seaplanes of *Seenotflugkommando* 2. The aircraft captains, namely Pilot Officer John Fenton, Pilot Officer Henri Gonay and Pilot Officer Leon Prévot, the latter two both Free Belgians, shared the victories equally. There were no survivors.

It was on this day that the use of Spitfires as high-altitude 'spotters' was formalised with the creation of 421 (Spotter) Flight, equipped with six Spitfire Mk IIAs, based at Gravesend. According to Air Chief Marshal Hugh Dowding, AOC-in-C, Fighter Command:

> it was later recommended that the Spitfires should be used in pairs, for reasons of security, and that the Flight should become a squadron [author's note: on 11 January 1941 421 Flight became 91 Squadron]. A special R/T receiving set was erected at Group HQ so that reports might be obtained without any delay from the Sector receiving station. There is reason to believe that the Germans also adopted a system of high-flying He 113s [sic] as scouts. Their information concerning our movements was transmitted to the ground and relayed to their bombers in the air.

The flight was originally a detached flight formed from Gravesend's 66 Squadron, under the command of Flight Lieutenant Charles 'Paddy' Green, an Old Harrovian, former Olympian and who had joined the 'Millionaire's Club', 601 Squadron, as an auxiliary airman in 1937. Green had seen action with 92 Squadron over Dunkirk, destroying a Me 109 before being wounded, only returning to operations on 1 October 1940. Now, he was given the task of forming this new unit, the 'main duties of which were to act as "Jim Crows" and report on enemy aircraft, their tactics in combat, camouflage etc' [ORB]. Amongst Green's original ten pilots was Pilot Officer Keith Lawrence:

> I had seen action with both 234 and 603 Squadrons when I was posted to 421 Flight at Hawkinge [author's note: on 8 October 1940]. I understood that the Flight had been formed at the instigation of the Prime Minister. Known as the 'Jim Crow' Flight, I found that our purpose, flying singly or in pairs, was to report on the movement of enemy shipping in the Channel, or the build-up of Luftwaffe formations. Conjecture is that here was cover to permit ULTRA secrets to be used to best advantage without giving the game away. From Hawkinge the Flight's first daily task was for a single Spitfire to fly a weather patrol along the Kentish coast between North Foreland and Dungeness to obtain Met 'actuals' on the cloud conditions and formations. At the same time we would listen out for any operational instructions from Control. The pilot detailed for

the weather flight would take-off between first light and sunrise. It was interesting and worthwhile work, we thought.

On the flight's first day of existence, two patrols were flown, a figure substantially increasing in days to come.

At Biggin Hill, 92 Squadron had occasion to celebrate: Flight Lieutenant Brian 'Kingpin' Kingcome DFC and Pilot Officer Tony Bartley received news that both had been awarded the DFC. Although unmentioned by squadron records, however, according to certain secondary sources two unknown pilots of 92 Squadron claimed a Me 109 destroyed and a probable, respectively, east of London at 09.15 hrs; certainly between 08.15 and 09.40 hrs eleven Spitfires of 92 Squadron patrolled base, but no record of this combat can otherwise be found. German fighters were over south-east England at that time, though.

At 08.50 hrs, Flight Lieutenant Bob Oxspring led Pilot Officer George Corbett and Pilot Officer Charles Cooke up on a 'Convoy and Interception Patrol' [ORB] from Gravesend. At 09.30 hrs, the Spitfires were attacked by Me 109s, Corbett being shot down and killed, his Spitfire crashing at Bayford Marches, Upchurch, in Kent; 5/JG 52's *Feldwebel* Ludwig Bielmeier claimed a Spitfire destroyed over 'NE London'.

At 09.00 hrs, Squadron Leader Ronald Kellett led the Poles of Northolt's 303 (Polish) Squadron on a fifty-minute patrol during which there was no contact with the enemy – but, nonetheless, the squadron suffered a devastating loss. The Hurricanes were recalled to base, but over Staines Czech Sergeant Josef František DFM broke formation, ignored R/T instructions to re-join the formation, and flew off to the east. News was later received that the gallant ace was dead, having been killed whilst making a forced-landing at Cuddington Way, Banstead, south-east of Ewell. František went to his grave at Northwood being the only person aware of why he broke formation and forced-landed; within 303 (Polish) Squadron it was widely believed that he had 'beaten up' his new girlfriend's home but everything went wrong when a wingtip clipped a tree or the ground, the pilot being fatally injured when his head hit the Hurricane's gunsight – suggesting that his harness was too loose. Whatever happened, it was a tragic and pointless end to the life of the Battle of Britain's top-claiming RAF fighter pilot, whose final number of claims amounted to seventeen enemy aircraft destroyed and one probable. In addition to having been awarded the DFM just a week before his untimely death, the Poles had honoured the Czech with the *Virtuti Militari* V Class, and he posthumously received the Polish Cross of Valour with three Bars, a Bar to the DFM, and the Czech Military Cross in addition to being commissioned in 1945. As Northolt's station commander, Group Captain Stanley Vincent, wrote to Squadron Leader Ronald Kellett, 'His name should stay forever in the Squadron History as a really fine fighter. I am proud to have known him myself and had him at Northolt.'

The day also began badly for Biggin Hill's 72 Squadron, ten Spitfires of which took-off at 09.57 hrs to patrol the Maidstone to Gravesend line at Angels 15. Soon afterwards, Sergeant Norman 'Sticky' Glew turned back with engine trouble, safely forced-landing at Halstead. Unfortunately, 'R/T transmission from Biggin Hill failed and Pilot Officer Robert Deacon Elliott was sent back to re-establish contact and, until repairs were made, orders were telephoned to Dispersal Point, thence radio-telephoned'

[ORB]. This communication breakdown may have contributed to why the Spitfires, when at 20,000ft, were jumped by Me 109s from above and up-sun. Two Spitfires were hit, both pilots (identities unknown) returning safely to base, unhurt. *Stab* II/JG 54 and 7/JG 54 were responsible, four Spitfires being claimed destroyed at the material time north of Folkestone. There was, though, a third Spitfire down: R6894 of Heston's PRU.

Flying Officer W.B. Parker, a New Zealander, was climbing over Kent prior to setting off for France at height when he also ran into the JG 54 Me 109s. Attacked by two German fighters, the defenceless Parker's Spitfire erupted into flame – forcing the pilot to bale out, despite the need for oxygen at high altitude. Passing out, Parker regained consciousness lower down only to discover that he was saturated in petrol, his uniform well ablaze, the flames encouraged by the descent. So intense was the pain that Parker decided to put an end to his suffering and release his parachute – but this failed to operate, only the shoulder harness coming away, pitching him down, head-first, held only by his thigh straps – and these slipped, holding him by his ankles. One strap then burnt through, and as the flames subsided Parker landed heavily, his parachute also damaged by fire, breaking an arm. Fortunately, his predicament had been witnessed by an army unit, which rushed orderlies to the scene and conveyed the wounded pilot straight to hospital. Thankfully, Parker survived, returned to duty and completed another tour as a reconnaissance pilot.

At 10.45 hrs, 222 Squadron's Spitfires scrambled from Hornchurch and 605 Squadron's Hurricanes likewise from Croydon, both to patrol south of the Thames. At 11.00 hrs, near Gatwick, the former squadron's Pilot Officer Tim Vigors and Pilot Officer Eric Edsall broke away to attack a Ju 88, which was rapidly disappearing into clouds – pursued by 605 Squadron's Flight Lieutenant Christopher 'Bunny' Currant and his 'A' Flight. Vigors reported that the Hurricanes 'got there first and delivered attacks', the raider then entering cloud with a smoking engine. The Spitfire pilot flew above cloud in the same direction and engaged the Ju 88 as it emerged, making the other engine pour black smoke. The bomber then dived, followed by Currant (also awarded the DFC on this day) who saw the Ju 88, of 4/KG 51, crash and explode at 11.20 hrs, at Three Bridges, Sussex. There were no survivors and the victory was equally shared between all pilots involved.

At the same time as the Ju 88's demise, the third fighter and fighter-bomber sweep of the day was incoming over Lympne, penetrating South and East London. From Gravesend, the Spitfires of 66 Squadron were scrambled at 11.35 hrs, with, according to Sergeant Harry Cook of 'A' Flight, orders

> to climb to 20,000 feet as quickly as possible. On reaching 16,000 feet information was received that bandits were approaching from the SW at 20,000 feet. Almost immediately we were attacked from the South by a number of Me 109s. The Squadron broke formation and advantage was taken of clouds at 3,000 feet. We were then ordered to re-form at 10,000 feet over base. On climbing through a clear patch over the Thames I saw a E/A diving to cloud level, going South. I turned and followed – catching the E/A at a point West of base and delivered an attack from directly astern, no result from fire observed. He used slight

cover of cloud but came into the open soon after – giving time to deliver another attack – with a result that pieces were seen to fall from him, and smoke came from his fuselage. I gave him the rest of my ammunition and he dived into clouds about ten miles SE of base.

Sergeant Cook claimed the 109 as damaged.

Sadly, 66 Squadron lost its second pilot of the day in this clash: Sergeant Rufus Ward was shot down over Rochester and baled out – but found dead.

According to an eyewitness, Peggy Whamond:

When we saw the pilot bale out from the falling plane a great cheer went up from the gardens all around – and when another plane began to fly around the parachute we thought he was one of ours protecting the falling man. Suddenly, my father shouted 'The swine is shooting at him' – this, in the bright sunshine of an Indian Summer. It seemed unbelievable but was so. I was thirteen at the time and the memory that has stayed with me all the years was not, I am afraid, the killing of the pilot but my Dad's sheer rage and frustration and his yelling 'You bastard, you bastard!' That was a dreadful word to use in those long-ago days and in front of the neighbours.

From Hornchurch, 603 Squadron had also scrambled at 11.35 hrs, to patrol base. Having climbed to Angels 20, 20 miles south of base fifty Me 109s were found, between 20,000–25,000ft, above and south of the Spitfires, which Squadron Leader George Denholm immediately ordered into line astern. The 109s split up and flew east; Pilot Officer Ronald 'Raz' Berry DFC, Yellow 1,

dived down an closed on two 109s. I caught one up as it entered cloud and I sent a good burst into E/A. Smoke and glycol came heavily from the E/A and it dropped out of cloud cover. I dived below clod but could not see E/A. I was attacked by the other 109 as I climbed through again. I took evasive action and E/A dived into cloud and was not sighted.

Pilot Officer Berry claimed a 'probable'.

In the skirmishes with 66 and 603 Squadrons, two Me 109s, in fact, were brought down: *Oberleutnant* Werner Voigt, *Staffelkapitän* of 4/JG 3, who was forced to ditch his badly damaged aircraft on the foreshore at Abbots Cliff, Folkestone, where he was captured, unhurt, most likely having been attacked by Berry, and *Feldwebel* Paul Boche of 5/JG 52, who crash-landed and hit a haystack at Woodham Mortimer, Essex, where the pilot was captured, injured. Given that the only Spitfire lost was Sergeant Rufus Ward of 66 Squadron, and the only German claims arising being for two Spitfires destroyed by pilots of *Stab* II and 6/JG 52, it is likely that Cook, of 66 Squadron, shot Boche down.

By 11.55 hrs, the PRU's Flight Lieutenant James Smalley DFC was at 33,000ft over the Friesians, having left Heston at 09.15 hrs to photograph the *Kriegsmarine* base at Kiel. The Germans, however, were mounting high-flying patrols to intercept these sky spies, and Smalley was shot down by *Oberleutnant* Adolf Kinzinger of *Stab* I/JG 54, who claimed a Spitfire destroyed 30 km south-west of Emden. Given the high altitude involved, at first Smalley had to remain with his doomed Spitfire, which, unlike Flying Officer W.B. Parker's had not become a 'flamer', eventually baling out at 2,000ft. Landing safely near Noordbrook in the Netherlands, this experienced reconnaissance pilot was captured, seeing out the war at the infamous Stalag Luft III camp.

By noon, what had begun as a bright and clear day had deteriorated into one of 'low cloud and very poor visibility', so bad, according to 229 Squadron's ORB, that the Northolt controller ordered the Hurricanes to land after an uneventful patrol 'outside the bad weather area'. Six aircraft, however, returned to base whilst five of 'A' Flight landed at Halton – then tragedy struck:

> Sergeant [John Robinson] Farrow, with Yellow Section, had been in formation up above cloud at 6,000 feet but as the Section climbed again into cloud. It was seen that he did not re-join it, after passing out of cloud again at 9,000 feet. His aircraft disintegrated in mid-air at about 200 feet over Bovingdon (Herts) and pieces were scattered over four fields ... So far as can be ascertained there was no sign of enemy action in the wreckage.

What caused the Hurricane to break up will never be known – but the 24-year-old former teacher, Sergeant John Robinson Farrow, from Eastleigh in Hampshire, would join 303 (Polish) Squadron's Sergeant Josef František in Northwood Cemetery.

At 12.25 hrs, two small formations of Me 109s, each numbering twenty plus, flew in over Folkestone and as far as Kenley and Biggin Hill before turning about; they were not intercepted and because of the worsening weather, this intrusion represented the last fighter sweep of the day. The low-lying cloud, however, lent itself perfectly to nuisance raids by lone Ju 88s, which became the main feature for the rest of the day.

The first of these lone Ju 88s to be intercepted was at 15.00 hrs, at 27,000ft over South Cerney in Gloucestershire. Pilot Officer Peter Matthews and Pilot Officer George Goodman made up Blue Section of Wittering's 1 Squadron, patrolling Hucknall. Goodman, Blue 2, sighted the raider at 26,500ft, about 5 miles away and heading west. Matthews, Blue 1, also saw the Ju 88 and both pilots gave chase. After five minutes the Hurricanes were still failing to close on the bomber, which was now over the Bristol Channel. Matthews got left behind but Goodman pursued the bomber in a dive, closing to 500 yards. At sea level the Ju 88 suddenly climbed towards a bank of thick cloud, but, Goodman reported,

> I opened fire at 300 yards with a three-second burst and silenced the rear-gunner. I could see the De Wilde ammunition hitting the fuselage and wing roots and engine nacelles. The E/A disappeared into cloud, steering a course of 220° South of Cardiff. I landed at Filton aerodrome.

The Ju 88 was accredited as damaged.

At 15.40 hrs, Fighter Command lost two more pilots – both in a training accident. Whilst 74 Squadron took its turn at Coltishall in 12 Group, although operational, undertaking convoy patrols and interceptions, under Air Chief Marshal Hugh Dowding's far-sighted Stabilising Scheme, as a 'B' unit the 'Tigers' there received and trained replacement pilots prior to returning south. At 15.10 hrs, Pilot Officer Frank Buckland, a new pilot, took-off with Pilot Officer Douglas Hastings, a combat veteran, for dogfight practice. At 15.40 hrs, the two Spitfires collided and crashed near Gillingham, Norfolk: both pilots were killed. Not yet having flown an operational patrol, however, the name of 20-year-old Buckland will not be found amongst 'The Few'. Five years older, Douglas Hastings was a married man – his wife giving birth to the daughter he would never meet on Christmas Day 1940.

Next to score against the nuisance raiders would be 312 (Czech) Squadron. Formed at Duxford on 29 August 1940, the fourteen original Czech pilots, the squadron diarist recorded

> report having between 600–2,000 hours flying experience and without exception have been in combat against the enemy in France. They all claim one or more victories but the exact number of individual successes is difficult to ascertain owing to the French practice of a squadron or flight each counting any enemy plane shot down as beginning to every pilot of the formation engaged. [ORB]

As with the two existing Polish squadrons, 302 and 303, and the Czech squadron, 310, a system of 'double-banking' was adopted wherein RAF commanding officers and flight commanders were shadowed by Czech officers. Consequently, the British CO, Squadron Leader Frank Tyson, was shadowed by Squadron Leader Jan Ambrus, and Tyson was first joined by Flight Lieutenant Denys Gillam AFC, from 616 Squadron, to command 'A' Flight, and Flight Lieutenant Harry Comerford, formerly a flying instructor, to lead 'B'. Whilst the latter had no combat experience, Gillam was a seasoned veteran and both an exceptional fighter pilot and leader – who had really held 616 Squadron together during its battering at Kenley the previous month. It is no surprise, therefore, that Gillam would greatly contribute to recording 312 Squadron's first aerial victory.

On 26 September 1940, the new 312 (Czech) Squadron moved from Duxford to Speke, near Liverpool, and by 3 October 1940 the unit's pilot strength stood at four British pilots and twenty-four Czechs. At 18.15 hrs that day a lone Ju 88 had flown across the airfield but was unsuccessfully engaged by ground defences, and Tyson prepared to give chase but was stood-down by Operations. Two days later Tyson's Yellow Section was vectored to intercept a raider over Hoylake, but heavy cloud led to the Hurricanes returning uneventfully to Speke. The following day, a lone Ju 88 dropped three bombs on Speke aerodrome, damaging a Boston bomber and destroying an Audax. On 7 October 1940 another solo raider over flew Speke but was not intercepted. Things would change on 8 October 1940.

That afternoon, Flight Lieutenant Denys Gillam was Yellow 1, leading Pilot Officer Alois Vašátko, Yellow 2, and Sergeant Josef Stehlík, Yellow 3, on patrol over the Mersey at Speke. At 16.15 hrs the attention of Yellow 3 was drawn first to AA fire exploding up river, then to a Ju 88 flying west at 1,200ft. As the bomber's crew sighted the RAF fighters the German pilot climbed steeply in an attempt to reach cloud cover; Pilot Officer G. McK Phillips, 312 Squadron's intelligence officer, reported,

> Shortly before entering the E/A received a burst from Yellow 3, which was followed by continual attacks from Yellow 1, 2 and 3, which weaved in and out, attacking from below and above, principally from the rear on account of bad visibility. The E/A received bursts from Yellow and 3 while still climbing through cloud and started gliding downward, Yellow 2 and 3 doing quarter attacks. By this time both E/A's engines were on fire and it was seen by Yellow 2 and a large number of ground observers to fall flat down on a meadow on the left bank of the Mersey. During the combat heavy and accurate return fire was experienced from the E/A up to the last moment before the crash. Slight damage was sustained by all our aircraft, a bullet hitting the windscreen of Yellow 1, another the exhaust manifolds of Yellow 2, while Yellow 3 sustained damage to petrol tank and the gun pipe line ... AA fire ceased immediately our fighters came into action.

The Junkers, a reconnaissance machine of 2/KGr 806, forced-landed at Bromborough Dock, Port Sunlight where the co-pilot was captured unhurt, and the air gunner and navigator, both of whom were injured in the crash; *Leutnant* zur See H. Schegel, the pilot, was killed, according to the 312 Squadron ORB, 'by a machine-gun bullet in the head while still in the air'. It was an historic victory, being 312 Squadron's first, prompting congratulatory signals from AOCs of 9 and 12 Groups. Further telegrams were received, including one from Wing Commander Alfred Basil 'Woody' Woodhall, station commander at Duxford, which accommodated 310, the other Czech squadron, and from 310 came 'We congratulate you on your great success in your first action and are looking forward to hearing of further successes'. Significantly, President of the Czechoslovak Republic in Exile Dr Eduard Beneš sent congratulations and good wishes for future successes. For men these men far from home, with no news of their families, this was the first blow struck against Germany from British soil.

Much further south-east, the final daylight combat on 8 October 1940 was not so successful, Red Section of Kenley's 501 Squadron, comprising two Hurricanes, were scrambled to intercept a bandit, Flight Lieutenant Eustace Holden managing to dame a Ju 88 off Rye before it disappeared into cloud.

The lone Ju 88 raiders achieved little during the day, isolated bombs reported at Bexhill, Hastings, Fairlight – and Yeovil. Westland Aircraft had, of course, been unsuccessfully attacked the previous day by heavily escorted Ju 88s of KG 51 in what was the last major daylight raid of the Battle of Britain and during which bombs fell on the town centre. On 8 October 1940, a lone Ju 88 tried to hit Westlands – but its bombs fell wide, missing the airfield and exploding in the adjacent suburban street of Preston

Grove. There, as Roy Madelin, a schoolboy at the time, recalled 'There was a direct hit on the shelter at 103, the corner shop owned by Don Harrison. My friend Laurence Sweet – known as "Peter" – was killed there'. 'Peter' Sweet, the son of Leading Seaman Ernest Sweet and his wife, Elsie, was 10 years old – but was not the youngest to die in that shelter: Anthony Maxwell Fitkin, who was only 3, also died there along with his parents, William, aged 31, and 29-year-old Olga Fitkin. Also 29 and who perished at 103 Preston Grove was Myrtle Harrison. Without doubt, the suffering of civilians, and children especially, brings into sharp focus that war is not a romantic or glamorous adventure but a baptism of fire indeed – and the reach of air power had even put the likes of young Fitkin and Sweet in the front line.

Throughout the day, having started with 235 Squadron's successes off Cherbourg, Coastal Command escorted twenty-three convoys and flew the usual round of coastal reconnaissance and sweeps; by night, six Blenheims attacked shipping at Gravelines, and FAA Swordfish mined the Ems Estuary. Owing to the weather, 2 Group only despatched two Blenheims on offensive sorties, one of which aborted, the other bombing Boulogne harbour. After dark, Bomber Command was active, thirty-seven Blenheims attacking the invasion ports, whilst Wellingtons hit docks and industrial targets in Germany, Whitleys attacked the Fokker works in Amsterdam, and an alloy plant at Hanau, whilst Hampdens targeted the *Tirpitz* at Wilhemshaven. From these operations a 53 Squadron Blenheim was shot down by flak near Calais, and one of 42 Squadron, and two of 82, crashed upon return, as did Whitleys of 58 and 77 Squadrons. By night, enemy air activity over Britain was concentrated on London, the night Blitz continuing to vex the defenders.

Having suffered heavy losses by day, on 1 September 1940, the handful of 264 Squadron's surviving Defiant turret fighters and crews had been withdrawn to Kirton, but on 13 September 1940, eight 264 Squadron crews, including Pilot Officer Harold Goodall and his air gunner, Sergeant Robert Bett Mirk Young, a New Zealander, flew to Northolt, to bolster the 'night operational flying defence of London' [ORB]. Britain's night defences remained inadequate, airborne interception radar, coordination with ground controllers and searchlights embryonic, and dedicated night-fighting aircraft had yet to reach the squadrons in numbers. Consequently, and for some time yet, single-engined day fighters, including the Defiant, were pressed into service after sunset. Having previously proved unsuitable for daylight operations when Me 109s were present, it would be at night that the Defiant would make an essential contribution. The Defiants, lacking the benefits of Airborne interception radar, were being used as a 'catseye' fighter, meaning that interceptions were reliant upon the crews' vision, seeking clues such as searchlights, AA fire, bomb explosions or the glowing exhaust's of enemy aircraft to guide them to a target.

No. 264 Squadron's 'B' Flight commenced night flying operations immediately from Northolt, Pilot Officer Harold Goodall and Sergeant Robert Young patrolling the Maidenhead to Halton line. The ORB reported that 'Pilot Officer [Eric Gordon] Barwell and Pilot Officer [Harold] Goodall both had a "Tally Ho", but the enemy evaded the searchlights and were not seen again. The guns were not fired. Some difficulty was experienced with the R/T and with Northolt Control'. A few days later, 'B' Flight moved to Luton 'due to the unsuitability of Northolt', continuing to patrol the Halton to Maidenhead, and Maidenhead to Guildford lines. This was not easy: without modern navigation aids and considering the blackout below, it was exhausting and dangerous work, especially given ongoing problems with ground communications. On one patrol by Goodall and Young, the transmitter broke down at Luton, making operations 'very difficult' [ORB]. The pair flew a further patrol four evenings later, but contacting the enemy in the night sky was proving virtually impossible.

At 21.50 hrs on 8 October 1940, Goodall and Young took off from Luton in Defiant N1627, to patrol the Maidenhead to Halton line at Angels 10. At 21.20 hrs, Goodall called up Luton control, reporting that he was investigating a suspected 'bandit some distance away' (accident report dated 18 October 1940). Nothing further was heard from the Defiant. However, 'at 2140 hrs, Operations at Northolt reported that a Defiant aircraft had crashed near Marlow'. Further investigation revealed that this was N1627, in which both pilot and gunner lay dead. It was ascertained that the 'colour cartridge of the hour had been fired', suggesting that the Defiant crew were uncertain as to whether the aircraft they stalked was friendly or hostile. Sadly, the latter was the case: the Defiant's wreckage was found to be riddled with German bullets.

Pilot Officer Harold Goodall, aged 25, was buried in Parkstone Cemetery at Poole, Dorset, where his mother and next of kin resided. Sergeant Robert Young, aged 22, was laid to rest at Northwood Cemetery – a long way from home in Wellington, New Zealand. Suffice it to say that for both men to have survived the virtual annihilation of 264 Squadron during the daylight battles, only to be killed in action in these circumstances was a travesty.

Weekly Report by Home Intelligence:

> An interesting comment on peace-aims comes from a Ministry speaker, who says that audiences are determined to win the war but are apprehensive about what will happen when peace comes. Will there be more unemployment? Will everyone bear their fair share in the work of rehabilitation? Will the peace terms sow the seeds of another war? Will justice be done to ex-Service men and their dependents? Similar comments are reported by working-men between the ages of 18 and 20 when asked what they will do after the war. Most reports show distinctly less talk about reprisals this week. This is attributed to ... the belief that 'the R.A.F. is delivering shrewder blows on Germany than they on us'. Our reports directly disagree with an analysis of the *Daily Express* postbag which is stated to show that 5 out of 6 people now want reprisals. At the same time, it is said that 'reprisals' are not an ethical problem; indiscriminate bombing has caused serious economic dislocation, and this has a real military value to the enemy. Many people feel that our pilots gaining experience over Germany might go in for the random bombing of large German towns, and that the loss of sleep and production would be well worth while. Another type of comment is: 'Just because I know some chap in Germany is being bombed in his bed, I don't enjoy being bombed in mine'.

Wednesday, 9 October 1940

Although mild, with a strong south-westerly, the weather remained overcast, Hornchurch 41 Squadron reported visibility being 'moderate to good' [ORB]. Elsewhere, at Wittering, 1 Squadron reported 'Bad weather' [ORB] – the regional variations being so typical of Britain's unpredictable autumn weather. It would be 1 Squadron, however, which drew first blood against the lone Ju 88s prowling over Britain.

Pilot Officer John F.D. 'Tim' Elkington had been shot down by *Oberleutnant* Helmut Wick on 16 August 1940, baling out, wounded; having returned to 1 Squadron's 'B' Flight on 1 October 1940, the 19-year-old found himself in action again, at 11.03 hrs, a few miles south of base:

> While on local flying with Blue 2 [author's note: Sergeant Maurice Davies], we were vectored by Control onto a Bogey. I saw a Ju 88 about 1,000 feet below, travelling on the same course. I went down to investigate and when about 800 yards away he started firing from top rear gun. He flew in and out of cloud and when he did so I climbed to await him emerging. Eventually I gave him two bursts of three seconds, from 600 yards, without effect. While in cloud I passed quite close to the E/A. This dodging in and out was kept up while I dived on him to 300 yards, firing a short burst. The E/A turned gently each time to avoid my fire. He eventually came out of cloud over the sea and the E/A came down to about 500 feet and started a dogfight with steep turns, the rear top gunner firing at about 700 yards. After flying straight at me I climbed into the sun and dived onto the E/A, which turned, and I pulled round to keep with him and fired the rest of my ammunition in a slight deflection from 200 yards, closing right in to 20 yards. I pulled out and upwards to 500 feet and blacked out, coming out on my back. When I had righted my aircraft I looked around for two or three minutes without seeing any trace of the E/A. Visibility was very clear and clouds about ten miles away, and I circled up to about 1,000 feet but could not see anything. I landed at Manby.

Sergeant Maurice Davies also attacked the bomber, reporting having last seen it 'some distance ahead and below, streaming white smoke'. The two pilots shared the Ju 88 as a 'probable'. Both Elkington and Davies returned from the combat unscathed, but 1 Squadron suffered a fatality later in the day, when Sergeant Stanley Warren, a new replacement pilot, inexplicably crashed into The Wash during a formation practice exercise – emphasising that flying was a dangerous activity, and not just because of enemy action.

Over the 11 Group area, at midday, Yellow Section of 213 Squadron was up from Tangmere and patrolling the Selsey Bill area when Sergeant Ernest Snowden was ordered to patrol base. A mile south of Selsey Bill the Hurricane pilot intercepted a Ju 88, the bomber's rear gunners immediately opening fire. Attacking twice from astern,

Snowden set the Ju 88's starboard engine on fire, and after using up all his ammunition on further attacks, watched the bomber flying 'South, losing height and flew into the sea about thirty miles South of Selsey Bill.'

The ever-constant stream of lone raiders was also an issue for 10 Group, 234 Squadron at St Eval flying nine interception scrambles throughout the day. At 13.20 hrs, Red Section, Pilot Officer Edward Mortimer-Rose and Pilot Officer Ernest 'Bertie' Wootten, engaged a Ju 88 over Falmouth, claiming it as probably destroyed. Similarly, at 14.35 hrs, 601 Squadron's Red Section, patrolling from Exeter, intercepted a 'He 111 [author's note: more likely a Ju 88]' at 2,000ft, 6 miles north of Dartmouth, which Pilot Officer Thomas Grier attacked, the bomber making off into cloud 'at top speed'; it was claimed as damaged. During these sporadic encounters, both 6/KG 30 and I/KG 54 lost Ju 88s over the sea, their crews all missing, and two of I/KG 51 crash-landed with combat damage back at Villaroche.

During the afternoon, slightly improved weather saw a resumption of heavily escorted fighter-bomber attacks on London. At 11.45 hrs, 72 and 92 Squadrons had scrambled from Biggin Hill to patrol base, and were then vectored to the Hawkinge – Dungeness area. The enemy was not sighted – but Sergeant Eric Frith of 92 Squadron was ambushed at 12.50 hrs and shot down by *Oberleutnant* Hans-Ekkehard Bob, *Staffelkapitän* of 7/JG 54; the Spitfire pilot baling out so badly burned that he would die of his wounds a week later. At 14.50 hrs, 41 and 222 Squadrons scrambled from Hornchurch with orders to climb to 25,000ft over base before proceeding to patrol Maidstone.

Flight Lieutenant Eric 'Tommy' Thomas, commanding 'A' Flight of 222 Squadron reported that at 15.35 hrs,

> I was leading the Squadron on patrol at 30,000 feet, roughly over Chatham. I followed 41 Squadron down to 28,000 feet and then saw about five Me 109s directly above at about 29,000 feet. I climbed up into them and they made for a layer of cirrus, through which I followed them. I increased revs to 3,000 and gradually outclimbed them and gave a four second burst into the belly of one enemy aircraft. Glycol streamed out of port radiator and he went down in a shallow dive. I followed him down and gave a series of one second bursts at 100 yards, down to 3,000 feet. During these attacks glycol came out of the starboard radiator and black smoke from the engine. The enemy aircraft landed with undercarriage up about four miles North of Hawkinge. I circled round, waggling my wings to attract attention. I saw the pilot get out and set fire to his aircraft, which burnt very slowly, a small amount of blue smoke coming out of the cockpit. Civilians then arrived and I saw them approaching the pilot who was standing about thirty yards from his aircraft, holding a white handkerchief and with his arms raised in surrender. The enemy aircraft had a completely yellow nose and rudder.

The enemy pilot was *Feldwebel* F. Schweser of 7/JG 54, who forced-landed and was captured, according to the victor's log book, '4 miles North of Hawkinge' at 16.00 hrs.

Pilot Officer James Walker, a Canadian was flying Yellow 3 with 41 Squadron when the first Me 109s were sighted above, which Squadron Leader Donald Finlay climbed the Spitfires to attack. Because of cloud, Walker lost sight of both his squadron and the enemy, but when at 21,000ft,

> [He] sighted a Me 109 at 17,000 feet, four miles away, diving towards the French coast. I dived after the 109 and caught the E/A up about ten miles from the French coast. The pilot of the 109 did not see me coming, so I closed up to 100 yards before firing a stern shot. I saw my tracer going into the fuselage and wings of the Me 109. Black and white smoke then came from the engine. He did a sharp left-hand turn. I then gave him a deflection shot. The enemy then did a steep right-hand turn when I did another five seconds deflection shot. All the time there was black smoke coming from the engine. The engine of the 109 then stopped, so that the prop was just turning over slowly. The enemy then made a controlled landing in the sea, two miles off the French coast.

Despite his controlled ditching on the sea, *Leutnant* Josef Eberle, 9/JG 54's signals officer, was killed, his body washing ashore at Chatham some days later.

No. 41 Squadron's ace, Pilot Officer Eric 'Sawn Off' Lock DFC, also claimed a 109 destroyed over the sea, so also attacked Eberle, in addition to two probables. Like Pilot Officer James Walker, Sergeant John McAdam, Blue 3, became separated from 41 Squadron and so patrolled Ashford 'in the hope of picking up a straggler'. At 12,000ft the Spitfire pilot saw a Me 109 ahead and below, flying south-east, so McAdam dived onto the enemy's tail, his burst of fire ripping holes in the German's rudder before the 109 disappeared into cloud. Squadron Leader Donald Finlay also damaged a 109, but in turn his Spitfire was damaged, resulting in a wheels-up landing back at Hornchurch – the German pilot responsible being *Oberleutnant* Hans-Ekkehard Bob, who claimed a Spitfire over Chatham and chalked up his second success of the day. There were no other RAF casualties.

In addition to Schewser, who was captured, and Eberle, who was killed, 1/JG 77's *Leutnant* Escherhaus also failed to return to France – not because of enemy action but owing to having lost control of his fighter due to an accidental inflation of his dinghy; crash-landing at Eastry, the hapless *Jagdflieger* was captured unhurt. No. 5/JG 51's *Unteroffizier* Rudolf Delfs, however, was killed when he crash-landed his damaged 109 at Calais.

German nuisance raiders continued being a problem over Britain during the evening, St Eval airfield being attacked by two bombers. Three sections of 234 Squadron's Spitfires were airborne at the time, but only Sergeant Charles Bell, Green 2, who had become separated from the squadron, sighted and attacked one of the raiders, 'a Do 17Z', at 19.15 hrs, west of base at 2,000ft. Having shot pieces off the bomber and hitting the port engine, Bell watched his target go 'into a steep vertical dive, seemingly out of control'. Although claimed as 'conclusive', the enemy aircraft was not seen to crash and no corresponding loss appears in Luftwaffe records. The enemy rear gunner, however, accurately returned fire, hitting the Spitfire, resulting in Bell crash-landing back at St Eval, unhurt.

For Coastal Command it had been a typical day, although only fifty-five aircraft were involved and just ten convoys escorted. That evening, Blenheims of Thorney Island's 235 Squadron attacked Le Havre but were intercepted by Me 109s. Pilot Officer James Kirkpatrick's Blenheim was shot down and crashed into the sea, the crew never seen again, and others possibly damaged. *Hauptmann* Otto Bertram, *Kommandeur* of III/JG 2, claimed two Blenheims destroyed 20km North of Le Havre, and, *Oberfeldwebel* Hans Klee of 5/JG 2 claimed a 'Hereford [*sic*]'. Although details are scant, there was also an action fought by 2/JG 26 against an unknown Blenheim north-west of Calais at some stage during the day, *Unteroffizier* Hans-Jurgen Fröhlich being shot down and wounded.

Only eight 2 Group Blenheims were despatched by day to attack targets in Germany and enemy occupied France: three aborted due to unsuitable weather, one reported hitting a Homburg oil facility, and the remaining aircraft bombing Boulogne. By night, Calais was attacked by Polish Battles, and Wellingtons and Hampdens successfully attacked industrial targets in Germany, and other Hampdens mined Lorient. Only one bomber failed to return, a 149 Squadron Wellington based at Mildenhall, which simply disappeared.

Weekly Report by Home Intelligence:

> Rumours of frustrated invasion are still current in many places – the Orkneys, the Shetlands, Brighton, Dover, Isle of Wight, Inverness, and letters with circumstantial accounts of thousands of bodies washed up on our shores contain abuse of the Ministry of Information for withholding the news. The enemy radio has tried very strongly to counter these rumours of frustrated invasion but without success.
>
> There are still a number of the usual Haw Haw rumours about places to be bombed, and a new version is that certain industrial concerns in Cardiff have not been bombed because of the German capital invested in them. There are also rumours that the AA defences of certain places, e.g. Falmouth, have been taken away to protect London.

Thursday, 10 October 1940

With the changed tactical scenario, on this day, Air Vice-Marshal Keith Park wrote to Air Chief Marshal Hugh Dowding requesting that Air Vice-Marshal Trafford Leigh-Mallory's 12 Group now take a larger share of the fighting – this was because, unlike in previous phases, 11 Group was no longer reacting to ponderous, large, formations of twin-engined and heavily escorted bombers, but the fast-moving single-engined fighter and fighter-bomber attacks at high altitude. Consequently, this required a greater state of alertness and an increasing amount of standing patrols. That the AOC 11 Group recognised that this was the right time for 12 Group's squadrons to be use over his group area is further evidence of the New Zealander's tactical awareness.

Air Vice-Marshal Keith Park also emphasised that certain 12 Group squadrons would need to replace some war weary 11 Group units. The only alternative, Park suggested, was for 12 Group not to rotate its squadrons, thereby remaining at its current strength, and the Duxford Wing operate under the control of either the Biggin Hill or Kenley sector for a short period each day. In this document, Park raised a valid point: Leigh-Mallory had so far not sent 19, 242, 302 (Polish), 310 (Czech) or 611 Squadrons for a tour of duty in 11 Group, which was inconsistent with the policy of rotating squadrons. Nothing, however, would change as the result of this request – because unbeknown to Dowding and Park, dark forces were conspiring against them in the corridors of power. Indeed, this was on an inconceivable scale.

By this time, certain influential officers in 12 Group and at the Air Ministry were convinced of the Big Wing's apparent superiority – among them 242 (Canadian) Squadron's adjutant, Flight Lieutenant Peter 'Boozy Mac' MacDonald MP. Without even reference to his CO, Squadron Leader Douglas Bader DSO and Bar DFC and Bar, station commander, Wing Commander Alfred Woodhall, or 12 Group's AOC, Air Vice-Marshal Trafford Leigh-Mallory, MacDonald spoke 'earnestly' with the Undersecretary of State for Air Harold Balfour, himself a decorated First World War fighter ace, then exercised his right as an MP to seek an interview with the prime minister. Winston Churchill, was at first 'gruff', but later 'thawed', spending an hour listening to MacDonald's concern that the battle was not being properly managed by Dowding and Park, and considering MacDonald's argument that attacking in strength was the way forward. Indeed, Churchill was sufficiently convinced to begin 'sending for various … commanders', according to Flight Lieutenant Robert Wright, who was Dowding's personal assistant, but their identities are unknown – except to say that neither Dowding or Park were amongst them. Dowding would not, in fact, learn of this MacDonald's disloyalty to his C-in-C until 1968; he was stunned, remarking that 'It does rather take your breath away', further commenting,

> Of course, so long as a squadron adjutant pays attention to his Service responsibilities, there's no harm done. Those responsibilities are clearly defined. But it is another matter when a squadron adjutant, serving under my command, starts by-passing the correct procedure and chain of command in order to get the ear of politicians. I think it was impertinent and quite extraordinary behaviour in engineering things in this way. And all done without my knowledge. No one could deny a Member of Parliament the right to attend to matters that were in his political sphere. But was it right for him to introduce this purely technical matter of the tactical use that was being made of my Command into such a political atmosphere?

The answer is simple: no. MacDonald's interference was totally inappropriate, not to mention insubordinate. Air Vice-Marshal Trafford Leigh-Mallory and his supporters, however, now enjoyed the immense benefit of prime ministerial interest – and support. Whilst 'Dowding's Chicks' continued fighting the enemy many Angels high, what would become known as the 'Big Wing Controversy' would soon come to a head.

So far as the fighting was concerned on 10 October 1940, the day dawned clear, turning to heavy rain, and began with the enemy undertaking now routine reconnaissance flights. At 07.10 hrs, nine Spitfires of 92 Squadron scrambled from Biggin Hill to patrol Maidstone at Angels 15, then sent to 20,000ft, patrolling at that height for forty minutes before being vectored to intercept a Do 17 east of Brighton. The Dornier was sighted, the squadron diving and splitting up to make individual attacks from astern, abeam, and above. Unfortunately, the pilots found their 'windscreens obscured by ice and reflector sights could not be used' [ORB]. Sergeant Walter Ellis reported that as he was approaching the Do 17 to attack it from abeam, he saw two Spitfires making quarter attacks from astern, one from port, the other starboard. Suddenly, the starboard wing of the right-hand aircraft contacted the other Spitfire's tailplane, causing both pilots to lose control. Pilot Officer Desmond Williams was killed when his Spitfire crashed near Brighton, and Pilot Officer John Drummond DFC baled out too low over Portslade, dying in the arms of a priest who administered last rites (both were experienced pilots, aces, particularly Drummond, a veteran of Norway). Ellis continued with his attack, chasing the Dornier through cloud and last seeing it diving vertically towards the sea; claimed as a probable, 12 miles off Brighton, it is likely that this was the Do 17 of 1/KG 2, which returned to France damaged, with a dead crewman aboard.

Across the Channel, there was a reshuffle in JG 53: *Oberstleutnant* von Cramon was posted to the RLM and succeeded as *Geschwaderkommodore* by the younger *Hauptmann* Günther Freiherr von Maltzhan, until then *Kommandeur* of II/JG 53, whose place there was taken by *Hauptmann* Heinz Bretnütz. On the morning of 10 October 1940, all three *Gruppen* of JG 53 escorted the *Jabos* of LG 1 to London. The mission was uneventful for I/JG 53, but II and III *Gruppen* clashed with the Spitfires of 603 Squadron, which had left Hornchurch at 09.45 hrs to patrol south of base. At 10.30 hrs, the Spitfires met II and III/JG 53 heading home, off Folkestone.

Flying Officer Brian Carbury was leading Green Section, the Spitfires going into line astern upon sighting the enemy: 'I remained at 33,000ft, saw two Me 109s and sent a burst into the last one. He went on his back and dived straight into the Channel.'

Pilot Officer John Soden, Red 3,

> [I saw] the two leading Spitfires attack the Me 109s on the left. I saw one Me 109 on the right, which I attacked. I fired a short burst at about 400 yards, which hit. I then got closer and gave a longer burst. Glycol etc streamed out of the machine and it spiralled down, apparently out of control. I saw it hit the sea.

The only 109 down in the Channel was that of 4/JG 53's *Staffelkapitän, Oberleutnant* Richard Vogel, who was killed; there can be no doubt, therefore, that Carbury and Soden claimed the same 109 destroyed.

Carbury then sighted a 109 climbing over his Spitfire, so pursued the enemy fighter to 31,000ft: 'He rolled on his back and I gave him a burst. The E/A went down vertical, so I followed, but he crashed on the beach at Dunkirk. One wing flew off and the rest shot along the beach. No parachute was seen.' Although no corresponding casualty appears in Luftwaffe records, given Carbury's experience and record there can be no doubt that this happened.

Fling Officer David Pinckney claimed a 109 damaged, 603 Squadron suffering no casualties in the fight – although on this occasion the Germans overclaimed: *Oberleutnant* Gerhard Michalski of *Stab* II/JG 53, *Hauptmann* Wolf-Dietrich Wilcke of *Stab* III/JG 53, and *Leutnant* Erich Schmidt of 9/JG 53 all claiming Spitfires destroyed. It is likely, however, that these were the Me 109s that 421 Flight's Sergeant Maurice Lee ran in to, who 'landed his aircraft safely in spite of the fact that a cannon shot from a Me 109 had damaged his controls while he was taking evasive action' [ORB]. Things had already got busier for the new 'Jim Crow' Flight, in fact, which flew sixteen spotting patrols on this day.

The next attack was mounted by *Luftflotte* 3, a fighter sweep by all three *Gruppen* of JG 2 with fifty-three Me 109s over the Portland and Dorchester areas of Dorset. Boscombe Down's 56 Squadron was operating from the forward base at Warmwell, and scrambled therefrom at 11.55 hrs to intercept the 'X-Raid' [ORB]. At 12.20 hrs, the Hurricanes were over Wareham, west of Poole and Studland Bay. Sergeant Peter Fox, who had survived being shot down and wounded on 30 September 1940, was flying with the Czech Sergeant Jaroslav Hlaváč: 'We were both weaving behind 56 Squadron as "Tail-end Charlies". Hlaváč was shot down and killed, but I didn't even see him attacked, we all just flew on, oblivious.' The unseen 109 pilot had executed the perfect bounce.

Having left Chilbolton at 12.05 hrs with orders to patrol base, Squadron Leader Harold Fenton's 238 Squadron was then vectored to Portland Bill:

> When due South of Warmwell [author's note: over the sea], about twenty-five E/A encountered comprising Me 110 [author's note: deployment of Me 110s is omitted from surviving Luftwaffe records] and Me 109 flying in very wide circle. Squadron was split up after encountering cumulous cloud. [ORB]

Flying Officer Bob Doe DFC, commanding 238 Squadron's 'A' Flight, was later critical of Hurricanes being used to counter these high-flying raids, given that it high-altitude performance was inferior to the Spitfire, which was comparable to the Me 109 at great height: 'In retrospect, I don't think Hurricanes should have been used for this purpose'. Doe also explained that when flying in cloud 'one odd property ... is that when you are in them you can't see out, but from outside you can see in for some distance. So that as I climbed out of the clouds, I could be seen for probably the last few hundred feet – but I was blind.'

As Doe 'broke clear', he was 'hit from in front and behind at the same time ... My first indication of it was of a tiny speck of light, which seemed to come over my right shoulder, into the instrument panel. A loud explosion under my bottom, a knock on my left hand and a thump as from a hammer on the left-hand side of my body'. The Hurricane slid back into cloud, which Doe considered 'almost certainly saved my life'. The hammer-blow had seemed like a death-blow to Doe, but still breathing seconds later he decided to vacate his doomed fighter – but having pulled the safety pin to release the Sutton harness, found himself trapped in the cockpit owing to negative 'g'. In 'sheer panic', Doe tore at the straps, and was 'catapulted into space' – then the sensation of 'peace and comfort … just floating down on the air … quite miraculous.' The Hurricane plunged to earth, crashing near Corfe Castle, a famous Dorset landmark.

Having deployed his parachute, then came the realisation that the cannon-shell explosion beneath his aircraft had damaged his parachute, as a result of which Doe was descending too quickly, landing heavily on his backside and passing out before coming to,

> lying in about six-inches of mixed water and sludge, with my head in a bramble bush, being asked by an ugly villain with an iron bar 'What are ya?'. Having explained in basic English just what I was, he became a good Samaritan and carried me some distance to a jetty from where a party of naval ratings took me to Cornelia Hospital in Poole.

There, it was found that Doe, who had landed on Brownsea Island in Poole harbour, had suffered a severed Achilles tendon, sliced through by shrapnel from the cannon shell, and the 'hammer blow' had been caused by a machine-gun round passing through his left arm. Having landed so heavily, however, Doe's spine was badly damaged, an injury which would afflict him for a lifetime; he was consequently hospitalised for some weeks and out of the Battle of Britain from now on.

So far as the remainder of 238 Squadron fared, 'only five pilots engaged' [ORB]. By this time, 238 Squadron had received a number of replacement Polish and Czech pilots, and two of these filed claims after this action, which occurred at 12.30 hrs. Pilot Officer Wladyslaw Różycki, Blue 2, managed a short burst from 50 yards range at a Me 109, which escaped into cloud, the Hurricane pilot then climbing 'and saw what I thought to be Hurricanes in formation, but when I got to within 200 yards I saw that they were Me 109s, which opened fire on me'; fortunately Różycki gained the sanctuary of cloud and lived to tell the tale. Czech Pilot Officer Rudolf Bohumil Roháček, Green 3, was the fourth aircraft in Squadron Leader Fenton's Section, and described firing 1,620 rounds at a Me 109, which 'went into cloud … considerably damaged'.

Although 152 Squadron's records are very poorly recorded, it is a fact that the squadron was also up, from Warmwell, and that Pilot Officer Dennis Fox-Male was shot-up by a 109 over Dorchester and returned to base unhurt but with a damaged cockpit and glycol tank.

On this occasion, JG 2 suffered no losses and claimed accurately: *Leutnant* Julius Meimberg of 4/JG 2 and *Feldwebel* Willi Reins of 1/JG 2 both claiming Hurricanes, and *Oberfeldwebel* Erich Rudorffer of 2/JG 2 a Spitfire – his nineteenth kill (Rudorffer would, of course, go on to become one of Germany's most successful *Experten*, with 224 aerial victories, decorated with the Knight's Cross, Oak Leaves, Swords and Diamonds, ending the war flying the Me 262 jet; he would ultimately die aged 97, in 2016, having been the last living recipient of the Knight's Cross with Oak Leaves and Swords). Once again, the Me 109 pilots had shown how dangerous they were given the advantage of height and surprise.

There were no other combats on this day – but other losses had occurred, to both sides, as the result of flying accidents. At 15.47 hrs, 249 Squadron's Sergeant Edward Bayley was killed when his Hurricane crashed at Cooling Marsh, east of Gravesend, whilst on a routine patrol, probably due to oxygen failure; at 15.55 hrs, 253 Squadron's Sergeant Harold Allgood was killed when his Hurricane inexplicably crashed, possibly also due to oxygen failure, into a row of terraced houses at Albion Place, Maidstone, also killing three women and five children, from two families. Up at Speke, the 312 Squadron Hurricane (L1547, actually the first production Hurricane) of Czech Sergeant Otto Hanzlíček caught fire over Ellesmere Port, the pilot baling out and falling into the Mersey, some way from shore. Unfortunately, when help arrived a few minutes later, the pilot was found to have drowned. Across the Channel, Me 109s of 6/JG 27 and 1/JG 51 were damaged in take-off and landing accidents, and two of III/JG 52 collided in mid-air, their pilots baling out unhurt. Whilst two of Fighter Command's non-operational losses were doubtless due to oxygen failure, the *Jagdwaffe* accidents suggest inexperience and/or increasing exhaustion.

Nonetheless, there were lighter moments, as the killing continued – as Flight Sergeant Frederick 'Taffy' Higginson DFM recalled,

> The main recollection I have of serving with 56 Squadron at Boscombe Down and Warmwell at this time is that we were a somewhat disorganised lot. As a result of the action we had seen we needed to re-equip and receive replacement pilots. The Station Commander at Boscombe was a group captain who, I believe, later took a unit to Russia and was killed. He was a first-class chap, good rugger player and liked by all. During the early part of our Boscombe sojourn I remember thinking that morale would perhaps be boosted if we had a Squadron mascot, so I went to the local town and bought a small monkey, which we named '109'. He was a great success and kept in a cage, on a lead. Anyway, the Station Commander gave a cocktail party for the Squadron and requested 109's presence. [The] 109 went down very well, until, that is, he started to undertake enthusiastic sexual self-gratification! Morals being what they were in those days we had to remove him quickly!

A busier day for Coastal Command was 10 October 1940, ninety-four aircraft being engaged on operations and nineteen convoys were escorted. A lack of cloud cover, however, led to a raid on Boulogne being aborted, the four Blenheims instead bombing a large ship, and two more ships were attacked without result in Heligoland. Two 42 Squadron Beauforts carried out an early evening torpedo strike against shipping at Boulogne, one crew claiming a hit on a ship, the other recording a miss. The Beauforts, though, were intercepted by Me 109s of 3/JG 77, *Oberleutnant* Karl-Gottfried Nordmann and *Oberleutnant* Günther Beise each claiming a 'Blenheim [*sic*]' destroyed south of Folkestone – only one was damaged, however, Pilot Officer G.S.P. Rooney DFC crash-landing back at Thorney Island; the pilot and Flying Officer Simmonds were wounded, whilst Sergeant R.F. Henry and Sergeant W.R.J. Little survived unscathed. By night, Coastal Command Albacore biplanes attacked German-held harbours, including Brest, and also dropped more mines. The weather had prevented 2 Group carrying out any offensive sorties by day, but after dark 157 aircraft of Bomber Command sallied forth to attack the invasion ports and industrial targets in Germany – there were no casualties.

Weekly Report by Home Intelligence:

> There is still much criticism of the official air raid bulletins. People still object to the phrase: 'A few people were killed'; and unnecessary anxiety, aroused when it is vaguely said that 'a large hospital in the London area' or 'a well-known public school in the Home counties' has been bombed, is commented on in the *Times* and also by the headmaster of Rugby school.
>
> The most severe criticism has been aroused in all parts of London by the official bulletin which stated 'that the raids on Monday night were on a somewhat smaller scale than the previous night', when in fact they were heavier.
>
> Two reports from Scotland criticise a picture of Lambeth people dancing on the ruins of their homes. It is described as 'ghoulish' and 'in the very worst taste'. In general, criticism of the Press has slightly increased this week. This is more probably due to bewilderment about the news rather than to antagonism'.

Friday, 11 October 1940

According to 41 Squadron at Hornchurch, the weather over south-east England dawned calm, the high winds, cloud and rain of the previous day having abated. An autumnal mist soon evaporated, giving over to 'cloudless visibility' [ORB]. For 73 Squadron at Castle Camps, it was 'a beautiful autumn morning with practically no cloud' [ORB]. Unsurprisingly, therefore, the *Jabos* of *Jafü* 2 were already preparing for the day ahead: 115 sorties would be flown against the 11 Group area throughout the day, during which there would be seven major attacks, 2 by fighters, the rest by formations comprising 75 per cent fighters and 25 per cent *Jabos*. The daylight hours would be busy for both sides.

Just before 07.00 hrs (BST), II/JG 53 left their base at Etaples, near Le Touquet, escorting *Jabos* to London. At 07.35 hrs, eleven Spitfires of 72 Squadron left Biggin Hill to patrol a convoy off Deal. The Spitfires, however, ran into II/JG 53, Pilot Officer Peter Pool baled out, wounded, his Spitfire crashing in flames at Milton Regis, Sittingbourne. Although this was the only RAF casualty, both *Hauptmann* Heinz Bretnütz and *Oberleutnant* Gerhard Michalski of *Stab* II/JG 53 both claimed Spitfires destroyed.

At 08.00 hrs, 72 Squadron's Flight Lieutenant John 'Pancho' Villa DFC was up from Biggin Hill on an engine test flight when, at 08.30 hrs, he saw a lone aircraft – subsequently identified as a Do 17 – above him. Informing the controller, the Spitfire pilot climbed at full throttle but experienced difficulty in catching up the raider at 30,000ft. After five minutes, the range had closed to 1 mile, and over the mouth of the Thames, Villa opened fire. After four attacks,

> one undercarriage leg fell right off the aircraft and the other one was hanging down. The starboard engine then stopped … The E/A tilted

steeply and dive vertically down, I last saw it disappear in haze at 3,000 feet ... Just before going down the E/A endeavoured to ram and I was only just able to avoid him by pushing the stick forward.

A De Wilde round exploded in the breech of Villa's port No. 2 gun, and a round from the bomber's rear gunner pierced his engine cowling, fortunately without causing any further damage – and this damage went unrecorded except in the pilot's personal combat report; no corresponding loss appears in Luftwaffe records for this Do 17, which was claimed as destroyed.

Whilst taxiing for take-off from Biggin Hill at 10.30 hrs, 72 Squadron's Sergeant Norman Glew recorded the day's first accident, damaging Spitfire R6777. Flight Sergeant Jack Steere led the remainder of two sections of three each to patrol base at 30,000ft. Having attained Angels 22, west of Haywards Heath, Steere was vectored 45°, then over Tonbridge three Me 109s were sighted, flying north. Ordering the other two members of his Red Section to 'take one each', Steere lost his Red 2, and whilst waiting a matter of seconds for him to reappear, the right-hand 109 became aware of the danger and turned to attack Red 1. Opening fire on the 109, Steere saw 'his hood break-up. I gave him a second burst and he pulled up into a stall and burst into flames and fell away.' Attacked by another Messerschmitt, being out of ammunition Steere broke away. Although claimed as destroyed, no German fighters crashed in England on this day, although several crash-landed back in France with combat damage.

At 09.05 hrs, 17 Squadron left Martlesham Heath, landing at Castle Camps at 09.25 hrs, to operate therefrom with 73 Squadron. Both squadrons were scrambled at 10.35 hrs, to patrol Hornchurch at Angels 20, 17 Squadron leading, and over Rochester condensation trails were seen above, at 30,000ft. None of what were obviously Me 109s were seen to dive and attack – but the Hurricane of Sergeant Robert Plenderleith – the vulnerable 'Tail-end Charlie' weaving, alone, behind 73 Squadron, was seen to plummet in flames, the pilot baling out at 15,000ft. At 11.08 hrs, the Hurricane crashed at Dillywood, Frindsbury, the pilot being admitted to Chatham Hospital suffering from burns. As happened so often, the weaver had yet again been ambushed and picked off by an unseen enemy – in this case *Oberleutnant* Karl-Heinz Lessmann of 2/JG 52.

No. 66 Squadron at Gravesend was also having a busy morning, the first patrol taking place at 07.30 hrs. Returning from this, Sergeant Peter Willcocks became disorientated in the haze and crashed near Newhook on approach to land at Eastchurch; the Spitfire was damaged, the pilot unhurt. That patrol was otherwise uneventful – but not so the squadron's third patrol over Kent, the Spitfires scrambling at 10.40 hrs. At 12.00 hrs, 'about Dungeness', Pilot Officer Hubert R. 'Dizzy' Allen, Blue 2, reported four Me 109s above, at 30,000ft. Unfortunately for 66 Squadron, this was the JG 51 *Stabschwarm*, led by the Luftwaffe's *Oberkanone, Major* Werner Mölders. Allen climbed, 'as fast as possible' and hit a 109, continuing to fire until 'white glycol appeared. The 109 appeared to stagger and went down vertically with black smoke issuing rom engine region' – this vertical, high-speed dive, full throttle producing voluminous black smoke from the engine's exhaust ports, actually being the 109 pilots' standard evasive tactic (although white glycol steam confirmed that the aircraft had been hit). Allen then turned for home, 'descending rapidly'. According to his personal diary, 'I was hit by British Ack-Ack returning from mid-Channel', but this detail is omitted from his combat report, which continues,

> When I had descended to about 20,000 feet I noticed oil appearing on my windscreen. Oil pressure vanished and the temperature rose rapidly. Accordingly I switched off and proceeded towards Hawkinge. My visibility was badly obscured by oil on the windscreen and side screens. I touched down about 250 yards from the aerodrome boundary and applied full brakes immediately. Unfortunately the grass was wet and I could not stop before reaching the boundary. I tipped onto my nose (or rather the aeroplane did) and hit my head and knees vigorously when I lost consciousness.

Over Folkestone, the Spitfire of Pilot Officer John 'Pickles' Pickering was hit by *Major* Werner Mölders – the forty-third aerial victory of the 'Father of Modern Air Fighting'. Pickering immediately sought to make a forced-landing:

> I looked for an aerodrome but could not find one, but managed to find a big field. After gliding down to 1,000 feet everything was still under control, but suddenly the cockpit and instruments became covered in thick oil and I could not see what airspeed I was travelling at. My speed must have been over 200 mph as I completely overshot the big field, also smaller ones, and my machine went straight through a hedge, leaving its radiator behind, knocked down four trees, at the same time relieving itself of its starboard wing, and then cartwheeled over a pile of felled trees which unfortunately decided to keep the engine. These little things did not seem to slow the machine down. My tailplane had to catch hold of a tree before the fuselage would consider slowing down, but not quick enough to enable to tail to stay attached to the fuselage.
>
> Once again the rest of the fuselage cartwheeled over a tree and then came to a standstill. For a few seconds I just sat in the remains of my machine and wondered what had happened, but suddenly noticed that the cockpit had caught fire, so I hopped out and ran like hell with my parachute for the nearest tree. Carefully I looked round the side of the tree. Hell! I could not see a thing out of my right eye. Was I blinded? In a few minutes crowds of people arrived and one person in particular decided that I must have been knocked out and had fallen in the cockpit. He climbed into the machine and lifted the seat up, and to his dismay could not find anybody. When I dashed up and tapped him on the shoulder he must have thought I was a ghost, as he just stared at me and did not say a word for a few seconds, and after that he only said 'Good God!' By now I was fully convinced that I had been blinded, but it was not so, all that had happened was that I had a beautiful black eye.

It had been quite a crash-landing – and a lucky escape indeed. The big field Pickering had first chosen for his landing was known as 'Bladbean', his Spitfire careering through Covert Wood, Elham, close to Hawkinge airfield, where the wreck burnt out at 11.15 hrs. From Kenley, the Hurricanes of 253 Squadron took-off at 10.30 hrs with unclear orders, but Pilot Officer Leonard 'Elsie' Murch 'was forced, whilst in combat with the enemy, to abandon Hurricane V6750 and was admitted to the Kent and Sussex Hospital, Tunbridge Wells, suffering with a broken arm and several minor injuries.' [ORB]. It appears that Murch spotted a 109 1,000 feet below the squadron, so attacked but came off second-best in the violent exchange.

Mr D.A. Barmby was a local resident:

> In the lunchtime alert we suddenly heard the high-pitched shriek of a fighter hurtling down out of control and watched it dive straight over the town to crash behind the railway viaduct at High Brooms. Then a small figure on a parachute became visible: it drifted lower and eventually landed in a tree in the garden of St Lukes Vicarage [author's note: just West of the railway line]. We always cheered the fall of a plane on the assumption it must be German, we heard how quite a crowd had advanced on the pilot with various weapons. However, he was found to be English and had an injury to his arm so was taken to the Kent & Sussex hospital, the plane being a Hurricane.

Unusually, there is no corresponding German claim for this loss, which was the only casualty suffered by 253 Squadron, which, like Kenley's 501 Squadron, otherwise patrolled without encountering the enemy.

Earlier in the day, at 11.00 hrs, bombs had been dropped on Folkestone's Riveria and Sandgate districts. A section of sea wall was destroyed, four houses seriously damaged and thirty-seven more less so; there were no casualties. At 12.03 hrs, thirty-six more houses were damaged by more bombs which fell on Grove, Julian and Wilton roads, which damaged another 193 dwellings. On that occasion 18-year-old Arthur Foreman of 68 Grove Road was fatally injured, dying later, two more males, six females and two children also being injured. More bombs were dropped at 12.45 hrs, damaging properties in Sidney Street, Alder Road and Golf Links, although fortunately there were no casualties. Given its location, just west of Dover, Folkestone, like other coastal towns in southern England was vulnerable to attack – as the destruction wrought this day alone confirms. Although the *Jabos* of 3 and 4/JG 53 reported having attacked Eastbourne at the material time, in all likelihood the target was actually Folkestone.

At 13.40 hrs, with more RDF plots on the board, Flight Lieutenant Bob Oxspring once more led 66 Squadron aloft from Gravesend to patrol the Chatham area at 30,000ft. Height was always the problem: the Me 109 was an excellent fighter at high-altitude and had the advantage of climbing over France and the Channel to enjoy the benefits of height and sun. Only the Spitfire could take on the 109s at such heights on equal terms – the Hurricane, quite simply, could not; the problem was there were insufficient Spitfires, so 11 Group's Spitfire squadrons were under particular pressure, flying multiple, physically tiring, sorties daily. Little wonder, then, that Air Vice-Marshal Keith Park was now asking for 12 Group to play a greater part in the fighting over 11 Group.

At 14.45 hrs, Pilot Officer Crelin Bodie was weaving behind 66 Squadron at 30,000ft over Chatham when AA bursts were seen to the east, drawing the Spitfire pilot's attention to thirty Me 109s flying north. The Spitfires, Bodie reported,

> cut them off at the coast and they turned South, passing underneath us. The rest of the Squadron climbed to attack, I was still weaving and saw six 109s in ragged line-astern about 500 feet above me, making no attempt to help their pals. I commenced a quarter attack on the rearmost, before I opened fire he dived vertically to cloud level ... I drew up to 100 yards, having to fire tracer as my sight had packed up. My windscreen was useless, iced up from the dive. He gave out a small amount of black smoke, and then, due to my windscreen, I lost him in haze.

Bodie searched for and found his quarry at 4,000ft, 0.5 mile out to sea:

> I overtook him without any difficulty (his engine must have been damaged) and pooped off all of my ammo. He went on losing height, I beat him up, and he turned about fifteen miles out and glided back, crash-landing in the sea ten miles SW of Dungeness Point. I didn't go below 2,000 feet and saw no sign of the pilot.

Bodie had shot down 5/JG 27's *Unteroffizier* Wiemann, who was wounded but rescued by the *Seenotdienst*.

In this action, Pilot Officer Stanley Baker and Sergeant Harry Cook shared a 109 damaged over Chatham; 'Clickety-Click' suffered no loss, but 3/JG 52's *Feldwebel* Karl Rüttger claimed a Spitfire at 14.40 hrs (BST).

So far, all the action had been over the 11 Group area, which indeed was the case until evening – although certain secondary sources state that at 15.30 hrs the Exeter, 10 Group-based 87 Squadron's Pilot Officer Roland 'Bee' Beaumont damaged a Me 110 south of Abbotsbury, no mention of this exists in 87 Squadron records, and nor does a personal combat report exist.

By mid-afternoon, *Major* Adolf Galland had led two *Geschwader*-strength escort missions without meeting the enemy. Now, the great ace was leading the day's third mission, and, at 16.05 hrs (BST), espied the 421 Flight Spitfire of Sergeant Charles Ayling, operating from Hawkinge, spotting for incoming trouble. Somewhere south-east of Chatham, Galland attacked the lone Spitfire, Ayling being killed in the resulting crash at Newchurch, on Romney Marsh. Just seven minutes later, Galland pounced again, this time hitting the Hurricane of 253 Squadron's Sergeant Robert Innes, up from Kenley on an 'Interception Patrol', and who crashed at Staplehurst, fortunately unhurt.

No. 41 Squadron's Spitfires had scrambled from Hornchurch at 15.45 hrs on their second sortie of the day, to patrol base at 30,000ft. This 41 Squadron did – but even at that height the Me 109s of JG 26 were 1,000ft higher still – forcing the Spitfires to climb and attack. During the ensuing melee, two Spitfires collided: Flying Officer Desmond

O'Neill was killed owing to parachute failure, his aircraft crashing at Crooked Billet, Ash, 10 miles east of Canterbury. Sergeant Leslie Carter baled out safely, his Spitfire crashing and burning out at South Ash Manor, West Kingsdon. Pilot Officer John Lecky Jr, however, was shot down and killed, crashing at Preston Hall, Maidstone. In this combat *Hauptmann* Walter Adolph, *Gruppenkommandeur* of II/JG 26, claimed two Spitfires destroyed.

The only pilot of 41 Squadron to strike back at the Me 109s was Pilot Officer Eric Lock, leading Yellow Section, the weaving rear-guard section. Having patrolled for 'some time', at 16.10 hrs, 5 miles off Dungeness, five 109s dived on the Spitfires, opening fire. Lock turned, with the sun to his advantage, and found himself behind five 109s, 2,000ft below him. Lock dived and attacked one from the blind spot, astern and below. The 109 executed a 'flick roll … then started to dive with smoke and glycol coming from the engine. I left him at 20,000 feet, diving steeply and his machine a mass of flames. This was over Dungeness.' Although not seen to crash, the 109 was awarded as destroyed.

At 15.40 hrs, five Spitfires of Biggin Hill's 92 Squadron, led by Flight Lieutenant Brian Kingcome scrambled with orders to co-join with 66 Squadron (callsign 'Fibus') at 30,000ft over Maidstone. At Angels 25, Kingcome, 'Ganic Leader', sighted fifty Me 109s over Thameshaven, but as the Spitfires set off in pursuit, the enemy fighters, they headed south-west. By 16.30 hrs, the Germans were crossing out over Dungeness when Kingcome 'fired short bursts at three of them, one of which dived away vertically with smoke pouring from it, and crashed into the sea, mid-Channel'. Again, given Kingcome's great experience and integrity, there can be no doubting that this happened – and yet, again, no corresponding loss appears in German records which cannot, as previously evidenced and argued, possibly be as complete as many believe.

No. 92 Squadron made no other claims against the withdrawing 109s, and the Spitfires suffered no loss in what was the last of the fighter sweeps and fighter-bomber assaults.

Having contributed to the Duxford 'Big Wing' operations, 12 Group's 611 Squadron was now split between Digby in Lincolnshire, its HQ and administrative base, and Ternhill in Shropshire, the latter being the squadron's operational base – from where Squadron Leader James McComb's Spitfires could afford some protection to Liverpool. In this quieter sector, the squadron was able to continue receiving new pilots and provide extra training, some operational.

That afternoon, *Kustenfliegergruppe* 606, based at Lannion in Brittany, planned a *Dämmerungsangriff* – a 'Twilight Attack' – by thirteen Do 17s. These would not fly to their targets in one large formation, however, but either singly or in sections of three, taking off between 15.15 and 16.12 hrs (BST). According to the Luftwaffe intelligence report arising, the targets selected were Liverpool, Liverpool-Speke, Rootes aircraft factory at Speke, and Rolls-Royce in Crewe.

At 17.30 hrs, six Spitfires of 611 Squadron's 'A' Flight left Ternhill to sweep Anglesey in North Wales, and another section took-off to patrol the Point of Ayr – both formations would intercept some of the *Kustenfliegergruppe* 606 raiders.

At about 18.20 hours, whilst 'A' Flight was making a wide orbit at 17,000ft in line astern, Yellow Leader, Flying Officer Douglas 'Dirty' Watkins, sighted three enemy aircraft flying in a wide vic formation about 12 miles away and approaching from the south-west at 14,000ft. After informing Red Leader, Flight Lieutenant Jack Leather, Watkins ordered his section into echelon starboard, and attacked the setting sun. The Merlin of Flying Officer Ian Hay's Spitfire cut out, however, forcing Yellow 2 to drop out of the fight. Pilot Officer Thomas Williams, Yellow Leader and Yellow 3, opened fire at a Do 17, which responded in kind. After Williams's last attack and explosive round hit his cockpit, rendering his ASI unserviceable, so Watkins ordered him to return to base, being 'certain' that the enemy would 'not get back'. Watkins then watched as the Dornier jettisoned five bombs into the sea from 200ft and hit the water at 18.35 hrs some 50 miles west of Holyhead. Before returning to Ternhill, seeing some of the German crew afloat in a dinghy, Yellow Leader first endeavoured to draw attract the attention of a passing cargo ship, then broke away; unfortunately, there would be no survivors rescued.

When the bombers were sighted, as Yellow Section attacked, Flight Lieutenant Jack Leather ordered his Red Section to attack the starboard Dornier, stopping its starboard engine. This aircraft rapidly lost height, 'finally crashing into the hills about ten miles South of Caernarvon' [ORB] – although that was not the case, because none of these bombers crashed on land. This 1st *Staffel* bomber actually ditched in Caernavon Bay, 16 miles off Bardsey Island; one crewman was killed, the rest picked up and captured by a passing trawler.

Red Section then turned about to engage the enemy leader and whilst closing for a third attack the Spitfire pilots saw two crewmen bale out over Capel Curig, *Unteroffizier* Johansen being killed, and *Feldwebel* Starf, who was captured. According to 611 Squadron's ORB, the enemy aircraft, with 'both engines on fire, glided down and crashed in flames at Capel Curig. Again, it did not: this 1st *Staffel* Do 17 returned to Brest, badly damaged.

At 17.45 hrs, Flying Officer Barrie Heath, Blue Leader, led Blue Section off from Ternhill, comprising two new replacement pilots, namely Sergeant Kenneth Pattison, Blue 2, and Sergeant Robert Angus, Blue 3, to patrol the Point of Ayr at 20,000ft. Over Prestatyn, Blue Leader 'Tally Ho'd' two Dorniers approaching from the south-west, 500ft below the Spitfires and quarter of a mile toy port. Heath attacked one bomber, ordering Blue 2 and Blue 3 to deal with the other, expending all his ammunition before returning to base. During the action the raider re-crossed the Dee and 1 mile west of Sealand, at about 10,000ft, glided south-west, jettisoning bombs of farmland near Flint. Heath then saw a Hurricane appear, which also attacked.

This fighter belonged to Speke's 312 (Czech) Squadron, Squadron Leader Frank Tyson having led Red and Yellow Sections up at 17.50 hrs to patrol Chester and the Point of Ayr. Flight Lieutenant Harry Comerford sighted and attacked a Dorner without visible effect, whilst the other five Hurricanes attacked another Dornier between Prestatyn and Chester, which they attacked, expending all ammunition before the bomber made off southwards – having returned fire, riddling the Hurricane of Pilot Officer Josef Jaske with 'explosive bullets' [ORB], although the Czech pilot was unhurt.

Meanwhile, Sergeant Robert Angus, Blue 3 of 611 Squadron, attacked the port Dornier of the vic engaged by his section, head on, and last saw it 'going down towards the sea in Liverpool Bay'. Sergeant Kenneth Pattison, Blue 2, however, was missing.

An inexperienced and OTU-fresh replacement pilot, it would seem that in the fading light and heat of battle, Pattison became disorientated and ultimately lost. At dusk and with no sophisticated navigational aids or lights on the ground to assist him, Pattison wandered across North Wales and Shropshire, then into North Worcestershire. With daylight fading fast, Harry Turner, the blacksmith at Cooksey Green, near Kidderminster, watched the Spitfire circling overhead with its landing lights on. The pilot selected a field adjacent to a farmhouse and was almost down safely when a herd of startled cows stampeded across the aircraft's projected landing path. Pattison instinctively heaved the control column back, but the Spitfire stalled, crashing into a pear tree, hitting the ground inverted and bouncing 15ft into the air, tearing along the field until coming to rest against an ancient tree stump. Mr Turner ran to the wreck, finding the pilot hanging upside down in his Sutton harness, which the blacksmith cut before releasing the trapped man. Thick black smoke, Turner recalled, belched from the wreckage as an ambulance arrived and conveyed the badly injured pilot to Barnsley Hall Military Hospital near Bromsgrove.

Sergeant Kenneth Pattison was a married man from Nottingham, his wife, Joan, rushing to hospital only to see watch her husband linger in great pain until he died two days later. A VR pilot, Pattison never met his daughter, Jean, who was born seven months after his death.

Pilot Officer Denis Adams, 611 Squadron:

> Sergeant [Kenneth] Pattison would have been better off making a wheels up forced landing, but his intention was no doubt to save his aeroplane, a valuable new Spitfire Mk II. I blame the CO and his Flight Commander for not briefing the new boy that his training was worth more than a Spitfire. In those days it was estimated that the cost of training a pilot to operational standard was £40,000, the cost of a Spitfire was £8,000.

Pilot Officer Peter Olver, 611 and 603 Squadrons:

> The mention of 'Pat' dying in Bromsgrove Hospital grabbed me rather strongly as I was at Bromsgrove School and once visited a sick friend in the hospital. The thought of Sergeant [Kenneth] Pattison also being there I find very sad, not implying any criticism of the hospital but rather that at such a young age I was unduly impressionable. At that period I was strongly under the impression that the war would be won before I could get there, so I applied for a posting straight from OTU to a squadron in the south of England. Fortunately for me, however, I was actually sent to 611 Squadron at Digby, a 'B' unit, on 30 September 1940, with which I remained for sixteen days and received eighteen hours of flying, some of it operational, until my posting came through to 603 Squadron, an 'A' unit, at Hornchurch. On my first subsequent operational trip, on 25 October 1940, I was shot down by an Me 109.

With only Sergeant Kenneth Pattison lost and Pilot Officer Josef Jaske's Hurricane damaged, with two Do 17s destroyed and another badly damaged, in fading light this was a successful action for 611 and 312 Squadrons. It was also exactly the short-range interception of unescorted enemy bombers for which the Spitfire and Hurricane were intended. And so closed the day fighting on 11 October 1940.

On this day, possibly in response to Air Vice-Marshal Keith Park's memorandum of 8 October 1940, 302 (Polish) Squadron, which had contributed to the Duxford 'Big Wing' operations the previous month, was transferred from Leconfield in 12 Group to RAF Northolt, in 11 Group.

During the day, the clearer weather had enabled PRU Spitfires to range widely over enemy occupied Europe, successfully photographing the invasion ports, various *Luftflotte* 2 and 3 airfields, but adverse weather over Germany and Norway rendered those sorties unsuccessful. Coastal Command carried out its typical duties, escorting twenty-one convoys, an Anson of 48 Squadron engaging and driving off a FW200 Condor attacking one of these. No. 2 Group's Blenheims uneventfully swept the North Sea by day, the night bombers hitting the invasion ports and secondary targets owing to ongoing bad weather shrouding Germany's naval bases. After dark, six Coastal Command Blenheims attacked Rotterdam, FAA Swordfish mined the Hubert Gat, and twelve Bomber Command Hampdens sowed mines elsewhere. There were no operational losses.

Weekly Report by Home Intelligence:

> Official schemes of evacuation 'on the whole have worked well'. The daily registration of mothers and children in London is now at the rate of 8,000, although the numbers who actually travel are always considerably below full strength.
>
> Much plan-less evacuation is still going on and causing a great deal of dislocation and some antagonism in many areas. This plan-less evacuation is largely westwards, particularly into Region V1. The billeting of penniless 'refugees' is made more difficult by the large numbers with money to spend who make their own arrangements.
>
> The reception of evacuees and 'refugees' varies considerably. Local authorities, although complaining of the burden on them, have risen to the emergency with good will and often efficiency. The efforts of voluntary organisations are also highly praised.
>
> Despite their eagerness for jobs, there is some prejudice against employing evacuees 'in case they re-evacuate', but in other areas they are settling down. 'Whatever happens to the majority it seems likely that many of those who have left London will not return to it after the war.'
>
> Complaints about profiteering in billets are not confined to any particular district, but 'the richer type of refugee are mainly affected'. 'Some people with comparatively small incomes rent rooms in safe areas in case they have to evacuate, and so prevent the use of them by those in more urgent need. Residents as well as refugees complain of this.' There is a good deal of criticism that richer homes evade billeting. Arrangements in many rural Rest Centres are unsatisfactory.

Saturday, 12 October 1940

As we have seen, although on 17 September 1940 Hitler postponed Operation *Seelöwe* 'until further notice', his intention remained to invade southern England in October 1940 in the event of the necessary conditions being achieved. Time, however, was never on Hitler's side – but now the situation was critical: the time when winter weather and sea conditions rendered a sea-crossing impossible was at hand. Moreover, on 2 October 1940 the OKW expressed concern regarding the RAF's attacks on the invasion ports, and these raids remained ongoing. On 26 September 1940, *Grossadmiral* Erich Raeder had asked Hitler to make a final decision about *Seelöwe* by 15 October 1940, because this high degree of readiness required to maintain the invasion fleet was negatively affecting *Kriegsmarine* strength elsewhere – not least the vital U-boat campaign. Four days later, the OKW also wrote, pressing for a decision by the same date, because the continued concentration of forces in the invasion ports had led to ongoing attacks by the RAF and 'continual casualties'. Moreover, Hitler's winter training programme was now being impeded, and specialist troops, including engineers, could not be released back to their parent units in eastern Europe, where their presence was required.

On 12 October 1940, Hitler made his decision: there would be no invasion in 1940, preparations hereafter being 'only a means of exerting political and military pressure on England' – more brinkmanship and bluff – and 'Should a landing in England again be considered in the spring or early summer of 1941, the required degree of preparedness will be ordered at the right time. Until then the military basics of a later landing will further be improved.'

Seelöwe, which had been in a gradual decline since 17 September 1940, was finally off. Although Hitler still considered the war already won, regardless, the fact was that the *Führer*'s intentions in 1940 had been frustrated – and for the first time Germany had suffered its first major failure of the Second World War.

If we are to accept that the Battle of Britain was fought to deny Germany aerial superiority over southern England, and thereby prevent a seaborne invasion, then this epic aerial contest must have begun on 2 July 1940, when the OKW announced the intention to invade – and ended on 12 October 1940, when Hitler finally abandoned *Seelöwe* and consigned this hazardous operation to the dustbin of history. This, then, challenges the dates of the Battle of Britain, as set by the Air Ministry – 10 July 1940 to 31 October 1940 – which we will explore further in due course. The fact of the matter is, though, that despite the ongoing fighting by day and bombing of British cities by night – the Battle of Britain, now that the immediate threat of invasion had passed – had very much been won. Nonetheless, whilst grand strategy was being decided by Hitler, the fighter forces of both sides once more prepared for battle.

This significant day dawned much the same as the previous, autumnal mists giving way, at first, to a mainly cloudless sky with good visibility, although this would deteriorate as the morning progressed. The usual dawn patrols were flown uneventfully, but despite the poor weather seven attacks were mounted by *Luftflotte* 2, five of which penetrated to London. Some 400 aircraft were involved in these raids – there would be no decrease in pressure on the defences, therefore.

At Gravesend, 421 Flight became the first unit to receive the Hawker Hurricane Mk II, taking on six of these new machines whilst retaining two Spitfire Mk IIAs. The Hurricane Mk II was a marked improvement over the Mk I, which, with its Rolls-Royce Merlin II or III engine had a maximum service ceiling of 33,200ft, and maximum speed of 318 mph at 20,000ft. The Mk II, however, with the equally new Merlin XX engine, had a two-stage supercharger providing a maximum service ceiling of 37,500ft, and a maximum speed of 342 mph. The Hurricane Mk II, therefore, compared favourably to the Spitfire Mk IIA, the Merlin XII of which allowed a maximum service ceiling of 37,500ft and maximum speed, at 17,000ft, of 357 mph. Whilst 421 Flight would put their new aircraft to good use, the majority of the original 'Jim Crow' Spitfires were distributed to fighter squadrons, the Spitfire Mk IIA having a faster rate of climb than the Me 109, which, most importantly, had a tighter turning ratio.

At 08.50 hrs, seven Spitfires of 72 Squadron, and five of 92 Squadron, left Biggin Hill to patrol Maidstone at Angels 15, and at the same time the Hurricanes of 249 and 257 Squadrons were brought forward from North Weald to patrol from Hornchurch to Biggin Hill at Angels 20.

At 09.45 hrs, over Deal, the pair of Hurricane squadrons were bounced by *Major* Werner Mölders's *Stab*/JG 51. No. 257 Squadron's Pilot Officer John Redman was hit by cannon fire which destroyed his ASI and causing him to crash-land, unhurt, at Saffrey Farm, Selling, east of Faversham, and Pilot Officer Kenneth Gundry was also hit, forced-landing at Detling, wounded by shrapnel in in the legs and thigh. No. 249 Squadron's *Adjutant* Georges Perrin, a Free French pilot, was shot down, baling out over Eastchurch, slightly wounded. Mölders's *Stabschwarm* claimed three Hurricanes destroyed, two by the *Kommodore* himself and one by *Oberleutnant* Georg Claus; a Hurricane was also claimed by *Hauptmann* Dietrich Hrabak of *Stab* II/JG 54. In response, only 249 Squadron's Sergeant John Beard managed to return fire, attacking a 109, which was diving on six Hurricanes, which was last seen 'going out to sea with glycol streaming out behind. He was losing height.'

The fight over the coast was seen by the Spitfires of 72 Squadron, from a distance but were unable to engage because deteriorating weather had split up the squadron, as pilots attempted to avoid collision 'with another squadron of Hurricanes with which they had joined up'. Only six of the Spitfires returned to Biggin Hill at 09.48 hrs, however: Pilot Officer Herbert Case crashed and was killed at Capel-le-Ferne, near Folkestone. The cause was never established but *Hauptmann* Walter Oesau of *Stab* III/JG 51 claimed a Spitfire destroyed over Dungeness, so it is likely that Case was ambushed. The same area remained the focus of the morning's next clash.

The Spitfires of 222 Squadron left Hornchurch at 09.15 hrs to patrol Gravesend before being vectored south to Maidstone at 30,000ft. Over Deal, at 10.15 hrs, 'A' Flight sighted three Me 110s, the Spitfires immediately going into line astern and diving to attack; before contact was made, however, the presence of twenty Me 109s sighted above changed the whole tactical scenario and 'A' Flight sensibly withdrew. South African Flying Officer Brian van Mentz was leading 'B' Flight and sighted a lone Me 110 5,000ft below him, at 25,000ft, travelling in the opposite direction; van Mentz dived after it, firing from long range, 800 yards, as it appeared that the 110 would make cloud cover, causing smoke to issue from the starboard engine. The Spitfire's windscreen then iced over, so van Mentz returned to base via Dover – where he received good news: he had been awarded the DFC.

On 9 October 1940, 145 Squadron returned to Tangmere after its rest period at Dyce. Although patrols were flown over the next few days, it was now that the replenished squadron contacted the enemy for the first time this tour. At 10.10 hrs, 145 Squadron was patrolling at 30,000ft off Dungeness, with vics in sections line astern, when two Me 109s attacked from the sun. In what was his first meeting with the enemy, Yellow 1, Flying Officer Paul Rabone, a New Zealander, turned into the attack and after both Hurricane and 109 turning tightly, 'The Me 109 was appeared to explode in mid-air. No black smoke was seen but plane spun downwards.' The leading Me 109 then fired at Rabone, who took evasive action, spinning down to 10,000ft. Upon pulling out he saw a 109, which the Hurricane pilot assumed to be the machine he had hit, 'crash into the sea and disappear, about five miles off coast, near Dungeness.' Rabone's Hurricane, however, had been so badly damaged in the exchange that although the pilot returned safely to Tangmere, and was himself unhurt, the aircraft was written off.

Two other 145 Squadron replacement pilots, also experiencing their first taste of combat, were not so lucky: Sergeant John Wadham was shot down and killed, his Hurricane crashing at Cranbrook, and Sergeant Peter Thorpe was also shot down and baled out, his Hurricane going in at Guestling; Thorpe later reported that he was deliberating fired upon by a 109 pilot during his descent.

Pilot Officer Roger Boulding of 74 Squadron made a pertinent comment: 'It is astonishing, upon reflection, how many new pilots failed to return from their first engagement. To see was to live, but your "eyes" only grew with experience.'

No. 145 Squadron had been bounced by 1/JG 77, *Leutnant* Bernd Gallowitsch, *Feldwebel* Alfred Rosen and *Unteroffizier* Harald Kolbe all claiming Hurricanes destroyed.

Five minutes after 145 Squadron was attacked, Squadron Leader Harry Hogan's 501 Squadron, up from Kenley and patrolling from Robertsbridge to Oxney, was being stalked from behind, over Hawkhurst, by Me 109s. A *Schwarm* of these enemy fighters then turned towards the sea, and Hogan dived 501 after them, from 27,000ft, the interception made at Angels 23, Hogan attacking the leading 109. Immediately, the 109 dived steeply towards the coast, pursued by Hogan who shot bits off his opponent and from whose aircraft black and white smoke streamed. Confident that the 109 was finished, Hogan broke off, his Red 3 reporting seeing the 109 'spinning down' and crashing into the sea 'five miles SW of Rye' – almost certainly the same 109 hit by 145 Squadron's Flying Officer Paul Rabone, and Flight Lieutenant Eustace Holden of 501 Squadron. Sergeant James Lacey confirmed that the 109 had hit the sea whilst he chased another, despite his windscreen frosting over. Clearing the screen, Lacey fired a short burst and watched the 109 make 'a pancake landing in the Channel, the pilot climbing out before the aircraft sank. When I returned to base he was still swimming around quite strongly.'

Clearly, two Me 109s had been shot down into the sea – and yet according to German records the only fighter down in the Channel was just one of 7/JG 54, the pilot of which, *Leutnant* Behrens, remains missing.

That morning, Squadron Leader Stanford Tuck, CO of North Weald's 257 Squadron, was at Biggin Hill, visiting his old squadron, 92, when the latter was scrambled at 08.55 hrs, to patrol Maidstone. Jumping into a 92 Squadron Spitfire in preference to his own Hurricane, Tuck flew the sortie as 'Ganic Yellow 1'. At 10.15 hrs, Tuck sighted the action off Deal and Dungeness, seeing 'several groups of Me 109s milling around with Hurricanes and Spitfires.' Tuck reported this to the Ganic Leader, then attacked the leader of a pair of Me 109s flying in line astern:

> I gave five short bursts from astern, abeam and quarter attacks, and he dived steeply, belching thick black smoke. Much evasive action at first, but this stopped after my third burst and he dived steeply, last seen going into haze at 5,000 feet with right wing down. Saw a large single black chevron on the starboard side of the E/A, just in front of black cross. No yellow nose observed.

Chalking up his twentieth combat claim, Tuck had shot down *Leutnant* Bernhard Malischewski of *Stab* II/JG 54, the *Gruppe* signals officer, who was captured after forced-landing near Chapel Holding, Small Hythe, Tenterden, at 10.20 hrs. No. 92 Squadron made no other claims in the engagement, and suffered no losses.

Of Tuck, Sergeant Reg Nutter of 257 Squadron said,

> I found [Robert Stanford] Tuck to be a very charismatic leader and this, combined with his exceptional combat record, immediately gave one a good deal of confidence in him. His style of leadership contrasted greatly with that of his-predecessor, Squadron Leader [Hill] Harkness. Tuck would make suggestions to the Controller as to how we would be better placed to make an interception, but Harkness would follow all instructions without question. There is no doubt that before Tuck's arrival, squadron moral had sunk to a very low ebb; under his leadership there was a tremendous improvement. In many ways he was an individualist but he would go out of his way to give sound advice to other pilots.

On 9 October 1940, 615 Squadron had returned to 11 Group from Prestwick, operating from Northolt. The squadron's first patrol from its new base was over Kenley on the morning of 12 October 1940, but owing to bad weather the Hurricanes landed at Croydon, thereafter patrolling in company with 605 Squadron. Amongst 605 Squadron's pilots was actually a local lad, Sergeant Peter McIntosh, whose interest in aviation had been inspired by Croydon airport from an early age. His sister, Mary Cooper, recalled that on the day in question, 'Peter telephoned home at about mid-day, telling us that he would be on "Ops" during the afternoon but would phone again later.'

At 12.15 hrs, Squadron Leader Archie McKellar, commanding 605 Squadron, scrambled from Croydon, leading off Flying Officer Ralph Hope, Pilot Officer James 'Spud' Hayter, a New Zealander, Pilot Officer Alec Ingle, Sergeant Jan Budzinski, Sergeant Harold Howes and Sergeant Peter McIntosh to patrol with 615 Squadron.

At 13.15 hrs, the Hurricanes met the enemy over Dungeness, as Pilot Officer Ingle, Green 1, reported:

> The Squadron was in sections, vic astern. At 25,000 feet, the Squadron paired into six sections, staggered line astern. After patrolling on various vectors, the Squadron was heading SE at 23,000 feet, towards Dungeness, when three small formations of Me 109s passed about 1,500 yards ahead, heading NW. We held formation in a SE direction for about one minute, when for enemy aircraft appeared out of the sun ahead of and dived on us. The leading sections, not already engaged, did a diving turn to the right and engaged the enemy aircraft below them, who were at that time being engaged by 615 Squadron. Various enemy aircraft broke out of the engagement and headed SE. I picked an isolated and unengaged one and chased it towards the coast. I expended all my ammunition on it in five equal bursts, in astern attacks, and after the third one saw oil come out of the starboard side. When about four miles out from the coast of Dungeness at about 1,500 feet, I broke off the engagement and watched the enemy aircraft descend into the sea in a shallow dive some ten to fifteen miles east of Dungeness. Whilst chasing this aircraft I saw another enemy aircraft plunge into the sea about two miles off Dungeness. I returned to base at 1340 hrs.

Sergeant Howes also claimed a 109 shot down into the sea off Dungeness – but back at Croydon 605 Squadron had a missing pilot.

Mary Cooper:

> When Peter neither telephoned or came to see us, our father called the Squadron and received the devastating news that Peter was missing. There was no other official news throughout the next day, but we knew from other pilots that there had been a combat over the Kentish coast. Our father and elder brother then travelled by car to tour the country area over which the combat had been fought. They stopped and questioned people regarding whether they had seen a British fighter crash on the day in question, and were eventually directed to Littlestone Golf Course, near New Romney, by a farmer who had seen a plane come down there. They subsequently returned home with a piece of fuselage bearing the number P3022, which identified the aircraft concerned as Peter's Hurricane. When approached by my father the Air Ministry said it had no personnel available to search for missing aircraft, and so, needless to say, in our house there was much bad feeling against the authorities. In the event, father still had difficulty persuading them that he had found Peter's crash site. Eventually, my brother's remains were recovered by the RAF and brought home. Ten days after his death in action, our dear Peter was buried in Shirley churchyard. A letter to the British press from

our father, criticising the authorities' efforts to establish the fate of pilots missing in action, was never published.

Sergeant Peter McIntosh was yet another RAF fighter pilot hacked down in a surprise attack by *Major* Werner Mölders, *Kommodore* of JG 51 – possibly the greatest ace of all – who claimed a Hurricane over Dungeness, his third victory of the day.

At 13.15 hrs the Spitfires of 66 Squadron scrambled from Gravesend to patrol south of London at 30,000ft. As usual, Pilot Officer Crelin Bodie was weaving above and behind 'Clickety-Click' when at 14.00 hrs AA fire drew his attention to a number of aircraft. Bodie reported this and set off, 2,000ft above the squadron, to investigate – confirming these to be forty yellow-nosed Me 109s, heading north, then turning south. Bodie turned to re-join 66 Squadron – but by mistake formated on Me 109s, weaving above them 'before I realised my error'. Bodie then 'saw that I was "protecting" six yellow-nosed Me 109s', which were diving to attack a large formation of friendly fighters from astern. Bodie attacked the 109s, a running battle commencing between London and Hastings. 'Bits' were 'knocked off one machine', which emitted black smoke, and another 109 was 'losing glycol fast', and dropped behind the others. Bodie prepared to 'finish him off' but 'more Me 109s came down at me from 1,000 feet above over the Channel in lime abreast'. Going into a steep turn, with '300 mph on the clock', Bodie fired at one of his assailants, which 'rolled over and went straight down'. Concerned about the presence of other 109s, Bodie turned so steeply that he blacked out, and upon recovery, as the sky appeared clear of the enemy, he returned to base, claiming two 109s probably destroyed and one damaged. No. 66 Squadron suffered no casualties and made no other claims.

To the west, at 15.30 hrs, Green Section of Westhampnett's 602 Squadron intercepted a Ju 88 'just out to sea from Beachy Head at 10,000 feet. This aircraft was left fifty feet above the sea with one engine stopped, the rudder badly damaged and the whole machine raked with our fire.' [ORB]. This was a machine of II/LG 1, which crashed on landing back at Orléans-Bricy. The rear gunner had returned fire, however, hitting and badly damaging two Spitfires: Sergeant Cyril Babbage crash-landed near Lewes, his Spitfire overturning, although the pilot was unhurt. Pilot Officer John Hart, a Canadian, returned to base with a bullet through his aircraft's mainspar, which required a new wing.

Late afternoon would see more heavy fighting over South London and Kent, as the relentless fighter-bomber raids persisted. With the Me 109s having increased their incoming height to 31,000ft, the Spitfires had to fly higher still.

At 14.45 hrs, eleven Spitfires of 603 Squadron left Hornchurch to patrol south of base. Pilot Officer David 'Scottie' Scott-Malden, a former Cambridge scholar with a first in classics, was about to meet the enemy for the first time:

> I was on patrol as Yellow 3 of 603 Squadron at 32,000 feet over the Maidstone area ... at 1615 hrs. AA fire drew our attention to 100 Me 109s 3,000 feet below and ahead of us, flying NW towards Central London, in no particular formation. As we dived down on them they turned round and headed down the estuary. I picked out one on the inside of the turn

and did a deflection attack, developing into a stern chase, firing long bursts. E/A was not hit by deflection attack but at first burst in line astern mixed black and white smoke appeared. E/A slowed up and began to lose height but took no evasive action. In the first burst I saw tracer from four starboard guns going into side and tail of E/A. When I broke off, owing to lack of ammunition and petrol, E/A was at 5,000 feet over Chatham area, losing height in a straight glide to the East, with engine coughing puffs of black smoke. Another Me 109 came and circled him as he went down.

It was 'Scottie's' first aerial victory, albeit only claimed as a probable: *Oberleutnant* G. Büsgen, *Staffelkapitän* of 1/JG 52, baled out, wounded, and was captured, his 109 crashing at Deans Hill, Harrietsham. Probables were also claimed by both Flight Lieutenant John Boulter and Pilot Officer John Soden. No. 603 Squadron suffered no loss.

At 15.50 hrs, 66 Squadron was up again from Gravesend, linking up with Biggin Hill's 92 Squadron at 3,000ft over the latter airfield to patrol Maidstone at 30,000ft, Flight Lieutenant Brian Kingcome and 92 Squadron leading. Kingcome, Ganic Leader, climbed 'the train' over London but at 16.15 hrs, whilst at 28,000ft and still climbing, travelling towards the patrol line, two 109s were sighted by the eagle-eyed Pilot Officer Crelin Bodie, Red 4 of 66 Squadron, a few hundred feet above him, 'with red, white and blue vertical stripes on their fins, and yellow noses'. Bodie attacked one of the enemy fighters, which 'gave out black smoke', and Kingcome dived the Spitfires from down-sun to intercept, according to 92 Squadron's Form 'F', 'a straggling mass of Me 109s ... 50+' flying east over the Thames Estuary. Ganic Leader 'became embroiled with twelve Me 109s', firing short bursts at several in the running battle developing back to the coast, and 'noticed one of them go over on its side and fall away vertically with black smoke coming from it NW of Margate, but I was too busy to see whether it actually crashed or not'. Kingcome then pursued a lone 109 southwards and watched as it 'finally crashed into the sea off Cap Gris Nez'.

Pilot Officer John 'Tommy' Lund of 92 Squadron chased a 109 down to 2,000ft over Dover, leaving it smoking, and Pilot Officer Trevor 'Wimpy' Wade fired at a 109 from just 15 yards, the pilot of which baled out. Wade then damaged two more 109s before heading home, his ammunition expended. Sergeant Donald 'Don' Kingaby hit a 109 'which crossed his bows' and dived away, streaming glycol; Kingaby then hit another 109, which Sergeant Walter Ellis saw crash 'near Rochester'. Meanwhile, 'Clickety-Click's Pilot Officer Crelin Bodie had chased the pair of 109s he had attacked to the coast, 'the engine of the smoky one was idling slowly', so the Spitfire pilot pressed home his attack, and five miles off Dungeness noted smoke 'definitely of the type which accompanies fire in an aircraft', whilst conceding that what could have been flames may equally have been 'the sun shining on his bright yellow nose.' The other 109 was then on Bodie's tail, and, out of ammunition and with more 109s above, 'Bogle' 'beat it'.

It had been a successful action. No. 66 Squadron suffered no loss, only Bodie making a claim, but for 92 Squadron it was 'a big day' [ORB]: three Me 109s were claimed destroyed, two probables and three damaged. No. 2/JG 52 lost *Oberleutnant*

Karl Sauer, who baled out and was captured slightly wounded, his 109 crashing at Hollingbourne, south-east of Maidstone, and *Feldwebel* S. Voss, who baled out and also captured, unhurt, his machine crashing near Ashford. Furthermore, *Unteroffizier* Reichenbach of 4/JG 52, went into the sea, so in terms of 109s destroyed, 92 Squadron claimed accurately. This success, however, was not without loss: Flying Officer Aberconway Pattinson, who had only joined 92 the previous day, was shot down and killed, his Spitfire crashing at Bartholomew Wood, Postling Wents, north-west of Folkestone; he was 21. Although the only Spitfire down, both *Leutnant* Franz Essl of 1/JG 52, and *Oberleutnant* Helmut Bennemann of 2/JG 52, claimed Spitfires destroyed south-east of London.

At 15.50 hrs, the Hurricanes of 46 and 257 Squadron had left North Weald to patrol Canterbury. At 16.40 hrs the Hurricanes were vectored south of London Docks. North Weald's station commander, Wing Commander Victor Beamish DSO and Bar DFC AFC, was patrolling alone and also saw the withdrawing 109s, some forty of which were flying west above the two Hurricane squadrons. Beamish attacked, breaking up the enemy formation and damaging a 109, but the Germans remained high above the Hurricanes, which could not, therefore, engage. Instead, 46 and 257 Squadrons flew on and were ordered to Dungeness where the latter clashed briefly with a formation of 109s; the Hurricane pilots made no claims but Pilot Officer Cardale 'Carl' Capon, who regularly flew as Squadron Leader Tuck's wingman, was shot down, baling out slightly wounded, his Hurricane crashing at High House Farm, Kenardington, inland of Dungeness. *Major* Günther von Maltzhan was responsible, Capon being his eleventh aerial victory and first since having become *Kommodore* of JG 53.

At 17.33 hrs, *Hauptmann* Heinz Bretnütz claimed a Spitfire at an unrecorded location, and at 18.05 hrs *Leutnant* Heinrich Tirnow of 4/JG 51 claimed another at 18.05 hrs north-west of Dungeness. After the skirmish between JG 53 and 257 Squadron, however, there were no further combats between RAF fighter squadrons and Me 109s. However, Flight Lieutenant Charles 'Paddy' Green, commanding 421 Flight, was spotting on 12 October 1940,

> [He] was flying at 30,000 feet, shadowing E/A when he iced-up inside the cockpit. He was attacked by yellow-nosed Me 109s and had his fore and aft controls shot away. With shrapnel wounds in arm and neck, Flight Lieutenant Green struggled to open his hood while his aircraft fell from 30,000 feet to 1,000 feet. Observers saw him finally bale out at 700 feet and he was picked up by sociable New Zealand troops at Pembles Cross Farm, Egerton, before being taken to hospital. [ORB]

Green's Spitfire crashed at Coldbridge, Boughton Malherbe, south-east of Maidstone; the pilot would not resume operational flying until 1 November 1940.

The final daylight combat of 12 October 1940 involved Flight Lieutenant Adrian Boyd DFC and Flying Officer Dudley Honor DFC of Tangmere's 145 Squadron who caught an Arado 196 floatplane of 1/*Bordfl.Gr.196* at 18.00 hrs, 12 miles south of St Catherine's Point and shot it down; *Hauptmann* Karl-Hugo Thewaldt, the *Staffelkapitän*, and *Unteroffizier* Kottwitz remain missing.

Coastal Command again flew its usual round of sorties throughout the day, and at night four aircraft attacked the power station at Lorient and another hit Quimper airfield. No. 2 Group sent six Blenheims on a North Sea reconnaissance, but the deteriorating weather prevented any other operations, and for the same reasons nocturnal raids were also reduced. No. 301 (Polish) Squadron's Battles attacked the ports of Calais and Ostend, and Blenheims targeted enemy shipping at Amsterdam, Dunkirk and Le Havre – these being the last major attacks on the invasion ports – and industrial targets in Germany, and the Fokker factory in Amsterdam, were also bombed. Neither command suffered any casualties.

The relentless fighter-bomber raids on London, however, had left 23 civilians dead and 149 injured. Nonetheless, on the Home Front, even in London, life had to go on: on this day, Raymond Husband of Ealing, a London underground worker and member of the Home Guard, married Eva Russell, a switchboard operator at Paddington Station. The uncertainty of life led to many a passionate wartime romance leading to a swift marriage, some sadly ending with the premature death of one or the other spouse, or perhaps divorce, but this union was not one of those: Raymond and Eva were childhood sweethearts and, thankfully, lived happily ever after, raising a family and eventually living in Pagham, by the sea. Nonetheless, the family was still touched by the blast of war: Eva's cousin, Rifleman Timothy Brophy of the Rifle Brigade would be killed on 26 June 1944, during the Normandy campaign.

On the night of 12 October 1940, the He 111s of the specialist *Beleuchter-gruppe* (fire-lighting unit, later known as *Pfadfinders*), *Kampfgruppe* 100, based at Vannes, equipped with the secret *X-Verfahren* and *Knickebein* radio beam navigation system, accurately bombed Coventry city centre with both incendiaries and HE. Nineteen civilians were killed and sixty-nine injured. It was the first heavy raid on the city – and an ominous portent of things to come for Coventrians.

Sunday, 13 October 1940

On 13 October 1940, Air Vice-Marshal Douglas Evill, senior air staff officer at Fighter Command HQ, sent Air Chief Marshal Hugh Dowding a set of minutes regarding various aspects of the battle to date. The SASO wrote that beyond daily combat reports, Fighter Command HQ had

> no regular source of information as to how groups are operating. We do not know whether their squadrons are sent up singly or in twos or threes, or to what heights they are sent. We have no indication as to how squadrons in the air are disposed or whether factory areas are specifically covered. There is, in fact, no general statement of the action taken. For instance, though 12 Group's wing was called in on afternoon of 11 October, as is indicated in their Form 'Y', there is no mention in 11 Group's report that they called for this reinforcement or what they did with it.
>
> We have, I know, received – after calling for it – a report from 11 Group on their method of operation in the first six weeks of this

battle, which contains very valuable information as to methods adapted by 11 Group in that period. We have also received from [Trafford] Leigh-Mallory reports as to why and how he employs his wing, and reports from Park as to why he does not. Apart from these communications we do not know a great deal about the way in which they conduct operations and there is certainly no recognised routine for reports from Groups as to what they are doing.

I fully understand that you delegate the tactical conduct of operations to the groups, and that we must neither bother them with demands for a lot of written information, nor show a lack of confidence in their conduct of operations, which would, indeed, be entirely unjustified in view of the results which they have achieved.

Evill's comments regarding Air Vice-Marshal Keith Park's reports are puzzling, given that the latter's are comprehensive and do not explain 'why he does not' use wings. Evill had completely missed the point, so far as the wing scenario went. Park was using wings, when appropriate, as his reports confirmed, and had been doing so for some time. Indeed, in this particular phase of the battle was even more necessary to operate squadrons in at least pairs, given the numbers of enemy fighters involved. Park's tactics, in fact, were clearly defined and flexible – but unbeknown to him, behind closed doors at the Air Ministry, a critique of his handling of the battle over south-east England was being prepared.

On 13 October 1940, the early morning mist of the previous few days had shifted to the eastern side of the Channel, reducing enemy air activity. Nonetheless, *Jafü* 2 would fly ninety-eight fighter-bomber sorties in three attacks aimed at London.

The first raid, of twenty-five plus, a fighter sweep, crossed coast at 12.48 hrs, over Hythe, and went out over Lympne twelve minutes later, without being intercepted. Next around 13.25 hrs, two waves of thirty plus flew up the Medway, the first penetrating to London, the second holding off over Dartford. Once again, Flight Lieutenant Brian Kingcome was Ganic Leader, at the head of 92 Squadron, climbing over London, with orders to patrol the Biggin Hill – Gravesend line at 30,000ft. At 25,000ft, control informed Kingcome that bandits had turned south, so the Spitfires headed for Dover, but upon arrival there was no sign of the enemy. Whilst flying towards the intended patrol line, further information was received of the raid heading in over the Medway, from the east. Kingcome made for the Thames Estuary and intercepted four Me 109s at 25,000ft, which were 'chasing a squadron of Hurricanes', but 92 Squadron was attacked by a single Me 109, which opened fire from astern. Kingcome immediately ordered his Red 3 to detach and engage the bandit – but Ganic Leader's R/T was unserviceable, and so the message was never received. A Spitfire went into a spin, the 109 still firing, so Kingcome gave chase – but as, unbeknown to him, his R/T was U/S, his order for the rest of the squadron to attack the other 109s went unreceived, and the Spitfires followed their leader. Realising what had happened, however, the pilots turned about, but found only Hurricanes. Kingcome shot down the 109 concerned, of 7/JG 3, the pilot of which, *Gefreiter* H. Rungen, forced-landed at Cuckold Coombe, near Ashford, and was captured unhurt. No. 92 Squadron suffered no casualties.

There were certainly many Hurricanes up over Kent: 46 and 249 Squadrons were patrolling together when Green Section of the former was ambushed over Dungeness by six Me 109s. Sergeant Leonard Pearce was hit and wounded in the arm, forced-landing at Biggin Hill. Typically, the 109s had attacked in a high-speed, diving, pass, and were gone before a counter-attack could be delivered. Nos. 17 and 73 Squadrons were patrolling Hornchurch, having scrambled at 13.45 hrs, and over Chatham AA fire opened up just behind the Hurricanes. At 14.55 hrs, both squadrons landed at Martlesham Heath to find 17 Squadron's Pilot Officer Jack Ross was missing. At the time, it was assumed that Ross – the squadron's vulnerable weaver – had been hit by AA fire, but Ross was much more likely picked off in another ambush by 109s. Fortunately, the Hurricane pilot baled out safely, his aircraft having been hit by a cannon shell, which sent splinters into his left side, leg and neck. On this occasion, however, the Germans substantially overclaimed, pilots of 4/JG 54 claiming eight Hurricanes destroyed.

At 14.55 hrs, Squadron Leader Rupert 'Lucky' Leigh led 66 Squadron up from Gravesend to patrol Maidstone, first at 15,000ft, then at 30,000ft. Leigh's Spitfires were, therefore, already airborne when at 15.35 hrs a raid of fifty plus came in and flew to Maidstone, where they separated, one formation proceeding towards Hornchurch, the other via Dartford to Central London. Having attained 22,000ft, the controller sent sixty-six back down to 15,000ft, then back up to Angels 30. Consequently, the Spitfires missed the incoming raid, which reached its targets without being intercepted. Leigh, however, led the Spitfires to 31,500ft when, vectored 20°. Over the Ashford area at 16.00 hrs, AA fire attracted Leigh's attention. Unable to see any enemy aircraft, Leigh patrolled 'across sun' – then the sharp-eyed Pilot Officer Crelin Bodie, as usual flying Red 4 and weaving, saw and reported the withdrawing Germans, which were 2,000–3,000ft below, heading south-east. With his Spitfires in line-astern, Leigh ordered Red Section to protect the remainders' tails – and attacked, hitting a 109, which Fibus Leader followed in a vertical dive. The 109, with its fuel-injected engine, pulled away from the Spitfire, and Leigh's engine cut-out and 'would not pick up. I landed in a ploughed field North of Maidstone.'

Bodie was attacked by Me 109s from above. Counter-attacking, Bodie hit a 109 with De Wilde ammunition in the engine cowling, cockpit and canopy; the 109 'flicked violently' and began extreme evasive manoeuvres, once almost ramming the Spitfire. Bodie, however, was hit by three cannon shells and machine-gun bullets, spinning away out of control. Eventually recovering, Bodie returned his damaged Spitfire to Gravesend.

Pilot Officer Charles Cooke was leading Red Section and attacked the Me 109s from 'out of the sun, apparently taking the enemy by surprise'. Cooke hit one 109, which emitted black and white smoke, which he then lost in the sun's glare; whilst attacking another 109, Cooke was fired upon himself and broke away.

Flight Lieutenant Bob Oxspring hit a 109, which dived, emitting white smoke, pursued by Red 1 who finished all his ammunition on the German, who flew on, with 'something definitely wrong with his engine'. During this combat, all four of Oxspring's port machine guns refused to fire due to the heating system failing.

Oxspring's Red 2, Pilot Officer Stanley Baker:

> I attacked one E/A ... he half-rolled down and ... employed violent evasive action and for about two minutes we fought for position.

Eventually, in a violent upward manoeuvre in which he opened fire, which was going well behind me, he allowed me to pull up inside him and get in a fairly long burst. Glycol smoke suddenly began to pour out and his aircraft stalled and fell away. This was at about 24,000 feet in the Ashford – Manston area. I did not follow E/A down as there were other Me 109s still in the vicinity and all my ammunition was not shot ... The aircraft was camouflaged darkly above with pale blue under-surface and had **not** red, white and blue stripes on the fin. The pilot seemed very experienced and fought the whole time without endeavouring to get away. It was very apparent, however, that a Spitfire could turn comfortably inside a Me 109 at high speed.

Sergeant Matthew Cameron, Blue 2, also hit a 109, which emitted black smoke, but then lost his target owing to his windscreen frosting over.

It was a sharp and furious fight, during which 66 Squadron claimed five Me 109 probables and another damaged. Sergeant Harold Cook was shot-up, but returned to base where his Spitfire was written off in the resulting crash-landing. The Germans claimed just one Spitfire destroyed, by *Oberleutnant* Roloff von Aspern of 4/JG 54; no Me 109s were lost.

AC1 Bob Morris, a Fitter IIE on 'Clickety-Click':

I remember Pilot Officer 'Bogle' Bodie coming back to Gravesend with his port mainplane knocked about by a cannon shell, and I had to rip part of the aileron off for him which he proudly took as a souvenir. I always remember a Spitfire coming in and making a horrible whistling noise – it had a bullet hole right through a propeller blade! As we didn't have a new propeller we smoothed the hole out and drilled corresponding holes in the other two blades – it then flew for another fortnight with that same airscrew! We had to drill the other holes because when a propeller is assembled it is very finely balanced to prevent vibration.

By 16.10 hrs, south-east England was clear of the enemy, and there were no further fighter-bomber attacks on this day.

Sadly, further north, up in 12 Group, there was, however, an unfortunate incident of so-called 'Friendly Fire'. With Liverpool being frequently visited by the enemy's night-bombers, the Blenheim night fighter of 29 Squadron had also been stationed at Ternhill in Shropshire. As we have seen, at dusk on 11 October 1940, 611 Squadron's Ternhill-based Spitfires had fought an action against several Do 17s of *Kustenfleigergruppe* 606 over the Mersey and North Wales, and this was a key time to intercept raiders in the last vestiges of daylight. At 17.35 hrs, therefore, on 13 October 1940, two 29 Squadron Blenheims took-off to patrol the Point of Ayr: Pilot Officer Jack Humphreys (pilot), Sergeant Ernest Bee (air gunner) and AC1 Joseph Fizel (radar operator), in L6637, and Sergeant Robert Stevens, Sergeant Oswald Sly, and AC2 Arthur Jackson, in L7135. Fifteen minutes later, Squadron Leader Frank Tyson led six 312 (Czech) Squadron Hurricanes up from Speke, also to patrol the Point of

Ayr. According to the latter's ORB, what followed was 'a most regrettable incident' arising from 'an unfortunate chain of circumstances.' Czech Squadron Leader Jan Ambrus was leading Yellow Section, and sighted the Blenheims below, 10 miles north-west of Liverpool. Assuming these to be Ju 88s, Ambrus attacked L7135, the pilot of which, Sergeant Robert Stevens, immediately firing two red flares – the recognition colours of the day – and warned Pilot Officer Jack Humphreys, in L6637, over the R/T. Flight Lieutenant Harry Comerford fired a short burst, as did Czech Sergeant Josef Stehlík (who later claimed to have been sighting his guns at a range of 1,100 yards). Whilst Humphreys's aircraft escaped serious damage and returned safely to base, the crew unhurt – but L7135 burst into flame and crashed into the sea; all three men aboard were lost. It was a tragic mistake – but an understandable one, given that the Blenheim Mk IF, with its glazed nose, twin rotary engines and dark night-fighter camouflage distinctly resembled the Junkers 88, especially in fading light and an area in which German bombers operated.

Nothing of note occurred so far as Coastal Command was concerned during the day, although at night shipping was attacked off Flushing and fires reported. No. 2 Group's Blenheims made no daylight raids, but at night the Battles of 142 and 300 (Polish) Squadron attacked the invasion port of Calais; Blenheims attacked Le Havre and industrial targets in Germany, and Wellingtons and Hampdens bombed German shipyards and Eindhoven airfield. A 142 Squadron Battle ran out of fuel returning from Calais and was abandoned by the crew over Lincolnshire, and a 300 Squadron Battle crashed at Oxton whilst returning to Swinderby, killing all three Polish airmen aboard. A 99 Squadron Wellington failed to return to Newmarket from Wilhelmshaven, disappearing without trace.

Weekly Home Intelligence Report:

> Anti-Semitism is still reported in evacuation areas, even as far afield as Pembrokeshire and Cardiganshire. In the big area round London to which many East-enders have evacuated, anti-Semitic remarks are common. A new development is that London Jews who have stayed behind are themselves showing signs of turning against the Jewish evacuees. In some evacuation areas people are refusing to give billets to Jews. In certain London shelters the Jews are segregated from the Cockneys, and remarks are made that the Jews arrive earliest at the shelters. Though the strong family and property ties of the Jews naturally cause comments, there is little evidence to suggest that in fact Jews are behaving any worse or better than Cockneys. If anything, the naturalised alien minorities tend to arrive at shelters before either Jews or Cockneys.

Monday, 14 October 1940

On 14 October 1940, Deputy Director of Home Operations Air Vice-Marshal Donald Stevenson, produced an 'Air Staff Note on the Operation of Fighter Wings' for the

DCAS, Air Vice-Marshal Sholto Douglas, this document being based solely upon Air Vice-Marshal Trafford Leigh-Mallory's report dated 17 September 1940. In due course, Stevenson's memorandum was shown to Air Vice-Marshal Keith Park, whose responses are shown below in italics:

> It has become apparent that on some occasions our fighters have been meeting the enemy on unequal terms both as regards numbers and height. In order to overcome or reduce this disadvantage, fighters must be operated in tactical units large enough to deal effectively with enemy formations and these units must be so controlled that they encounter the enemy without tactical disadvantage.

2. It is the purpose of this note to examine the circumstances in which fighter units of more than single squadrons should be operated and to evolve general principles for their employment.
3. It would be well first to summarise the disadvantages under which our own fighters have in some instances operated. These are briefly as follows:

    (i) Numerical Inferiority: Squadrons have been sent up singly or in pairs to meet large formations of bombers escorted by still larger formations of enemy fighters. The operations of three squadrons have not been effectively coordinated with the operations of other squadrons in the same group, and adjacent groups, with the result that fighters have operated independently and effectively.

    (ii) *Pairs of Spitfire squadrons engage high fighter screen. Pairs of Hurricane squadrons to each raid and escort. Wing formations from Tangmere, Northolt, Debden, North Weald. Not 'adjacent Groups': only 12 Group.*

    (iii) There have been few opportunities for fighter formation leaders to discuss or concert operations with leaders of other fighter formations.

    Group and Sector conferences are frequent.

    (iv) Fighters are frequently told to patrol at a height which puts them at the mercy of high-flying fighters.

    See Instruction to Controllers No. 25.

    (v) Fighters are vectored towards enemy formations in such a way that by the time they reach the plan position of the enemy, they are below him.

    For many units assemble at height over base or on their patrol line.

(vi) The limitations of High Frequency Radio Telephony preclude the possibility of operating a number of squadrons on the same frequency.

4. Examination of the disadvantages leads us to recommend the adoption of the following principles for operating fighter formations larger than squadrons.

Is an aim to engage bombers _before_ they reach target?

FIGHTER WING

5. The minimum fighter unit to meet large enemy formations should be a wing of three squadrons.

Depends on time available and clouds. Impossible for _London_ sectors!

'BALBO'

6. When necessary, to secure superiority in numbers or to reduce inferiority as far as possible, a force of two fighter wings should be operated as a tactical unit. This tactical unit of two wings will be referred to in this paper as a 'balbo'.

Too clumsy and rigid for Home Defence fighting.

COMPOSITION OF A WING

7. A wing should be of three squadrons of the same type and if possible mark of aircraft.

Yes.

8. All squadrons of a wing should operate from the same aerodrome, or failing this, from aerodromes within two or three miles of each other.

No. Dispersment reduces vulnerability.

COMPOSITION OF A BALBO

9. A balbo should be of two wings. One wing may be of one type of aircraft and the other wing may be of another. Wings composing a balbo should be so disposed that the wing having the aircraft of higher performance is further back from the zone of operations.

CONTROL OF A WING

10. In order to ensure sympathetic and effective control of the wing, one of the squadron commanders from the squadrons composing the wing should supervise the controlling wing from the Sector Operations Room.

Continuous Watch in daylight?

CONTROL OF A BALBO

11. The wings composing a balbo will come from different sectors. The control of each wing will be supervised by a squadron commander from the wing, but the Group Headquarters should detail one of the sectors to coordinate the operations of the two wings of the balbo. The Direction Fixing positions of both wings should be shown in the Operations Room of the controlling sector.

VARIATIONS IN CONTROL NECCESSITATED BY VHF OR HF R/T

12. VHF facilitates the control of balbos, but if squadrons are fitted with HF it is considered that difficulties in inter-communications are outweighed by the advantages in meeting large enemy formations with large fighter formations.

CONTROL OF BALBOS WITH VHF R/T

13. All the squadrons in each wing should operate on sector frequency (Button 'B') and would have to be controlled on this frequency. Inter-communication between wings is in a balbo would be by means of the Command frequency through aircraft on watch on this frequency.

    Yes.

CONTROL OF BALBOS WITH HF R/T

14. Squadrons should operate on their squadron frequency; inter-communication between squadrons by R/T is impracticable except through ground stations. It will frequently happen when using HF that balbos will pass out of R/T range of their sectors. When this happens it may be confidently expected that weather will be such that large enemy formations will be clearly visible from a distance, and vectoring, therefore, will be unnecessary.

    Yes.

15. The control of balbos operating at a distance from their controlling sectors even with VHF is complicated by the sectors not having operations tables big enough to show the whole area over which balbos may have to fight. It is recommended that smaller scale 'balbo tables' should be provided to show the tracks of enemy formations of more than, say, fifty aircraft. These tables should be small-scale replicas of the Fighter Command table (say 10 miles to 1 inch). Consideration would have to be given to the method by which this information might be passed to sectors.

One group must **control all** squadrons in its sectors.

UNITY OF WINGS

16. 'Espirit de Wing' and consequent operational efficiency would be fostered by regarding wings as units and moving them complete from one station to another when rest or reinforcement is necessary, but this is obviously impractical at present. It would be difficult to engender in a balbo the same spirit of unity which should inform a wing, but much could be done to promote good cooperation by encouraging personal contact between the pilots and particularly the leaders of the squadrons concerned.

LOCATION OF WINGS

17. Wings should be located at stations from which they can gain advantage in height over the enemy before they meet him, without having to turn. This may be impracticable except in special cases.

GROUP COMBINED TACTICAL PLAN

18. The tactical plan on which the primary group should work ought to be based on the principle that although the aim is to destroy enemy bombers, the enemy fighters must be contained to enable the bombers to be destroyed.

Need to protect vitals of area?

ROLE OF WINGS

19. The wing with higher performance aircraft should take on enemy fighters. The wing with the lower performance aircraft should take on bombers, if any.

Yes.

Clearly, Air Vice-Marshal Keith Park had all the answers to every detail in Stevenson's note – hardly surprising given that by now he was the most experienced fighter leader outside Germany. That being so, it is incomprehensible that such a memorandum was compiled and circulated by the Air Ministry without consultation with Air Chief Marshal Hugh Dowding or, indeed, Park. Stevenson's fifth point makes abundantly clear the thinking at the Air Ministry and traction achieved by 'Big Wing' supporters: 'The minimum fighter unit to meet large enemy formations should be a wing of three squadrons'. This is irrefutable evidence of the inflexibility of the 'Big Wing' theorists' thinking. The Air Staff note was circulated, notifying the AOCs of 10, 11 and 12 Groups that the CAS was holding a conference on 17 October 1940 to discuss day-fighter formation tactics and hear a report from Dowding regarding the progress of nocturnal defences. Stevenson's note was to 'form the basis for discussion'. The agenda for this forthcoming meeting was circulated; again, Park's comments are italicised:

Is it agreed that the maximum fighter unit to meet large enemy formations should be a wing of three squadrons?

To meet enemy bomber formations only.

Is it agreed that a larger fighter formation than a wing should operate as a tactical unit? If so, is it agreed that this unit should consist of two wings?

Not over UK but on offensive sweeps.

By what name should such a unit (referred to in this agenda as a 'Balbo') be known?

Are any insurmountable obstacles foreseen in operating all the squadrons of a wing from the same aerodrome?

No, but congestion, take-off delay and all being bombed on the ground together should be considered.

Is it agreed that the wing and 'Balbo' should be controlled by a squadron commander from one of the squadrons composing the formation?

No, by Ground Sector Controller.

Are there likely to be any difficulties in coordinating the operations of the two wings or 'balbo'?

Yes, limitation of R/T and clouds.

In weather conditions which enable the enemy to operate in mass formation, it is likely that the fighter leader may be able to dispense with sector control. Is it agreed that in these conditions he should inform the sector controller and take over control of the wing or 'balbo', being informed by the Controller of the location, size, speed, course and height of the enemy mass?

These conditions are best suited for Sector Controller, as he gets good information from Observer Corps, recce aircraft, AA units and Group HQ.

Has the Conference any comments on the method of R/T control of 'balbos' described in 12–15 of the attached Air Staff Note?

VHF as common frequency.

Can wings be regarded as permanent units and moved complete when necessary, from one station to another?

No, unless squadrons are added.

Is it agreed that wings should be deployed at stations from which they can gain advantage in height over the enemy without having to turn?

No, depends on length of warning.

Short report by C-in-C Fighter Commander on present position regarding night interception.

Whilst Air Vice-Marshal Keith Park prepared for what was, so far as he and Air Chief Marshal Hugh Dowding were concerned, a routine conference in two days' time, the fighting continued.

The weather, according to 249 Squadron at North Weald, was 'bad' [ORB], and operations were much reduced; indeed, across the Channel, JG 53 was given its first rest day in weeks. Nonetheless, the threat of further fighter-bomber attacks dictated that 11 Group maintain standing patrols.

At 11.35 hrs, 249 Squadron left North Weald and at 12.00 hrs was 22,000ft over Folkestone. Pilot Officer George Barclay was Yellow 1 and described how the Hurricanes were attacked by thirty Me 109s, which rained down from 30,000ft, a *Schwarm* of these singling Barclay out, who dived to 15,000ft. A 109 then crossed his bows, the Hurricane pilot quickly firing, the 109 diving towards the sea, pursued by Barclay. The 109 streamed glycol but Barclay 'was obliged to break off attack when E/A was at about 1,500ft, upside down. Owing to an attack by seven other E/A, so that I did not observe E/A crash in sea'. Claimed as a probable, no 109s were actually lost, and nor did 249 Squadron sustain casualties.

Inevitably, given the poor weather and reduced fighter operations, lone Ju 88s made a nuisance of themselves. At 12.30 hrs, Red Section of Biggin Hill's 92 Squadron, comprising Pilot Officer Robert 'Bob' ('Dutch') Holland and Pilot Officer John Lund, found the bandit they were searching for at 10,500ft over Ashford. The Spitfires were 500ft below the Ju 88. Both pilots attacked but the bomber disappeared into cloud, which had descended to just 200ft. Similarly, at 12.30 hrs, Flying Officer Brian Carbury and Flight Lieutenant John Haig were scrambled from Hornchurch to patrol base at 10,000ft; the Spitfire pair climbed to 10,000ft in 10/10ths cloud, which they climbed above at 15,000ft. Control then informed the pilots that a bandit was at 7,000ft, but as Carbury and Haig descended, the Ju 88 was seen above, at 17,000ft. Carbury 'climbed ahead of the E/A and carried out a frontal attack, saw one engine stop and the last I saw of the E/A he was waffling into cloud at 6,000 feet.'

At 14.40 hrs, Flying Officer Count Manfred Czernin and Pilot Officer Geoffrey Pittman of 17 Squadron were scrambled from Martlesham

and intercepted a Do 17 with British markings on tail fin, upper wing surfaces and fuselage. As the E/A turned away, black crosses were seen on the underside of the wings and Flying Officer [Manfred] Czernin attacked, leaving the port engine on fire. The E/A fired two rockets, which were, however, incorrect colours. Later, Pilot Officer [Geoffrey] Pittman attacked, but the Do 17 escaped by flying through Harwich balloon barrage.

The Do 17 was claimed as damaged – and was a machine of 9/KG 2, which crash-landed back at Cambrai-Sued.

It was a rare occasion that the Me 109s made no combat claims, and neither fighter force suffered any losses in action – but this had been one such. What is significant, however, is the large number of flying accidents suffered by Fighter Command on this day. A 152 Squadron Spitfire was damaged when landing at Warmwell, wheels-up; a 213 Squadron Hurricane was damaged when landing on water-logged Merston airfield; two 601 Squadron Hurricanes overshot Exeter's runway, one of which was damaged, and a 616 Squadron pilot was unable to lower his undercarriage and landed wheels-up at Kirton. No. 605 Squadron, based at Croydon, however, suffered a sad fatality.

Ralph Hope was an Old Etonian and former Oxford scholar, related to Britain's former prime minister Neville Chamberlain. From Birmingham, Hope joined the family business, manufacturing metal window frames, and whilst working in New York, began flying lessons, receiving his Aero Certificate at Reading Aero Club in 1938 – after which he joined 605 'County of Warwick' Squadron of the AAF. On 9 May 1940, Hope shared in the destruction of a Do 17, and survived being shot down himself by Me 109s on 28 September 1940. According to 605 Squadron's ORB,

> [It was] A grey day, clouds coming down to ground level by 13.00 hrs. In the morning a He 111 [author's note: more likely a Ju 88] came over the airfield at 1,500 feet and dropped a bomb quarter of a mile away. Two sections of two aircraft went up at 1230 hrs, only one aircraft landing here, two at Gatwick …

In the bad weather, however, Flying Officer Ralph Hope wandered into London's Inner Artillery Zone, striking a barrage balloon cable. Realising that had if he baled out the Hurricane would crash onto dwellings below, Hope remained with the Hurricane, managing to steer it towards open ground before baling out – too low. The Hurricane crashed harmlessly into an allotment at Tennison Road, South Norwood at 12.50 hrs, but the Hope was killed. His squadron commander, Squadron Leader Archie McKellar, said 'Ralph Hope was the type of fellow who would do a thing like that and think nothing about it. He was very brave and thought little of his own safety where the safety of others was concerned.' Hope was, in fact, the last original auxiliary member of 605 Squadron, and 'his charming personality and quiet sense of honour and stability will be missed by all' [ORB]. The gallant airman was 27.

Owing to the weather, sorties by Coastal Command were much reduced, but a Hudson of 233 Squadron, based at Leuchars, was shot down off Norway by *Oberleutnant* Horst Carganico of *Stab* II/JG 77, the crew lost. No. 2 Group's daylight operations were largely scrubbed, but by night seventy-eight Whitleys, Wellingtons and Hampdens attacked Berlin, Stettin, Böhlen, Magdeburg and Le Havre. A Hampden of Waddington's 44 Squadron was shot down west of Gardelegen by 2/NJG 1's *Leutnant* Hans-Georg Mangelsdorf, and a Hampden of 50 Squadron was shot down near Kalbe by *Hauptmann* Werner Streib of I/NGJ 1; a Wellington of 9 Squadron was destroyed by *Oberfeldwebel* Gerhard Herzog of I/NJG 1 over Salzwedel – indicating that Germany's night defences were getting well organised. Conversely, Britain's cities continued to be attacked after dark.

Pilot Officer George Pushman, a Canadian, commented,

> We of 23 Squadron were based at Wittering, but flew mostly from Ford during the Battle of Britain, which was a very busy period. We used to have ten days on duty followed by two days off. Flying at night in our Blenheims, we prowled around the East coast, but I never even caught a glimpse of a German aircraft.

Tuesday, 15 October 1940

On 15 October 1940, Air Vice-Marshal Keith Park sent a memorandum to his sector commanders, the following being the relevant extract for our purposes:

USE OF WING FORMATIONS AGAINST PRESENT ENEMY TACTICS

1. The use of wings of two or three squadrons is effective against enemy bombers with close fighter escorts for the following reasons:

   a) Much more warning from RDF plots is received while the enemy bomber and fighter formations are assembling over the French coast; this gives the Group Controller plenty of time to order squadrons up to operational height, in some cases well before the enemy raids commenced to approach our coast;

   b) The bomber formations fly mostly between heights of 15,000–20,000 feet;

   c) Formations of enemy bombers and escorting fighters can be sent over to this country only in good weather conditions which are suitable for interception by wings.

2. Against the present enemy tactics, very high fighter patrols or raids, the use of wing formations has been found to have serious disadvantages for the following reasons:

   a) The warning received from RDF plots is insufficient to place squadrons at the required height in time to intercept the **first** wave of enemy fighters;

   b) The heights of enemy aircraft are much greater, thus requiring more time to intercept from above;

   c) The present enemy tactics are generally confined to days when considerable cloud is present.

3. Results have shown that wings or pairs of squadrons have only been successful in intercepting when there is a second or third wave

of enemy fighters, and this can be only done if the squadrons take off and climb to operational height and then effect a rendezvous. When two or three squadrons take off and climb together, the rate of ascent is found to be slower, thereby wasting valuable minutes during which time one or two squadrons, operating singly, could attain position above the enemy fighter formations.

4. The first wave of enemy fighter aircraft has usually been intercepted only by the Spitfire squadron carrying out Standing Readiness Patrol, and sometimes by one or two Spitfire squadrons from 'Stand-by'.

5. Rigid squadron formations and wing formations have been found to be ineffective against very high fighter raids for the following reasons:

    a) They can't be broken up easily by attacks from above by small formations of enemy aircraft. Instances have occurred of even one or two enemy fighters having broken up a pair of squadrons.

    b) If enemy fighter aircraft happen to be below they can usually see a large formation of our fighters, and on account of their superior speed at high altitude they are able to withdraw before we can engage.

The first paragraph 'a' of the foregoing memorandum is significant, and relates exclusively to 11 Group. Supporters of the 12 Group 'Big Wing', however, argued that Duxford's squadrons should be scrambled immediately RDF indicated an enemy formation assembling over the Calais, so that the wing could be at height in time to intercept the incoming enemy over Canterbury. As previously explained, however, the reality of this theory in practice was impractical, because the technical limitations of RDF meant that it was unable to differentiate between assembling raids and the constant heavy enemy air traffic over the Pas-de-Calais. The earliest warning of a raid, therefore, was when one began moving out over the Channel, towards the English coast – just seven minutes flying time away. In this scenario, time, distance and height are the key factors, so the following must be borne in mind:

1. From the time a plot appeared on the RDF screen, it took around five minutes before the first RAF fighters were scrambled.

2. The distance between Duxford and Canterbury is some seventy miles.

3. Pilot's Notes indicate that the Spitfire Mk IIA's average climbing speed was 180 mph. Thus it would take twenty-three minutes to travel from Duxford to Canterbury, longer for a number of aircraft in formation. Moreover, not all the aircraft were new Spitfire Mk IIs – most were inferior Hurricanes. Then, the time between the first indication of an incoming raid and squadrons being scrambled has to be added, and all this time German aircraft are approaching Britain. Arguably, then, it would potentially take over thirty minutes from the raid's first detection by RDF to the Duxford Wing arriving over Canterbury.

4. A German bomber formation incoming at three miles per minute, it would take approximately fourteen minutes to fly from Calais to Canterbury, assuming a direct course – half the time it would take Duxford's squadrons to be in position.

Whilst the foregoing mathematics indicate the impossibility of the Duxford Wing scrambling and intercepting an incoming raid over Kent, the wing could certainly be positioned to attack the retiring enemy – after the target had been bombed. This, though, was unacceptable to Park – the defender of London – who referred to the matter in his robust response to Stevenson's Air Staff note. On the same day that Park wrote his report on the use of wing formations, he replied to Stevenson, enclosing copies of his instructions to 11 Group sectors of 1 and 5 October 1940, suggesting that these should be circulated prior to the conference, 'in order to save a great deal of valuable time'; unsurprisingly, it was caustic in places, and indicates how one sided Stevenson's communication had been:

> Your Air Staff Note is, apparently, based on the experience of 12 Group on the five occasions in which they have reinforced my Group. We in 11 Group used wings of three squadrons in May, June, July, August, September, and are still using them when conditions of time, space and weather make them effective.
>
> During the last big attack by the German long-range bomber force, the squadrons in 11 Group, operating in pairs of squadrons destroyed 115, plus 28 probably destroyed, plus 41 shot down damaged, for a cost of 15 pilots. [No.] 12 Group employed their large wing formation on that date ... they destroyed 13 enemy aircraft, plus 6 probably destroyed, plus 3 damaged, for a cost of 2 pilots. As you have included in the papers for the conference detailed results by 12 Group wings, I think you should include the attached statement, showing the results by 10 and 11 Groups on the last big battle with bombers over England. We were both using mainly pairs of fighter squadrons as our geographical situation does not afford the time to despatch, assemble and engage with wing formations BEFORE THE BOMBER RAIDS HAVE REACHED VITAL OBJECTIVES. I may be wrong in imagining that our primary task is to protect London, aircraft factories, sector aerodromes, against enemy bombers, and not merely to secure a maximum bag of enemy aircraft after they have done their fiendish damage.
>
> You must appreciate, of course, that conditions of time and space do not permit squadrons in 12 Group to engage incoming raids, but mainly outgoing raids after they have been attacked by pairs of Spitfire and Hurricane squadrons located around London and have had their close escort and themselves pretty badly shaken by AA fire.
>
> It beggars belief that Park even had to write the foregoing. If the proposed conference was genuinely to review tactics to date and consider what, if any, improvements could be going forward, surely

the AOC 11 Group would logically, as the most experienced group commander by far, should have been the first consulted? Moreover, that Stevenson's critical memorandum only included data from 12 Group speaks volumes.

Park also made out his own 'Points for Air Ministry Conference', reiterating the content of his previous reports concerning the use of wings, making several noteworthy comments:

Our AIM has been to engage bombers BEFORE they reach vital objectives, using maximum force in time given – wings or pairs, or single squadron, or even Station Commanders.

FLANK SECTORS, North and South, been used in wings of three frequently, but can only engage out-going bomb raids with good results because:

   i) Raids coming in been being engaged by pairs of Spitfire and/or Hurricanes and so lost their escorts.
   ii) Have been subjected to heavy AA fire.
   iii) Have expended much of their ammunition.

DUXFORD WINGS, 4/5 squadrons, like the Debden and Tangmere wings have arrived to intercept out-going bomb raids.

DANGER TO MORALE of squadrons being taught by northern groups that it is not safe to enter the south-east area except in wings of 4/5 squadrons. [Nos.] 616, 266, 66 Squadrons from 12 Group possibly imbued with Big Wing idea not fought so well as 13 Group squadrons trained to fight singly …

DEBDEN squadrons found to be TOO FAR NORTH, so moved one squadron to North Weald.

DUXFORD ROVING WINGS caused considerable confusion to London defences and prolonged Air Raid Warnings through wandering uninvited and unannounced over East Kent **after retreat of enemy**.

REINFORCEMENTS from 10 Group; arrangement entirely satisfactory because:

   a) They proceed to the place and height requested.
   b) They do not delay to form up wings of 4/5, so arrive after Brooklands, Kingston, Kenley etc have been bombed.
   c) They remain under the direction of 11 Group, so avoid confusing Observer Corps, 11 Group squadrons and ARW system.

Although Park was wrong about the Duxford Wing wasting time forming up, it is impossible to argue with what he says.

On 15 October 1940, the 242 (Canadian) Squadron ORB recorded that 'Squadron Leader [Douglas] Bader proceeded on four days leave.' This would shortly prove significant.

Early on in the morning, the weather improved, the overcast becoming cloudless and visibility substantially improving – perfect for a resumption of the heavy fighter-bomber raids. Throughout the day, five such attacks would be made on London, involving over 500 enemy aircraft.

At Kenley, 501 Squadron came to readiness at dawn – with welcome news: Pilot Officer Kenneth MacKenzie had been awarded a well-warned DFC. At 07.55 hrs, the squadron scrambled in company with 253 Squadron, vectored to Redhill. Squadron Leader Harry Hogan was leading 501 Squadron and at 08.25 hrs when 24,000ft south of Kenley, twelve Me 109s passed overhead, heading north, which then turned about, flying south-east. Hogan led the Hurricanes to intercept the intruders, flying east, more 109s approached the Hurricanes from astern but broke away as the squadron went into a more open formation. Whilst re-forming the squadron, two 109s were seen going south-east, one of which Hogan pursued and who was

> surprised that the second of these half-rolled, making it easy for me to get on his tail. I caught him up and after two long bursts from 80 yards he half-rolled onto his back, with black and white smoke belching out. He then disappeared vertically into the cloud. As the base of this was down to 15,000 feet I came out cautiously below it and saw the wreckage of a burning aircraft on the ground near Ashford.

No. 501 Squadron had been engaged by JG 51, which lost *Unteroffizier* Erich Höhn of 4/JG 51, who baled-out and captured, unhurt, his 109 crashing at 08.25 hrs, on Owls Castle Farm, Lamberhurst; although 25 miles west of Ashford, this was the aircraft Hogan destroyed. Hogan's Red 2, Sergeant Stanley Fennemore, however, was shot down and killed, at 08.15 hrs crashing at Postern Gate Farm, Godstone, near Rye. No. 253 Squadron, the pilots of which made no combat claims, was also attacked, at 08.30 hrs Sergeant Ernest Kee crash-landing his severely damaged Hurricane at Dunton Green, Sevenoaks; the pilot was unhurt. In this sharp skirmish, *Major* Werner Mölders, JG 51's famous *Kommodore*, *Oberleutnant* Josef 'Joschko' Fözö, *Staffelkapitän* of 4/JG 51, and *Leutnant* Hans Kolbow of 5/JG 51, all claimed Hurricanes destroyed south of London.

Sergeant Maurice Lee of 421 Flight had left Gravesend on a 'spotting patrol' at 08.15 hrs, running into the withdrawing Germans at 08.50 hrs, south of Maidstone, attacking and claiming a 109 shot down at 27,000ft, which was 'the first victim of the Flight' [ORB]; Lee also claimed another 109 damaged. No other 109s, however, crashed in Kent at this time.

The Spitfires of 41 Squadron scrambled from Hornchurch at 08.25 hrs with unknown orders and no combat claims arose – but Sergeant Phillip Lloyd was shot down and killed at 09.00 hrs over the sea, his remains later washing ashore in Herne Bay.

Flight Lieutenant Christopher 'Bunny' Currant DFC led 605 Squadron's Hurricanes off from Croydon, also at 08.25 hrs, to patrol Maidstone, and at 28,500ft, at 09.05 hrs, between there and Rochester the controller warned of enemy aircraft approaching from the south-east, 4 miles east of the squadron, at 18,000–20,000ft. Looking down, sure enough, Currant saw fifty Me 109s flying north-west at 23,000ft, led by a *Schwarm* of five Me 109s, 'the rest straggling behind'. Currant informed his pilots of the enemy's presence, then dived on the leading Messerschmitt from out of the sun. Just before the Hurricanes got within range, however, they were seen, the 109s consequently splitting up in all directions. From 200 yards, nonetheless, Currant attacked the leading German fighter, damaging it before the 109 disappeared into 10/10ths cloud below, as did a second 109 he fired at. Then, Currant was attacked by another Me 109 and took 'violent evasive action', noticing that 'Me 109 was turning almost as steeply as I was. I had full boost and 2,800 revs.' The German dived away, but the Hurricane 'could not catch it in the dive'. Currant claimed two damaged 109s, and Pilot Officer James Hayter damaged another, whilst Flying Officer Cyril Passy and Sergeant Eric Wright each claimed a probable. No. 605 Squadron suffered no loss and the Hurricanes returned to Croydon at 09.30 hrs. *Oberfeldwebel* Willi Bauer of 4/JG 3 suffered combat damaged to his radiator, as a result of which he was forced to land below the high-water mark at Prince's Golf Club, Sandwich, at 09.15 hrs, where he was captured unhurt. More *Jabos*, however, were incoming, and at 09.20 hrs the *Stab* I/LG 2 Me 109 fighter bomber of *Leutnant* Ludwig Lenz blew up over Elham, its SC250KG bomb having inexplicably exploded, killing the pilot.

Eleven Spitfires of 92 Squadron scrambled from Biggin Hill at 08.45 hrs, rendezvousing with 6 Squadron over base, the latter leading the formation which climbed to height over London. Sergeant Ronald Fokes was Blue 1, weaving ahead and below of 92 Squadron, and 'noticed a mass of Me 109s heading South'. No. 92 Squadron gave chase, catching the retreating 109s over the Channel, between Dover and Cap-Gris-Nez. Fokes attacked a section of three 109s, one of which 'turned onto its back and dived into the sea'. He then fired at another 109, which also dived away, but was then attacked himself, so broke away, seeing a Spitfire below, heading back towards England, streaming glycol fumes and with a 109 on its tail.

> [Fokes] followed it and in mid-Channel met a He 111 and ten – fifteen 109s circling a bomber or flying boat which was in the sea. They were flying at about 200 feet, I attacked the He 111 and fired a long burst into it from across its starboard quarter, the Me's were firing at me the same time, as was the He rear-gunner also. When I broke away and looked behind, the He had gone into the sea. I then used maximum boost and came home with the Me's in pursuit, but outpaced them.

German records, however, indicate just one Me 109 down in the Channel, at an unspecified time, this being *Feldwebel* Freis of 6/JG 27, who remains missing; no He 111s are recorded as being lost in these circumstances. Sergeant Donald Kingaby also claimed a 109 destroyed over the sea, but the Spitfire pilot to whose aid Fokes went failed to return: Sergeant Kenneth Parker crashed into the Channel and was killed (not Hoo Marina, as often stated elsewhere), his remains washing up on the Dutch coast days later.

At 09.30 hrs the newly arrived 302 (Polish) Squadron took off in company with and leading 229 Squadron to patrol Biggin Hill, 'at maximum height, but were subsequently vectored over the Thames Estuary ... Near Canterbury a formation of 109s was encountered at 20,000 feet, followed a mile behind by a second formation of some twenty-five Me 109s.' [No. 229 ORB]. Squadron Leader Arthur Banham, previously a flight commander in the Defiant-equipped 264 Squadron and who had survived being shot down in flames in a turret fighter, immediately ordered 229 into line astern, ready to engage the rear formation of 109s, but before doing so the Hurricanes were hit by five 109s from above. At 10.00 hrs, Pilot Officer Ronald Brown, Red 2, fired a full deflection shot at a 109, which, after his second burst, 'burst into flames and spiralled down through the clouds ... The combat was between Canterbury and Manston' (although credited as destroyed, no German fighters crashed on land, but several, during the day, returned to France damaged). Flying Officer Vernon Bright and Pilot Officer Geoffrey Simpson, a New Zealander, also damaged 109s – but Squadron Leader Arthur Banham was 'set on fire, and he was forced to bale out, landing near Winchelsea, with face and neck burns' [ORB]. Flight Lieutenant William Smith's Hurricane was also damaged, his 'tail and rudder were shattered by cannon fire from a Me 109, but he brought the aircraft back to base' [ORB]. In this action, *Leutnant* Wilhelm Wiesinger of *Stab* II/JG 27, who claimed a Hurricane over Bethersden.

Over Canterbury at 10.15 hrs, 302 (Polish) Squadron was at 28,000ft but found seventy Me 109s incoming, flying north, 4,000ft above, which the Hurricanes were unable to reach. Other 109s, however, made diving passes at the Hurricanes, which went into a defensive circle, one of these shooting down Sergeant Marian Wedzik, Blue 3, whose aircraft erupted into flames, the pilot baling out over Chatham; Wedzik would be admitted to the hospital there, suffering from burns. Flight Lieutenant William Riley, Blue 1, and his Blue 2, were unable to catch Wedzik's assailant, as another large enemy formation passed over the Hurricanes, heading south-west. Thirty more German fighters then dived on 302 (Polish) Squadron from the north; Riley 'attacked formation, selected one Me 109 and fired a three-second burst at fifty yards. Immediately after fired a one-second burst at Me 109, twenty-five yards ... then took evasive action and in neither case had time to watch for results.' Somewhat surprisingly, Riley was credited with a Me 109 destroyed; it was 302 (Polish) Squadron's only claim in this action. *Unteroffizier* Erhardt Scheidt of 1/JG 26 claimed a 'Spitfire' destroyed over Maidstone, which, as no Spitfires were involved, was more likely Wedzik's Hurricane.

Sergeant Maurice Lee of 421 Flight took-off from Gravesend at 10.40 hrs on his second spotting patrol of the day, but was not as fortunate as on his previous sortie: south of Maidstone the Spitfire pilot was shot-up by a 109, crash-landing at Broad Oak and later admitted to hospital, wounded.

Still the waves of Me 109s were incoming, however, and at 11.45 hrs, 605 Squadron suffered a sad loss when Flight Lieutenant Ian Muirhead was shot down and killed, his Hurricane crashing at Speke's Bottom, near Garland, near Gillingham; no claims were made in response.

At 11.19 hrs, 249 and 257 Squadrons scrambled from North Weald to patrol over Kent together, but east of Dover at 11.50 hrs the two Hurricane squadrons lost contact owing to the presence of Me 109s directly above. At 25,000ft, Pilot Officer Percival Mortimer, Green 1 of 257 Squadron's 'B' Flight, was engaged by three Me 109s on four occasions but fortunately only hit by a single machine-gun round, which passed cleanly through his starboard wing. Mortimer pursued one of the enemy fighters, which he hit before it headed back towards France. Attacked head on by another 109, Mortimer delayed firing in order to be sure that the rapidly closing machine was not a Spitfire – luckily there was no collision and the 109's fire passed harmlessly overhead. Pilot Officer Gerald North, however, was shot down and successfully forced-landed at Hawkinge, unhurt. For 249 Squadron, there was 'Nothing to report' [ORB].

No. 46 Squadron left Stapleford at 12.30 hrs to patrol Sevenoaks and Gravesend at 20,000ft:

> At 1255 hrs and when six – eight miles south-east of Hornchurch, Blue 1 (Flight Sergeant Eric Williams), who was leading the Squadron, reported on the R/T having sighted twenty to thirty Me 109s milling overhead at 25,000 feet, and the Squadron at 15,000 feet were not in a position to engage the enemy. The Squadron continued to climb as rapidly as possible, 120 mph, and were then vectored nine zero. [Form 'F']

No. 46 Squadron was then jumped by Me 109s, which attacked from out of the sun. Pilot Officer Robert Reid, Green 1, had slid into the Blue 3 position when Blue 2 had left the formation owing to oxygen trouble, 'saw tracers entering the cockpit of Blue 2 and also tracers hitting Blue 1 with effect.' An Me 109 then appeared just 50ft above Reid, who opened fire, the 109 emitting grey smoke and spiralling down, pursued by the Hurricane pilot until the 109 entered clouds. Upon being attacked, Red and Yellow Sections broke up, not being in a position to engage the enemy. It was a perfect 'bounce' from the Germans' perspective: Pilot Officer Peter Gunning was shot down and killed, his Hurricane crashing at Little Thurrock, and Sergeant Albert Gooderman's Hurricane was set of fire, the aircraft crashing at Gravesend; the pilot was slightly burned and admitted to hospital. Of Blue 1, Flight Sergeant Eric Williams, however, there was no news.

According to the Kent County Council War Diary,

> One British plane down at Albion Parade ... Pilot missing, plane burnt out, slight damage to wharf buildings. Royal Engineers subsequently investigated the site of this aircraft, which had crashed through the roof of Barton's Timber Wharf and buried itself deep in the mud below. Although able to identify the wreckage as being a Hurricane, and recovering a flight sergeant's crown, recovery proved impossible.

Nobody doubted that this could only be 46 Squadron's missing man, Flight Sergeant Eric Williams. Indeed, despite campaigning by various enthusiasts and historians (including this author), Flight Sergeant Williams, a married man, remains buried with his aircraft to this day, a recovery attempt by the authorities in 2006, following pressure from both enthusiasts and the developer building flats on the Albion Parade site, also being unsuccessful. Nearby, however, a memorial exists commemorating the missing airman.

JG 26 was responsible for 46 Squadron's casualties, *Oberleutnant* Eberhard Henrici and *Unteroffizier* Erhardt Scheidt of 1/JG26, *Hauptmann* Walter Adolph,

Gruppenkommandeur of II/JG 26, *Oberleutnant* Harald Grawatsch of Adolph's *Stabschwarm*, and *Unteroffizier* Hugo Dahmer of 6/JG 26 all claiming Hurricanes destroyed.

At 11.20 hrs, 92 Squadron had taken-off again from Biggin Hill, this time patrolling Sevenoaks area, and, once more, Flight Lieutenant Brian Kingcome was Ganic Leader. At 13.00 hrs at 27,000ft over Ashford, the Spitfires intercepted fifty Me 109s, stepped-up, in open formation, from 23,000–25,000ft. No. 92 Squadron broke up after the initial attack, Pilot Officer Robert Holland, Yellow 1, diving after a 109, which he hit and saw 'a panel or something fly off the starboard wing', before the target disappeared in cloud to be claimed as a probable. Sergeant Ronald Fokes, Blue 1, was again 'weaving around Ganic Squadron', attacking a Me 109 from astern 'which burst into flames, giving out black smoke and white glycol fumes', this being claimed as destroyed, as indeed it was: *Oberleutnant* G. Diecke, *Staffelkapitän* of 8/JG 27 baled out to be captured unhurt, his 109 crashing at Olantigh, north-east of Ashford. Pilot Officer John Lund, however, was shot down over Medway Having baled out and landed in the sea, Lund was fortunately rescued by the RN.

Having expended his ammunition for a nil result, Flight Lieutenant Kingcome, as so often happened, found himself alone, with only three Spitfires in the far distance. Base, Biggin Hill, could be seen in the distance, so Kingcome headed home, throttling back and preparing to execute and practice a dead-stick landing. As 'Kingpin' later wrote,

> It was breathtakingly stupid behaviour. It was so irresponsible that it would never even have occurred to me to warn new pilots against it. The skies of Kent were at all times a hostile environment, whatever the illusion of emptiness … an over-confidence fostered by exposure to the dawn-to-dusk rotation of 'take-off, climb, engage, land, re-fuel, re-arm, take-off, climb, engage …' two, three or sometimes four times a day, familiarity reducing what had begun as exciting, adrenalin-pumping action to mere routine. In other words, I had become *blasé*.

The inevitable happened: Kingcome, an exceptional and highly respected fighter pilot and leader, was ambushed by a Me 109. Fortunately, 92 Squadron's heart and soul, the 'Kingpin', baled out safely, his Spitfire crashing at High Halstow; wounded, Kingcome was admitted to the RN Hospital at Chatham and would not return to the squadron until 23 December 1940 – by which time his well-earned DFC has been gazetted.

Both *Major* Adolf Galland, JG 26's *Kommodore*, and *Leutnant* Gustav 'Mickey' Sprick of 8/JG 26 accounted for 92 Squadron's two lost Spitfires.

Having left Kenley at 12.30 hrs, 501 Squadron was vectored towards the trouble over the Sheppey area, but when at 21,000ft the Hurricane pilots sighted Me 109s, which were too far away to engage. Other Me 109s, however, jumped 501 Squadron, *Oberleutnant* Rudolf von Aspern of 4/JG 54, shooting-up Blue 3, Sergeant Raymond Jarrett, who was wounded and forced-landed at Rochester. Sergeant James Lacey reported having been 'shot at by a Hurricane' [ORB], fortunately surviving the experience unscathed, and Pilot Officer Bob Dafforn also landed at Rochester 'with glycol trouble' [ORB]. The Hurricane pilots made no claims. Yet more enemy formations, however, were incoming.

No. 222 Squadron scrambled from Hornchurch at 13.00 hrs to patrol Maidstone, but did not meet the enemy until 14.30 hrs, when still climbing, between Maidstone and Sheerness. Sergeant Jack Dunmore, Green 3, sighted a *Rotte* of Me 109s heading south, 5,000ft above and at 31,000ft. Dunmore gave chase, attacking one from below, the 109 flicking over, dived and stalled. Dunmore then pursued the second Me 109, coming within range 10 miles off Dover, hitting his target which streamed glycol. Uniquely, Dunmore reported that 'the E/A was firing from a fixed gun, pointing back beneath the fuselage', which could only have been an individual, local, experiment if the case. After evasive tactics the 109 'bounced on the water, as it come up I got in another burst of five seconds' – but then ammunition was expended. Breaking away, Green 3 forced-landed near Dover, out of petrol, claiming the 109 as destroyed – although it was not seen to crash; no 109 appears in German records to have crashed in the sea at this time, but a machine of 2/JG 77 did crash-land after combat at Cap-Gris-Nez. The remainder of 222 Squadron, however, were not engaged, Flying Officer Ian Hallam recording in his log book that the enemy had not been seen, although it was a long patrol: Hallam also ran out of fuel, landing at Detling, as did Sergeant John Burgess, who forced-landed at Eastchurch.

At 15.00 hrs, 302 (Polish) Squadron was up again from Northolt and patrolling the Maidstone line, barring the way to London, at 20,000ft. Pilot Officer Waclaw Kroll reported that 100 Me 109s passed overhead (direction not stated). The 109s did not attack immediately, only doing so after the Hurricanes had formed into a defensive circle. Kroll saw a 109 attack a Hurricane 300 yards away, and hastened to assist, but only managed a very short burst at the German fighter before being attacked himself and taking evasive action: 'On orbiting I saw a parachute open' Kroll then attacked another 109 and 'noticed that the pilot had baled out and that he was not wearing a "Mae West"'. Short of fuel, Kroll landed and re-fuelled at White Waltham before returning to Northolt. No. 302 (Polish) Squadron suffered no casualties and made no other combat claims; Kroll was credited with one Me 109 destroyed, but the parachutes he claimed to have seen remains a mystery: certainly, two Me 109 pilots baled out over Kent on this day, *Unteroffizier* Höhn of 4/JG 51 at Lamberhurst, south-east of Tunbridge Wells, and *Oberleutnant* Deicke of 8/JG 27 at Olantigh, north-east of Ashford – but recorded as occurring at 08.35 and 13.00 hrs respectively. As there were no RAF fighter pilots at this time, who may have baled out, those times are, therefore, questionable.

Squadron Leader George Denholm and 603 Squadron had left Hornchurch at 15.15 hrs to patrol Kent, but only South African Pilot Officer Basil 'Stapme' Stapleton, Blue 2, sighted the enemy, at 16.00 hrs, when at 25,000ft over Bethersden; Stapleton 'informed Viken Leader, and as he did not understand', broke away and attacked the rearmost of a *Schwarm* of Me 109s 5,000ft below. After four attacks from both astern and head on, the 109 'dived very slightly and continued to do so until it was 100 feet over the sea. Then it dived vertically into the sea between ten and fifteen miles off Dungeness.' No German fighter, however, is recorded as lost in these circumstances, the only machine down in the sea, according to Luftwaffe records, being the 6/JG 27 machine which 'ditched' of Cap-Gris-Nez and the pilot of which was reported missing, and, as we have seen, various RAF pilots claimed 109s destroyed over the sea on this day.

Thus ended the day fighting over the eastern Channel and Kent. Given the relentless waves of escorted fighter bombers, it was inevitable that some would reach Central London – and, indeed, they did. Southbound lines out of the capital were blocked at Waterloo and Vauxhall stations, and lines were also damaged between Richmond and Twickenham. Factories at West Ham were hit, as was the King George V Dock. Six civilians were killed in Southwark and forty injured, and during both morning and afternoon, domestic properties were damaged in Folkestone, where three females were injured. Unsurprisingly, with so many 109s involved, a toll was taken of RAF fighters: five Spitfires were destroyed and one damaged, with two pilots killed and one wounded, along with four Hurricanes written off and five damaged, two pilots killed and three wounded. Inevitably, both sides overclaimed: only four Me 109s crashed in Kent but how many more returned to France damaged or crashed into the Channel is impossible to determine. If, however, Luftwaffe records really are comprehensive, which this investigation has proven to be unlikely, unpalatable though it is, certain RAF pilots' combat reports can only be considered questionable indeed.

Whilst these heavy attacks were being fought off over Kent, there was concurrent action further west. At 12.20 hrs, Yellow Section of Warmwell's 234 Squadron was patrolling base when Sergeant Alan Harker, Yellow 1, sighted AA fire over Falmouth at 15,000ft and 'a smoke trail heading North', 10 miles away. Investigating, Harker and Sergeant Hugh Sharpley, Yellow 2, attacked what was a Ju 88 from the sun, noting no result, before the raider was lost in cloud. This, however, is likely to have been the Ju 88 of *Luftflotte* 3's 1/LG 1, which failed to return to Orleans-Bricy, its crew missing. At the same time, *Jafü* 3 was in the process of mounting a fighter sweep over the Southampton and Portsmouth areas.

At 12.30 hrs, Squadron Leader Adrian Boyd was up with his 145 Squadron from Tangmere and patrolling The Needles at 15,000ft. At 10,000ft above, however, Boyd sighted a *Schwarm* of four Me 109s and 145 Squadron climbed to attack. This, however, was bait. At 20,000ft Boyd

> looked behind and saw four Me 109s diving onto our rear Section. I immediately gave a warning over R/T and turned sharply to meet the attack. The E/A opened fire on the rear Section and then passed over our heads. I was able to put in a quick burst and saw cowling come off bottom of E/A. Other pilots of the Squadron observed the pilot to fall from his machine and he was later observed descending into Christchurch Bay by parachute.

Boyd, who made 145's only claim, was credited with a 109 destroyed over the sea – but what his pilots had actually seen was not a German pilot descending by parachute but one of their own: Czech Pilot Officer Jiří Jaromír Macháček was shot down and baled out, being picked up, wounded, from Christchurch Bay.

Tangmere's 213 Squadron was also patrolling over the Isle of Wight, Sergeant Gordon Bushell flying Yellow 2, astern of Yellow 1, Flight Lieutenant James Strickland, commander of 'B' Flight. Bushell reported that, at 12.48 hrs, a Me 109 came down on Yellow Leader's tail. I immediately opened fire on him at fifty yards range, pieces came away from his starboard wing and he dived away. At this moment I noticed two Me 109s on my tail, I was fired at and dived, following my leader who was hit and in obvious distress. The two Me 109s followed us down for a short time but made off. I flew round and round my Leader until he was able to make a 'crash' forced-landing in a field.

Strickland was unhurt, having been shot down by *Oberleutnant* Siegfried Bethke, *Staffelkapitän* of 2/JG 2, who claimed a Hurricane over the Isle of Wight at the material time. For his conduct in protecting his Flight Commander, Bushell was mentioned in despatches; sadly neither pilot would survive the war.

Polish Pilot Officer Bolesław Andrzej Własnowolski was Blue 3 in 213 Squadron and upon being attacked broke right in a climbing turn. Seeing two Me 109s, 'one a long way off', another below, over the 'Centre of the Isle of Wight', the Hurricane pilot attacked the latter, surprising the enemy pilot with five or six bursts: 'After my attack he did a stall turn away and then vertically dived to the ground. Smoke was pouring from his engine.' Accredited with a 109 destroyed 'on land', there was no mistake: *Feldwebel* Horst Hellriegel, a former flying instructor, of 3/JG 2, forced-landed at Newport, virtually in the centre of the island, as Własnowolski reported, and was captured.

Having had a very busy start to the Battle of Britain, of late 609 Squadron, based at Warmwell, inland of Weymouth in 10 Group, was having a comparatively quieter time – and would have a lucky escape indeed on this particular day. At 12.15 hrs, 'A' Flight of 609 Squadron scrambled to patrol Winchester at Angels 20, and 'B' to cover base at Angels 16 – a somewhat suicidal height.

Pilot Officer David Crook of 'B' Flight:

> We all got off the ground and started to climb towards the coast. At about 10,000 feet there was some cloud and as soon as we got above this, I looked round and above, and saw many thousands of feet above us at least 30 Messerschmitt 110s accompanied by a lot of Me 109s.
>
> At first, I thought they were our own fighters and called up to the C.O. and suggested that they were the Hurricanes of 234 Squadron. The C.O. took one look and replied 'No, their formation is much too good – they must be Huns!' And so they were, as I recognised them a moment later.
>
> We were in a hopeless position – a long way below them and outlined against the white cloud underneath us – altogether a very vulnerable position. However, we continued to climb in the hope of somehow managing to get in one attack, and all the time we watched the Messerschmitts like cats, as sooner or later they would obviously drop down on us. Altogether rather an unpleasant few minutes!
>
> It was very difficult watching them, as they were almost in the sun and the glare was awful.

Suddenly I saw two Me 109s just behind John Dundas's Spitfire. How they got there I don't know – I never saw them come down and nobody else did either. They must have dived very fast indeed, and they had just opened fire when I saw them – I remember distinctly their yellow noses and the white streaks caused by their cannon shells.

I immediately shouted on the R.T. 'Look out, Messerschmitts, they're coming down.' I have never seen the squadron break up so quickly – everybody turned sharply away in all directions and dived hard for the cloud. I went down with everybody else, pulled out after a few thousand feet and looked round. Apart from a few Spitfires dashing around, there was nothing to be seen.

No. 609 Squadron had been flying west over Christchurch, and in addition to the Me 109s reported by Pilot Officer Crook, Flying Officer John Dundas DFC, Blue 1 of 'B' Flight, three vics of Me 110s flew 'over our heads about 5,000 feet above'. Climbing south-west, the Spitfires were silhouetted against 9/10ths cumulus cloud when Crook's warning came of three yellow-nosed Me 109s, which attacked Blue Section; Dundas reported that as only Blue 2 was hit by a single bullet, 'their aim must have been very poor'. According to Dundas, after the squadron broke up, he unsuccessfully attempted to re-form 'B' Flight at 12,000ft when his 'transmitter began to fade'. With communications compromised, Dundas claimed to have made two beam attacks on a 'circus of fifteen – twenty Me 110s at 18,000ft over or near Christchurch'. After his second attack on the 110s, Dundas described being 'chased for some time by two Me 109s, which I eventually lost'; he then joined up with Flight Lieutenant Frank Howell DFC, Yellow 1 and commander of 'A' Flight, and Flying Officer Terence Forshaw, Green 1, and upon orders from Squadron Leader Michael Robinson, Sorbo Leader, orbited the 'West end of Isle of Wight at 15,000 feet till Control ordered us to land'. Dundas added to his report the following: 'As I was apparently the only pilot in this or any other squadron to attack a Me 110, and as a Me 110 crashed in Christchurch Bay after this engagement, I feel entitled to claim it, though I did not at the time observe results.' Dundas was credited with a Me 110 destroyed – but no Me 110 crashed into Christchurch Bay – only the Hurricane of 145 Squadron's Pilot Officer Jiří Jaromír Macháček.

When attacked by the Me 109s north, Green 2, Pilot Officer Noël le Chevalier Agazarian 'Aga' ('Aggy'), a half-Armenian, half-French aristocrat, stayed at height in order to attack any Me 109s, which followed 609 Squadron down. None did. Whilst climbing, 'Aggy' was then fired upon by a 109, a tracer round richochetting off his canopy. Diving and then climbing in a steep turn, the Spitfire pilot returned fire, the leading 109 diving away at full throttle. The second 109 was then hit, by a five second burst, after which 'thick black smoke was coming from his engine. I gave him the rest of my ammunition from astern and he went on down in his dive, going south-west, obviously on fire.' Credited with the Me 109 destroyed between Southampton and Poole, it is like that this was the machine of a wounded 4/JG 2 pilot who crash-landed back at Beaumont-le-Roger.

A few minutes after being attacked by the Me 109s, at 12.45 hrs, north of Southampton, Flying Officer Tadeusz Nowierski, Green 3,

> saw an Me 109 slightly above me and opened fire from astern. He went into a left-hand spin and pieces fell off the machine. He disappeared into cloud and I lost him, but Flying Officer [Zbigniew] Olenski [author's note: also Polish] followed him down and saw him crash. The pilot did not get out and was lying or sitting with his parachute near the crash (believed between Milton and Lymington).

Once more, however, the combat report is incorrect. The German pilot, *Gefreiter* Alois Pollach of 4/JG 2, did bale out, as Crook recounted in his memoir, *Spitfire Pilot*:

> When the machine was near the ground the pilot got out and just managed to open his parachute in time, but landed very heavily and lay on the ground, probably winded by the fall. Novi circled round and said afterwards, in his rather broken English: 'I circle round, bloody German lies down, he is dead, ok. But I look again, he is now sitting up – no bloody good!' He was very disappointed in his opinion the only good Germans are dead Germans.

Pollach, who was 19, was lucky to survive, and was captured, shaken and winded but otherwise unhurt. Many years later, in 2015, friends and I excavated the crash-site of his Me 109E-1 at Everton Nurseries, discovering countless fragmentary remains and a large amount of both live and exploded 7.92mm machine-gun ammunition. The Me 109E-1 was not armed with 20mm cannon, so this made sense, as did the fragmentary remains – this was a *Jabo*, the bomb of which had exploded upon impact, disintegrating the aircraft.

No bombs fell on either Southampton or Portsmouth during this raid. Two Me 109s were down, their pilots prisoners, and another returned to base damaged. In total, pilots of 145, 213 and 609 Squadrons claimed four Me 109s destroyed and one damaged, and the unreconcilable Me 110 accredited as destroyed to 609 Squadron. Just one Hurricane was destroyed, another damaged, one pilot being wounded, and when attacked north of Southampton just one round pierced the wing of a 609 Squadron Spitfire. On this occasion, therefore, JG 2 substantially overclaimed, pilots of *Stab* I, *Stab* II, 1, 2, 3, 4/ JG 2 being awarded a total of six Hurricanes and five Spitfires destroyed. Amongst the supposedly successful enemy pilots, yet again, was *Major* Helmut Wick, claiming his first victory following award of his Oak Leaves as the result of recording his fortieth and forty-first victories on 5 October 1940. On this occasion Wick claimed a Spitfire destroyed over Portsmouth: none of these claims are substantiated.

So ended the fighting by day: by night, Pilot Officer Phillip Ensor, a Blenheim pilot of Wittering's 23 Squadron, would claim a He 111 probably destroyed over the Redhill – Sevenoaks area, and Pilot Officer Fred Hughes and Sergeant Fred Gash, a highly successful Defiant crew of 264 Squadron, operating from Northolt, claimed a He 111 destroyed over Brentwood.

Coastal Command had flown its usual routine patrols, and by night Blenheims. French ports: owing to the absence of cloud over the Continent, 2 Group's daylight raids were scrubbed, but by night Bomber Command sent 134 aircraft to attack the Channel ports, the German naval bases at Kiel and Hamburg, industrial targets in Germany, and sowed mines off Kiel. There were two losses: a Coastal Hudson of Bircham Newton's 206 Squadron disappeared, and an 83 Squadron Hampden forced-landed returning from Magdeburg having run out of petrol, the crew surviving unhurt.

Weekly Report by Home Intelligence:

> Reports this week show a varying state of morale throughout the country; variations are also noticed among different groups of people in the same places. In Yorkshire, although confidence is strong, there is an 'almost dangerous complacency'. This is attributed to the absence of raids in the area, and the unconcern of the great mass of people with matters abroad. The propaganda for 'the island fortress' has succeeded almost too well. In the same area intellectual people are said to be depressed because they do not see how bombing Germany can win the war for us, if bombing London cannot win it for the Nazis.

Wednesday, 16 October 1940

AC1 Bob Morris, Fitter IIE, 66 Squadron, Gravesend:

> Once I watched some dogfights over Biggin Hill. We were in an aircraft bay and saw a German aircraft on fire. Four parachutes came out, two of which were on fire. We saw these two German aircrew falling faster and faster, until their parachutes were completely burnt away and they fell to their deaths.
>
> We rarely got to see shot down enemy aircraft … but once I had the chance to look over an Me 109 which was on the Station and virtually complete. I looked in the cockpit and by our standards it was nowhere near up to the Spitfire's instrumental standards, it was very bleak.

A cloudless dawn on 16 October 1940 gave over to an overcast, as a result of which the enemy fighters and fighter-bombers rested following their maximum effort of the previous day. Some forty solo intruders were active over Britain throughout the day, but few bombs were dropped and only minor damage arose. Nonetheless, Fighter Command maintained standing patrols, and on one of these, at 13.15 hrs, 249 Squadron was patrolling over Kent when Flight Lieutenant Keith Lofts, Red 1, and Sergeant Henri Bouquillard, Red 2, a Free Frenchman, were detached to intercept a bandit approaching Maidstone from the south. At 12,000ft over Tenterden, Red Section sighted the intruder approaching, head on, identifying the raider as a 'Do 215' [author's note: much more likely a Ju 88], which was damaged:

[Lofts] noticed a rather uncomfortable thud against my aircraft and shortly afterwards my engine stopped and I noticed I had been hit. The cockpit filled with fumes and smoke but were not sufficiently overcoming to warrant an emergency descent by parachute. I chose a field and parked the machine there with wheels up.

This was the only interception by day, although Fighter Command suffered several aircraft damaged in flying accidents, and unfortunately two pilots were killed.

Only two days before, Sergeant Ian Pearson had joined 65 Squadron at Turnhouse, direct from 7 OTU, together with fellow Sergeant D. Rees and Sergeant W. Moncur. The following day, both Moncur and Pearson flew practice flights, the latter twice, sorties of forty and fifty-minutes duration. At 14.50 hrs on 16 October 1940, Pearson and Moncur took-off from Turnhouse on another practice flight – Pearson heading north over the Firth of Forth towards his parents' home at Bannatay Mill Farm, Gateside, Fife, north of Dundee. There, the spirited young pilot commenced showing off his skills, performing unauthorised low-level aerobatics. Tragically, Pearson lost control of his Spitfire less than a mile from the farm and was killed in the crash, watched by his parents. Sadly, the 20-year-old would be far from the only RAF fighter pilot killed in such circumstances.

On 14 October 1940, Sergeant Jan Chalupa (a Czech and not to be confused with Polish Sergeant Józef Stanisław Chałupa, as is so often the case), was amongst three officers and three sergeant-pilots who joined 310 (Czech) Squadron at Duxford as replacements direct from 6 OTU, Sutton Bridge; on 16 October 1940, Chalupa was 'accidentally killed while engaged on a training flight near Ely' [ORB].

Whilst a routine day for Coastal Command, ninety-five of the usual sorties were flown, during which a Blenheim destroyed a He 115 off Bishop's Rock, two U-boats were inconclusively attacked by a Sunderland and an Anson, and four Blenheims attacked Cherbourg Harbour. By night, six more Blenheims bombed Brest; Coastal Command lost just one aircraft, a Hudson of RAF Aldergrove's 224 Squadron, which hit a mountain, the crew all being killed. Six 2 Group Blenheims uneventfully swept the North Sea, but the continued lack of cloud cover led to further operations being cancelled. By night, the Wellington and Hampden forces started fires at Bremen and Kiel, attacked an oil facility at Merseburg, and dropped incendiaries in the Hartz Forest; four Hampdens also dropped mines off Bordeaux, and others scattered propaganda leaflets over enemy occupied Europe. These nocturnal operations, however, were costly: one Hampden was shot down by flak on the Bordeaux run, its crew all killed, six more crashed in England upon return from operations, and one was abandoned over the sea. A Wellington was abandoned over Cumberland, and another over Penrith, and *Leutnant* Ludwig Becker of 4/NJG 1 shot down a 311 (Czech) Squadron Wellington over the Zuider Zee; two of the crew were captured, the other four killed. Due to icing, another 311 Squadron Wellington was abandoned over Nottinghamshire, the crew all landing safely – but Pilot Officer M. Vejrazka was mistakenly shot and killed by the Home Guard. A third 311 Squadron Wellington was returning from Kiel when it hit a balloon cable near Bentley Priory and crashed; the crew survived, but Sergeant F.

Truhlar suffered serious burns. Only one of the four Wellingtons despatched by 311 Squadron, in fact, returned safely to East Wretham.

Weekly Report by Home Intelligence:

> In rural districts and in country market towns, there is little talk of the war.
>
> The big provincial towns, which have been bombed, continue to show determination. On the South coast there is no despondency but some lowering of morale, thought to be due to the cumulative effects of warnings, raids, prolonged tension, long hours of work, the coming of winter, and more indirectly the absence of any spectacular war success.

Thursday, 17 October 1940

It was on this day that the 'Big Wing Controversy' came to a head.

The following RAF officers assembled in the Air Ministry's air council room:

AVM W.S. Douglas	DCAS
ACM Sir H.C.T. Dowding	AOC-in-C Fighter Command
AM Sir Charles Portal	AM(P)
AM Sir Phillip P.B. Joubert de la Ferte	ACAS I
AVM K.R. Park	AOC 11 Group
AVM Sir C.J. Quintin Brand	AOC 10 Group
AVM T.L. Leigh-Mallory	AOC 12 Group
AC J.C. Slessor	D of P
AC D.F. Stevenson	DHO
AC O.G.W.C. Lywood	PDD of Signals
GC H.G. Crowe	ADAT
WC T.N. McEvoy & Mr J.S. Orme	Secretaries
SL D.R.S. Bader	CO 242 (Canadian) Squadron

The presence of a mere squadron leader at this high-level meeting of senior officers is astonishing – especially without the knowledge and consent of his C-in-C, Air Chief Marshal Hugh Dowding. Later, the Parliamentary Secretary of State for Air Harold Balfour contested this view:

> Maybe it was against service discipline and custom for such a junior officer to be present at this high-level conference but even today I can see no real objection. Here were a lot of middle-aged experts meeting to resolve differing views on fighting strategy and tactics. Here among them was one of the men actually doing the daily job and I think it must have brought a refreshing breath of reality that Bader was there to give his views.

This perspective is skewed – and Balfour was sympathetic to the 'Big Wing' argument. Were this an open and genuine analysis of tactics, however, to agree best practice for the future, surely Air Vice-Marshal Keith Park and Air Vice-Marshal Sir C.J. Quintin Brand would have been invited to bring along one of their squadron commanders, so as to afford a fair hearing to all perspectives, enabling the most informed decision to be made? Squadron Leader 'Sailor' Malan, CO of 74 Squadron, immediately comes to mind, a highly experienced fighter pilot and leader who had flown extensively in 11 Group and even with the Duxford Wing, while resting in 12 Group. Likewise, Brand had had no shortage of experienced squadron commanders to choose from, not least Squadron Leader Harry Fenton (238 Squadron) or Squadron Leader George Darley (609 Squadron), whose squadrons had frequently reinforced 11 Group.

Clearly, whatever Balfour's post-war perspective, the whole thing was undoubtedly a *fait accompli*, and Dowding and Park realised – too late – that the meeting's purpose was purely to push forward the adoption of wings as standard practice in responding to large enemy formations. Of Acting Squadron Leader Douglas Bader's involvement, Park later wrote that 'he was used to make room for [Trafford] Leigh-Mallory'. Dowding, who was unaware of Flight Lieutenant Peter MacDonald MP's disloyalty at the time, commented that 'Leigh-Mallory had quite enough incentive of his own, without bringing Douglas Bader in'; the AOC-in-C was not to learn of Leigh-Mallory's statement to Air Vice-Marshal' Park that he would 'move heaven and earth' to get Dowding sacked until 1968.

Lord Dowding:

> I do not think Bader would ever have allowed himself consciously to become embroiled in such a move. It would probably have come as a shock to him to hear that [Trafford] Leigh-Mallory ever entertained such an idea. It was one thing to disagree with my views, and to express criticisms forcibly, but it was another altogether to intrigue against his own Commander-in-Chief, which is why I think that latter was out of the question.

While 'out of the question' so far as Squadron Leader Douglas Bader's involvement went, that was clearly not the case where both Trafford Leigh-Mallory and Peter MacDonald were concerned. Mutiny may be too strong a word – but arguably that is, in truth, what was happening.

So that there can be no ambiguity about this infamous meeting, the minutes, which are lengthy, are herewith reproduced verbatim:

1. DCAS explained that he was presiding at the meeting as CAS was unable to be present owing to indisposition.
2. There were three propositions that he would like the meeting to consider:

    i) We wish to outnumber the enemy formations when we meet them.

ii) We want our superior numbers to go into the attack with a coordinated plan of action so that the protecting fighters are engaged by one part of our force, leaving the bombers to the remainder.

iii) If possible, we want the top layer of our fighter formation to have the advantage of height over the top layer of the enemy formation.

3. This was the ideal, but it was obviously not always possible of attainment. For instance, the time factor might not allow us to do what we wanted. It might be necessary to engage before he reached some vital objective, and in such cases, there might not be time either to collect a superior force or to obtain superior height. DCAS then invited comments on the propositions he had outlined.

4. AOC of 11 Group said that with factors of time, distance and cloud that were often involved in the operations of 11 Group it should not be laid down as a general principle that the wing of fighters was the right formation to oppose attacks, even those made in mass. He felt that the satisfactory use of the wing by 12 Group related to ideal conditions when enemy bombers were in retreat, separated from their escort. [No.] 11 Group, using formations of one or two squadrons had, on the other hand, quite recently obtained results against bombers on their way in which compared not unfavourably with those of the wing sorties from 12 Group.

5. The AOC outlined to the meeting the principle that applied in 11 Group for operations against enemy bombers with a fighter screen; this involved the use of squadrons in pairs at different heights to engage separately the top fighter screen, the close escort and the bombers.

6. AOC-in-C Fighter Command said that the great problem was to obtain early knowledge as to which of perhaps many raids was a major one. The Observer Corps did good work but were often baffled by the extreme height of enemy formations. He therefore attached great importance to the development of GL and LC organisation; Kent and Sussex would be covered by the end of November. This beam control had, of course, the disadvantage that the plot of only one formation at a time could be brought through into a Sector Operations Room, but it would be a big help when a big raid was known to be coming in.

7. AOC 11 Group referred to experiments he had been making with reconnaissance Spitfires, which, in favourable conditions, were useful for obtaining early reports of big formations. The general installation of VHF would give better results from this reconnaissance work.

Top, middle and bottom: Ju 88s of I/KG 77 at Laon, autumn 1940. (Peter Taghon)

Left: *Leutnant* Otto Bischoff of I/KG 77, who successfully bombed Worcester's MECO factory on 3 October 1940 – mistakenly believing he had hit Coventry's Daimler works.

Below: Repair work ongoing at the MECO factory.

The Ju 88 of *Oberleutnant* Siegward Fiebig, *Stab* I/KG 77, shot down by Hatfield airfield's defences on 3 October 1940.

Jabo: an Me 109E fighter bomber.

Above left: *Jabo* pilot: *Oberleutnant* Lothar Siegfried Stronk of 8/JG 53, killed in action, 2 October 1940.

Above right: Stronk's grave a Cannock Chase.

Below: Range, or the lack of it, was a constant problem for Me 109 pilots throughout the Battle of Britain – this one only just regained the French coast after an escort mission to London.

Major Helmut Wick, *Kommodore* of JG 2, at the international press conference following award of the Oak Leaves to his Knight's Cross, having claimed his fortieth and forty-first on 5 October 1940 – no evidence exists to substantiate these victories.

'MacKenzie's Knock' – the damaged Hurricane of 501 Squadron's Pilot Officer Kenneth MacKenzie DFC after using his wingtip to knock a Me 109 into the sea on 7 October 1940.

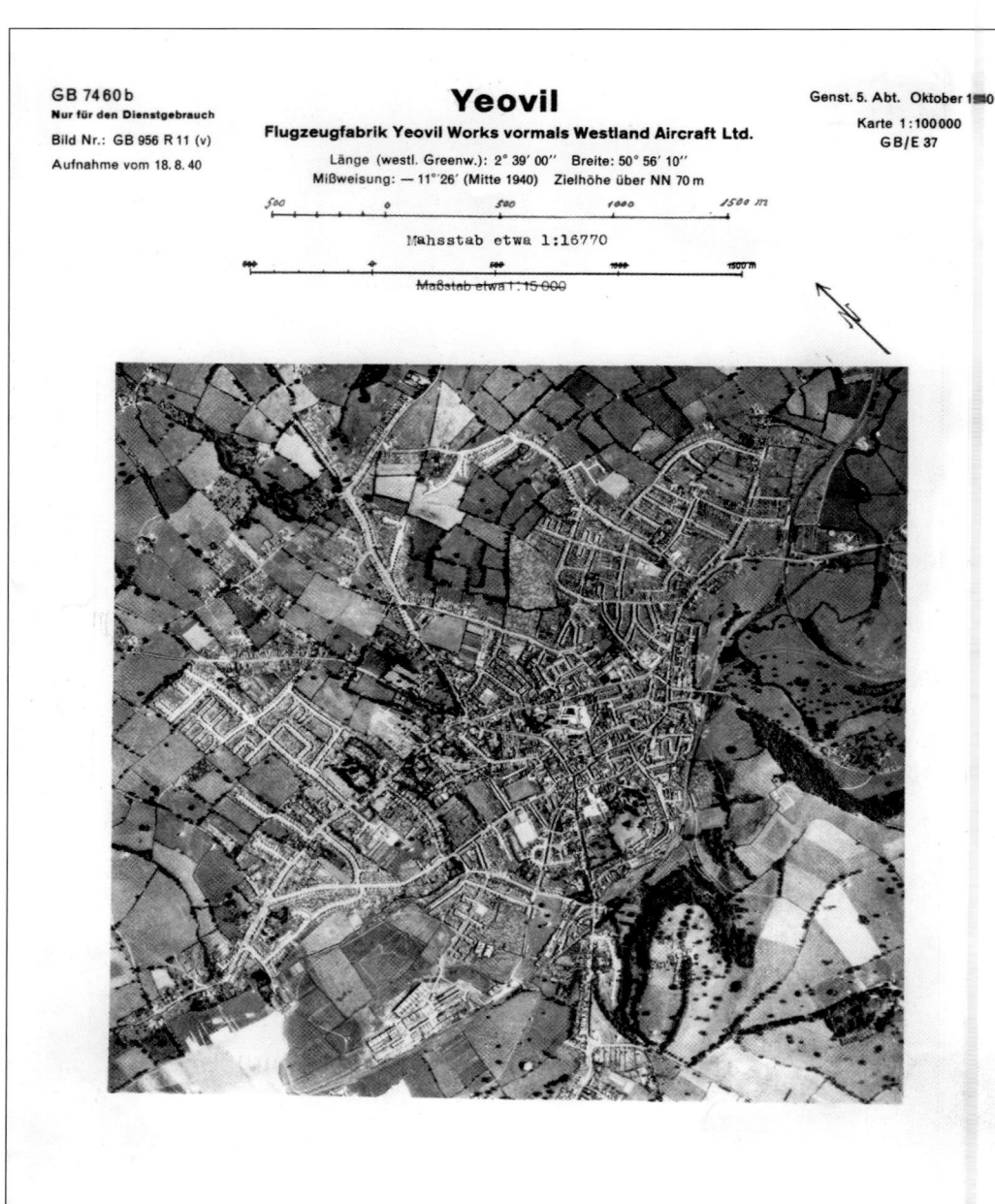

Yeovil

Flugzeugfabrik Yeovil Works vormals Westland Aircraft Ltd.

Länge (westl. Greenw.): 2° 39′ 00″   Breite: 50° 56′ 10″
Mißweisung: — 11°26′ (Mitte 1940)   Zielhöhe über NN 70 m

Genst. 5. Abt. Oktober 1940

Karte 1 : 100 000
GB / E 37

500 · · · · 0 · · · 500 · · · 1000 · · · 1500 m

Maßstab etwa 1:16770

500 · · · 0 · · · 500 · · · 1000 · · · 1500 m

Maßstab etwa 1:15 000

A Luftwaffe target map of Yeovil, showing the Westland Aircraft Factory, which was attacked on 7 October 1940.

Right: Suffer the little children: 10-year-old Laurence 'Peter' Sweet, killed when a shelter in Preston Grove, Yeovil, received a direct hit on 8 October 1940.

Below: A Short Sunderland of Coastal Command on an essential – but forgotten – convoy protection sortie.

Above: The crew of a Coastal Command Hudson safely back at base after their Hudson was holed by flak off Norway.

Below: More unsung heroes: an Observer Corps post in south-east England.

Bristol Blenheim Mk IVs of 2 Group, Bomber Command, heading out to attack a German airfield in France – unescorted and in daylight, these crews fought a forgotten battle.

A Hampden of Bomber Command being 'bombed up' for a night raid on Germany.

Night bomber: a Wellington of Bomber Command heading for Berlin.

A Wellington crew of Bomber Command safely back at base after a night raid on Germany.

Life went on: the wedding, in London, of Raymond Husband and Eva Russell on 12 October 1940 (Georgia Stone).

'Dad's Army': Raymond Husband and friends of the Home Guard (Georgia Stone).

Above and below: The Me 109 of *Oberleutnant* Egon Troha, *Staffelkapitän* of 9/JG 3, who was shot down and forced-landed at Shepherdswell, a few miles inland of Dover, on 29 October 1940.

Above: Down on the beach: the Me 109 of *Unteroffizier* Arno Zimmermann of 7/JG 54, who forced-landed at Lydd on 26 October 1940.

Right: The grave of the Czech ace, Sergeant Josef Frantisek DFM and Bar, at Northwood – killed in a flying accident on 8 October 1940, whilst serving with 303 (Polish) Squadron at Northolt.

Pilot Officer Peter 'Sneezy' Brown of 41 Squadron at readiness, Hornchurch, October 1940 – wearing the lifejacket of *Feldwebel* Ludwig Bielmaier of 5/JG 52, shot down by Brown on 20 October 1940.

Squadron Leader Peter Brown AFC photographed by the author in 1995.

Pilot Officer Crelin 'Bogle' Bodie DFC of 66 Squadron, pictured at Kenley – an exceptional fighter pilot, Bodie did not survive the war.

Above: During October 1940, Flight Lieutenant Eric Thomas was a flight commander on 222 Squadron at Hornchurch, later becoming wing leader at Biggin Hill and surviving the war a decorated ace (Sylvia Lewis).

Right: Canadian Pilot Officer Hugh Reilley of 66 Squadron, killed in action on 17 October 1940.

The grave of Knight's Cross holder *Hauptmann* Hans-Karl Mayer, *Gruppenkommandeur* of I/JG 53 at Hawkinge Cemetery, killed in action on 17 October 1940 – note incorrect details on headstone.

Flight Sergeant Eric Williams of 46 Squadron, shot down and killed on 15 October 1940 – and who remains buried with his Hurricane at Gravesend, the nature of the crash-site preventing recovery.

Pilots of 501 Squadron at Kenley – 501 was in the front line throughout the entire sixteen weeks of the Battle of Britain, losing nineteen pilots – more than any other squadron.

Polish Pilot Officer Franciszek Surma of 257 Squadron – who scrambled from North Weald on 29 October 1940 during a Jabo raid – and then survived being shot down by *Hauptmann* Gerhard Schöpfel, *Gruppenkommandeur* of III/JG 26.

The Polish Flying Officer Tadeusz Nowierski of 609 Squadron, pictured at Warmwell.

The youngest RAF casualty of the Battle of Britain and probably the entire Second World War: 16-year-old AC1 Harry Clack of 54 MU, at Eaton Socon, near St Neots, electrocuted whilst recovering a crashed German bomber on 24 October 1940.

Above: Pilot Officer John Curchin, Flight Lieutenant Frank Howell and Pilot Officer David Crook of 609 Squadron attending their DFC investiture at Buckingham Palace.

Below: No. 12 Group pilots of 19, 249 and 310 (Czech) Squadrons' pilots having received decorations at Duxford.

Above: The German bombers were defeated in daylight – but with Britain's nocturnal defences still in their infancy, the night blitz on Britain's cities was a terrible ordeal throughout the winter of 1940/1941.

Left: Leader of 'The Few', Air Chief Marshal Sir Hugh Dowding was made 1st Baron of Bentley Priory – but, scandalously, was never made a Marshal of the Royal Air Force.

8. Incidentally there has been two recent occurrences of extremely experienced pilots on reconnaissance being shot down over 25,000 feet by raids of which RDF had given no indication.

9. Experience showed that this reconnaissance work was not suitable for young pilots, whose commendable keenness led them to engage, rather than shadow, the enemy.

10. Reverting to the general question of fighter tactics the AOC said that to meet the present 'Tip-and-run' raids he felt that the only safe system was that now employed in 11 Group. The reconnaissance Spitfire section was always backed by a strong Spitfire squadron patrolling on the Maidstone patrol line at 15,000 feet, as soon as the first RDF warning was received this squadron went up to 30,000 feet and then to 35,000 feet, so as to cover the ascent of other squadrons; one of these was always at instant readiness and, generally, the present situation demanded an exceptionally high degree of readiness throughout the Group.

11. AOC 12 Group said that he would welcome more opportunities of using the wing formation, operating, say, from Duxford and coming down to help 11 Group. We could get a wing of five squadrons into the air in six minutes and it could be over Hornchurch at 20,000 feet in 25 minutes. If this type of counter-attack intercepted a big formation only once in ten times the effort would have been worth it. On two recent occasions good results had again been obtained, once against fighters alone.

12. ACASI drew attention to the shortness of some of the warnings that groups had recently received.

13. AOC-in-C Fighter Command said that he had recently given written orders that an 'Arrow' should go down on the operations table on receipt of the first 'Counter'. It must be realised that the enemy's approach at great height presented a difficult problem.

14. AOC 11 Group said that he could face the problem when it was a large bomber raid that was coming in. Could it not be accepted that if his group had, say, 20 squadrons at readiness, that was generally sufficient to meet any enemy formation?

15. Discussions followed on this question and it was generally agreed that additional fighter support would often be advantageous, since the more we could outnumber the enemy the more we should shoot down. The AOC-in-C said that he could, with his group commanders, resolve any difficulties of control in sending such support. The other main difficulties to be met, it was agreed, were those involving the time factor, though in this connection it was mentioned that the Me 109s carrying bombs had not, so far, been found over 22,000 feet.

16. Squadron Leader Bader said that from his practical experience time was the essence of the problem; if enough warning could be

given to bring a large number of fighters into position there was no doubt they could get most effective results.

17. Air Marshal Portal inquired how such a local concentration might affect the responsibility of a group commander for the defence of all the area of his group. AOC 12 Group said that satisfactory plans were prepared to meet the possibility of other attacks coming in: he was satisfied that the concentration of a wing was not incompatible with his general responsibilities as Group Commander.

18. This raised the question of whether some of 12 Group's squadrons might be moved to 10 Group, which was, the C-in-C agreed, at present somewhat weak should any concentrated attack develop in the West. On the other hand, the protection of the Midlands and of the East coast convoys was a big commitment for 12 Group. Though it was a serious limitation he had, as C-in-C, to keep in mind the necessity of meeting every threat with some force.

19. Further discussion followed in which the importance of a long warning from the RDF was stressed. ACAS said that was everything being done to get the south-east coast RDF stations back to full efficiency following the damage suffered from enemy attacks. He mentioned the recent example when a 25 minute, steady, RDF warning had not been received without delay in 11 Group. It was decided that 11 Group should have the services of a certain member of the Stanmore Research Station, who had previously been of assistance to them.

20. DCAS said that he thought the views of the meeting could be summarised as follows:

The employment of a large mass of fighters had great advantages, though it was not necessarily the complete solution to the problem of interception. In 11 Group, where the enemy was very close at hand, both methods described by AOC 11 Group and those of AOC 12 Group could, on occasion, be used with forces from the two groups cooperating.

21. The AOC-in-C said that it would be arranged for 12 Group wings to participate freely in suitable operations over the 11 Group area. He would be able to resolve any complications of control. In reply to DHO, the C-in-C said that cooperation of this kind, in the present circumstances, hardly be employed generally throughout the Command, as similar conditions seldom arose elsewhere.

22. With reference to the formal agenda prepared for this meeting, the following observations were made:

Items 1 and 2
Items 1 and 2 formed the basis for the general discussion as shown above. It was agreed that when conditions were suitable, wings of three squadrons should be employed against large enemy formations, and that

where further forces could be made available without detriment to other commitments, larger fighter formations than wings should operate as tactical units. It was agreed that it would, on occasion, be convenient to operate two wings together as a unit and that, for want of a better name, such a unit should be provisionally known as a 'Balbo'.

Item 3

It was agreed that it would not always be practicable to operate the combined squadrons of a wing from the same aerodrome, particularly in winter when aircraft might be confined to the runways. It was, however, agreed that all squadrons of a wing should operate from the same sector.

Item 4

It was agreed that, as was now the practice, the wing or 'Balbo' should be controlled by the sector commander. It was considered undesirable for a squadron commander from one of the squadrons to control such a formation.

Item 5

No major difficulty was foreseen in coordinating the operations of the two wings of a Balbo; it was agreed that one sector commander should control the two wings, and that when possible the two wings of a Balbo could work on a common frequency.

Item 6

It was agreed that, in the conditions which enable the enemy to operate in mass formation, the fighter leader could dispense with sector control and that if he was given information about enemy movements he should be responsible for leading his formation to the battle.

Item 7

It was agreed that all squadrons of a Balbo could operate effectively on the same frequency with HF R/T and that by using VHF a theoretical maximum of seven Balbos could be operated.

Item 8

It was not thought that wings could be regarded as permanent units to moved complete, but that whenever possible the same squadrons should operate together as a wing.

Item 9

It was agreed that where practicable, wings should be deployed at stations from which they could gain advantage in height over the enemy without having to turn.

Item 10

23. AOC-in-C Fighter Command, in amplification of his earlier reports, gave the meeting an interim account of the development of the Airborne Interception Beaufighter. As yet, troubles with the Mk VI AI Beaufighter, and its engines, were causing much unserviceability, but he was satisfied that the system was sound in principle.

24. The method of using searchlights in clumps promised good results and was about to be developed in the South.

25. DCAS and DHO referred to the grave problem of maintaining civil morale in London, in the face of continued attack, over the two or three months that might be expected to pass before the system outlined by the C-in-C was practically efficient. To bridge the gap during the intervening period it was suggested that a temporary wing of two Defiant and two Hurricane squadrons should be formed to specialise in night-fighting on a 1914–1918 basis. C-in-C Fighter Command said that continual experiments had been made on these lines, many of them by AOC 10 Group who had, since the last war, been a specialist in night interception, but with the height and speed of modern night raids the old methods had not so far proved effective. He felt certain that now the only sound method would be a combination of AI and GL (or LC); his Defiant squadrons were, however, now being normally employed on night interception. While it was his considered opinion that the diversion of Hurricanes to night interception was a dangerous and unsound policy, with our present strength of fighter squadrons he had nevertheless agreed with reluctance to implement the Air Staff decision to do so. These aircraft, he felt, might show reasonable results in clear weather when the controlled clumps of searchlights began to work round London towards the end of November, but a real solution to the problem would only be found through the logical development of a system based on the two new radio aids to interception.

26. AOC-in-C said that he would be prepared to experiment with a 'Fighter Night' over London, but this was not a course he could recommend. As people heard the fighters over London they would imagine that the noise represented so many more enemy aircraft, and the experiment would be justified only if it succeeded.

27. A preliminary draft of the scheme which the DCAS and DHO had explained to the meeting was handed to the C-in-C Fighter Command, who undertook to examine it.

Copies of the minutes were sent to Hugh Dowding, the three group commanders present – and Douglas Bader.

Dowding had typically placed little importance on the meeting prior to attending, his feeling being that the Germans' tactics had changed so much that any thought of using massed fighter formations from a defensive perspective was now 'out of the question'. To him, the Air Staff were not looking ahead, as the meeting claimed, but to the past. This error of judgement rapidly dawned on Dowding in the air council room when he realised that this was actually a postmortem of Fighter Command tactics – and both he and Keith Park were being called to account. At that point, Dowding acknowledged that he had 'possibly made a mistake in allowing my group commanders so much liberty in running their groups their own way'.

Of the two AOCs, Park and Leigh-Mallory, involved in what was now an open dispute. Hugh Dowding said,

> I was entirely on [Keith] Park's side without, up to that time, having to say much. There was no need for me to say it. He was carrying out his assigned task and there was no need for any comment from me. But I had come by then to realise that Leigh-Mallory was not conducting the affairs of his group in the way I expected of him. I did not want to say you mustn't do this and you mustn't do that. I expected more of my group commanders. And that was why, by mid-October, I had come to realise I would have to do something about what was going on and get rid of [Trafford] Leigh-Mallory.

Dowding's style of command was one of trusting his group commanders to operate in accordance with his broad strategic wishes, deploying tactics consistent with that aim and within the parameters of the system. It was now clear that where Leigh-Mallory was concerned, that trust had been both misplaced and betrayed. Equally, Dowding's failure to heed warnings also came into sharp focus. Although Dowding later argued that because of his 'hands off', trusting, management style, Leigh-Mallory had been able to connive behind the scenes, the AOC-in-C himself largely unaware of 'what was going on', Park had, as we have seen, expressed his concerns about 12 Group in writing to Dowding on 29 September 1940. No action, however, was taken, and Air Vice-Marshal Douglas Evill, Dowding's SASO, had failed to deal with Park's complaint.

In his memoir *Years of Command* (see Bibliography), Air Vice-Marshal Sholto Douglas, the DCAS, referred to a 'clash of personalities' between Park and Leigh-Mallory culminating in 'an unnecessarily heated argument' between them 'one afternoon at the Air Ministry'. The DCAS claimed that from this point on, he was personally,

> drawn into the argument, and just as Dowding's name has since become linked with Park's, so mine has become associated with Leigh-Mallory's ... It has since become clear that Dowding, also, was not as deeply involved in what has come to be called the 'Wings Controversy' as many writers and historians would have us believe.

Dowding disagreed: 'I don't see how it would be possible for me to have become more deeply involved.'

When later reporting on the meeting, Sholto Douglas wrote,

> At this meeting it was confirmed that wings of three or more squadrons were the proper weapon to oppose large enemy formations when conditions are suitable … It was my view that the best way of defending an objective was not so much as to interpose a screen of fighter squadrons between that objective and the enemy, as to shoot down a high proportion of the enemy force sent to attack it, irrespective of whether the objective was bombed on a particular occasion or not.

It is doubtful that Britain's civilian population would have agreed.

Dowding, Brand and Park objected to the meeting's minutes, and prepared to write to the DCAS accordingly. The matter, therefore, remained ongoing – to say the least.

For the fighter pilots of 11 Group, surviving another day was doubtless uppermost in their minds, rather than grand strategy. Indeed, perhaps if Squadron Leader Douglas Bader had been fully occupied as a squadron commander in 11 Group, there would have been no 'Big Wing Controversy'. Throughout the day, the pilots of 11 Group would have to deal with four fighter sweeps over Kent, comprising some 300 German fighters and fighter bombers.

At 08.45 hrs, 421 Flight's Sergeant Arthur Spears took-off from Gravesend on a spotting patrol, flying one of the new Hurricane Mk IIs [ORB, Form 541], but 'dived steeply to escape Me 109s at 32,000 feet and had to land at Detling with seized engine' [ORB]. At the material time, *Feldwebel* Erwin Fleig of 1/JG 51 claimed a 'Spitfire', doubtless assuming Spears's fighter to be such and not expecting to find a Hurricane at such high altitude.

Whilst Squadron Leader Douglas Bader was on leave, Flight Lieutenant Eric Ball DFC had assumed command of 242 (Canadian) Squadron, which was operating from its home base at Coltishall, instead of Duxford, to which it had not flown since 5 October 1940 – which, considering Air Vice-Marshal Keith Park's recent request that it was now the right time for the Duxford Wing to take a larger part in the fighting over London and the south-east, is surprising. From Coltishall, 242 (Canadian) Squadron patrolled base and the east coast, and at 08.45 hrs this day, a section of three Hurricanes took-off to patrol off Yarmouth. At 09.00 hrs, Pilot Officer Marvin Brown and Pilot Officer Norman Campbell, both Canadians, and Pilot Officer Bruce Rogers intercepted a Do 17 off Yarmouth – but on this occasion the lone bomber came out on top: Brown's Hurricane was hit, resulting in throttle jammed in open position' [ORB] and Campbell was shot down and killed; no counter combat claims were filed, but a Do 17 of *Stab* KG 2 crashed and burnt out at Eroillers, killing the crew, possibly due to combat damage.

According to JG 53 historian Jochen Prien (see Bibliography), on this day all three *Gruppen* participated in a *Jabo* attack on London, taking-off before 09.00 hrs (BST), the five fighter bombers of 5/JG 53 dropping bombs on London and Margate. Nos. I and II *Gruppen* reported no contact with the enemy, but 9/JG 53's *Feldwebel* Schramm apparently claimed a Spitfire destroyed over Dungeness – which, as there was no RAF fighter lost, or combat reported, is unconfirmed. Indeed, this first raid does not appear to have been intercepted.

Much later, at 13.15 hrs, 421 Flight's Sergeant James Gillies left Gravesend in a Hurricane Mk II but, at 14.20 hrs returned to crash-land 'his aircraft after it had been badly damaged in a fight with Me 109s. Plane wrecked and Sergeant Gillies injured.' [ORB].

JG 53 was then briefed for another fighter-bomber attack on London, take-off time 14.45 hrs (BST). At 14.55 hrs, 66 Squadron scrambled from Gravesend to patrol Maidstone, and five minutes later, 222 Squadron took-off from Hornchurch to patrol base. At 15.10 hrs, this latest raid, totalling eighty Me 109s, headed for East London, Kenley and Biggin Hill – so 222 was vectored to reinforce 'Clickety-Click' over Maidstone. Two days previously, 74 'Tiger' Squadron had concluded its rest period in 12 Group and had flown south, to Biggin Hill. Now, at 15.10 hrs, that legendary South African freedom fighter, Squadron Leader 'Sailor' Malan, climbed his Spitfires hard, up-sun, to 26,000ft, also with orders to intercept the rapidly approaching enemy.

By 15.30 hrs, Squadron Leader John Hill's 222 Squadron had climbed over Hornchurch and was at 24,000ft when he sighted a formation of Me 109s – 222, therefore, went into action over the Thames Estuary and east coast, before reaching Maidstone. Yellow Leader, Flying Officer Desmond McMullen, attacked the rearmost of a *Schwarm* 'slightly apart from the main formation.'

> I opened fire at 100 yards and closed in. E/A became enveloped in black smoke and appeared to be out of control. About 10,000 feet E/A straightened out and kept on diving, doing gentle turns. We went below cloud, almost to sea-level, where E/A dived into sea. The camouflage was battleship grey, with very prominent crosses. The pilot made no real attempt at evasive action and appeared to have little more than the bare knowledge of how to fly.

As he actually saw his victim crash into the sea, it is possible – but, as we will see, far from certain, that he shot down the ace and Knight's Cross holder *Hauptmann* Hans-Karl Mayer, *Gruppenkommandeur* of I/JG 53 – who is the only 109 pilot to have been killed on this day in those circumstances. Apparently, according to Prien, Mayer had previously been forced to abort the mission owing to engine trouble – but, being aware from R/T traffic of combat over London and knowing that another JG 53 formation leader had turned back with technical trouble, the *Kommandeur* raced off again in a newly delivered and unarmed Me 109. Mayer subsequently 'disappeared' – until his body washed ashore at Littlestone ten days later.

Sergeant John Burgess was attacked by twenty Me 109s, and breaking away to damaging a yellow-nosed Me 109 before fired upon again himself; optimistically, Burgess claimed a probable. Flying Officer Ian Hallam was leading Green Section and dived with the rest of 222 Squadron onto the twenty Me 109s; finding a 109 in front of him, with 'a yellow nose and wingtips', Hallam delivered 'a longish burst from astern. Bits flew off his tailplane and he turned over and dived straight down.' Almost certainly, one of these pilots was responsible for shooting down *Oberleutnant* Walter Rupp, *Staffelkapitän* of 3/JG 53, who managed to put his damaged 109 safely down on

Manston airfield, where he was captured, unhurt. Whereas it was a particularly bad day for I/JG 53, 222 Squadron suffered no loss.

Squadron Leader 'Sailor' Malan and 74 Squadron met the enemy north of Ashford, the Spitfire pilots' attention drawn to AA fire:

> At approximately 1530 hrs, we suddenly saw two yellow noses (Me 109s) crossing our bows and surprised them from the sun. I gave the right-hand one a two second burst with quarter deflection from 200 yards and closed to 150 yards astern, and delivered another two second burst. I then closed to 100 yards and delivered a four second burst which appeared to damage elevator controls as his nose went vertically downwards very suddenly, instead of the usual half-roll.
>
> My engine naturally stopped when I followed suit but it picked up again and I closed to 150 yards on half-roll and gave another four second burst.
>
> I found myself doing an aileron turn to keep direction and delivered another four second burst. He then started to smoke but I blacked out completely and lost consciousness for a couple of seconds, and eventually pulled out at 9,000 feet above 10/10ths cloud.
>
> My port guns failed to fire during the whole engagement.'

The 109 was claimed as a probable. The 'Tigers' also claimed three more German fighters destroyed, having intercepted III/JG 53 approaching London. One was destroyed by Pilot Officer Bryan Draper, who also claimed a probable. When first attacked, Draper, Yellow 3, hit a 109 in the engine, a cloud of black and white smoke bellowing forth, the aircraft apparently 'in difficulties'. Draper then ambushed another 109 from astern, shooting it 'down in flames', but this was not seen to crash. Flying Officer William Nelson – a Jewish-Canadian pilot – hit a 109, which half-rolled away, streaming glycol; Nelson followed, still firing, and much smoke belched from the enemy fighter which entered cloud at 2,000ft and disappeared. Flying Officer Peter St John closed to such short range that he was buffeted about by the 109's slipstream and 'had difficulty in keeping my sights on ... I noticed white smoke coming from underneath, which gradually turned black, and then I noticed flames coming from the machine, it rolled slowly over onto its back and fell away in a dive.'

No. 74 Squadron was responsible, it seems, for the demise of *Oberleutnant* Heinze, *Staffelkapitän* of 8/JG 53, who nursed his crippled 109 nearly as far as France, ditching off the French coast and being rescued by the *Seenotdienst*. Flying Officer Alan Ricalton, however, was shot down and killed, his Spitfire crashing at Hollingbourne, the victim, it seems, of *Feldwebel* Eduard Koslowski of 8/JG 53; Ricalton – another veteran of the Fall of France – had been amongst the first batch of replacement pilots posted to 74 Squadron at Wittering, and had been lost in his first combat. Pilot Officer Roger Boulding, who joined the 'Tigers' with Ricalton, commented that 'There before the grace of God ...' Ricalton was 74 Squadron's first casualty during this tour of duty at Biggin Hill – but would not be the last.

No. 66 Squadron's Flight Lieutenant Bob Oxspring's subsequent report describes events befalling 'Clickety-Click':

> Throughout the patrol we were warned by Operations that there were enemy fighters about, but all we saw were friendly. It was after we had been to investigate some aircraft we had seen, and which proved to be Spitfires, that I noticed Pilot Officer [Hugh] Reilley, who was Red 4 and doing the duties of look-out above the Squadron was no longer with us. I called him up but there was no reply. I also called up Red 1, who replied that he had not seen Pilot Officer Reilley for some minutes. The Squadron had landed at 1605 hrs and Pilot Officer Reilley was still missing.

But what happened to Pilot Officer Hugh Reilley – 66 Squadron's vulnerable weaver?

Reilley crashed at 15.25 hrs, in Spitfire LZ-N, R6800, the usual mount of his squadron commander, Squadron Leader Rupert Leigh, at Crockham Hill, Sevenoaks. The 22-year-old Canadian, a married man with a new-born son, was killed – the forty-eighth aerial victory of none other than *Major* Werner Mölders, *Kommodore* of JG 51. No. 66 Squadron suffered no other losses in the combat, after which no claims we made.

AC1 Bob Morris:

> Having lost so many pilots at Kenley, replacements arrived at Gravesend, although several of these were also killed. Amongst them was one I had got to know quite well, Pilot Officer Hugh Reilley. By this time, however, we were quite accustomed to losses, it sounds terrible to say now but I think you can get used to anything. I remember I was on my half day, fast asleep on my bed at Cobham Hall, as we usually were on our half days off, when the Sergeant stuck his head round the door and said 'Everybody on Half Day – outside, best blue, best greatcoat, webbing belt round your waist and get in the lorry!' He did not tell us what for, but we got dressed and piled onto the lorry, which took us to the church near Gravesend. It was then we realised that we were going to be the guard of honour at Pilot Officer Reilley's funeral. We sat in the church for the service. A four-wheeled trailer was hitched up to our truck, and the coffin was placed on this trailer, which we marched behind, through the middle of Gravesend to the cemetery, where the burial took place.

No. 66 Squadron's favourite pub was the 'Leather Bottle' at Cobham, the regulars of which adopted 66 as 'their' squadron. When Pilot Officer Hugh Reilley was buried, they and their families turned out in large numbers, lining the route through Gravesend, paying their respects as the cortege passed.

There would be one more clash between the opposing fighters before the day was done. At 15.40 hrs, 41 Squadron scrambled from Hornchurch, and headed for the Maidstone line. Although ordered to patrol at the questionable height of Angels 15, 41, an experienced Spitfire squadron, climbed to 31,500ft. Yellow Section, led by Pilot

Officer Eric Lock, became separated from the rest of the squadron whilst climbing into the sun. Suddenly, Lock died, and Pilot Officer Frederick Aldridge, Yellow 2, followed – and realised that Lock 'was diving on nine Me 109s in line-astern formation', but the Spitfires were unable to catch them. Continuing towards Chatham, the sharp-eyed Lock then, at 17.00 hrs, 10 miles south of Chatham, 'went down after a Me 109 and I climbed just above him, after a single Me 109, which I fired upon. He staggered in flight and went down into the haze' – an addendum to Aldridge's combat reports reads that Lock, who was below, 'saw E/A go hurtling past him, spinning and smoking, and still out of control at 2,000 feet' – this was claimed as a probable.

The rest of 41 Squadron split up on attacking a formation of Me 109s, and at 17.15 hrs, Pilot Officer Edward 'Hawkeye' Wells, a New Zealander and outstanding fighter pilot, sighted a 109 returning from London, heading towards the Channel. Wells, 2,000ft above the retreating enemy, which flew south at 15,000ft, gave chase – closing 'until he exactly filled the sight bar, range 250 yards':

> [After a] preliminary burst ... glycol smoke immediately poured away in large quantities and the machine started a shallow dive which he continued until about 7,000 feet, when he suddenly dived very sharply straight down into the sea. No pilot attempted to leave the machine at any time. I circled over the spot on the sea at 500 feet, nothing came to the surface.

And there is the mystery. Historically, the loss of *Hauptmann* Hans-Karl Mayer has been attributed to Flying Officer Desmond McMullen DFC of 222 Squadron, who claimed a 109 down in the sea during the clash with I/JG 53 off the eastern Kent coast. However, if Prien's account is accurate and Mayer was late on parade, as it were, having returned to base with engine trouble, and listening to his *Gruppe*'s hectic radio transmissions, before taking off again in a new, unarmed, Me 109, the time of McMullen's claim, when 222 fought against the rest of I/JG 53, simply does not fit. Wells's claim, nearly two hours later, for a lone Me 109, would, given time and distance, although nowhere in Luftwaffe records can a time be confirmed for Mayer's take-off, or, indeed, loss. The other question arising is, if McMullen did not shoot Mayer down, and if Wells did, who did McMullen down, and vice versa? As is so often the case, it is impossible to be certain, and yet more unanswerable questions have gone with these men to the grave. No. 41 Squadron recorded no casualties in the engagement.

At 16.25 hrs, Tangmere's 213 Squadron scrambled to patrol from Mayfield to Tenterden, and at 17.15 hrs were at 23,000ft above Romney Marsh when twenty Me 109s were sighted, returning to France from London. Squadron Leader Duncan MacDonald turned the Hurricanes towards the enemy, the CO, Red Leader, personally hitting a 109, which streamed white smoke and disappeared into cloud. Sergeant Maurice Davies also damaged a 109, 10 miles north of Dungeness, where Sergeant Gordon Bushell also hit a 109,

> a great stream of black substance coming back from the E/A and hit my windscreen, this was oil, a warning that I was being attacked from

behind caused me to turn away sharply, the E/A when last seen was at 1,000 feet, losing height rapidly, and with oil and other substance gushing from it, disappeared into the haze.

It was claimed as a probable.

No. 213 Squadron's Pilot Officer Ronald Atkinson, a 19-year-old veteran, was shot down and killed, his Hurricane crashing at Weeks Farm, Egerton, near Pluckley, near Ashford.

Sergeant Geoffrey Stevens:

We of 213 Squadron were scrambled late in the afternoon, getting on for 1700 hours, and as we climbed away from Tangmere I remember thinking that I wished Flight Lieutenant Jackie Sing, the commander of 'A' Flight, was leading us, as in my opinion he was the best. Neither did we have a Tail End Charlie, for reasons that escaped me.

We climbed to about 17,000 feet when I noticed AA shells bursting ahead and below. I reported this and at about the same time we had a course correction starboard. As we turned I saw strikes on Red 2, just ahead of me. We were flying the stupid close formation 'vic' of three aircraft in line astern (I was Yellow 2). Simultaneously, I was hit in the engine by three or four cannon shells. The rev counter went off the clock and smoke and flames enveloped the outside. The standard practice if hit was to get out of the action as quickly as one could. I therefore shoved the stick over and went into a spiral dive. Flames, smoke and glycol fumes were everywhere, and I went down switching off everything I could think of.

I entered cloud at about 10,000 feet, coming out at 5,000 feet whilst preparing to bale out. The flames appeared to have stopped. I lifted up my goggles to have a look round and saw that I was over a town. I knew that if I baled out my aircraft would cause some severe damage, possibly loss of life. A field containing an AA gun was within gliding distance and so I opted for a forced-landing.

I did not appear to be in any immediate danger at this stage and so settled into a straight glide towards the field. Having sorted everything out in my mind, knowing exactly what I was going to do, I was dismayed to see what I have since described as electric light bulbs, but what were in fact tracer shells, going past my cockpit. Looking in my rear-view mirror I saw a yellow-nosed Me 109 on my tail. Without power, evasive action is limited, especially with so little height to play with. I used rudder to skid out of the German's sights, and am told that fortunately he'd been chased off by another Hurricane. I had lost height, however.

The effect of this on my carefully planned approach was disastrous. I opened the hood and blinded myself with glycol fumes. I put my goggles on again, but by this time I was very low, about 100 feet, travelling much too fast and in the wrong position for an approach to the field.

Everything was wrong! I did a steep left-handed turn towards the field and slammed the Hurricane onto the ground, it was all I could do. It was unfortunate that I had been forced to choose the one approach that ended up with my wing root against a four feet thick tree stump. The aircraft shot into the air and over onto its back, into a sort of marsh. With all that had gone on leading up to this, I had omitted to lock the sliding cockpit hood open, and my harness back. The hood consequently slammed shut and I was propelled forward upon impact with some force, cutting my head on the reflector gunsight.

I was now hanging upside down with blood running down my face. I could smell the petrol leaking out everywhere and hear the hissing of the cooling engine in the wet marsh. Otherwise everything seemed dead quiet. I tried to open the hood but it was useless. I was expecting the aircraft to go up in flames at any time and seemed powerless to effect an escape. I carefully released my straps and let myself down so that I lay on my back on top of the cockpit hood. I think that this was more to do *something* than continue hanging upside down doing nowt!

Although it seemed like an age, assistance actually came very quickly. People seemed to come from nowhere, including the Army. One helpful farmer got himself a corner post with a pointed metal end and rammed it through the hood. Had I still been hanging upside down it would have gone straight through my head, as it was it went just past my nose! To cut a long story short, one wing was lifted enough to allow the hood to slide back. The small clearance from the ground was sufficient for me, I was out of the wrecked Hurricane like a bullet from a gun! I'd never moved so fast in my life!

When I got out I could not stand up because the stick had come back and whacked my knee and I was somewhat shaken. However, with two men supporting me on each arm we made it to HQ and I remember being amazed at the number of people there. As we walked up the field it was a crescent of people all looking to the centre. I only mention this because shaken though I was it left a clear impression that I can remember to this day.

Having come down near Tenterden, they took me to Ashford Hospital, and later the soldiers returned and invited me to join them for a drink that night. Although I was willing the doctor was having none of it!

The Spitfires of 603 Squadron had hurried from Hornchurch at 17.10 hrs to reinforce the squadrons over Kent, and at 17.30 hrs (not 13.45 hrs as per pilot's combat report), Pilot Officer Basil Stapleton 'sighted E/A dead ahead'. Having reported the sighting to Squadron Leader George Denholm, Stapleton was ordered to lead the Spitfires towards the Germans. Stapleton caught the Me 109s, which were stepped up from 18,000–25,000ft, over the Channel, off Dungeness, and engaged the leading five. One of these 'Stapme' hit, which 'wobbled and went vertically down, emitting both black and white smoke ... at great speed.' The plummeting Me 109 was last seen at 10,000ft and claimed as a probable.

According to Luftwaffe records, in this engagement with 41, 213 and 603 Squadrons, I/JG 77 lost a single machine, which ditched in the Channel off Cap-Gris-Nez, the pilot being rescued by the *Seenotdienst*. Although only two Hurricanes of 213 Squadron had been shot down, pilots of *Stab* I, 1, 2 and 3/JG 77 claimed eight Hurricanes and two Spitfires destroyed, all south of Tunbridge Wells – once more proving the point that Luftwaffe combat claims are from as accurate as many have assumed.

After dark, a lone Ju 88 dropped bombs on Kenley airfield, seriously damaging four 253 Squadron Hurricanes and one of 501 Squadron – the raider was not intercepted.

For Coastal Command it had been another routine day, with just forty-five sorties flown, although three U-boats were attacked, one of which was claimed destroyed by a Sunderland of 10 RAAF Squadron, west of Bishop's Rock. A 22 Squadron Beaufort was damaged by flak from shipping off the Dutch coast, crash-landing at Sutton Bridge; the crew survived, two being injured, but a Blenheim of 59 Squadron was lost over the sea on a sortie to attack German destroyers at Brest. Adverse weather conditions, however, led to all Bomber Command operations, by day and night, being scrubbed.

Weekly Report by Home Intelligence:

> There is neither fear nor expectation of invasion. The demand for reprisals continues to decline and Beable's 'bomb Berlin' posters have aroused little interest [author's note: this was a private and unofficial initiative by one J.M. Beadle, which were distributed in London during October 1940, the message being 'Bullies are always cowards – bomb Berlin and save London']. There are, however, strongly worded demands that we should bomb the Rumanian oil wells, and it is suggested that our hesitancy is due to fear of hurting international financial interests. People wonder also why we do not bomb Italy more heavily as the Italians are considered likely to 'crack' easily. There is criticism of the R.A.F.'s failure to raid Germany in bad weather, since this does not prevent the Germans raiding us.

Friday, 18 October 1940

At dawn, coastal observation posts sited between Dover and nearby Folkestone reported a flotilla of E-boats approaching Dungeness. At Warren Halt Sidings, the 9.2-inch gun 'EE Gee' was already dressed for action – and opened fire. The round splashed down beyond the target, but was a sufficient deterrent for the E-boats to turn about and return to France. Having fired at a right-angle to its carriage, however, the recoil made the 86-ton gun jump back off its rails – taking twelve hours to rectify.

Fog, however, prevented *Jafü* 2 launching any fighter sweeps or *Jabo* attacks. Typically in such conditions, enemy operations comprised nuisance raids by lone Ju 88s, although damage caused was slight. Two of these raiders were intercepted, both by Northolt squadrons: at 15.47 hrs, 229 Squadron's Pilot Officer Ronald Bary, a New Zealander, Pilot Officer Victor Ortmans, a Belgian, and Pilot Officer Vernon Bright damaged a Ju 88 over Redhill, and 302 (Polish) Squadron's Squadron Leader Jack Satchell and Polish Sergeant Eugeniusz Nowakiewicz claimed a probable Ju 88 over the south coast at 17.05 hrs. No. II/KG 51, however, lost a Ju 88 and crew, which failed to return from an attack on London, and another of III/LG 1 also went missing on a similar mission; another Ju 88, according to Luftwaffe, records, crash-landed at Calais with combat damage, and a III/LG 1 machine returned to Fécamp with a wounded crewman aboard, although only two interceptions appear in RAF records. Three I/KG 54 Ju 88s crashed upon returning to France due to the poor weather conditions.

After the early morning British shelling of enemy shipping off Calais, the German railway guns responded at midday: eight shells fell on the harbour area, damaging Admiralty Pier and a trawler, and killing two male civilians; military and further civilian casualties were suffered when Connaught Park was also hit.

Although there were no combat casualties, both sides lost fighters and pilots owing to bad weather, partially due to the conditions, inexperience and fatigue.

Coastal Command Blenheims reconnoitred the Norwegian coastline, one escaping from Me 109s, but night operations were cancelled. A lack of cloud cover led to a 2 Group Blenheim aborting a raid on Hamburg, although by night Bomber Command Hampdens and Whitleys attacked the port and industrial targets in Germany. A Whitley of Scampton's 83 Squadron was abandoned upon return, having got lost, the crew safely baling out over Yorkshire, and a 102 Squadron Whitley was abandoned after running out of petrol whilst returning to Linton-on-Ouse, two of the crew sustaining slight injury.

Weekly Report by Home Intelligence:

> Invasion rumours seem to have ceased, but rumours of excessive air-raid damage are still very prevalent. There are several suggestions that listening to the German wireless is increasing, because the B.B.C. is off the air so much nowadays. Haw Haw rumours of places bombed or to be bombed are still common (Pimlico, Willesden, Welwyn, Stevenage, Canterbury etc.), but in no case do they bear any relation to the actual material broadcast from Germany. Rumours are common that certain objects, such as reservoirs, serve to guide German planes, and the public asks why barrages are not concentrated at these points.

Saturday, 19 October 1940

The bad weather persisted, continuing to much reduce air operations, which followed a similar pattern to the previous day, with lone raiders making a nuisance of themselves, as intended. Substantial damage was caused to civilian property at Margate, where three people were killed, and a lone Ju 88 bombed Coventry at lunchtime, damaging twenty-seven houses and strafing the Coventry bypass, although no casualties were inflicted. A few bombs were dropped around London, but damage was slight.

At 11.00 hrs, Red Section of Warmwell's 152 Squadron, namely Flight Lieutenant Derek 'Bottle' Boitle-Gill and Pilot Officer Graham Cox, took-off to patrol Dorset when five minutes later they intercepted and attacked a Ju 88 over Dorchester. After both pilots fired at the intruder, which was pursued southwards, the bomber 'disappeared into the mist … and finally lost ten miles SSW of Portland'; it was claimed as damaged.

Flight Lieutenant Dennis David DFC took-off from Tangmere at 10.55 hrs with his 'B' Flight on a practice flight. Soon afterwards control ordered Green Section to land whilst David, leading Blue Section, was ordered to intercept a bandit. At 11.10 hrs, a Ju 88 was sighted 4 miles north of Manston, which the Hurricanes dived to attack. David 'delivered a long, steady burst … his right engine and wing caught fire and his fuselage glowed' before 'diving into a misty cloud which covered the sea 800 feet'. Although claimed and credited as destroyed, this aircraft was not seen to crash and nor, apparently, did it.

At 13.25 hrs, the two Spitfires of St Eval's 234 Squadron's Red Section, Flight Lieutenant Cyril Page, commanding 'A' Flight, and Sergeant Hugh Sharpley, scrambled to patrol 'Point 10 at Angels 5'. At 13.40 hrs over Falmouth, three Ju 88s were sighted approaching from the south-east. In the ensuing combat, Sharpley set the port engine of one Ju 88 ablaze, which he last saw 40 miles south-west of Land's End, 'going down in a vertical dive, still burning fiercely, with clouds of black smoke enveloping it.' Again, this was claimed as destroyed, but was not seen to crash.

At lunchtime the weather and visibility improved, so at 13.30 hrs Flying Officer Dennis Parrott and Pilot Officer Keith Lawrence left Gravesend on a spotting patrol; for unknown reasons, however, Parrott forced-landed at Old Swanley, and was slightly injured.

Having not flown at all the previous day due to the bad weather, 92 Squadron left Biggin Hill at 14.25 hrs to patrol the Maidstone line. During this patrol, Sergeant Leslie Allton's Spitfire dropped out of formation at high altitude, the pilot being killed in the resulting crash at Smarden, oxygen system failure being the most likely cause. The patrol was otherwise uneventful.

Up at Castletown, 3 Squadron suffered a sad and unnecessary fatality when Flying Officer George McAvity, a Canadian, was engaged on an AA cooperation sortie and crashed attempting a slow roll – not having flown an operational flight between the Battle of Britain's official dates (10 July 1940 – 31 October 1940), McAvity's name will not be found amongst those of 'The Few'.

On this day, for reasons which will soon become all too apparent, Squadron Leader Douglas Bader's 242 (Canadian) Squadron began its permanent move from Coltishall to Duxford.

Once again, owing to the weather, Coastal Command's sorties were much reduced, although a 210 Squadron Sunderland depth-charged a 'suspected' U-boat; night operations were cancelled. No. 2 Group sent six Blenheims on an uneventful North Sea sweep, but all other daylight sorties were scrubbed. By night, only three Bomber Command sallied forth, due to the poor weather over the British Isles, to bomb Osnabrük and Berlin. Neither command suffered any losses.

Weekly Report by Home Intelligence:

The belief that black-out infringements are due to Fifth-Columnists is still prevalent, and penalties for the careless use of torches are widely approved. There are still complaints that the lighting of cars and railways is unnecessarily bright and there is even some anxiety about the modified street lighting. Many people contrast the severity shown towards householders with the apparent leniency towards motorists.

Sunday, 20 October 1940

Air Vice-Marshal Keith Park continued to try and find a way forward in terms of cooperation with 12 Group, writing to Air Vice-Marshal Trafford Leigh-Mallory that he would be 'delighted' to have the Duxford Wing's assistance provided that it patrolled where requested until engaged. Park emphasised that the wing's position would also have to be communicated to the 11 Group controller, to avoid throwing the Observer Corps and AA units into confusion, as had Douglas Bader's previously unauthorised fighter sweeps over 11 Group. Indicating exactly which direction any antagonism was coming from, Leigh-Mallory refused, arguing that he could maintain R/T control from Duxford and fix the wing's position south of the Thames using Direction Finding. This was completely unhelpful to 11 Group, which needed immediate information and communication with squadrons operating over its area. Park's exasperation can only be imagined – but Leigh-Mallory had his sights firmly set on a greater aim than cooperating with Park: he was determined to replace him as AOC 11 Group.

Although the morning remained dull, *Jafü* 2 resumed the fighter-bomber attacks, with five aimed at London throughout the day, during which, so typical of a British autumn, the weather improved by afternoon. Despite the pressure these attacks maintained on 11 Group, the enemy pilots remained sceptical: the previous day, thirteen fighters of III/JG 53 escorted just four *Jabos* to London, three of which were forced to turn about for various reasons, leaving just an officer cadet to drop his single SC250KG bomb on the capital. Clearly, the damage inflicted was hardly going to end the war, and the pilots, aware of the futility, mocked the propaganda spouting forth from Berlin, that the next bomb may be the bomb to break Britain's spirit to resist. Being at the forefront of these operations, the *Kanaljäger* were best placed to be in touch with reality.

Over the Filton sector of 10 Group, the morning weather was so poor that only one Hurricane, flown by Flight Lieutenant William Royce, was scrambled at 09.01 hrs and vectored to intercept a bandit over Gloucester, some 30 miles or so to the north. Having climbed to 24,000ft, when over Gloucester Royce was informed by Filton control that the bandit was approaching from the north and ordered to orbit. AA bursts to the west then alerted Royce's presence to a lone Ju 88 flying south-west, 2,000ft below him. A stern chase ensued, Royce setting the raider's starboard engine on fire over Hullavington, at 09.28 hrs, and expending all his ammunition as the German dived to 5,000ft and levelled out, flying south. According to 504 Squadron's ORB, the Ju 88 was 'in difficulty, dropped its bombs and was last seen very low over the sea at Bournemouth and later plotted over the sea'. Claimed as damaged, this may have been a Ju 88 of II/KG 76, which crashed on landing at Creil with combat damage.

At 09.25 hrs, Squadron Leader Archie McKellar scrambled with his 605 Squadron from Croydon, to patrol over Kent, on what was now 'A wonderful, still, warm autumn day' [ORB]. Whilst climbing, McKellar ordered the squadron into pairs at 10,000ft, and when over Ashford at 26,000ft, twenty Me 109s were seen 2,000ft above. Immediately, the Hurricanes formed a defensive circle – as the 109s dived to attack. Pilot Officer Peter Thompson, Red 3, reported that a 109 'came down steeply' over his left shoulder, damaging his propeller as the Hurricane went into a steep left turn. The German pilot overshot, however, pursued by Thompson, firing all the way for three seconds, pieces coming away from the 109's wing and aileron, by which time the combat had progressed south-east. Owing to the propeller damage, though, Thompson's aircraft 'was vibrating badly', so Red 3 returned to base. At 10.20 hrs, Squadron Leader Archie McKellar destroyed a 9/JG 54 Me 109 over New Romney, *Feldwebel* Adolf Iburg forced-landing in flames at North Fording House, where he was captured wounded and suffering from burns. No. 605 Squadron's CO also damaged another 109, but Pilot Officer John Rothwell, however, 'had part of his controls shot away and half the canvas of one side of the fuselage of his aircraft' [ORB]. He also returned safely to Croydon. Considering that only 605 Squadron was involved in this battle, and just two Hurricanes were damaged, the pilots of *Stab* II, 4 and 9/JG 54 rather optimistically claimed four Hurricanes destroyed.

Between 10.30 and 11.30 hrs, Pilot Officer Henry Baker of 421 Flight was spotting when his Spitfire was attacked by 'twenty Me 109s but took successful evasive action and resumed "Jim Crow" work' [ORB]. Sergeant Arthur Spears was also up spotting in a Spitfire, between 11.20 and 11.55 hrs and was likewise shot-up, returning to Gravesend where he 'made a good landing of his Spitfire with only half a rudder and cannon shells through his radiator and elevator controls' [ORB]. Although the time and place is unclear, *Oberleutnant* Freidrich-Wilhelm Strakeliahn of 2(J)/LG 2 claimed a Spitfire destroyed, so may have been responsible for one of these incidents.

At 10.15 hrs, Squadron Leader Athol Forbes DFC, who had taken over command of 66 Squadron from the outgoing Squadron Leader Rupert Leigh three days before, led seven Spitfires of 66 Squadron up on an unspecified 'Interception Patrol'. Apparently, Sergeant Harry Cook was 'shot down, but landed at base, he was uninjured' [ORB]. Details are scant, but interestingly Cook was flying a presentation Spitfire, X4599, one of two Spitfires provided by the Portsmouth & Southsea Spitfire Fund, and named, appropriately, 'Portsmouth & Southsea I'. Following Lord Beaverbrook's manipulation of what began as a simple enquiry regarding a Spitfire's purchase price by an overseas newspaper, the Spitfire Fund had given the Home Front an opportunity to hit back, albeit indirectly, and the enthusiasm around the scheme was phenomenal. Funds had sprung up all over the country, Empire and Commonwealth, the figure of £5,000 being set on a Spitfire, which countless people contributed to, from wealthy individuals, organisations, businesses – and even school children, who donated pocket money – and having begun in July 1940, these named aircraft had now started to appear.

Although the Me 110 had been defeated as a day fighter and fighter bomber over Britain by 27 September 1940, when 504 Squadron routed over Bristol he raid bound for Yate, like the Boulton Paul Defiant, which had fared badly in daylight, the type was sufficiently versatile to significantly contribute in other roles. Both types, in fact, found themselves pressed into the night-fighter role, and the 110 continued its reconnaissance role. A Me 110 of 7(F)/LG 2, engaged on a mission to photograph damage to London's docklands, however, was now about to fall foul of Spitfires.

Flying Officer Desmond McMullen, 'Cotal Leader', led 222 up from Hornchurch at 11.15 hrs to patrol Maidstone at 30,000ft, and Biggin Hills 92 Squadron was led off five minutes later by Flight Lieutenant John Villa, 'Ganic Leader', with identical instructions.

In the air, 222 Squadron was ordered down to Angels 15, then vectored towards an X-Raid. At 12.00 hrs, whilst over Maidstone, a 222 Squadron pilot reported a 'smoke trail' to McMullen, who gave chase with Red Section, leaving Yellow Leader in charge and continuing to patrol with the squadron. During the flat-out climb to 28,000ft, McMullen outpaced his Red 2 and Red 3, and upon sighting the approaching Spitfire the German pilot, *Oberleutnant* Roland Semmerich, turned to attack, head on. McMullen out manoeuvered the German and attacked from astern, as both aircraft dived. At 5,000ft McMullen got in a five-second burst

> and a glow appeared in the E/A's cockpit. E/A then went to ground level and tried to lead me into a high-tension cable. I was on the E/A's tail to within 50 feet of the ground. I then finished my ammunition into E/A, passed it, and dived at it, head-on, turning each time.

McMullen's Red 2, Pilot Officer Hilary Edridge, after losing sight of the 110 then 'saw four Spitfires milling around the same E/A at ground level'. Diving, Red 2 fired twice, noting 'white smoke coming from E/A.'

The other Spitfires belonged the 92 Squadron, which were also at 15,000ft when the 'smoke trail' was first sighted. As 222 Squadron attacked, 92 split up to cut off the 110's retreat. Flight Lieutenant John Villa joined the chase to ground level, but was hit on his second attack, there being 'a very strong smell of petrol'. Attacking twice more, the enemy aircraft's starboard engine stopped and Villa reported that this 'probably killed the rear-gunner'. He was right: *Unteroffizier* Rudolf Ebeling was killed outright. Pilot Officer Cecil Saunders of 92 Squadron also managed a burst at the doomed 110 before it crashed in a field at Bockinford, Horsmonden, at 12.50 hrs, where Semmerich was captured. The victory was shared by all pilots involved, but afterwards McMullen 'felt sick owing to petrol fumes and noticed that I had practically no petrol left. I climbed up to 3,000ft and started for West Malling. The engine cut out on approaching aerodrome and I forced-landed, wheels down.'

With improving weather, at 13.00 hrs 421 Flight sent up another spotter, and until landing at 14.55 hrs, Flying Officer James O'Meara DFC 'successfully shadowed formations of twenty and thirty Me 109s raiding the south-east'.

Between 12.30 and 13.30 hrs the Hornchurch-based Spitfires of 41 and 603 Squadrons patrolled the Maidstone line. Then, 41 was ordered to 'pancake', but having descended to 12,000ft were ordered back to the patrol line. Just as 41 Squadron had left Maidstone, at 13.30 hrs, 603 Squadron sighted a large formation of Me 109s, flying south-east. The Spitfires set off in pursuit, attacking individually. Pilot Officer Basil Dewey attacked a 109 'which was diving at high speed out to sea, and followed it down to about 500 feet, when after several further bursts, it hit the water in a slight turn'. South-east of Folkestone, Dewey was then attacked by another 109, at which he managed 'a few short bursts' before his windscreen iced over; the 109 was last seen 'going out to sea at almost sea level at high speed, with a stream of white glycol smoke coming from it'. No Me 109 is recorded as having crashed into the sea, but two 3/LG 2 machines did return to France with battle damage. Pilot Officer Colin Pinckney also claimed a 109 destroyed, and both Pilot Officer Basil Stapleton and Sergeant Andrew Darling subsequently filed claims for 109s probably destroyed, and Squadron Leader George Denholm DFC damaged one. No. 603 Squadron incurred no casualties.

Whilst 41 Squadron climbed back to height, at 20,000ft AA fire was seen over Chatham, and control advised of bandits approaching from the south-east. Regaining 30,000ft, 41 Squadron was 7,000ft above fifty to sixty Me 109s which were wheeling about, intending to return home. 41 Squadron then attacked the rearmost 109s, individually, at 13.45 hrs over the Biggin Hill area. Pilot Officer Eric Lock was patrolling alone, 2,000ft above 'Mitor Squadron', and attacked. The first a pair of Me 109s which passed below, between him and 41 Squadron. Lock claimed that 'after two short bursts from behind, he dived steeply, with glycol coming from underneath the starboard wing'; after another burst 'the engine started smoking and he dived into the sea about ten miles from Dover'. Lock then attacked another 109 lagging behind a formation crossing out over Dungeness; after three bursts, Lock claimed that 'he spun towards the sea', then attacked a third 109, which he left 'smoking in a shallow dive'. Although in Lock's opinion 'These two Me 109s would not get home', none of these enemy fighters were seen to crash but he was awarded one destroyed. As previously stated, there is no German record of a 109 crashing into the Channel.

Although Squadron Leader Donald Finlay was 41 Squadron's CO, on this occasion 'Mitor Leader' in the air was Flight Lieutenant Tony Lovell, who attacked a Me 109 in the centre of the rear formation, which 'fell into a spin and burst into flames', before he was attacked himself and broke away; Lovel was credited with a 109 destroyed, although this was not seen to crash. Just before Finlay attacked, he saw 'bombs fall from five Me 109s flying level in vic'. Firing at a 109 from astern, 'glycol immediately poured out', but the 109 turned into the sun, Finlay losing sight of it, so 'turned to chase numerous others'.

Pilot Officer Peter 'Sneezy' Brown was Finlay's Red 2 and at 13.45 hrs attacked one of the rearmost Me 109s from 'astern and slightly underneath. The E/A half-rolled and I followed him down. The aircraft crashed in a wood north-west of West Malling aerodrome and the pilot, who baled out, landed at Rooton. I then landed at West Malling.' Years later, Brown recalled,

> As Fighter Command had previously almost always refused to accept my claims, I decided on this occasion to get evidence. I landed at West Malling and went with the Intelligence Officer to see the German pilot, who was in the lock-up. After introductions we had a friendly chat through our interpreter. Finally, we shook hands and I wished him the best of luck. Why? Well, he was obviously not a Nazi but he was a fighter pilot and for some reason this made for a common bond. I took as a souvenir his life jacket, which was superior to our Mae Wests, ad wore it for the rest of my time on 41 Squadron. [No.] 11 Group allowed this claim to be confirmed!

The German pilot concerned was *Feldwebel* Ludwig Bielmaier of 5/JG 52, whose machine crashed at Mereworth.

Sergeant Aubrey Baker concluded 41 Squadron's scoresheet, claiming a Me 109 probable; all Spitfires returned safely to Hornchurch. Surprisingly, however, between 14.05 and 14.15 hrs, Squadron Leader 'Sailor' Malan scrambled with 74 Squadron from Biggin Hill to intercept another raid in the Maidstone area – where, Flight Lieutenant John Mungo-Park, Blue Leader, reported the Spitfires, flying at 29,000ft at 14.35 hrs, found thirty plus Me 109s 500ft, below – which were immediately attacked. The 109s first 'dived away', he reported, 'then zoomed up', pursued by Mungo-Park who hit one, which 'immediately spun. I followed him for about 4,000ft when his tail unit broke away'. Attacked by other 109s, Blue 1 broke away. The 109's pilot, *Unteroffizier* Franz Maierl of 3/LG 2, baled out but fell to his death with a burning parachute – his 109 crashed at Lenham Heath.

Pilot Officer Harbourne Stephen was Blue 2, 'at the tail end of the Squadron' and attacked a *Schwarm* of four Me 109s which dived for Dungeness. Stephen caught up at 9,000ft, engaging the left-hand 109, the tail of which 'started to break up as well as the top of his cockpit flying off'. In the ensuing melee with the other three 109s, Stephen gave one a six-second burst, and saw 'the pilot bale out and his machine went into a wood'. This was *Feldwebel* Karl-Heinz Wilhelm of 3/JG 77, who was captured unhurt, his aircraft crashing at Waldron, near Uckfield.

Pilot Officer Bryan Draper flying Yellow 2, and 'singled out a Me 109 which turned North across the Thames and then tried to return South'. After two bursts, the 109 went down 'obviously out of control' – but then Draper was hit from behind and his radiator damaged, forcing him down with a seized engine. Draper had, however, shot down *Oberleutnant* Albert Friedemann of 6/JG 52, who was killed when aircraft broke up mid-air, crashing on Plumstead Road, Welling, near Bexleyheath. Sergeant Thomas Kirk was Yellow 4 and followed Draper, firing at a 109 from which 'large pieces ... fell off fuselage and wings'. Kirk. However, was then attacked and shot down, baling out over Maidstone; admitted to Preston Hospital there, he died of his wounds on 22 July 1941.

It was a successful action for 74 Squadron, freshly returned to the fray from 12 Group, although Sergeant Clive Hilken was also shot down, and baled out wounded over Cowden. During the afternoon's fighting, 41 and 603 Squadrons had suffered no damage, and 74 Squadron had lost two Spitfire destroyed, their pilots wounded, whilst another was shot-up and forced-landed; pilots of 5 and 7/JG 54 claimed five Spitfires destroyed.

At 15.25 hrs (BST), *Hauptmann* Heinz Bretnütz, *Gruppenkommandeur* of II/JG 53, claimed a Hurricane destroyed whilst on an escort mission to London – his twentieth victory, for which Bretnütz became only the third member of JG 53 to receive the coveted Knight's Cross. Furthermore, at 15.40 hrs (BST) a Spitfire was claimed by *Oberfeldwebel* Wilhelm Donninger of 5/JG 54, his fifth victory, making him officially an ace. There were not, however, any combats or aircraft of any type lost at these times – although it cannot be entirely discounted that the times were wrongly recorded.

Despite the succession of attacks, overall little damage was caused – but twenty-five people were killed in London and fourteen more elsewhere. The night, however, would see heavy raids on London, the Midlands and Liverpool.

Coastal Command again flew its typical round of sorties, during which two Blenheims of 248 (F) Squadron were shot down off Norway by Me 109s of 4 and 6/JG 77, their crews lost. By night, FAA Swordfish mined Flushing, without loss. No. 2 Group's daylight operations again involved an uneventful North Sea sweep, but other sorties were aborted owing to poor weather. Bomber Command's night bombers – 135 – successfully attacked the Channel ports, German naval bases and industrial targets in addition to factories in both Italy and Czechoslovakia. A 58 Squadron Whitley on the Pilsen raid, however, was shot down by *Hauptmann* Karl Hulsoff of I/NJG 1, who staked the bomber home and shot it down over Yorkshire, and a 44 Squadron Hampden raiding Berlin was lost to flak; five other aircraft ran out of fuel returning from these raids and were either abandoned or ditched by their crews.

Weekly Report by Home Intelligence:

> The expense of burying several members of one family is a very real problem in poor districts, despite the waiving of clergy's fees, etc. As a result, some relatives are refusing to claim bodies, whose burial thus becomes the responsibility of local authorities. The natural distress of relatives in these circumstances is increased by the fact that such burials are often made without coffins. Local Information Committees in London report 'that public feeling would be greatly relieved if Local Authorities were empowered to make grants in certain cases to those who wish to bury their own dead.'

Monday, 21 October 1940

On this day, the ever-exasperated Air Vice-Marshal Keith Park issued a lengthy statement to the Air Ministry concerning minutes of the 17 October 1940 meeting:

1. The AOC 11 Group pointed out that the Air Staff Note and proposals attached to the Agenda were based on the experience of 12 Group using wing formations only on five occasions, whereas 11 Group had accumulated five and a half months' experience in using wings of three squadrons when the conditions were suitable. The first essential is adequate time to despatch, assemble, climb and move across country the wing formation. The short warning given to squadrons situated around London seldom gave sufficient time for the employment of wing formations. To be effective, wing formations required sky mainly clear of cloud layers. Lastly, the possibility of employing squadrons in wing formations was dependent on the State of Preparedness of squadrons at each sector, and this was directed by the intensity of enemy activity.

2. The primary aim of 11 Group has been to engage the enemy bomber formations BEFORE they reached vital objectives, such as aircraft factories, ammunition factories, London and sector

aerodromes. When conditions were suitable, squadrons were employed in wings, otherwise in pairs, and in emergency in single squadrons, if necessary to save an important factory from being bombed. On several occasions, single aircraft flown by station commanders have saved sector aerodromes by means of head-on attacks which broke up the enemy bomber formation when about to attack. The AOC 11 Group emphasised that if he had delayed engaging enemy bomb raids until after his squadrons had been put to operating height in wing formations, they would seldom have intercepted before vital objectives had been effectively bombed, and that to have adopted this policy would probably have led to the German long-range bomber force achieving decisive results in their heavy scale attacks on the south-east of England during August and September. The DCAS, C-in-C Fighter Command and Air Marshal Portal agreed that AOC 11 Group had followed the correct policy, and must continue this against future mass attacks by bombers.

3. The AOC 11 Group described how sectors on the North and South flanks of London had frequently despatched their squadrons in wings of three into Kent, in order to intercept bomb raids, but owing to inevitable delay in forming up and manoeuvring in wing formation, these squadrons arrived in time to intercept the outgoing bomb raids. These outgoing raids had been fairly easy to deal with, because during their inward journey they had already been attacked by pairs of Spitfire squadrons and Hurricane squadrons which had effectively dealt with the high fighter screen and close escorting fighters, and frequently broken up bomber formations which were retreating, having expended much of their ammunition. The AOC 11 Group pointed out that the Duxford Wing operated under these favourable conditions, and therefore it was not sound to compare their results in air combat with squadrons stationed around London, which were forced to engage the incoming bomb raids, fighter screen and close escorts. In spite of the difficult conditions under which 11 Group squadrons fought, mainly using pairs of squadrons, the results obtained on the last two occasions when the enemy employed his long-range bomber force compared very favourably with the results obtained by the Duxford Wings. For example, on 27 September, 11 Group squadrons destroyed 102, plus 28 probably destroyed for a loss of 15 pilots, and on 30 September destroyed 31, plus 20 probably destroyed for a loss of only 2 pilots.

4. The AOC 11 Group mentioned the danger to the high morale of squadrons in being taught by 12 Group that it is not safe to enter the south-eastern area except in wings of four or five squadrons, and that he had to issue special instructions to squadrons recently

trained in 12 Group and now in 11 Group emphasising the entirely different conditions under which squadrons located around London must operate, because of the close proximity of the German Air Force.

5. The AOC 11 Group stated that the arrangements in the last two months for obtaining quick reinforcement from 10 Group had been entirely satisfactory, and had on a number of occasions resulted in saving from heavy bombing the aircraft factories at Brooklands, Kingston and Langley, as well as sector aerodromes to the west and south-west of London. The reasons for this were that 10 Group squadrons had always proceeded immediately to the place and height requested by 11 Group, and had placed themselves under 11 Group's direction, so avoiding confusion to the Observer Corps, Air Raid Warning system and 11 Group squadrons. Moreover, 10 Group squadrons did not delay in forming wings which would have prevented their arriving in time to engage the enemy before he had bombed the vital factories.

6. The AOC 11 Group then proceeded to describe the confusion that had been caused to the fighter defences, the ground defences and the ARW system in the south-east through his Group not being informed when Duxford Wings had been unable to patrol the area requested, but had proceeded unknown to 11 Group, to the Kentish coast between 20,000–25,000 feet, thus causing new raids to be originated by the Observer Corps and AA units. This had not only prolonged the air raid warnings, but had necessitated the despatch of 11 Group squadrons to intercept friendly formations which had reported as fresh raids, indicating a third or fourth wave of attack.

7. The AOC 11 Group explained that he had not made a practice of calling for reinforcements from 10 and 12 Groups if he had adequate squadrons to meet the enemy bomber attacks, because he understood that the other groups had only sufficient squadrons to meet daylight attacks in their areas. As 12 Group stated they could always spare four of five squadrons from their area, he agreed, however, to call of them for a wing, whenever it was reported to be available in time to make effective interception, provided it would go where requested and 11 Group could be constantly informed of the position of the reinforcing wing.

Air Vice-Marshal Sholto Douglas, however, refused to allow Air Vice-Marshal Keith Park's comments to be added to the minutes – nor did he consider the AOC 11 Group's remarks concerning the Duxford Wing's failure to comply with instructions to be 'appropriate' to the document.

Air Chief Marshal Hugh Dowding objected to a statement in which it was said that he agreed with a particular point of view: 'Please do not say that I agree, reluctantly or otherwise. I am carrying out orders which I believe to be dangerous and unsound with our present strength of fighter squadrons.' Dowding's comment was ignored, and no correction made.

Air Vice-Marshal Sir C.J. Quintin Brand of 10 Group also suggested amendments – which were likewise ignored.

The only possible conclusion from all of this, and Air Vice-Marshal Trafford Leigh-Mallory's complete lack of cooperation of late, is that the meeting's outcome was a foregone conclusion, and the minutes arising are not a fair or accurate record of what was said that day in the air council room.

The war in the air, however, was still being fought. On 21 October 1940, Park issued a memorandum to all 11 Group sectors concerning '11 Group offensive sweeps':

1. When weather conditions are suitable and enemy activities justify their use, the Group may order offensive sweeps to be made.

2. At present, during daylight, there is almost continuous enemy air activity about the French coast and within the area Calais – Cap Griz [sic] Nez – Dungeness – Dover. This activity may develop into a mass attack by enemy bombers under cover of fighters. The enemy cannot, however, assemble and launch mass raids from north-west France later than about one-and-a-half hours before sunset and land back in daylight. It is proposed, therefore, to make use of this period whenever possible to surprise the enemy by making a sweep in strength through the Dover Straits.

3. For this purpose a wing of three squadrons, from North Weald or Northolt, may be ordered to provide sweeps. The executive order for the despatch of these sweeps will be issued by the Group Controller on the authority of the AOC.

4. Wings are to assemble, squadrons in company, in the vicinity of their bases and proceed to the area of sweep at a height of 25,000 feet.

5. Dispositions within the wing, the direction and method of approach to the sweep are to be decided by the Wing Leader in the light of the weather conditions prevailing.

6. Units comprising a sweep are not to remain in the vicinity of hostile territory, but are to make their sweep from SW–NE, engage any hostile aircraft encountered, and are to return immediately to their bases unless otherwise ordered by the Group Controller.

7. Fighter cover for the withdrawal of a sweep will be arranged on each occasion by the Group Controller as follows:

   i) Two Spitfire squadrons, on common R/T frequency, patrolling one squadron at 30,000 feet, one at 25,000 feet, on the Canterbury patrol line during the sweep. The Group Controller is to withdraw these squadrons to the Maidstone patrol line as soon as the sweep has withdrawn inland over Kent.

ii) Two Hurricane or Spitfire squadrons on Readiness Patrol at 15,000 feet on the Maidstone patrol line to counter any late raids by the enemy.

8. In case of additional cover for London area being required during the course of, or withdrawal of, a sweep, squadrons at the disengaged sectors will be brought to a specially high state of Preparedness.

These instructions are further evidence that Park was not simply thinking in defensive terms, and inflexibly using small formations. On the contrary and as this narrative has evidenced, the AOC 11 Group had been using wing formations for some time in defence, when appropriate, and was very much looking to go on the offensive, using whatever formation size was conducive to the operation concerned, and balancing offensive operations with the ongoing and concurrent need to defend the group area. The matter, however, was far from resolved.

At Gravesend, there was good news for 66 Squadron: both Flight Lieutenant Bob Oxspring and Pilot Officer Crelin Bodie had been awarded well-earned DFCs.

AC1 Bob Morris, Fitter IIE, 66 Squadron, Gravesend: 'It was at about this time that we started seeing DFM and DFC ribbons on certain of our pilots' tunics, well deserved every one [*sic*], we were all very proud.'

These decorations reflected on the squadrons as a whole – and there were many, from groundcrews to orderly clerks, from station medical personal and firemen, meteorological experts to operations room staff, and more besides, who provided the essential but unsung support to keep 'The Few' in the air.

On this day, the weather was extremely bad, so much so that at four RAF airfields fighters remained grounded until 11.00 hrs. Nonetheless, the enemy's Ju 88 force was active, flying lone intruder missions, blind through 10/10ths cloud, attacking Liverpool, Portland and Weymouth, the London area, Northampton, Bedford and the Gloster Aircraft Company airfield and factory at Brockworth. These skilled and brave Luftwaffe crews made long, unescorted, flights in bad weather to targets deep inside the British Isles – like the *Jabos*, the damage inflicted was slight overall, but nonetheless represented a growing investment of disruption and pressure on the RAF and civilian population alike.

In addition to its Brooklands facility, the Hawker Aircraft Company had a factory and airfield at Langley, 3 miles east-south-east of Slough, to the west of London, where the Langley Defence Flight maintained a sole Hurricane, fuelled and armed, in which a Hawker or RAF test pilot could intercept any raid on the location. At 11.55 hrs on this day, a civilian Hawker pilot, Mr T.B. Fitzgerald, flying an experimental cannon-armed Hurricane, intercepted and damaged a Do 17 over Henlow, north of London. From Kenley, Flying Officer Spencer Peacock-Edwards, a South African, and Pilot Officer Denis Pennington scrambled at 12.45 hrs, flying various vectors over Kent and Sussex. Over Mayfield, flying just above cloud, Peacock-Edwards sighted a Do 17 approaching from the south-east – and attacked it from above, head on and abeam, aiming at the cockpit. Pieces flew off the bomber, but it disappeared into cloud. No. III/KG 76 lost a Do 17 and crew on operations over England, which may have been either of these raiders, both of which were claimed as damaged.

At Wittering in 12 Group, at 12.00 hrs, Pilot Officer Wycliff Williams, a New Zealander, was scrambled alone to patrol base below cloud and intercept an enemy aircraft approaching. No contact was made, so the Spitfire was vectored towards 'a raid attacking Cambridge. Chased E/A out in easterly direction but did not make contact. Landed at Stradishall for refuel. Pilot crashed on taking-off from Stradishall to return to base and was killed.' Witnesses described how the 20-year-old pilot had flown low across the airfield but stalled and crashed; they buried him at St Margaret's, Stradishall, a long way from his Dunedin home.

The enemy was also active over 10 Group, and at 13.00 hrs, Flight Lieutenant Frank Howell, commanding 'A' Flight, and Pilot Officer Sydney Hill, patrolling from Warmwell, intercepted a Ju 88, 3 miles north of Lymington

> which had been reported to be posing as a Blenheim and, inter alia, machine-gunning Old Sarum RAF station from a height of fifty feet. Howell dived to decide what it was, and even after making sure that it was a Ju 88 with a big black cross was surprised to see the rear gunner signalling with smoke cartridges. Both pilots attacked in turn and after an unusual chase above and below tree tops the E/A hit the ground and blew up near Lymington. [ORB]

The bomber crashed at Manor Farm Field, Black Bush, Milford-on-Sea at 13.47 hrs, where the crew were all killed. This was 609 Squadron's 100th combat claim.

At 17.35 hrs a lone Ju 88 flew over Kenley airfield, Flight Lieutenant Myles Duke-Woolley scrambling to intercept. At 10 miles north-west of Dungeness the lone Hurricane pilot sighted the bomber, 5 miles behind him, at 16,000ft and 1,000ft above. Curiously, the enemy crew three a 'large red ball' [ORB] out of the aircraft; Duke-Woolley attacked from the beam, damaging the Ju 88, which dived for the sea and cloud cover, returning fire. Setting off in pursuit, Duke-Woolley reached 400 mph IAS, but was still unable to catch the raider, so returned to base, claiming it as damaged; a Ju 88 of KGr 806 crashed at Caen aerodrome due to combat damage.

There were no casualties arising from combat, but 245 Squadron at Turnhouse lost Sergeant E.G. Greenwood, whose Hurricane dived into Lough Neagh at high speed and exploded – as the pilot, who was reported missing, was on a 'battle climb' [ORB], oxygen system failure was the most likely cause.

Coastal Command suffered an unfortunate loss on this day. A 53 Squadron Blenheim took-off from Detling at 07.58 hrs on an unknown sortie, and whilst later flying over Manston, towards base, was given four signals before passing over Detling, when rockets were fired: 'low cloud and bad visibility apparently caused pilot to lose direction … Jettisoned bombs before crew baled out' – the aircraft, however, crashed onto Dernier Road, Tonbridge, demolishing two houses, killing a civilian and injuring sixteen more. 'Pilot later stated that he was hit between 1000 hrs and 1030 hrs, which caused his machine to become unmanageable' [ORB]. What Pilot Officer H.J.W. Meakin was 'hit' by is unclear, however, as there are no corresponding claims by the Luftwaffe or the defences.

No. 2 Group's Blenheims attacked Boulogne and shipping off the French coast, and swept the North Sea. Due to bad weather, the Battle and Hampden forces were grounded, but Wellingtons and Whitleys attacked Hamburg and Cologne. A 75 Squadron Wellington hit a balloon cable upon return, crash-landing at Manston, and another of the squadron's aircraft crashed near its Mildenhall base after raiding Hamburg, due to fog; the crew were injured. A Whitley of 10 Squadron, however, simply disappeared during a raid on Stuttgart.

Weekly Report by Home Intelligence:

> Criticism and concern about official news of aerial warfare and bombing is reported. The fact that German losses are now approximating to those of the British has been realised by the public and they are asking for an explanation; this they would like to come from Joubert or Sinclair.

Tuesday, 22 October 1940

Operations over southern England continued to be restricted due to fog and low cloud, which cleared sufficiently after lunch for Convoy FRUIT to be attacked off Dover.

As the weather cleared, two fighter sweeps were incoming, one over Kent, the other heading towards south-east London and the Thames Estuary. Squadron Leader 'Sailor' Malan and 74 Squadron were scrambled from Biggin Hill at 13.40 hrs to patrol Maidstone.

Malan, 'Dysoe Leader', reported,

> We were then given various vectors for single high raiders but did not connect.
>
> We were then told to join 92 Squadron at 32,000 feet over Maidstone and intercept raids approaching from south and south-east.
>
> I stayed at 30,000 feet for a while in order to push out exhaust condensation trail to frighten the bomb carriers.
>
> I then connected with 92 Squadron over Maidstone and came down to 28,000 feet to stop exhaust trail.
>
> Over Ashford at 28,000 feet, 92 gave a 'Tally Ho' below and circled, but I could see nothing. I then proceeded on vector 270° as ordered but did not connect and came back towards Ashford to join 92 Squadron.
>
> Suddenly, at approximately 1410 hrs, I saw six Me 109s just below at 26,000 feet, steering SE and attacked with my five-remaining aircraft (Yellow Leader had gone down with oxygen leak and Yellow 2 had followed him), Yellow 3 and Red 2 having dropped back earlier as they could not keep up and told to land.
>
> I attacked a leading Me 109 in a fast dive at ranges from 200 to 50 yards. He started to smoke heavily after second burst but levelled out at 8,000 feet on south westerly course. I continued to fire at him intermittently because he wouldn't go down, and I had to break off unexpectedly to wipe ice layer off armour windscreen.

Eventually he crossed the coast on southerly course at Hastings. I patrolled coast and watched smoke trail.

About one mile off coast smoke trail suddenly went down and I saw a splash. I returned through lack of petrol and bad visibility.

This Me 109, of 3/JG 51, which was also hit by Flight Lieutenant John Mungo-Park, who claimed a probable, was credited as destroyed, *Leutnant* Kurt Müller baling out to be rescued by the Hastings lifeboat, spending the rest of the war as a prisoner. Malan's number two, the comparatively inexperienced Pilot Officer Bob Spurdle, a New Zealander, survived being shot down and baling out, his Spitfire crashing near Tonbridge, but sadly the popular Flying Officer Peter St John was killed, crashing at South Nutfield.

At 14.00 hrs, twelve Hurricanes of 605 Squadron scrambled from Croydon to patrol base, and when at 22,000ft, flying east, in pairs astern over Tunbridge Wells, the Hurricanes followed eight Me 109s, heading south-east. Five other Me 109s, however, dived on 605 Squadron's rear sections from out of the sun, shooting down Pilot Officer John Milne, a Canadian, 'who forced-landed near Dorking, slightly wounded in his back. He put up a very fine show in managing to land his machine beyond the own, but in doing so fractured his hip, which will take a long time to mend' [ORB]. In response, Sergeant Eric Wright claimed a 109 damaged.

No. 257 Squadron left Martlesham Heath at 15.45 hrs for its first patrol of the day, rendezvousing with Stapleford's 46 Squadron over that airfield and climbing towards Dungeness at 20,000ft. Over Folkestone, AA fire was noticed in the direction of a force of seven twin-engined German bombers, which were crossing the coast, heading north – but then, to avoid the flak, turned about, heading back to sea. No. 46 and 257 Squadrons then turned west, flying along the coast, when Flight Lieutenant Peter Brothers DFC, who was leading 257, sighted the bombers approaching the coast again further west, 3 miles ahead of the Hurricanes. Owing to the limitations of the TR9 radio, however, the two squadrons were on separate frequencies, so 257 was unable to alert 46 to the enemy's presence. Suddenly, at 16.30 hrs, 257 Squadron's Yellow 1, Flying Officer The Honourable David Arthur Coke, his Yellow Section weaving above and behind, shouted a warning of nine Me 109s attacking from astern. The two Hurricane squadrons immediately scattered.

North of Rye, Coke attacked a Me 109 head on – 'my bullets hitting him from the engine right through to the tail' – but lost his target in the sun. This 109 was later confirmed as having broken up mid-air, wreckage partially falling in the sea and at Littlestone Golf Links; the pilot, *Unteroffizier* Heinrich Arp of 2/JG 26 was killed. Brothers pursued a Me 109 5 miles out to sea, hitting the enemy machine, from which pieces came off its fuselage and wings. The 109s, however, had the upper hand: 46 Squadron's Sergeant Joseph Morrison was shot down and killed, crashing at Newchurch, and 257 Squadron lost Pilot Officer Norman Heywood, who was killed when his Hurricane crashed near Lydd – the victim of 'friendly' AA fire – and Sergeant Robert Fraser, shot down and killed at Shadoxhurst. Sergeant Reg Nutter's Hurricane was badly damaged in the combat, but the pilot was unhurt and landed at Gatwick.

That afternoon, *Major* Werner Mölders claimed three Hurricanes destroyed north-west of Maidstone – but as the action fought with 46 and 257 Squadrons occurred over the coast, more likely these were the two Spitfires lost by 74 Squadron, and the Hurricane by 605 Squadron. This combat over the Kentish coast brought the day fighting to a close.

Coastal Command flew thirty sorties, escorting fourteen convoys, and 2 Group sent just one Blenheim to Amsterdam, which scored a direct hit on a merchant ship off the Hook of Holland. All Bomber Command night operations were scrubbed.

Weekly Report by Home Intelligence:

> Planned and voluntary evacuation still continues on a large scale. As the number of evacuees grows, difficulties of smooth organisation increase and, 'This week the result seems to be more chaotic than ever, especially in S.E. England.' A striking trend seems to be increased ill-feeling towards the upper classes 'who are accused of being the first to leave bombed districts, of taking the best places in reception areas, and of refusing to accommodate poorer evacuees.'

On this day, there was a perhaps surprising turn of events: the start of 'Operation Cinzano' – fascist Italy's contribution to the Battle of Britain.

Back on 16 July 1940, Count Gian Galeazzo Ciano, the Italian foreign minister and son-in-law of the Duce, the Italian dictator Benito Mussolini, recorded in his diary how Hitler had written to Mussolini, declining 'in a definite and courteous way the offer to send an Italian expeditionary force' to contribute to the aerial assault on and proposed invasion of Britain. Hitler explained that 'logistic difficulties would arise in supplying two armies. Hermann Göring too, in a conversation with Alfieri [author's note: Dino Alfieri, Mussolini's ambassador in Berlin], said that Italian aviation had too important a task in the Mediterranean to scatter its forces in other sectors'. Both Hitler and Göring were right, and at that time, entirely confident that the war was virtually won and defeating Britain simply a question of time, had no need of an Italian intervention or complications arising therefrom. In truth, Italy was unprepared for war, but Mussolini wanted war – and had ignored the advice of many, including the air strategist Marshal Italo Balbo, to side with Britain. The Germans' attitude, however, to the *Italiano Regia Aeronautica* – the Italian Air Force – changed as the conflict ground on.

By early September 1940, Mussolini had ordered creation of the *Corpo Aereo Italiano* – CAI, the Italian Air Corps – the specific task of which was to contribute to the Battle of Britain. The new force, commanded by *Generale* (Air Marshal) Rino Corso Fougier and based around Milan, comprised three *Stormi* (wings): one of the Fiat *Falco* (Falcon) CR 42 biplane fighter, and two of Fiat BR 20Ms, twin-engined, monoplane bombers; 20 *Gruppo* (group) was equipped with the new Fiat G 50 *Freccia* (Arrow) single-engined monoplane fighter, Cant Z1007bis of the 179 *Squadriglia* (squadron) provided tactical reconnaissance, plus various types fulfilled the communications role. Fougier had 200 aircraft at his disposal, and it was agreed that the CAI would transfer to bases in Belgium, where the firstd Italian airmen arrived on 25 September 1940. By 22 October 1940, the CAI was fully on station in Belgium, the bombers based at

Melsbroek and Chievres, the fighters at Maldeghem and Ursel, whilst Fougier's HQ was at Sint-Genesius-Rode a village between Waterloo and Brussels.

On 22 October 1940, *General* Petro Badogolio, the Italian Chief of Staff, gave orders, Ciano recorded, 'for a limited air action (against Britain). The Duce does not agree. He wants us to attack very vigorously, because he would like everything to go to pieces at first clash.'

Wednesday, 23 October 1940

Already, news of the CAI's arrival in Belgium had reached the Air Ministry in London. On this day, the Weekly Intelligence Summary shared with Churchill and the War Cabinet referred to the matter, concluding that the Italians' purpose 'appears to be solely reconnaissance'.

Due to the bad weather, all air operations were vastly reduced, and it was not until 17.10 hrs that there was any daylight action all. At that time, Flying Officer Robert Yule, a New Zealander, and Sergeant John Haire, an Irishman, intercepted and damaged a Ju 88 off Beachy Head. There were no other combat claims or losses by either side.

Coastal Command continued its usual operations, and attacked Le Havre by night, FAA Swordfish also mining the Maas Estuary. No. 2 Group attacked the invasion ports, and by night Bomber Command attacked Hamburg, Hannover and Berlin, these raids supplemented by seven aircraft from OTUs.

Weekly Report by Home Intelligence:

> The big provincial towns, which have been bombed, continue to show determination. On the South coast there is no despondency but some lowering of morale, thought to be due to the cumulative effects of warnings, raids, prolonged tension, long hours of work, the coming of winter, and more indirectly the absence of any spectacular war success.

Thursday, 24 October 1940

Again, due to the weather, there was little air activity, mainly involving the usual lone raiders targeting the aircraft industry, a large fire being started at Fairey Aviation in Hayes, Middlesex, and railway networks, the Great Western Railway line being blocked at Yatton in Somerset. Damage remained slight, however, and there were few casualties.

At 09.25 hrs, 74 and 92 Squadrons left Biggin Hill to patrol Maidstone at 15,000ft, Sergeant Donald Kingaby with Red Section weaving behind the latter. Cloud was 10/10ths and down to 2,500ft but clear above 6,000ft. Kingaby went to investigate an aircraft just above the clouds, and descended to 7,000ft. Identifying the aircraft as a Do 17, Kingaby attacked, hosing the cockpit, after which the bomber's port wing dropped, the machine diving vertically. Kingaby 'spiralled down and came out over the sea. A moment's search revealed a large green patch on the water and I am certain it was the last of the Dornier.' The combat had taken place at 10.20 hrs, 20 miles east of

Deal; Luftwaffe records indicate no such loss, but several Do 17s did return to France with combat damaged.

At 11.45 hrs, Sergeant Donald McKay of 421 Flight was sent up from Gravesend on an R/T test flight in one of the new Hurricane Mk Iis, and thirty minutes later was above cloud when he saw 'a single aircraft East of me, near Ashford. On investigation I discovered it to be a Me 109, and engaged. After a short dogfight the Me 109 turned over on its back and dived vertically back into the clouds.' That was the last McKay saw of his target, which he claimed as damaged. What the Me 109 pilot was doing alone over Kent is unknown, but presumably reconnaissance.

At Wittering in 12 Group, Red Section of 1 Squadron, Flight Lieutenant Mark 'Hilly' Brown, a Canadian, Pilot Officer Arthur Clowes DFM and Pilot Officer Anthony Kershaw, scrambled at 12.04 hrs to intercept Raid 10. When 3,000ft above cloud over St Neots, a Do 215 was sighted, attacked and shot down, the bomber crashing behind the Crown Inn, Eaton Socon, at 12.35 hrs. This was a machine of 3/*Aufkl.Gr.Ob.d'L* on a mission to photograph Coventry; one of the crew baled out low and was captured injured, but the other three did so too late and were killed. This bomber was also attacked by Flying Officer Count Manfred Czernin, who was half Austrian, Czech Pilot Officer František Fajtl and Sergeant Robert Hogg of 17 Squadron, patrolling from Castle Camps, who all made attacks and watch their target burst into flames and crash in a field near St Neots. The sections of both squadrons equally shared the victory – so, they again, this single enemy casualty became two on the scorecard. Sadly, this incident also led to the Battle of Britain's youngest service casualty.

No. 54 Maintenance Unit was based nearby, at RAF Cambridge, and sent a crew to recover the crashed Dornier. Disastrously, the mobile crane used contacted overhead electricity cables and tragically electrocuted AC1 Harry Clack. A Halton apprentice, and from South Norwood, Harry Clack was 16. On 8 August 1940, AC1 Raymond Wheeler, aged 17, had been killed aboard an RAF rescue launch, and on 16 August 1940, the youngest of 'The Few', Pilot Officer Martin Aurel King of 249 Squadron, who was 18, was killed in action over Southampton – both were interred at All Saints Church, Fawley, near Southampton. Without doubt, poor Clack was the youngest RAF serviceman to die during the Battle of Britain, and quite possibly the war.

Fighter Command suffered no combat casualties on this day, but there were more flying accidents: two Hurricanes of Exeter's 87 Squadron collided whilst on a routine patrol, Pilot Officer Trevor Jay baling out but killed when he struck his aircraft's tailplane; Australian Pilot Officer John Cock forced-landed back at base, unhurt. Up at Usworth, 43 Squadron also suffered a fatal accident when Sergeant D.R. Stoodley, a replacement pilot still non-operational, crashed upon landing during a dusk-flying exercise.

Coastal Command escorted twenty-two convoys and attacked enemy shipping, a Hudson of Wick's 269 Squadron being shot down off Norway by *Leutnant* Deuschle of 6/JG 77, the crew all missing. No. 2 Group carried out reconnaissance of the French ports, some of which were attacked, and North Sea, without loss. Bomber Command sent 113 night bombers to attack industrial targets and dockyards in Germany, a 38 Squadron Wellington failing to return, and a 102 Squadron Whitley was shot down shortly after taking-off from Linton-on-Ouse by *Feldwebel* Hans Hahn of 3/NJG 2; the aircraft crashed 4 miles from base, only one crewman surviving. Clearly, the *Nachtjäger* were becoming increasingly confident: this was the second bomber lost to a German intruder pilot in a matter of days.

Weekly Report by Home Intelligence:

> A considerable decrease has been noticed in the amount of talk about Mr Churchill. At one Postal Censorship Centre he is mentioned only one tenth as much as formerly, though, with one exception, all the remarks were favourable. The Censor comments that 'whereas in June people seemed to feel that only Churchill stood between them and disaster, now the ordinary people of England have shown that they too could play just as stubborn and important a part.'

It was on the night of 24/25 October 1940, that the Italians first attacked Britain. Captain Franco Bassi, a decorated Spanish Civil War veteran of the of 3 *Squadriglia*, based at Melbroech, led the mission: an attack on the east coast port of Harwich from 16,400ft, take-off time 20.35 hrs (BST). The operation was ill-fated: within minutes of taking off, one bomber crashed at Houtem. There were no survivors. Disorientated, a BR 20M crash-landed at Lille, another at Cambrai, and a crew abandoned their machine between Namur and Charleroi. The remaining Italian airmen found Harwich obscured by mist, and obviously blacked out, so were unsure whether any bombs hit the target. They did not, and four aircraft had been lost for nothing: it was an inauspicious start.

Friday, 25 October 1940

On 25 October 1940, Air Vice-Marshal Trafford Leigh-Mallory at last requested 11 Group's permission to send the Duxford Wing on a patrol over Kent. Air Vice-Marshal Keith Park agreed, and asked that the wing patrol the Sheerness – Maidstone line at 25,000ft. Once the 12 Group formation passed south of the Thames, however, 11 Group received no reports on its progress or position. This was clearly impractical and inappropriate, and so Leigh-Mallory finally agreed to the sensible operating procedure Park had already suggested five days previously. With the Battle of Britain almost over, it can only be regretted, with the benefit of hindsight, that this agreement was not reached three months before.

At 08.00 hrs, 501 Squadron at Kenley reported the weather as being 'Poor ground visibility and low cloud. The Squadron was at readiness from dawn to 09.00 hrs. One section took-off at 08.08 hrs to patrol Eastbourne. They attacked a Ju 88 but did no apparent damage before it escaped into cloud.'

Cloud was down to around 7,000ft, but was clear above, the slightly improved weather enabling a resumption of *Jafü* 2's fighter-bomber attacks on London, four waves of which would be unleashed throughout the day.

At 09.25 hrs, 46 Squadron, up from Stapleford, was patrolling south of Maidstone at 24,000ft when twenty Me 109s were sighted 1,000ft above and to starboard. Climbing, the Me 109s outpaced the Hurricanes and no contact was made, and similarly the squadron was unable to reach forty more high-flying Me 109s approaching from the north. When over the Biggin Hill area, Pilot Officer Blair Pattullo was 'flying guard to the Squadron at 27,000ft, made a beam ahead attack on these latter E/A and damaged one Me 109, pieces of the wing and fuselage being observed to fall off' [ORB].

The Spitfires of 66 Squadron were up from Gravesend at 08.35 hrs, also to patrol south of Maidstone, at 30,000ft. At 09.25 hrs, 66 Squadron was at 31,000ft and over 10/10ths cloud between Maidstone and the south coast when nine Me 109s were sighted 3,000ft below, flying south-east, very fast. The Spitfires dived to attack from astern, all but three, which broke right, diving away. A general dogfight ensued, during which Pilot Officer Stanley Baker, Green 4, gave one of these a long burst, closing from 180–50 yards:

> The E/A caught fire, apparently by the wing root, and went into a steep right-hand aileron turn at over 300 mph; this was at about 8,000 feet. We went through cloud at about 6,500 feet with flames enveloping the cockpit. I followed but the cloud was fairly thick in parts and at about 2,000 feet I ran into a heavy rain storm. I levelled out and found myself in very bad visibility over the sea.

The Spitfire pilot flew north, safely landing at Hawkinge and reporting that the 'E/A must have come down between Lympne and Hawkinge, about three miles out to sea. The pilot had not baled out. When the machine entered cloud the cockpit was well ablaze.' This Me 109, however, was not actually seen to crash – but at 09.30 hrs, 5/JG 54's *Oberleutnant* Joachim Schypek forced-landed and was captured at Lydd, owing to a damaged radiator.

Pilot Officer John Kendall was flying at the rear of 66 Squadron when battle was joined, hitting a Me 109, which dived steeply and was last seen 'beginning to spin and going straight down into cloud'; Kendall recorded his position as being 'near Hawkhurst', and 'unknown' damage being caused to the 109, which was actually destroyed: 5/JG 26's *Oberleutnant* Kurt Eichstädt's aircraft broke up, throwing him clear, but the pilot fell dead at Shovellers Green with an unopened parachute.

Flight Lieutenant Bob Oxspring, however, suddenly felt something smash into the fuselage behind his seat

> with an arse-twitching crash … It was something I had been expecting for the past two months, but when it arrived it surpassed all expectations. The stick felt loose in my hand and there was no elevator control … I saw flames spreading along the cockpit floor between the rudder bars … it was obviously time to depart. The Spit was starting to dive again as I strove to get upright and as my shoulders cleared the cockpit I was plucked out into space. The initial sensation was one of profound relief.

Oxspring landed safely by parachute, his trust Spitfire, X4170, which had carried him into many successful battles, crashing near Capel. The Home Guard 'whisked me away to the Kent & Sussex General Hospital for a check-up. There the super medical staff gave me a sympathetic going over, produced a most welcome four fingers of brandy and pronounced me fit for further adventures.' Before leaving hospital, Oxspring visited a badly burnt Hurricane pilot, swathed in bandages: 'As I left he wished me luck. I felt very humble.'

At 09.00 hrs, the Spitfires of 41 and 603 Squadrons had left Hornchurch, the two squadrons joining up at 23,000ft and continuing to climb towards Maidstone. Near Biggin Hill, at 09.50 hrs, the formation ran into thirty Me 109s. Sergeant John McAdam was Blue 3 of 41 Squadron, and together with the test of 'B' Flight providing the rearguard. McAdam sighted two Me 109s several thousands of feet below, but was unable to attract the attention of his formation leader, Flying Officer John MacKenzie. Giving chase alone, one of the 109s pulled away, McAdam attacking the 'straggler', firing a long burst whilst still diving. According to McAdam, 'The E/A then steepened its dive and hit the water about seven or eight miles SE of Dungeness'; a 9/JG 51 was shot down and crashed into the sea off Dover, the pilot of which was rescued.

During the great dogfight following the initial interception, Flight Lieutenant Norman Ryder, Pilot Officer Eric Lock and Pilot Officer Edward Wells all claimed Me 109s probably destroyed, and Pilot Officer John MacKenzie and Sergeant Terence Healey all claimed one each damaged. Pilot Officer Frederick Aldridge reported that 'Near Maidstone' he had shot the canopy from a Me 109, which 'came off and hit me in the radiator', only slightly damaging his Spitfire, which was only recorded in the pilot's personal combat report. No. 41 Squadron suffered no losses, and on this occasion was led in the air by Flight Lieutenant Norman Ryder, of whom Flying Officer Peter Brown wrote,

> I flew many times with him and his tactics were always to put the Flight or Squadron in such a position that all pilots could engage. This was different to the headlong rush I had experienced when flying with 611 Squadron in the Duxford Wing. Although Norman Ryder led his Flight during the Battle of Britain and afterwards in an outstanding manner, he received no decoration or recognition from Fighter Command – another unsung hero indeed.

Of 41 Squadron's 'second and unsung legend', Pilot Officer Eric Lock, Brown wrote,

> He was basically a loner who personified the Squadron's motto of 'Seek and Destroy' – but it did seem to be a one-man battle. Although he took-off with the Squadron he often disappeared, landing later on his own reporting another victory. Fighter Command was suspicious of his claims and refused to confirm some of them.

During the engagement in question, 603 Squadron, fared badly, making no claims but losing two Spitfires to the Me 109s: Pilot Officer John Soden and Pilot Officer Peter Olver were both shot down and baled out, wounded, both Spitfires crashing at Brede. Pilot Officer Ludwik Martel was also shot-up, returning to base unhurt (in Spitfire

Mk IIA, P7350, still flying today with the RAF Battle of Britain Memorial Flight). Squadron Leader George Denholm's pilots made no response.

At 09.20 hrs, 229 Squadron left Northolt to patrol the Guildford line, possibly with 302 (Polish) Squadron, the orders of which are unrecorded. The former squadron 'encountered no enemy aircraft and returned to base' [ORB], but Flight Lieutenant Franciszek Jastrzębski of 302 (Polish) Squadron failed to return, who had been 'seen to leave formation and glide towards France' at 10.50 hrs; the 34-year-old airman's body later washed up on the enemy coast, at Sylt.

At 11.24 hrs, 249 Squadron scrambled from North Weald and again joined up with 46 Squadron from Stapleford over base, to patrol at 25,000ft. Some Me 109s were soon seen, which headed back to the coast, but the RAF formation's rearguard, apparently a mixed formation of 46 and 249 Squadrons' pilots, 'were chased by 109s. Two Hurricanes went into flames.' [Form 'F']. These were the aircraft of 249 Squadron's Sergeant John Beard, who baled out wounded over Maidstone, his Hurricane crashing at Linton, south of the town, and the Free French *Adjutant* Henri Bouquillard, who forced-landed near Rochester, wounded. Yellow 1 of 249 Squadron, Pilot Officer Tom Neill DFC, attacked the leader of the attacking Me 109s, from which 'large pieces broke off', the enemy fighter diving away vertically to be claimed as a probable. No. 46 Squadron's Pilot Officer Blair Pattullo, however, was shot-up during the 109s' attack and whilst subsequently attempting a forced-landing crashed into a house at Woodstock Road, Romford, and was killed.

No. 46 Squadron made no claims in response, but 249 Squadron's Blue 2, Pilot Officer Pyers Worrall and four other Hurricanes headed north-west, after another group of Me 109s thought to be *Jabos*. Worrall attacked on of these over the Sevenoaks – Woolwich area, and saw it 'fall to pieces with its petrol tank alight'. A second 109, probably short of fuel, made no effort to attack Worrall, who 'chased this aircraft all over the sky towards the South', but lost it north of Dover. Patrolling there, Worrall found six Me 109s, which he suspected were awaiting the *Jabo*'s return and which made no effort to attack a Lysander, which passed beneath them.

Blue Leader of 249 Squadron, Pilot Officer William Millington claimed a 109 destroyed, which '*presumably* [this author's italics] crashed in the vicinity of Hastings or the sea'. After a stand-off with various groups of Me 109s, the Hurricanes returned to base.

Flight Lieutenant Eustace Holden was leading 501 Squadron, up from Kenley, patrolling over Ashford at 30,000ft, travelling north-east, when at 12.10 hrs and after two vectors a dozen Me 109s were seen to starboard, flying south-east. No. 501 Squadron attacked, Holden chasing a 109 in a vertical dive, which he lost in cloud. Holden's Blue 2, Czech Vladimir Zaoral, followed Blue Leader into attack, firing at the left-hand Me 109 and watching 'the left wing fall from the E/A, which dived away out of control'. This could only have been the Me 109E-4 flown by *Hauptmann* Hans Asmus of *Stab*/51, which broke up mid-air and crashed near Marden. Finding himself sat in a wing and engine-less aircraft, Asmus baled out and was captured. The 109 involved was a famous machine, in fact, being the usual mount of *Major* Werner Mölders, who, since 22 October 1940, had been testing a new Me 109F, still with the Rechlin codes SG + GW. Curvaceous in appearance, with rounded wing tips and lacking the

109E's tail struts, square wingtips and more angular design, the new Franz, looked not altogether unlike a Spitfire – and its performance, when it entered operational service the following year, outclassed the Spitfire Mk II.

Holden, who, with had also very likely fired upon Asmus, then attacked another Me 109, from out of the sun, over Hawkinge, having dropped to just above the thick cloud layer which was at 7,000ft. Attacking from out of the sun, 'glycol streamed out of both his radiators', but then Holden broke away when attacked by two other 109s; the one he hit was not seen 'to hit the ground' but was considered 'undoubtedly destroyed'. Indeed it was: *Feldwebel* Leonhard Birg of 7/JG 51 forced-landed with an overheated engine and was captured at Hunton. An Me 109 was also claimed destroyed by Pilot Officer Vivian Snell, Red 3 (although no combat report appears to have survived).

Further west, standing patrols were also being maintained by Tangmere's squadrons, 145 and 213 Squadrons having been up over base at Angels 10 between 09.20 and 11.00 hrs without event. Then, at 11.25 hrs, 145 Squadron scrambled again to patrol Dungeness and Tenterden. Whilst heading east along the Sussex coast at 20,000ft, however, Pilot Officer Baudouin de Hemptinne, a Belgian, suffered engine failure, so glided inland to forced-land. At 1,000ft the Merlin completely cut-out 'and fumes and flames started up from the engine. He forced-landed at Hayward's Heath Golf Course and five minutes later his petrol tanks blew up. He was somewhat bruised and later, when seen by the MO, was put off flying for seven days.'

Whilst 145 Squadron's Pilot Officer Robert Yule was patrolling with the squadron over Kent, at 12.30 hrs he saw Me 109s below:

> [He] tried to communicate by R/T but someone had left their transmitter on. After repeated attempts to get into communication, he broke formation and dived. He was joined by two Spitfires and next he knew was being fired at. A bullet entered his left leg and another penetrated his glycol tank. He forced-landed at Burwash and was taken to Pembury Hospital. The bullet extracted from his leg was of German manufacture.

The squadron made no combat claims.

At 12.31 hrs, Squadron Leader Robert Tuck and 257 Squadron left Martlesham Heath with orders to meet Northolt's 615 Squadron and patrol together over that aerodrome; North Weald's station commander, Wing Commander Victor Beamish flew on this patrol with 257 Squadron.

From Rochford, at 13.00 hrs, with yet another threat incoming, 222 Squadron was scrambled and ordered to join 74 and 92 Squadrons, up from Biggin Hill, at 10,000 feet, but as the 'Tigers' sighted enemy aircraft in the meantime, 222 were instructed to climb to 30,000ft, in 74 Squadron's direction, which was Maidstone.

Squadron Leader Robert Tuck led 257 Squadron north-west, towards Central London, at 25,000 feet, sighting twenty Me 109s below and ordering individual attacks. In the dogfights ensuing, Tuck claimed two damaged Me 109s. By 13.25 hrs the battle had ebbed south-east and was over the Maidstone area, where 92 and 222 Squadrons were also in action, in what had become a confused mass of whirling fighters. Tuck reported diving on a 109 3,000 feet below, firing and seeing 'bits fly off him' before the target dived away, south-east. After 'two good bursts from dead astern at close range saw a large cloud of sparks suddenly burst from his starboard wing root-end and then the whole starboard wing came off and back and narrowly missed my aircraft', Flight Lieutenant John Villa, 'Ganic Leader' of 92 Squadron, reported attacking a 109 from which 'a large amount of glycol poured out of the E/A and it dived vertically down. Half the tail fell off in the dive and part of the starboard mainplane. E/A dived vertically through cloud.' Clearly, both pilots had hit and claimed the same 109, which again became two on the scoresheet: the Me 109 concerned crashed a mile south of Sevenoaks; the pilot, *Leutnant* Hermann Ripke of 8/JG 26, baled out but fell dead 5 miles away.

No. 92 Squadron's Blue 3, Pilot Officer Thomas Sherrington, was also successful, attacking a 109 diving for cloud cover, 'firing all the time. He took no evasive action except climbing slightly and I think I started a fire in the cockpit. I broke away and saw him go onto his back and dive through the clouds where he crashed near Sevenoaks.' This 109 was also attacked and claimed by Flight Lieutenant Eric 'Tommy' Thomas, who was leading 222 Squadron on this occasion:

> I got on the tail of a Me 109 and opened fire at 200 yards, closing to about seventy-five yards, when the E/A completed about three downward flick rolls and pulled straight up. I followed and put in another burst and glycol streamed from both radiators. Pilot Officer Edridge also fired at the E/A after this. I got on his tail again and he went straight down. At about 20,000 feet the pilot jumped out and I narrowly missed colliding with him. I followed the E/A down and it disappeared in the clouds, vertically. I came below the cloud and recognised West Malling airfield.

The vanquished German pilot was *Feldwebel* J. Gärtner of 8/JG 26, who was captured, his aircraft crashing at Congelow Farm, Yalding – and was another multiplied statistic.

Wing Commander Victor Beamish, flying with 257 Squadron, claimed a probable and a 109 damaged, and Pilot Officer Gerald North and Flying Officer David Coke of 257 Squadron also claimed a probable each. The squadron's only casualty was Sergeant Harold Shead, who was shot-up, his brakes failing upon landing back at base, causing the aircraft to overrun the landing strip; the pilot was unhurt. No. 92 Squadron's Sergeant Donald Kingaby also claimed a Me 109 damaged, over the Channel, only Pilot Officer John Mansell-Lewis being shot-up and forced to land at Penshurst, unhurt. In the hectic action over Maidstone, 222 Squadron's Flying Officer Desmond McMullen also chased the 109s back to the Channel, claiming one destroyed, which crashed into the sea, and damaging another which was left heading home trailing black smoke; 222 suffered no loss. Finally, Squadron Leader Joe Kyall DSO DFC, commanding 615 Squadron, damaged two Me 109s over Maidstone, there being no other action for his Hurricane pilots.

As the enemy withdrew, in addition to the two pilots killed over Kent, two others were also left behind: 3/JG 77s *Gefreiter* Karl Reisinger was attacked and his radiator damaged, forcing him down near Saltdean, and 5/JG 54's *Leutnant* Ernst Wagner became disorientated and forced-landed on the Lydd Ranges, near Dungeness. Both enemy pilots were captured unhurt. Both sides overclaimed, with III/JG 26 and II/JG 54 pilots claiming a total of five Spitfires destroyed – no Spitfires were lost. The raid had achieved little, indeed, in view of the fighter opposition, JG 53's *Jabostaffel* dropped their bombs on the eastern Kentish coastal town of Ramsgate.

Having been withdrawn from Biggin Hill on 14 October 1940, to recuperate at Leconfield, six days later 72 Squadron was moved to Coltishall, changing places with 74 Squadron. Since arriving at the Norfolk sector station there had been little operational flying, owing to the bad weather, but at 14.00 hrs on 25 October 1940, Blue Section, were scrambled and when over Aylesham vectored to intercept a bandit plotted at 27,000ft north of Cromer. As the Spitfires climbed to intercept what was a 2(F)/122 Me 110 on a sortie from Brussels-Everéto photograph the Rolls-Royce works at Derby, 'an object, apparently square and flat was jettisoned from the E/A. It left a trail of smoke behind it as it fell. The E/A waggled its wings and did a sudden stall turn over our aircraft, and dived down towards a cloud bank, heading out to sea.' [ORB]. Blue 1, Pilot Officer Norman Norfolk attacked the 110: 'There was a flash and a big puff of smoke from the E/A, which dived down through cloud and was last seen at about 1,500 feet, fifteen miles NE of Great Yarmouth'. The enemy pilot, *Leutnant* Konrad Wacker, ditched in the North Sea, and was picked up by HMS *Widgeon*, but his *Bordfunker*, *Gefreiter* Gerhard Gneist, remains missing.

Mid-afternoon, the *Jabos* and fighters were back on what would be the day's final raid on London. No. 66 Squadron was patrolling over 10/10ths cloud, over the usual Maidstone line, when Pilot Officer Crelin Bodie became separated from the squadron. When flying at 15,000ft, the Spitfire pilot sighted a lone Me 109 heading home and followed, using 12lb boost. The 109 pilot saw the danger and dived, Bodie being unable to close further than 500 yards. Firing, he 'got in a lucky one, for a small amount of white and black smoke issued'. Now, the Spitfire caught up the Me 109, from which glycol splashed over Bodie's windscreen. The. German then disappeared into cloud and claimed as a probable. No. 66 Squadron had no other contact.

No. 501 Squadron, led again by Flight Lieutenant Eustace Holden, left Kenley at 14.43 hrs to patrol Biggin Hill, encountering a formation of Me 109s at 27,500ft between Tenterden and Cranbrook. The Hurricanes had a height advantage of 500 feet and attacked. Holden, Blue Leader, hit a 109, which 'streamed out glycol. I sat on his tail ...' Sergeant Raymond Gent had singled out the same 109, and saw Holden's Hurricane ahead of him in the chase. Being higher than Holden, Gent dived faster, got ahead and fired: 'at first white smoke appeared then black, followed immediately by flames behind the cockpit. The 109 then started entering the clouds, losing speed, and passing over the top of it I noticed that inside the cockpit was a mass of flames'. Holden had already 'at point blank range let it have all my ammunition. Everything poured out and bits flew off. The pilot jumped at 2,000 feet and landed at Idlesham.' This machine, of 7/JG 51, crashed into a drainage ditch on Lidham Hill Farm, Guestling, inland of Hastings; the pilot, *Feldwebel* Willi Koslowski baled out and was captured seriously wounded. Yet again, the same 109 was claimed destroyed by two pilots, both of whom were accredited accordingly. During this action, both Pilot Officer Tony Whitehouse and Pilot Officer Vivian Snell were shot down and baled out; both were returned to Kenley, unhurt, by army transport.

The final defending squadron to contact the, now withdrawing, enemy was 41 Squadron, as Squadron Leader Robert 'Bob' Beardsley DFC, at the time a sergeant-pilot, later recalled,

> This day, the CO, Squadron Leader Don Finlay, had lent me his new Spit Mk II, donated by the Observer Corps, as my aircraft was unserviceable, with the admonition that I was not to 'bend it'! We were patrolling Maidstone and attacked our usual target, the escorting fighters. I hit my target, which caught fire and was immediately hit myself with a cannon shell through the engine. I made for Hawkinge and landed safely without causing any damage. I was greeted by the Station Commander (again!) who said 'I hope you are not going to make a habit of this, Sergeant!' I returned to Hornchurch by train and underground via London – parachute on my lap! I was greeted by my CO who demanded to know what I had done with his aircraft! He was not amused – well, it was a *new* Spitfire and a *Mk II*! The CO of Hawkinge apparently recommended that I was put up for a DFM but our own CO was not at that time recommending for an award anyone who had not achieved five kills. The aircraft was apparently repaired and fought again.

Beardsley had been shot down by *Oberleutnant* Eduard Schröder of 6/JG 53, the *Jabostaffel* of which had randomly scattered bombs between Ramsgate and South London.

No. 41 Squadron had met the enemy south-east of Maidstone at 16.00 hrs, the fight rolling south to Dungeness. In this aerial mayhem, in addition to Beardsley's claim for a 109 destroyed and one damaged, Flying Officer Guy Cory claimed two damaged, and Pilot Officer John MacKenzie and Pilot Officer Edward Wells one damaged 109 each. Afterwards, MacKenzie, ran out of fuel, forced-landing at Tandridge, unhurt; his Spitfire was undamaged.

During the day, 35 people were killed in London and 200 injured, with 7 more being killed beyond the capital. At night, the German bombers returned to the capital, leaving ninety-nine Londoners more dead by dawn.

By day, it was a typical day for Coastal Command, which by night sent Blenheims to attack shipping at Antwerp and Brest's power station; a Hudson patrolling a convoy failed to return to RAF Aldergrove. Apart from uneventfully sweeping the North Sea, 2 Group's daylight operations were aborted due to bad weather. At night, Bomber Command sent ninety-two aircraft to attack docks, marshalling yards and industrial targets in Germany, and the big guns around Calais. From these operations a 61 Squadron Hampden simply disappeared, and a 144 Squadron Hampden crashed near Gainsborough, injuring the crew.

Weekly Report by Home Intelligence:

> From a study of those sheltering in the tubes, 'it seems that about one Londoner in twenty-five shelters in the tubes more or less regularly, though not necessarily going there every night. Much the largest single

group is still that which uses home shelters.' One of the major difficulties in home shelters is dampness; this is also reported in many public shelters in the London area.

Saturday, 26 October 1940

On this day, Secretary of State for Air Sir Archibald Sinclair visited both Duxford and Fowlmere to discuss wing tactics with its pilots. A subsequent visitor was Undersecretary of State for Air Harold Balfour:

> Sinclair asked me to go to Duxford fighter station and listen to what Douglas Bader and other formation leaders felt. Churchill had visited 12 Group units at Duxford and also the Secretary of State just the week before he asked me to pay my visit. Sinclair had come away feeling that there was a conflict of operational views between the two groups which was felt acutely by units at Duxford. So up to Duxford I flew. I had my talk with Douglas Bader and others. To my chief, in compliance with his request, I wrote for him a true account of what I found. This was the famous 'Duxford Memorandum'.

So, here we have politicians interfering in service matters, and only visiting 12 Group – without even discussing the matter with Fighter Command's C-in-C. The whole thing had become a Machiavellian farce.

The weather on 26 October 1940 was typically autumnal, 41 Squadron at Hornchurch reporting 6/10th–9/10ths cloud and visibility at 4,000 yards, improving to 12–15 miles as the day wore on – and 92 at Biggin Hill noted the weather as 'Dull with low cloud' [ORB]. Consequently, fighter-bomber raids were reduced to one major assault on London, whilst small formations of Me 109s prowled around the south-east, and, as usual in such cloudy conditions, a constant stream of lone Ju 88s were active over Britain – all of which maintained pressure on Fighter Command.

After a quiet start to the morning, at 10.05 hrs 92 Squadron scrambled from Biggin Hill, leading 74 Squadron, to patrol base, then join with 66 Squadron, up from Gravesend, to patrol Maidstone at Angels 30. Concurrently, the Me 109s of II and III/JG 53 were incoming, the fighters escorting just four fighter bombers of the *Jabostaffel* to attack London.

At 10.40 hrs, when at 20,000ft over the Tunbridge Wells area, 92 Squadron's Sergeant Ronald Fokes, Blue 1, was weaving around Ganic Squadron when thirty Me 109s were sighted 10,000ft below, which had 'already dropped their bombs', according to Flight Lieutenant Robert Holland, Yellow 1. Individual attacks were ordered and Fokes dived on and attacked a 109, firing from astern: 'glycol fumes streamed out of the E/A. He continued to go down and I followed, holding my fire. We went through the clouds and the enemy pilot jettisoned his hood and flames came from the cockpit. The E/A turned over on its back but I did not see the pilot bale out.' Nonetheless, Fokes claimed the 109 destroyed, as indeed it was: 6/JG 53's

Unteroffizier Karl Geiswinkler was killed and crashed at Pembury. Geiswinkler was also attacked by 92 Squadron's Red 2, Pilot Officer Roy Mottram: 'Small bits seemed to fly off the wings and white smoke came from the starboard side of the fuselage ... Another Spitfire did a quarter attack and I broke off the engagement.' Mottram claimed a probable but was credited with a 109 destroyed – so Geiswinkler also became two on the balance sheet. Pilot Officer Trevor Wade and Pilot Officer Cecil Saunders also damaged Me 109s over Tunbridge Wells, whilst Flight Lieutenant Robert Holland, forced to break off his first attack owing to a Spitfire crossing his sights, pursued two retreating Me 109s to Dover, the enemy fighters descending to 7,000ft and dodging in and out of cloud: 'I eventually got in range dead astern of the left-hand rear one and gave three short bursts. I think the pilot was killed as the aeroplane dived away to the right and hit the sea.' *Oberfeldwebel* Kaufmann of 4/JG 53, however, was not killed and baled out over the sea, to be rescued by the *Seenotdienst*, and two Me 109s of 6/JG 53 returned to France severely damaged. Nos. 66 and 74 Squadrons took no part in the action, during which, although no Spitfires were lost, *Feldwebel* Stefan Litjens of 4/JG 53 claimed one destroyed over Tonbridge.

With JG 53 having penetrated much lower than usual, at 10,000ft, at 10.55 hrs 229 and 302 (Polish) Squadrons were scrambled from Northolt to patrol Croydon at 15,000 feet, 302 (Polish) Squadron leading, and bar the way to South London. Squadron Leader Jack Satchell, commanding 302, reported seeing fifteen Me 109s on his starboard bow, flying north-east. Apparently, the 109s saw the Hurricanes simultaneously as they turned south:

> I followed with the Wing and after a long chase the E/A commenced to dive down and I got in one burst of about two seconds, closing from 300 to 100 feet, and saw one large piece and several small pieces of the E/A fly off – he then disappeared in cloud. Just before opening fire I noticed, through a hole in the cloud, that we were almost over and just to the East of Boulogne Harbour. I also saw an aerodrome with a number of Me 109s landing and taking-off. I also saw a little flak fire. As there were, by the time I ceased fire, no other E/A above the clouds, I rallied the Wing and returned to England. I attacked from the direction of the sun at about 8,000 feet. I was later informed that two crashed Me 109s had been seen on the ground. The E/A were at 18,000 feet when first sighted, with clouds 10/10ths at 7–8,000 feet.

Sergeant Antoni Markiewicz, Blue 3 in 302 (Polish) Squadron, broke away from his section to chase a lone 109, which was disappearing into cloud. Taking the German by surprise, Markiewicz opened fire, the 109 breaking-upwards, steeply, with 'intense black smoke issuing from the starboard wing and centre section. After executing a loop the E/A turned on its back and went out of control.' The Polish Hurricane pilot followed the diving 109 before being attacked by two Me 109s on his port bow and three on the starboard bow, forcing him to take evasive action and escape in cloud. Having also noticed the German airfield below, Blue 3 made off back to base.

The French coast was a dangerous place indeed for the Hurricane pilots to be, the combat occurring at 11.30 hrs, both Satchell and Markiewicz claiming probables. The Poles suffered no loss, but 229 Squadron fared less well.

As the Poles chased the 109s across the Channel, 229 Squadron followed on behind, but, according to the 229 Squadron ORB, 'This was subsequently proved to be a trap and the two squadrons found themselves over the French coast and returned to base without having engaged the enemy'. That, however, was incorrect as 302 (Polish) Squadron had engaged over Boulogne. Emerging from cloud at 4,000ft, Flying Officer Geoffrey Simpson, Blue 1 of 229 Squadron, saw a He 59 just offshore, which he followed with his Blue 2 and 3, namely Flying Officer Donald McHardy and Sergeant Rupert Omanney. After two bursts from the latter, the lightly armed communications aircraft of *Seenotflugkommando* 3, engaged on an ASR mission, alighted on the water – both crewmen were killed. The Hurricane pilot, who was then 'hotly engaged by Me 109s from the rear, and gun fire from the shore, made off and flying low across the Channel reached home base' [ORB]. Both Simpson and McHardy, however, were reported missing. Both had been shot down, Simpson crashing into the Channel, never to be seen again, whilst McHardy crash-landed near Boulogne, hitting his face on the gunsight in the process, breaking his jaw. He survived, and was captured. In this action, *Leutnant* Friedrich Geißhardt of I(J)/LG 2 and *Oberleutnant* Egon Troha of 9/JG 3 claimed Hurricanes destroyed west of Boulogne, and *Feldwebel* Otto Junge of 6/JG 52 another over Cap-Blanc-Nez.

At Kenley, 501 Squadron had been held at fifteen minutes availability from dawn until 09.00 hrs, when brought to readiness. At 11.35 hrs, the squadron scrambled with orders to join Croydon's 605 Squadron, then patrol towards the south-east coast. Squadron Leader Archie McKellar reported combat occurring at 12.15 hrs over Mayfield:

Leading Turkey Squadron with 501 Squadron following above and behind my Squadron in pairs and at 28,000 feet. Control had passed information about several lots of bandits and detailed me to a raid that was approaching and heading NW. Shortly after this I noticed about sixteen E/A at 2 o'clock when I was flying 0.10°. I informed the Squadron of this and checked up that there was nothing above and about except 501 Squadron, as far as I could see. The Squadron then carried out an attack in pairs from out of the sun. I selected one of the further back Me 109s and attacked from a quarter to dead astern, at once saw my De Wilde hitting and vapour pouring from the fuselage, more like petrol tank being punctured. At the same time, another Me 109 passed in front and very slightly above about 100 yards away. I therefore engaged this Me and could see DW again hitting. This machine rolled very slowly onto its back and I could see pieces flying off the underside as I was continuing to fire, it then dived away inverted. I followed, still firing, and then saw black smoke pour from it, followed by flames, it then entered cloud and although I followed I could see no sign of it, but presume it crashed somewhere in the Mayfield area. These Me 109s, instead of the usual dull yellow nose had bright orange noses.

McKellar was accredited with a 109 destroyed, although not seen to crash, and one damaged. Similarly, Green 2, Pilot Officer James Hayter, attacked one of the rearmost Me 109s, and just before breaking away, 'black smoke appeared from it and it rolled over on its side and dived down vertically, South of Mayfield'; awarded as damaged, this was clearly the same machine hit by McKellar – which was also fired upon by Pilot Officer Bob Foster, who claimed it as damaged: 'Pieces fell off ... he turned over on his back and dived almost vertically through the clouds.' This was also the same Me 109 hit by Pilot Officer Alec Ingle, Blue 1: 'I saw the greater part of the wing root and starboard side of the fuselage disappear and petrol and glycol steam out. E/A broke down to the right in a vertical dive ... disappeared into cloud at about 8,000 feet.' This time, the 109 was awarded as a probable. Sergeant Eric Wright, Yellow 1, attacked a different Me 109, which emitted 'black and white smoke and oil from him covered my windscreen and leading edges. He discontinued his climb and was gliding in a SW direction at 15,000 feet, still emitting smoke' – this being *Unteroffizier* Arno Zimmermann of 7/JG 54, who forced-landed on the beach at Lydd, where he was captured, wounded. Four of 605 Squadron's five claims, therefore, referred to the same Me 109, only Wright clearly attacking a different machine. Although no corresponding Luftwaffe claims are apparent, Flying Officer Cyril Passey 'landed near Rotherfield, having been shot in the prop, the machine being wrecked but he was uninjured' [ORB].

Flight Lieutenant Eustace Holden was leading 501 Squadron, which climbed to 30,000ft and was vectored north, towards bandits. As 605 Squadron climbed to attack,

[Holden] singled out the highest E/A. He tried every evasive action, losing height meanwhile. I got in several short bursts followed by a five-second burst which struck E/A and caused glycol to emit from one radiator. I noticed my bullets igniting on E/A. I eventually lost him in cloud at 8,000 feet, still smoking, and as this was West of Hastings it is improbable he reached land.

Ten miles north of Beachy Head, Sergeant James Lacey, Yellow 2, had been unable to single out an enemy aircraft during 501 Squadron's diving attack and so descended to 14,000ft. Seeing a pair of 109s flying at 7,000ft, just above cloud, Lacey attacked

the rearmost ... which had apparently been in a fight before as it had a thin white trail of petrol or glycol streaming out behind. Almost as soon as I opened fire the Me 109 caught fire and dived into the clouds, the rear portion of the fuselage burning fiercely. The second Me 109 now turned and attacked me and after a short while I found it expedient to dive into cloud to escape it.

Holden was credited with a probable, and Lacey a 109 damaged – but, again, this was clearly one and the same aircraft. That day, 1/JG 52 lost *Oberfeldwebel* Oskar Strack, who was shot down and crashed into the Channel off the south-east coast, so it is likely that his was the Me 109 concerned. No. 501 Squadron suffered no loss in the clash.

For most 11 Group squadrons, there was little or no operational flying as the weather closed in, with a thick ground mist, but at 15.30 hrs 605 Squadron was scrambled again to patrol north-east Kent. Pilot Officer James Hayter, who had damaged a Me 109 on the previous patrol, sighted a *Schwarm* of Me 109s but owing to R/T being faulty was unable to communicate with the rest of 605, so attacked the enemy alone. Hayter, however, was shot down, his Hurricane crashing near Cranbrook, although the pilot baled out and was unhurt. Hayter, had, it would seem taken on *Major* Adolf Galland and his *Stabschwarm*, the JG 26 *Kommodore* claiming a Hurricane destroyed near Maidstone. There were no other combats, claims or losses over south-east England that afternoon.

To the west, over the 10 Group area, there was considerable reconnaissance activity by lone German aircraft, twelve of 234 Squadron's Spitfires scrambling on ten interception patrols throughout the day, although only one interception took place. At 14.41 hrs, Red Section intercepted and attacked a Ju 88 south of the Lizard, but lost it in cloud; Pilot Officer Edward Brian Mortimer-Rose DFC and Bar, Red 1, claimed it as a probable.

Well to the north, at 18.30 hrs RAF Lossiemouth in Scotland was attacked from 100ft by three 3/KG 26 He 111, from Beauvais – one of which was hit by the airfield's defences and exploded in mid-air; there were no survivors. However, when the raiders appeared, six Blenheims of 21 Squadron were awaiting take-off for night-flying:

> One bomb fell on the landing field, destroying aircraft T2233, damaging beyond repair aircraft R3760 and severely damaged aircraft L1878 and L8744. Of the aircrew, Pilot Officer Slater and Sergeant Jones were killed, and Sergeant Green and Sergeant Bristow injured. Of the groundcrews, Corporal Holland was killed and AC Windelar injured. [ORB]

A Hudson of Coastal Command 269 Squadron, Coastal Command, was also destroyed in a raid on Wick airfield.

Coastal Command's Blenheims set fire to Brest power station during the morning, and a Hudson attacked shipping off Den Helder, recording a near miss. A Hampden patrolling off the east coast attacked and damaged a He 115 floatplane of 1/506, which was forced to land on the sea, the two crewmen taking to their dinghy, landing at Yarmouth the following day, where they were captured. There were, however, Coastal Command losses: a FAA Swordfish of 821 Squadron disappeared; 42 Squadron lost two Beauforts and crews off Norway to 4/JG 77 Me 109s, and a Hudson of the Heston-based PRU was shot down off Walcheran by *Leutnant* Hans-Erich Heinbockel of *Stab III/JG 54* – the crew were lost.

Blenheims of 2 Group uneventfully patrolled the North Sea, all other daylight operations being scrubbed owing to unsuitable weather. By night, Bomber Command was busy, ninety-seven aircraft attacking Berlin, oil and communications facilities, the invasion ports and mining the Gironde, an 83 Squadron Hampden and crew failing to return from the latter operation, and a 102 Squadron Whitley, on a raid to Politz, was hit by flak whilst returning over the enemy coast, the crew abandoning the aircraft and baling out safely over Yorkshire.

Weekly Report by Home Intelligence:

> There have been fewer rumours this week, though the usual crop of Haw Haws come from Ashchurch, Eastbourne, Hailsham, Lewes, Polegate and Rochester. In a good many places in North Wales Haw Haw is reported as saying: 'You may think you're safe in North Wales, but your turn is coming!' Rumours are not uncommon that the lull in raids is due to our use of a secret weapon. Some people believe that places which exhibit German planes 'receive special attention' from bombers; so strong was this feeling in Streatham that a Messerschmitt exhibited in aid of a Spitfire fund was removed 'in deference to public opinion'.

Sunday, 27 October 1940

The weather improved slightly, with cloud varying from 5/10ts to 10/10ths and, in the Hornchurch sector 41 Squadron reported visibility at only up to 5 miles. The enemy, however, was determined to launch another day of heavily escorted fighter-bomber raids targeting London.

At 07.50 hrs, 66 Squadron left Gravesend to patrol over Kent – but landed without Pilot Officer John Mather, who had apparently dropped out of formation and was killed when his Spitfire (P7539, currently being restored to flying condition) crashed behind the Half Moon public house at Hildenburgh, near Tonbridge. At the time, it was assumed that anoxia owing to oxygen system failure was responsible, but eyewitnesses on the ground heard a single burst of machine-gun fire before the roar of an over-revving Merlin. Although the Spitfire pilots saw no enemy fighters, and no corresponding claim apparently survives in German records, it is quite possible that Mather was ambushed and picked off by an unseen assailant.

The first recorded combat of the day, however, involved the Hurricanes of 249 Squadron, five of which took-off from North Weald at 07.35 hrs to patrol Hornchurch. Almost immediately airborne, the pilots sighted a Dornier

> dropping bombs near North Weald aerodrome. This aircraft was chased in and out of cloud and Pilot Officer Neil caught it up about ten miles from the Thames Estuary. He fired nearly all his ammunition, saw smoke pouring from the starboard engine and port engine. Smoking from both engines, this aircraft disappeared into the clouds and was claimed as a probable. [ORB]

Several Do 17s of KGs 2 and 3 returned to base damaged by RAF fighters throughout the day.

At 08.00 hrs, Gravesend's 421 Flight's Flight Lieutenant Billy Drake was on his second 'Jim Crow' sortie of the morning, flying a new Hurricane Mk II, when he was 'attacked by twelve Me 109s over Channel. Evaded and shadowed them, saw them

183

joined by six other Me 109s, the formation extending line abreast over five miles.' [ORB]. Most of Fighter Command's squadrons had caught on and abandoned the suicidal vic formation prescribed by the Air Ministry, individual squadron commanders experimenting by flying sections in pairs or fours in line astern – but it would take until May 1941 before the Tangmere Spitfire Wing finally imitated and perfected the German *Schwarm*. In line abreast, stepped up, with at least 200m between each aircraft, the German pilots flew without having to concentrate on formation flying and, in the words of Air Vice-Marshal Johnnie Johnson, the RAF's officially top-scoring fighter pilot of the Second World War, 'looked lean and dangerous, like a pack of hunting dogs'.

Across the Channel, *Oberleutnant* Ullrich Steinhilper and comrades of 3/JG 52 in Coquelles, near Calais, 'were beginning to feel the effects of being constantly mauled by the RAF'. Contrary to faulty Luftwaffe intelligence assessments of Fighter Command's strength and damage inflicted upon Fighter Command, Steinhilper and friends, at the *Kanalfront*, knew the reality: Hurricanes and Spitfires still appeared in numbers and were ever-ready for combat. Whilst Fighter Command remained under pressure, and had problems of its own, the truth was the *Jagdwaffe* on the *Kanalfront* were, Steinhilper realised, 'slowly but inexorably bleeding to death'. Since arriving in the Pas-de-Calais on 1 August 1940, Steinhilper had flown over 150 missions over England, once completing seven sorties in a single day – and these statistics were not uncommon. It was, it seemed, a constant round of take-off for an operational flight of an hour, land, re-arm and re-fuel, repeat, in what was a typically regimented German schedule – but, every time, the defending fighters were waiting. And the Spitfire Mk II, with its service ceiling of 37,200ft, as opposed to the 36,500ft of the Me 109E, was making its presence felt.

The Spitfires, Steinhilper lamented, would climb to their patrol height, as the waves of German fighters approached, then as the 109s turned the defenders attacked. Having landed and replenished, the defenders were up again, ready to meet the next raid, which, with Teutonic precision, would come in twenty minutes or so later. So far as Steinhilper was concerned, the whole thing had degenerated into a war of attrition, 'an airborne version of the dreadful trench-warfare of 1917/1918. Sooner or later, one side had to run out of aircraft and young men to fly them.' And with 60 per cent of the *Jagdflieger*'s flying time being spent over hostile territory, it was clear against whom 'the odds were well and truly stacked'. 'Time', Steinhilper knew, 'was now against us and time was running out'. In truth, time had been stacked against Germany since Hitler's uncertainty and lack of decision back in July 1940 – and time would certainly run out on this day for *Oberleutnant* Ulrich Steinhilper.

Like the Allied 2nd Tactical Air Force in the build-up to and after D-Day in 1944, most of the German fighter units in the Pas-de-Calais had operated from temporary airfields and tented accommodation. The 3/JG 52 was no exception and on 27 October 1940, Steinhilper awoke in his camp bed with the damp and cold autumn morning discouraging him from leaving the warmth and comfort of his blankets. Rising, Steinhilper wondered 'When would my time come', and with traumatic visions of combat flashing before his eyes, he wondered 'How much more could we take?' It was a fair question: of the thirty-six pilots I/JG 52 began the Battle of Britain with, precious few remained alive, and only four with more than three years' experience. Early that morning, Steinhilper was off on a pre-breakfast escort mission – just eight Me 109s being all that remained of the whole *Gruppe*. After taking-off, the 3/JG 52 Me109s climbed to 32,000ft, above the *Jabos*, and headed for London. Historically, the *Jagdflieger* had always enjoyed the height advantage – but now the new Spitfires and Hurricanes Mk II were turning the tables. Steinhilper remembered that the patrolling Spitfires were at 35,000ft, following the Germans, ready to attack when the 109s turned for home, and when, therefore, at the tactical disadvantage, the RAF pilots now having the benefit of height and speed.

With trouble inbound, at 07.50 hrs, Squadron Leader 'Sailor' Malan, Dysoe Leader, scrambled from Biggin Hill with 74 Squadron, with orders to patrol base at 30,000ft. In the air, orders were received to 'intercept "Snappers" over Maidstone – Gravesend', as reported by Canadian Flying Officer William Nelson of 'A' Flight, who was flying as Malan's Red 2. *Oberleutnant* Ulrich Steinhilper was flying his usual Yellow 2, but experiencing pitch control difficulties, causing him to straggle behind the JG 52 formation, which was providing top cover, in company with his friend and *Rottenhund*, *Feldwebel* Lothar Schieverhöfer; Steinhilper watched the Spitfires, and hoped he 'would survive the attack' then came the warning '*Achtung! Sie Kommen! Sie Kommen!*' ('Danger! They are coming! They are coming!') as the Spitfires curved towards the 109s.

Flying Officer William Nelson:

> We climbed rapidly and at 26,000 feet saw some gun bursts and turned towards them. Two Me 109s suddenly appeared by themselves across our bows and the Squadron Leader immediately got on tail of leading E/A and I closed with the inside E/A. He took no evasive action as we came out of the sun and I got a five-second burst, slight deflection, at 150 yards. He immediately started a half-roll down with white smoke streaming out, obviously glycol. I followed him easily at first and gave three two-second bursts and more (illegible) came from his engine, almost blinding him from me. At 2,000 feet he entered the cloud vertically and I pulled out in order to avoid hitting ground, having got up tremendous speed.

It is likely that Pilot Officer Peter Chesters, Yellow 4, attacked the same Me 109:

> The E/A I attacked was diving down to the clouds and then I followed him. E/A saw me and attempted to turn onto my tail. I managed to turn inside him and put a burst into his engine, causing it to stop. E/A forced-landed on Penshurst Aerodrome with wheels up. ... As I did not know my position and was short of petrol I landed on the same aerodrome. Engagement took place at 3,000 feet.

So ended the war for *Feldwebel* Lothar Schieverhöfer, who was captured at 09.15 hrs, unhurt, having come down on the emergency landing ground at Penshurst, west of Tonbridge.

Flight Lieutenant John Mungo-Park, commanding 'B' Flight and was Blue Leader,

> turned on to two E/A which had become detached from the main body. On opening fire I realised that only a few of my guns were working, owing to freezing. I closed right in to fifty yards and saw pieces of tail unit falling off before I broke away owing to lack of ammunition. Blue 2 [author's note: Sergeant Bill Skinner, whose personal combat report has not survived] attacked the E/A and I saw it going down with black smoke coming out and Blue 2 still firing from astern.

Mungo-Park and Skinner had hit Steinhilper, who recalled, 'A staircase of Spitfires queuing for the attack'. Having been ordered to right-turn for home, being on the inside of the German formation with the least distance to travel in the turn, Steinhilper had been relieved – but owing to transmission difficulties the rest of JG 52 had turned left – leaving Schieverhöffer and Steinhilper alone, exposed and vulnerable, Then, the inevitable had happened. Steinhilper's Battle of Britain, however, was not quite over.

Pilot Officer Harbourne Stephen was Yellow Leader:

> I was slightly below the rest of the Squadron and as I saw a Me 109 shoot at a Spitfire I tried to attack the E/A but was out of range. The E/A turned and dived and I followed and gave him two more bursts. At the end of the third burst the E/A burst into flames.

This was *Oberleutnant* Anton Pointer, the *Staffelkapitän* of 8/JG 27, who baled out and was captured, unhurt, his 109 crashing at Hooks Wood, Lenham, between Maidstone and Ashford.

No. 74 Squadron, however, lost a pilot: Sergeant John Scott, who had only joined the 'Tigers' four days before, was shot down and killed, his Spitfire exploding at Dundas Farm, Elmsted, near Ashford; *Oberleutnant* Erbo Graf von Kageneck, *Staffelkapitän* of 9/JG 27, claimed a Spitfire destroyed over Ashford. Squadron Leader 'Sailor' Malan returned to base with a damaged Spitfire, *Hauptmann* Max Dobislav, *Gruppenkommandeur* of III/JG 27, claiming a Spitfire south of Maidstone.

The Hurricanes of Croydon's 605 Squadron were also patrolling that morning, having scrambled at 08.50 hrs; the previous day, 605 had become the first fighter squadron to re-equip with the new Hurricane Mk II, only trialled so far by 421 Flight, and now Squadron Leader Archie McKellar and his pilots flew these into battle. Leading Turkey Squadron, McKellar climbed to the west and was informed of 'a lot of enemy aircraft about and above'. At 18,000ft, Squadron Leader Harry Hogan's Hurricanes, up from Kenley, joined with 605 Squadron, and at 23,000ft McKellar informed Biggin Hill control that the formation was ready to intercept a raid, and was told that four bandits were heading north-west. Flight Lieutenant Alec Ingle, Blue 1, then notified McKellar of bandits below, and, dropping his nose, Turkey Leader saw some sixty Me 109s, all heading south.

Oberleutnant Ulrich Steinhilper, nursing his damaged Me 109, emerged from cloud, having escaped the Spitfires of 74 Squadron, only to realise that he was now flying just above and behind a formation of Hurricanes. Valiantly, Steinhilper prepared to attack, alone, but then his windscreen iced over, preventing this, so he prudently retired back into the clouds – knowing that if spotted by the Hurricanes it was game over. By now, however, his engine was dangerously overheating, his temperature gauge showing 130°C, leading the pilot to conclude that his radiator had been damaged. At first, Steinhilper, radio call-sign *Euele* (Owl) 2 was unable to raise Coquelles on the R/T, but then made contact, informing *Hauptmann* Förster at the Calais ground station that he was now gliding towards the coast and would hopefully make the Channel. Reminding Steinhilper that 3/JG 52's *Adjutant* had recently ditched but drowned, Förster advised *Euele* 2 only to ditch is absolutely necessary, and alerted the *Seenotflugkommando*. Down to 1,600ft, the doomed 109 was fired upon by light AA fire, from a small town Steinhilper did not recognise, and re-started his engine, to get another burst of power. Soon cutting the engine, Steinhilper reported that he was now gliding across Pegwell Bay, but even at minimum throttle the engine was rapidly overheating again – and when full throttle was applied, seized completely. Not wanting to forced-land in Kent and deliver a 109 to RAF intelligence, there was only one option: bale out.

As Steinhilper descended by parachute, his Yellow 2 crashed at Upstreet, near Canterbury, into a field of cows – the 20mm ammunition immediately exploding, which Steinhilper mused was 'a kind of ridiculous last salute'. Landing near a canal embankment, wounded in the left leg, after being fired upon by a civilian with a shotgun, who took the wounded enemy pilot in custody. Steinhilper reflected on the events bringing him 'to this bleak and inhospitable place. My schooling, the Hitler Youth, Labour service, early flying training and then my years and tribulations in the Luftwaffe. A long, long journey for one still so young.' The 'journey' would continue, as a prisoner of war in England and Canada, and later as the inventor of word processing – Ulrich Steinhilper, a five-victory ace, would die peacefully in Stuttgart, aged 91, in 2009.

As *Oberleutnant* Ulrich Steinhilper reflected on his predicament, however, the fighting above continued; for I/JG 52, the losses incurred meant that the *Gruppe* was rendered non-operational and withdrawn to rest and re-fit at Krefeld.

Upon sighting the Me 109s over Redhill, at 09.15 hrs Squadron Leader Archie McKellar ordered 605 Squadron to attack, from above and abeam, himself diving on a 'mass' of Me 109s. The 109s and Hurricanes scattered all over the sky, McKellar attacking and hitting a 109 from astern, which 'slowly rolled onto his back', flying south, pursued by McKellar, who was eager 'to destroy him before he could enter cloud'. Unfortunately, the Hurricane pilot's windscreen iced over and his target was lost in cloud, 'twenty miles South of Croydon' – but was shot down: *Gefreiter* Carl Bott of 2/JG 52 baled out and was captured unhurt, his aircraft crashing near East Grinstead.

Green 3, Pilot Officer Douglas Scott, hit a Me 109, from which black smoke emitted, claiming it as damaged. Sergeant Eric Wright, Yellow 1, chased a 109 south, to the East Sussex coast, firing a two-second burst before 'on firing my guns the nose of my aircraft fell away'. The German was flying south-east when Wright caught up and fired again, when 'large pieces fell away from him and glycol smoke poured from him and he fell away and continued straight down, out of control. I last saw him going into haze at 1,000 feet in a vertical dive, either just inland or out to sea from Beachy Head. Nobody baled out.'

Flight Lieutenant Alec Ingle, Blue 1, had been first to sight the bandits, leading 605 Squadron towards them until Squadron Leader Archie McKellar could see them and took over. Ingle then attacked two Me 109s without result, before, somewhat boldly, tacking onto the rear of a formation of enemy fighters,

> heading south-east in the hope that I would not be identified, this was the case and I closed right up behind a 109. The enemy aircraft at this time were in a loose formation, mainly abreast, stretching over a distance of about 10 miles at 25,000ft. I observed one machine peel off from the right to attack two Hurricanes flying 4,000 feet below in close formation, when a second machine peeled off I followed him and attacked from ¾ astern, diving, a two second burst had no visible result. I closed to 100–150 yards, during which time he alternately climbed and dived, violently and frequently. I gave him a five second burst from directly astern and he pulled out of the dive at 20,000 feet, glycol and petrol streamed out of him followed by dense black smoke, rapidly gathering in intensity.

Years later, Ingle recalled what happened next:

> I was returning to base from an engagement, flying at about 12,000 feet when I was hit from an unexpected quarter by quite heavy fire.
>
> I dived into cloud below me, whereupon the engine seized and black oil covered the screen. When I came out of cloud I looked for a suitable field on which to land but most were heavily obstructed. However, I sighted a field within which I estimated I could make a wheels-up landing and headed towards it by peering around the windscreen. To do this I had to release the shoulder lock on my Sutton Harness.
>
> At about 800 feet I decided to turn into the field but there was no response to the ailerons, so had to proceed straight ahead. On looking at the starboard wing I noticed a large hole with two jagged ends of wire protruding through it. I then saw a row of large trees ahead and by jinking, saw that there appeared to be a gap between them ahead. I was low, had no ASI and could not turn. I tried the flaps but got no result and suddenly a railway cutting appeared – but I just managed to jump the aircraft over it and arrived somewhat heavily on the other side among the trees.
>
> My head was obviously impinged on the gunsight because I could not lock my harness, and, somewhat dazed, I was surprised to see a number of people around me, including the District Nurse. She stuck a plaster on my head and the next thing I knew I was back at Croydon. I vaguely remembered that I should recover the radio crystals, as they were in short supply, but whether I did or not I cannot recall.
>
> The aircraft had been hit by cannon shell and machine-gun bullets from below; the aileron controls were severed, airspeed indicator damaged, the oil and hydraulic pipe lines fractured and, of course, engine seizure.

Flight Lieutenant Alec Ingle, who had been promoted to command 'B' Flight this very day, came down at Barcombe, and was 605 Squadron's only casualty in the action.

As 605 Squadron attacked the Me 109s, Squadron Leader Harry Hogan, Red 1, leading 501 Squadron, led his Hurricanes to attack 109s which broke away from the main formation. At 09.40 hrs over Redhill, Hogan attacked one which half-rolled away, which he pursued at 'tremendous speed', hitting the fighter's port radiator, which streamed glycol. The German then entered cloud, but although Hogan could see the enemy aircraft he was unable to attack further owing to his throttle jamming fully open for a couple of minutes.

As 501 Squadron attacked, Pilot Officer Kenneth MacKenzie, a skilled and wily fighter pilot, held back at 23,000ft, awaiting 109s emerging from cloud having taken evasive action. Sure enough, a yellow-nosed Me 109 came out of cloud at 16,000ft, upon which MacKenzie crept up from astern, firing two short bursts: 'He developed a glycol leak almost at once, and then flames began to lick out below the pilot, behind the engine; he appeared to be out of control, going down in a gentle spiral. I followed to 3,000 feet and saw more smoke and flame going back along the fuselage.' Considering his opponent 'finished', Red 2 returned to base, claiming a 109 destroyed. Another was claimed as damaged by Pilot Officer Denys Jones, who managed a three-second burst at a diving Me 109, which 'disappeared in a cloud of white smoke'. No. 501 Squadron suffered no losses in this engagement.

Two Me 109s were lost in this skirmish: 4/JG 53's *Unteroffizier* Hermann Schlitt was reported missing, and 7/JG 54's *Unteroffizier* Arno Zimmermann belly-landed on the beach at Lydd, where he was captured unhurt. With so many RAF pilots claiming to have hit 109s which streamed glycol, it is impossible to say who was responsible for the demise of these two enemy airmen. Only Flight Lieutenant Ingle of 605 Squadron was shot down, but *Oberleutnant* Hans-Ekkehard Bob of 9/JG 54, *a Jabostaffel*, claimed a Hurricane destroyed 10km east of Tunbridge Wells, and *Unteroffizier* Heinz Wiest of 3/JG 77 one at Tonbridge.

The Spitfires of 66 Squadron were also patrolling over Biggin Hill area, Pilot Officer Charles Cooke flying Blue 4 and reporting, at 09.45 hrs, seeing twenty Me 110s being engaged by Hurricanes at 17,000ft; no other squadron, however, making claims or otherwise, reported the presence of Me 110s, which seems somewhat unlikely. Nonetheless, Cooke claimed to have attacked and damaged two Me 110s before landing back at base at 10.15 hrs.

The Hurricanes of 17 Squadron had left North Weald at 09.30 hrs to patrol Hornchurch, Polish Flying Officer Pawel Niemiec and Sergeant Glyn Griffiths being detached to seek and destroy a Do 17. This they found over Canterbury at 10.15 hrs, both pilots attacking before the raider disappeared into cloud west of the Isle of Sheppey; it was shared as damaged.

On 14 October 1940, Flight Lieutenant James Sanders DFC formed 422 Flight (later 96 Squadron) at Shoreham, which equipped with Hurricanes to evaluate the use of single-seater fighters in the night-fighter role. For the remainder of the month, several Hurricanes were maintained at readiness as a defensive measure, enemy aircraft being 'sighted and given chase on numerous occasions, but only in one instance was contact made with the enemy' [ORB]. This occurred at 11.00 hrs on 27 October 1940, when

Sergeant Alfred Scott sighted a He 111 at 8,000ft south of Guildford; attacking from above, black smoke emitted from the port engine and 'the airscrew faltered. The E/A disappeared into cloud and was not seen again.' [ORB].

Whereas previously the lone German raiders had primarily sought targets connected with aircraft manufacture and general industry, recently they had returned to harass RAF airfields. Three He 111s of I/KG 1, for example, flew low across the Channel in an effort to avoid RDF detection, then hedge-hopped to attack the Coastal Command aerodrome at Detling. One hangar was damaged, at 11.30 hrs, but one of the bombers was hit by AA fire and subsequently ditched off the Essex coast; the crew took to their dinghy and were captured unhurt.

To the west, lone raiders were also active. At 11.50 hrs, Green Section of Warmwell's 609 Squadron, Flying Officer Terence Forshaw and Flying Officer Piotr 'Osti' Ostaszewski, a Pole, and Pilot Officer Paul Baillon, caught and

> fired upon an elusive enemy bomber, believed He 111 or Ju 88 near Andover with uncertain results. The E/A was believed by the controller to have been shot down, but this report was not confirmed. Baillon received return fire which damaged his oil system, compelling him to bale out over Upavon. His machine landed near Central Flying School and burnt up. Green 1 highly praised the vectoring of the duty controller, again Flight Lieutenant Fieldsend. These recent bouquets for the Operations Room were no doubt appreciated coming, as they did, after a long series of brickbats. [ORB]

Again to the west, 145 and 213 Squadrons were up from Tangmere and patrolling base, then vectored to Mayfield and Tenterden, climbing to 31,000ft. The Hurricanes returned to base at 12.20 hrs, after an uneventful patrol, but both Flying Officer Dudley Honor and Sergeant Duncan Sykes of 145 Squadron forced-landed, at Halton and Amersham respectively, having run out of petrol; both Hurricanes were written off, but the pilots were unhurt. Now, the action swung back in the direction of London and Kent.

At 12.55 hrs, 66 Squadron scrambled from Gravesend to join up with 603 Squadron, up from Hornchurch. Sergeant Harold Cook of 'Clickety-Click' reported that at 13.40 hrs, Me 109s were seen below, so the Spitfire wing dived to attack – but the formation of 109s disappeared into cloud. Orbiting, Cook saw a pair of 109s beneath the cloud layer, at 7,000ft, attacking the closest from starboard and below. Black smoke issued forth but Cook broke away when attacked by the other Messerschmitt. This combat had progressed over the sea, south of Dover, Cook watching 'a motor boat put out from Dover and approach the spot where I estimated the E/A would crash'. No Me 109, however, came down in the Channel at this time.

East of Folkestone, at 14.15 hrs, 603 Squadron sighted and dived to attack Me 109s; Pilot Officer Ronald Berry was 'guard leader' and upon seeing other Me 109s approaching the Spitfires went below cloud, south of Dover, and also saw the 'patrol boat speeding out'. Attacked from out of the sun by two Me 109s, Berry took refuge in cloud, and upon emerging a mile west of Folkestone, he saw a Spitfire shooting at a 109, and another 109 attacking the Spitfire. Berry went to assist, firing at the Spitfire's assailant from close range, which 'took violent evasive action and dived eastwards to the Channel'.

No. 603 Squadron, however, had been roughly handled by JG 51: South African Flying Officer Claude Goldsmith was shot down and killed, crashing near Waltham, and Pilot Officer Robert Dewey was also killed, crashing at Chartham Hatch, south of Maidstone; Pilot Officer David Maxwell was shot-up and forced-landed at Throwley, fortunately unhurt. Berry's was the squadron's only combat claim in this action.

In these lunchtime battles, *Stab* I/JG 3 lost *Leutnant* Ernst Busch, the *Gruppe* signals officer, who was apparently shot down by Spitfires at noon, baling out and captured slightly wounded at Addington, his 109 crashing at West Wickham; surprisingly, however, there is no corresponding RAF combat claim. Enemy pilots of *Stab*/JG 54, and 4 and 6/JG 51, however, claimed five Spitfires destroyed, four over Folkestone and two at Ashford, between 14.05 and 14.13 hrs (BST).

Reconnaissance aircraft were also active during the early afternoon, Yellow Section of 72 Squadron, up from Coltishall, intercepting a Me 110 at 14.00 hrs, 20 miles west of Yarmouth, at 26,000ft. All three Spitfire pilots, Pilot Officer Robson and Pilot Officer Secretan, and Sergeant Staples, attacked, causing 'whitish smoke' to come 'from the E/A's starboard motor', the aircraft then 'disappearing into cloud' [ORB].

During the afternoon, 41 Squadron also patrolled over Kent, entering into a diving chase with Me 109s retreating back to France. At 15.20 hrs, off Folkestone, Flying Officer Denis Adams attacked a Me 109 from astern and 'saw bits fly off the E/A, but my guns stopped during the burst. I noticed that my air pressure had dropped to zero and had to break off the engagement.' There were no other claims or losses and it is likely that 41 Squadron pursued *Stab* and II/JG 53, which reported an inconclusive clash with Spitfires – which brought the day's fighter-bomber raids to a close: four more Londoners had been killed and twenty-three injured, and beyond the capital nine more civilians had been killed.

At 11.00 hrs, the majority of 17 Squadron had landed at and operated from North Weald. During the Hurricanes' absence from Martlesham Heath, at 16.40 hrs the airfield was subjected to a dive-bombing attack by a number of Me 109s. As the first salvo of bombs fell, Flying Officer Count Manfred Czernin scrambled and inconclusively attacked on the raiders. Two minutes later, Sergeant Robert Hogg took-off in another spare Hurricane, chasing the 109s. Having landed at 17.00 hrs, Czernin went off again at 17.20 hrs, with Pilot Officer Jack Ross, having been warned of another raid incoming. In the air, the pair were joined by Hogg, but apart from Ross seeing a Do 17 briefly in cloud, at which he fired without observing the result, the patrol was otherwise uneventful. Ross, however, had contributed to the loss of the 7/KG 76 Do 17, previously hit by AA fire having bombed Ipswich and which crashed into the River Stour at 18.00 hrs. There were no survivors.

The late afternoon also saw *Luftflotte* 3 launch a raid on Portsmouth, the enemy formation comprising twenty Ju 88s escorted by Me 109s of JG 2. Such a formation of German bombers was, by now, a rare sight in October's daylight skies.

At 16.19 hrs, the Spitfires of 602 Squadron scrambled from Westhampnett to patrol base, as RDF detected the incoming raid, climbing to 23,000ft. From Tangmere, the

Hurricanes of 145 Squadron went off at 16.25 hrs, to patrol north of the Isle of Wight at 24,000ft, and at 16.45 hrs 213 Squadron took-off to patrol Selsey Bill at 20,000ft.

Whilst climbing into the sun, Sergeant Andrew McDowell DFM, Green 2 of 602 Squadron, lost his squadron and whilst orbiting saw five Ju 88s below, in cloud, travelling south over The Solent. At 17.25 hrs, between St Catherine's Point and Selsey Bill, McDowell dived towards the enemy formation, emerging from cloud 3 miles ahead and 3,000ft above, at 11,000ft. Attacking the leading bomber head on, McDowell noted that 'E/A caught fire between engines and dived vertically through bottom layer of cloud, burning furiously'. Breaking away left, above and into the sun, McDowell then attacked the Ju 88s again, which were re-forming after his initial pass. Firing at the aircraft on the extreme right, 'Glass hood was shot off and starboard engine caught fire. The E/A dived out of formation again. I lost E/A owing to knocking my head against dashboard ... position ... thirty–thirty-five miles South of Selsey Bill.' McDowell claimed one Ju 88 destroyed over the sea, the other as a probable. No corresponding loss appears in Luftwaffe records, but a III/LG 1 Ju 88 crash-landed back at Manneville, inland of Le Havre, in *Luftflotte* 3, with combat damage.

Pilot Officer William Hopkin, Blue 2, 'pursued a Me 109 which went too far out to sea, and on his return got in a short burst at a Ju 88 before it escaped in cloud' [ORB]. Hearing the gunfire out to sea, Flight Lieutenant Robert Boyd hurried off from Westhampnett and found a vic of five Ju 88s, chasing one which 'dived to sea level ... whereupon the others attacked Flight Lieutenant [Robert Findlay] Boyd, who broke off the action and returned home without firing.' [ORB].

Whilst 213 Squadron patrolled Selsey uneventfully, 145 Squadron fared badly against the escorting Me 109s of JG 2. With Blue Section leading, when 25 miles east of the Isle of Wight, 145 Squadron was ordered to 'gate', which is to fly at maximum boost and make haste, but during this hurried return to the south coast the squadron's three sections became separated. As Blue Section approached the coast AA fire could be seen to the north, over Portsmouth, and the Belgian Pilot Officer Jean Offenberg, Blue 3, flying at 29,000ft, sighted seven Me 109s flying south. His section leader, however, had not seen the enemy and turned left, away from the Me 109s:

[When I was 5 miles south-east of Bembridge, Offenberg I] suddenly saw on my right about 150 yards away a Me 109 in a very steep dive. I think this plane must have just delivered an attack on Blue 2, Pilot Officer Jottard, who had been flying about fifty yards behind me. As he passed, I dived towards him and fired a deflection shot from 150 yards, giving a two-second burst. I then followed him down in a steep dive and gave him two further bursts of five seconds, each from astern. I saw the tracer bullets enter his aircraft and a burst of flame was observed, apparently just behind the pilot. The E/A then turned on its back and continued to dive very steeply.

Offenberg then broke away and, finding himself alone, returned to base. The Me 109 appears to have got home, but Pilot Officer Alexis Jottard, also Belgian, was shot down and crashed into the sea, never to be seen again.

Red Section was bringing up the rear, and the first indication of an attack was when Sergeant Jack Weber, Red 4,

> suddenly felt something strike his aircraft. He looked up and saw incendiary bullets all around. Before he had time to take evasive action, smoke and flames filled his cockpit and controls became inoperative. The aircraft went into a steep dive, the engine became rough, and at 5,000 feet the pilot baled out and landed in the sea, two miles of Gosport. [Form 'F']

Fortunately, Weber 'was picked up and brought ashore in a Motor Torpedo Boat' [ORB]. Sergeant John Haire, Red 3, weaving behind 213 Squadron, was also hit, voluminous black smoke and glycol issuing from his exhausts and filling the cockpit with fumes and sparks; the pilot managed to bring his Hurricane safely down to land just offshore at Bembridge, wading ashore, unhurt.

During this engagement, 145 Squadron lost three Hurricanes, but, surprisingly, only one claim appears to have been recorded by the enemy, 1/JG 2's *Oberleutnant* Hermann Reifferscheidt recording his first aerial victory off the Isle of Wight. The raid, however, was turned about before the majority of Ju 887s reached Portsmouth, but some bombs were dropped, causing minor damage and few casualties.

During the evening, there were more attacks aimed at RAF airfields by lone raiders. At 18.00 hrs, one of these, a Ju 88 of 7/KG 4, was shot down by AA fire whilst attacking the Bomber Command aerodrome at Linton-on-Ouse. The *Staffelkapitän*, *Oberleutnant* Freidrich-Franz Podbielski, managed to get 20 miles away before the damage forced him to belly-land in Duggleby, Yorkshire; one of his crew, *Unteroffizier* Karl von Kidrowski was severely wounded and later died of his injuries.

Blue Section of Wittering's 1 Squadron, Pilot Officer George Goodman, Pilot Officer James Robinson and Pilot Officer John Elkington, were returning from patrolling Clacton just after 18.00 hrs when the Bofors guns at Feltwell airfield could be seen firing at a Do 17. The Hurricanes dived low over the aerodrome but were forced to scatter as the Bofors' barrage continued unabated. All three pilots managed to attack and damage the raider before losing it in cloud.

At 18.10 hrs, Blue Section of 64 Squadron scrambled from Coltishall to intercept an incoming threat. Five minutes later, 10 miles north-west of base and at 5,000ft, AA fire from the aerodrome drew the attention of Blue 3, Sergeant Eric Limpenny, to a Do 17, which he attacked, damaged, but lost in cloud.

Up at Catterick, at 17.55 hrs Flight Lieutenant George Gribble DFC led Red Section, Pilot Officer Gordon Bachelor and Sergeant George Swanwick, scrambled to intercept two enemy aircraft, first intercepting and damaging a Ju 88 over the Cleveland hills. Gribble, Red Leader, then spotted another aircraft, south-east of Leeming, at first thought to be a Blenheim but upon closer inspection transpired to be a Ju 88, the rear gunner of which opened up from 1,000 yards. Gribble managed several attacks before also losing this bomber in cloud, descending below which Gribble saw the enemy aircraft's bombs explode harmlessly on moorland.

At 08.14 hrs, a Blenheim of Coastal Command's 53 Squadron left Detling on a North Sea sweep, sighting fourteen enemy ships which the pilot, Pilot Officer Plumtree, set course to attack. Upon emerging from cloud cover, however, Plumtree realised that he had overshot and was now over Den Helder, where eight more motor vessels could be seen in docks, and eight more outside. Another two were then sighted in dock, which Plumtree bombed at 09.45 hrs. The Blenheim's presence, however, had not gone undetected and the pilot had to take evasive action owing to heavy flak. Setting course for home, the crew

saw a large gun or emplacement near Dutch coast which was attacked with front machine-gun fire from diving level, and believes some casualties inflicted. On leaving coast due West of Den Helder aircraft was attacked by three Me 110s and rear-gunner replied with three bursts which made one E/A turn away. Our aircraft was hit by cannon shells on port side and cowling and gills of port engine damaged but armour plate saved crew from serious injury, although all were hit by splinters. The wireless transmitter received a direct hit. [ORB]

Plumtree managed to escape the German fighters and crash-landed at Martlesham Heath. No claims of recorded for Me 110s, which is a mistake in 53 Squadron records, but Me 109 pilot *Leutnant* Waldemar Wübke of 9/JG 54 claimed a Blenheim destroyed at 09.35 hrs (BST) 10km north-west of Den Helder.

Between 11.31 and 11.40 hrs, eight more Blenheims of 53 Squadron took-off from Detling to bomb various enemy shipping off Calais, the original intention having been that fighter cover would be provided, but these were drawn away owing to the presence of Me 109s over Kent. Three of the Blenheims were unable to locate their targets and returned home, Pilot Officer James Ritchie being 'chased over the English coast by an Me 109' [ORB]. The Me 109s of 2/JG 51 lurked in the 'clouds above ships' [ORB] and attacked several of the Blenheims. Pilot Officer Barbour was 'chased by three Me 109s to a position ten miles over the English coast', and Pilot Officer Maurer was 'chased out to five miles of the English coast'; both returned safely. Having attacked shipping off Cap-Gris-Nez, Pilot Officer Wigmore reported seeing 'a Blenheim going down' [ORB]. Without doubt, this was the machine of 20-year-old Pilot Officer Ronald Buckley and crew, namely Sergeant Cecil Henderson and Sergeant Percival Neale, who were shot down by a Me 109 and reported missing. 'Two crash boats recovered part of a parachute and a flying jacket, and identification established the death' of this crew. Pilots of 2/JG 51, however, claimed three Blenheims and a Westland Whirlwind destroyed, although none of the latter type was involved.

No. 2 Group Blenheims uneventfully swept the North Sea, and of nine sent to attack *Kriegsmarine* targets just one reported having attacked minesweepers off Terschilling. At night, eighty-two Whitleys, Wellingtons and Hampdens attacked industrial targets in Germany and the occupied lands. One aircraft was lost: a Hampden of Scampton's 49 Squadron, returning from Hamburg was stalked by an intruder, *Leutnant* Heinz Völkner of 2/NJG 2, who shot the Whitley down into the North Sea, off Skegness. There were no survivors.

Clearly, for the aircrew of all RAF commands, death was an ever-present and unpredictable companion. Of this, Squadron Leader 'Sailor' Malan had this to say,

> Fear and intense physical danger and the discomfort of battle was more than compensated by the very positive feelings nearly all of us had of satisfaction at being the only human beings able to stand between Hitler and world freedom. We knew that any day we might be shot down to death, but I will swear this feeling of being the only spearhead, the only instrument between German domination and democracy, was the one that kept us going and beat the Luftwaffe. It gave us an elation that transcended all else.

On the same subject, Polish Pilot Officer Jerzy Poplawski of 229 Squadron commented,

> Flying Officer Franek [Franciszek] Surma was a good friend of mine, a bit shy when you talked to him. Perhaps we were all a bit quiet, trying not to think of tomorrow. It would be wrong to say that we had no fear. After all, we were human beings and as such we all knew what fear was. But we also had a code of how we conducted our lives, a sense of duty, that made us control our fear. And that fact was perhaps the most important in our lives. We both talked about it a lot.

Monday, 28 October 1940

With cloudy weather persisting in the morning, predictably the first enemy air operations involved lone reconnaissance bombers. The first of these was intercepted by Red Section of 310 (Czech) Squadron, which had taken off to patrol Duxford at 07.55 hrs. Squadron Leader Douglas Blackwood led Flight Lieutenant Jaroslav Maly and Pilot Officer Vaclav 'Vic' Bergman to intercept a Do 17 at 08.15 hrs a few miles south-west of base; the Hurricanes attacked but the bomber escaped in cloud. Similarly, at 08.30 hrs, Flying Officer Count Manfred Czernin and Sergeant Leonard Bartlett of 17 Squadron intercepted a Do 215 10 miles off Orfordness, which was last seen losing height with its starboard engine on fire. At 10.10 hrs, 249 Squadron's Pilot Officer William Millington damaged a Do 17 north of Hawkinge, and at 10.45 hrs, Millington, together with Pilot Officer Tom Neil DFC, Pilot Officer Antony Thompson and Pilot Officer William McConnell, claimed a Ju 88 destroyed off Dungeness. After 17 Squadron's first patrol, Pilot Officer Leary had landed at Debden, and whilst returning to Martlesham at 10.40 hrs attacked a Do 17 near North Weald, which went down in a spiral glide before disappearing into the gloaming.

Polish Pilot Officer Franciszek Surma, Red 2 of 257 Squadron and patrolling from North Weald, attacked a He 111 between Romney and Folkestone at 11.00 hrs:

> I was Red 2 of the leading section of 257 'Burma' Squadron. We were following 249 Squadron when we were ordered to look for an enemy

bomber. While searching in the Ashford area I lost the Squadron in the clouds. When I came out of the cloud I saw seven aircraft of either 257 or 249 Squadron, which I intended to follow, then I saw a twin engined aircraft flying in their direction and below them. I went to investigate and saw the crosses on the wings when I dived down on him, but could not attack head on as it was too late. I zoomed up and made an astern attack. When I was about three hundred yards behind the enemy aircraft, a He 111, the rear gunner opened up from below me. I gave a short burst to un-nerve them. When I was 150–200 yards behind the enemy aircraft's tail, on the port side, I gave a three–four second burst at the cockpit. Passing over him I fired at the starboard engine from about 80 yards. He continued to fly on level and I gave him another burst of about four seconds from about 100 yards at the starboard engine. Seeing no result I followed up the attack with another burst at the starboard engine. I noticed a small explosion from the engine and saw grey smoke pouring out. At this time the aircraft lurched to the right and, as I passed him, a piece of the aircraft flew by my Hurricane, almost hitting it.

We went into cloud at about 4,500 feet. I levelled out, came out of the layer and searched above and below. As I came below cloud I saw that I was directly above the coastline, I looked for the enemy aircraft but did not find it.

The He 111 was credited as 'probably destroyed'.

Over 10 Group, the enemy was also active, 234 Squadron's Flying Officer James Ritchie, patrolling from Warmwell, damaged a Ju 88 at 12.20 hrs, 15 miles west of base.

As the weather improved as the day wore on, *Jafü* 2 launched its first escorted *Jabo* attack at 13.00 hrs, twenty to thirty Me 109s crossing in over Dungeness, occupying a five-mile front, and flying towards Biggin Hill. Before reaching there, however, *Jabos* dropped bombs on Maidstone before turning about and crossing out over Dungeness at 13.15 hrs; they were not intercepted. Ironically, the Duxford Wing had patrolled Biggin Hill between 11.45 and 13.00 hrs, and had done so equally uneventfully on 20, 25 and 26 October 1940, returning to Duxford just before the Germans appeared.

Shortly afterwards the next attack came in, eighteen plus crossing in over Dover and heading towards Maidstone and Biggin Hill. At 13.10 hrs, 603 Squadron scrambled from Hornchurch, and 222 Squadron from Rochford, joining up over the Maidstone line at 30,000ft. No. 603 Squadron was being led in the air on this sortie by Flight Lieutenant John Haig, with 222 Squadron following on behind. Haig reported that at 14.30 hrs, north of Maidstone, fifteen Me 109s were sighted below, at 25,000ft, on which the Spitfires dived from 31,000ft, attacking from astern. Haig hit one, which streamed white smoke, but broke away when attacked by another 109, which kept him 'fully occupied'. Pilot Officer George 'Sheep' Gilroy DFC, Red 3, attacked a 109 at 14.32 hrs, south-east of London: 'Smoke, followed by flames, issued from E/A and it dived vertically with cowling and hood coming off. The pilot was not seen to jump but may have delayed opening parachute upon reaching cloud.' The enemy pilot, *Unteroffizier* Anton Gonschorrek of 5/JG 27, did bale out, and was captured slightly wounded, his

109 crashing near Maidstone. The Me 109 attacked by Pilot Officer Bill Read, Red 2, broke away and nearly collided with another; pursued by Read, after further bursts the 109 streamed white smoke and went vertically down. Attacked himself by another 109, Read broke off. Pilot Officer Ronald Berry was flying as 'guard aircraft' and orbited the Channel, sighting several Ju 88s and Me 109s 'apparently going home. I then sighted two "He 113s [*sic*]" at 25,000 feet, going down towards the Channel, and gave chase'. Another Spitfire then attacked the closest 109, into which Berry put two more bursts, causing black smoke to issue from both radiators. With 420 mph IAS, Berry turned back close to the French coast.

No. 222 Squadron, however, had patrolled at 30,000ft for an hour-and-a-half before forced to descend to Angels 17 owing to oxygen shortage. AA fire was seen over Detling, but the shortage of life-giving oxygen prevented the Spitfires from investigating, and the pilots began returning to Hornchurch individually. Flying Officer Desmond McMullen, however, sighted five unidentified aircraft at 15,000ft, flying in line abreast, which investigated and confirmed as Me 109s, with another *Schwarm* of four 'some way off, over Dungeness'. Attacking one from astern, glycol poured out and the 109 dived, but McMullen was then attacked from behind, so made himself scarce.

Although neither 222 or 603 Squadrons suffered any casualties, *Oberleutnant* Ernst Düllberg, *Staffelkapitän* of 5/JG 27, and *Oberfeldwebel* Otto Schulz of 4/JG 27, both claimed Spitfires destroyed.

Next, the action briefly shifted to 10 Group, when at 15.00 hrs Pilot Officer Kenneth Dewhurst, Blue 1, and Sergeant Michael Boddington, Blue 2 of 234 Squadron, were patrolling 20 miles south of Cornwall's famous Lizard Point at 15,000ft when a Ju 88 was spotted 2,000ft below and to port. The Spitfires attacked, Dewhurst considering that the bomber was 'badly damaged' before it disappeared into cloud.

Then, the third fighter-bomber attack was made by *Luftflotte* 2: at 16.05 hrs, raids of fifty. Thirty plus and fifty crossed in over Beachy Head and Dungeness, one of which headed for Hornchurch whilst the other two flew towards Biggin Hill.

At 15.40 hrs, in anticipation of further attacks, 249 and 257 Squadrons scrambled from North Weald to patrol Maidstone. At 16.11 hrs, 222 and 603 Squadrons scrambled from Hornchurch on patrol, and when at 24,000ft received orders to intercept the approaching raid.

Squadron Leader Tuck and 257 Squadron were over Tunbridge Wells area at 29,000ft when at 16.45 hrs the Hurricanes found themselves astern and up-sun of 60 Me 109s 1,000ft below. Tuck watched the 109s wheel about – and ambushed the Germans from out of the sun, 257 Squadron's CO hitting one which left the formation, left-wing down, going down in a spiral 'belching out thick black smoke'. This attracted the other 109s' attention, however, but Tuck still had the advantage, being up-sun, and raked another 109 with fire, closing to 50 yards and seeing both the enemy fighter's tail struts break off. Almost stalling and dropping 500ft, Tuck watched the 109 pull up gently before stalling and entering a left-hand spin, trailing white smoke.

Perhaps surprisingly, given 257 Squadron's strong tactical position and benefit of surprise, apart from Tuck's claim for two probables, the squadron's only other claim was submitted by Sergeant Bernard Henson, Green 1, who attacked a 109 over Dungeness, Sergeant Reg Nutter, Green 2, confirming 'glycol pouring from underneath the Me 109'. Tuck, however, had actually destroyed a 109: 4/JG 53's *Feldwebel* Alfred Berg baled out and was captured unhurt, his 109 crashing at Hayward's Heath. The 'Burma' Squadron suffered no loss, but *Oberleutnant* Gerhard Michalski, *Stab* II/JG 53, claimed a Hurricane destroyed south of London.

Pilot Officer Archie Winskill was flying Red 2 in 603 Squadron and at 16.55 hrs, 27,000ft over Dungeness, saw a Me 109 pass in front of his leader. Attacking immediately, 'a little black smoke came from the machine and he went into a slight dive. I followed him and at about 100 yards range I gave him another burst ... He then poured out volumes of black smoke and went into an uncontrollable spin.' Winskill claimed a probable.

Five minutes later, 'near Dungeness' and at the same height, Sergeant Andrew Darling, 'Guard 1', attacked one of fifteen Me 109s:

> immediately I pressed the firing button, the 109 seemed to burst up and belch out thick black smoke, and turned over immediately and went down. This was observed by other pilots of the Squadron. I immediately attacked another 109, without a second glance at the first ... Observed glycol pour out of this aircraft.

The first 109 attacked was that of II/JG 51's *Adjutant Leutnant* Werner Knittel, a famous pre-war sport flier and Spanish Civil War veteran, who was reported missing (in September 1973, however, enthusiasts excavated a crash site at Burmarsh, on Romney Marsh, recovering the wreckage of a Me 109 from a depth of 24ft – along with its pilot's remains; *Leutnant* Werner Knittel, no longer missing, was buried at the Soldatenfriedhof on Cannock Chase, with full military honours).

At 17.15 hrs, Flying Officer Desmond McMullen was leading Red Section of 222 Squadron when ordered to investigate a raid, and at 17.15 hrs over Dungeness found a dozen 'Me 109s in a long line abreast'. On sighting the Spitfire the Germans separated into sections of four in line astern, the rearmost *Schwarm* trying to get on McMullen's tail. Going into a turning contest, a 109 broke out of the circle, enabling the Spitfire pilot 'to get in two deflection bursts, while the remaining E/A cleared off. The result being that the E/A shot down in a vertical dive in flames a few miles out to sea from Dungeness.' Only one Me 109 is recorded as having gone into the sea, 4/JG 51's *Feldwebel* Dieter-John, who was killed, although recorded at noon.

So ended the day fighting over Kent, a feint on Portsmouth, which caused little damage, concluding the daylight fighting. As ever, Coastal Command had flown its usual escort sorties, and three Blenheims scored four direct hits on Lorient power station, and four Beauforts attacked shipping off Norway. At night, adverse weather prevented all but one FAA Swordfish and a Blenheim attacking Boulogne; results were not observed. A 22 Squadron Beaufort based at North Coates crashed into the sea shortly after leaving for a patrol, the crew all killed. No. 2 Group's Blenheims carried out reconnaissance and attacked airfields and barges, and Bomber Command sent ninety-four night-bombers to various targets in Germany and the low countries. No. 105 Squadron at Watton lost one Blenheim which disappeared on the Hamburg raid, and another crashed at Fakenham on the return, killing the crew. A 102 Squadron

Whitley, having confirmed successfully bombing Bremen, became lost returning and crashed into the sea off Aberdeen – the crew remain missing.

Weekly Home Intelligence Report:

> A further detailed study by Listener Research has been made on the subject of radio listening during air raids. It was confirmed that even in London the great majority of people shelter in their own homes; the great majority therefore still have access to a radio set. Comparatively few people have radio sets in their private garden shelters and the number of sets in public shelters is negligible. In any place when severe raids begin, there is general reluctance to keep the radio on, but as raids become more frequent people once more start listening, particularly to the news and to light entertainments. The general deterioration of reception during air raids at night has caused both bewilderment and resentment. Most people are quite unaware of why this happens. A typical comment comes from the Leicester Information Committee: 'The British command of the air does not extend to the ether.'

Tuesday, 29 October 1940

Enemy operations on this day would be similar to the two preceding days. Five heavily escorted *Jabo* raids were made on the south-east, two in The Solent area and further attacks on aerodromes as far afield as Yorkshire.

The first raid involved some fifteen Me 109s, which swept up to London at 10.25 hrs, randomly dropping bombs in Westminster, Kensington, Paddington and Lambeth, killing four people. By 11.15 hrs the Germans had gone, but were not intercepted. A second formation of just nine Me 109s swept over Manston at 10.45 hrs, but dropped no bombs and no combats occurred. *Major* Adolf Galland had led JG 26 on an escort mission to London, during which the only action was when 7/JG 26 strafed a train near Dungeness.

The third raid was incoming at 12.20 hrs, followed by another at 12.53 hrs, each of twenty-five Me 109s, which penetrated to West London before turning east; bombs were dropped on Camberwell, where the South Metropolitan Gas Company was hit, causing four fatalities, Beckenham, and an optical works in Lewisham was also damaged. These two raids, however, were met by 11 Group.

At 12.00 hrs, Squadron Leader Joe Kyall scrambled from Northolt with his 615 Squadron to patrol over Kent. At 12.40 hrs the Hurricanes were over the Dungeness area at 25,000ft, and sighted Me 109s. Sergeant Eric Cosby, Red 3 in the leading section, saw two 109s – one below, the other above; stealthily climbing 1,000ft above the latter. Cosby then dived, picking up speed to overtake the German, opened fire and saw 'thick smoke streaming from the engine … after second burst the cockpit cover flew off and engine stopped. The plane spun into the sea fifteen miles SE of Dungeness.' Sergeant Jack Hammerton, Yellow 3, became separated from the squadron but over the Canterbury area at 12.40 hrs, together with an unknown Hurricane, engaged and damaged a Ju 88, which was last seen losing height over the sea 'with clouds of smoke coming from it'.

However, Pilot Officer Eric Edmunds, a New Zealander, was also separated from 615 Squadron and met three Me 109s half way across the Channel at 29,000ft – and was shot down. A cannon shell exploded in the Hurricane's cockpit, severely wounding Edmunds and saturating him in hot glycol. Having passed out, fortunately, the pilot came to in time to crash-land on Romney Marsh with a fractured skull and other head injuries, shrapnel in both lungs, back and legs, and a 7.92mm machine-gun bullet in his right leg. Near West Malling, *Adjutant* Henry Lafont, at 20 the youngest Free French pilot amongst 'The Few', wrecked his Hurricane during a forced-landing, apparently due to a glycol leak – but two Hurricanes were claimed destroyed over Dungeness, one by *Major* Werner Mölders, *Kommodore* of JG 51, the *Oberkanone* recording his fifty-fourth victory, and *Oberleutnant* Hermann-Friedrich Joppien of *Stab* I/JG 51, who chalked up his twenty-third. *Stab* I/JG 51 lost *Oberleutnant* Ernst Terry, the *Gruppen Adjutant* and an eight-victory ace, who was reported missing, having been shot down by Sergeant Eric Cosby.

At 12.25 hrs, Flight Lieutenant Christopher 'Mickey' Mount, commanding 'A' Flight, was Villa Leader and led 602 Squadron up from Westhampnett to patrol Mayfield at 27,000ft, being reinforced at 12.45 hrs by Flight Lieutenant Eric 'Tommy' Thomas, commanding 'A' Flight of 222 Squadron, again led the 'Natal' Spitfires up from Hornchurch to patrol Kent at 30,000ft.

At 13.30 hrs, control informed Mount of a raid travelling west over Canterbury, then plotted north-east of Biggin Hill. Mount was alerted to AA fire at 14.00 hrs, then 21.00 hrs, and saw 'a large and loose formation' of Me 109s 'in two main bodies', each of around twenty-five aircraft, heading south-east. No. 602 Squadron, however, were 3,000ft above the enemy, 'with some advantage from the sun and the supreme asset of greater height' [ORB]. Ordering the Spitfires into line astern, Mount, an Old Etonian and former member of the Oxford University Air Squadron, attacked the Me 109s from astern. Firing at a 109 in the right-hand formation, Mount reported that 'a great mass of black smoke was seen to come from port side of engine. He half-rolled to the left and dived vertically downwards, totally enveloped in smoke', the combat taking place between Biggin Hill and Maidstone. Although not seen to crash, this 109 was claimed as destroyed.

Sergeant Andrew McDowell DFM, Green 1, 'operating independently as Green 2 and 3 were weaving', was about to attack the leading 109s when he noticed five more curving round behind the Spitfires, so 'turned into the sun to head them off'. Getting on the 'tail of one Me 109 (bomb carrier)' McDowell fired, 'the E/A catching fire, rolling over and diving vertically into the ground'. Blue 3, Flying Officer Gerald Fisher, also attacked the same 109, a 'large hole appeared in underside of E/A ... then emitted clouds of white smoke, turned over on its back and dived straight in. Crashed on land roughly in area of initial attack.' This 109 was also hit by Pilot Officer Archibald 'Pat' Lyall, Yellow 1, who first fired at a Me 109 from dead astern in the first pass, from which white smoke issued, then another, shooting off a 'small portion of his starboard wing'; Lyall then resumed his assault on the first 109, which poured black smoke, 'rolled over and dived over the vertical with flames coming from the underside of the fuselage. I watched him dive for 5,000 feet and he went on down.' Pilot Officer Nigel Rose, Yellow 2, also attacked it, noting 'cowlings or cockpit cover came off. E/A was last seen diving steeply with white vapour still streaming. Yellow 3 saw bits of this aircraft falling off, and thick white trail.' Sergeant William Smith was Yellow 3, and attacked a 109, which 'flicked over and went into a spiral dive, streaming black smoke.'

Flight Lieutenant Eric Thomas and 222 Squadron were also on the scene, finding 'eight Spitfires already engaging from astern' and the Me 109s 'flying in a great mass of wide line abreast, stepped up'. Thomas fired at a 109, which 'emitted black smoke', then, seeing five 109s above, he climbed into the sun before attacking the right-hand 109 of a group of five. Closing to 'dead astern', Thomas fired and 'the E/A sheered-off to the right', but he was unable to 'follow him down as I was right underneath about ten E/A who would probably have followed me'. This exchange was seen by Sergeant John Burgess, one of Thomas's 'B' Flight pilots, and after his leader broke away he saw the 109 flatten out just above cloud and the white smoke cease. Burgess attacked from astern and watched the pilot bale out, 'The machine crashed just to the South of Pluckley Station (West of Ashford). I forced-landed at Lanham as I was shot myself and hit in the glycol system.'

Although descriptions of the action differ, the fact is that only one Me 109 crashed in south-east England as a result of this combat, so presumably 602 Squadron's McDowell, Fisher, Rose, Lyall and Smith, and 222's Thomas and Burgess, all attacked the same enemy fighter: *Oberleutnant* Otto Hintze, *Staffelkapitän* of 3/*Erprobungsgruppe* 210, on his fifty-third combat mission, baled out and was captured slightly wounded, his 109 crashing at Sheerlands Farm, Pluckley.

After this initial combat, McDowell chased four other Me 109s east of Dungeness, attacking one which 'caught fire and dived away over the vertical' – not seen to crash, this was also claimed as destroyed, possibly being a pilot of 6/JG 52 who was rescued from the Channel by the *Seenotdienst*. No. 602 Squadron's Blue 2, Pilot Officer John Hart, a Canadian, climbed above the enemy with Sergeant Andrew McDowell, chasing the Me 109s beyond the coast, hitting a 109, which 'burst into flames' over the sea. This was confirmed by Blue 1, Flight Lieutenant Donald Jack, and was undoubtedly the same enemy fighter claimed over the Channel by McDowell. Jack then attacked the other 109, flying with that ablaze, and after a five-second burst 'flames and smoke were observed coming from front of E/A'. Not seen to crash, this was also claimed as destroyed. Sergeant George Whipps, Red 2, claimed a 109 damaged, concluding 602's claims, At the time, having claimed seven Me 109s destroyed, two probables and three damaged, this was considered to be 'perhaps the most successful' action 'the Squadron had yet fought'. As we have seen, multiple pilots, from 602 and 222 Squadron were responsible for the demise of a single Me 109, and two pilots of 602, it seems, shot down the same Me 109 over the sea. Nonetheless, it was still a successful action, in which 222 Squadron suffered no casualties and the only damage 602 recorded was minor, to the Spitfire of Pilot Officer Hugh Niven, a Canadian, who returned safely to base. Furthermore, no combat claims were made by the enemy, and the capture of *Oberleutnant* Otto Hintze, a most experienced pilot and leader, was a bonus – his Knight's Cross would be announced the following month, whilst Hintze remained in Allied custody.

The next raid was mounted by *Luftflotte* 3, a *Freie Hunt* by Me 109s of JG 2, which spilt up over the Isle of Wight at 14.30 hrs, one formation heading towards Portsmouth, the other to Thorney Island. No bombing occurred and two Me 109s were hit by AA fire: *Oberleutnant* Wolf, *Adjutant* of III/JG2 crashed into The Solent and was killed, and I/JG2's *Unteroffizier* Bader returned his damaged fighter to France, crash-landing at Cherbourg.

No. 145 Squadron was already airborne when this raid approached, having scrambled from Tangmere at 14.15 hrs to patrol Portsmouth, followed by 213 Squadron, at 14.25 hrs, ordered to patrol base. At 14.50 hrs, the Hurricanes were flying east, towards 'Pompey', when Pilot Officer Peter 'Stunning Black' Dunning-White, Blue 2, sighted two Me 109s below, which he attacked, closing from 600 yards. The leading aircraft turned over onto its back, emitting white smoke, and later seen 'falling and emitting white smoke' by Australian Flight Lieutenant Robert Bungey; it was claimed as a probable. No. 145 Squadron suffered no loss, but 213 Squadron's Pilot Officer Richard Hutley was shot down over Selsey Bill, baled out over the sea but later picked up dead by the Selsey lifeboat, and Pilot Officer Thomas Thomson was shot-up and wounded over Fareham, returning his severely damaged Hurricane safely to Tangmere. Somewhat optimistically, but typically, *Major* Helmut Wick and friends of *Stab*/JG 2 overclaimed, the *Kommodore* himself claiming both a Hurricane and a Spitfire destroyed over Portsmouth, although none of the latter type were involved, and *Oberleutnant* Erich Leie, *Oberleutnant* Rudi Pflanz and *Oberleutnant* Karl-Heinz Krahl all claimed a Hurricane each, as did *Oberfeldwebel* Fritz Stritzel. The Richthofen *Geschwader*'s only losses were the two 109s hit by AA fire.

As JG2 retired, *Jafü* 2 was already preparing its fifth raid of the day: an attack aimed at Hornchurch and North Weald. At 16.15 hrs, 17 Squadron scrambled from North Weald, joining up with Stapleford's 46 Squadron to patrol North Weald at 25,000ft, and at the same time, the Duxford Wing scrambled with orders to patrol Hornchurch. For the last four days, the Spitfires of Wittering's 266 Squadron had flown to and operated from Duxford with the wing, joining with 19, 242 (Canadian) and 310 (Czech) Squadrons, and the Wittering Spitfires joined the party on this occasion. The wing, however, was, according to the 19 Squadron ORB, 'unable to set favourably' because 'Squadron Leader [Douglas] Bader's radio was unserviceable'. In such a circumstance it is difficult to understand why Bader did not return home and hand control over to one of his flight commanders. Sadly, shortly after take-off, the 310 (Czech) Squadron Hurricanes of Pilot Officer Emil Fechtner DFC and Flight Lieutenant Jaroslav Maly collided. Fechtner, who, together with Squadron Leader Sacha Hess, had been one of the first two Czech pilots to receive the DFC, crashed at Whittlesford and was killed, but Maly survived, forced-landing at Fowlmere.

With the enemy advancing towards the mouth of the Thames Estuary, at 16.30 hrs 253 and 501 Squadrons left Kenley to patrol the Kenley – Brooklands line at 15,000ft, and two minutes later 92 Squadron scrambled to patrol Hornchurch, also at Angels 15, leading 74 Squadron and joining up with Hornchurch's 222 Squadron.

Pilot Officer Charles Ambrose, Red 1 of 46 Squadron, reported that at 16.30 hrs, when at 23,000ft over Maidstone, AA fire was seen east of Dungeness, and eight Me 109s were seen avoiding it, flying west. The Hurricanes turned south-west but before intercepting more Me 109s appeared on the squadron's starboard beam, flying the same course – which dived to attack. Angel Leader, Flight Lieutenant Alexander Rabagliati, followed one down and after his second burst 'he turned over and dived into the Estuary between Isle of Sheppey and Essex coast'. Red 1 closed with the companion of the 109 destroyed by Angel Leader, which, after a five-second burst, poured glycol and oil from both radiators: 'He then stalled and the E/A, apparently out of control, fell into a vertical dive, crashing into the sea.' Pilot Officer Robert Reid claimed a 109 probably destroyed – but Sergeant Herbert 'Bert' Black was shot down and baled out, his Hurricane crashing at Hothfield. Black was admitted to Ashford Hospital with leg wounds and facial burns, the mortally injured pilot being joined there by his wife, Gwen, to whom he described how two fellow Hurricane pilots had followed him down, protecting him during his parachute descent. Sadly, having had both legs amputated, the 26-year-old pilot died on 9 November 1940 (his widow never re-married and joined 'Bert' in his grave at St Denys' churchyard, Ibstock in 2004).

Concurrently with 46 Squadron's engagement, the incoming raid was now coming in low and fast, attacking North Weald at 16.40 hrs. The twelve *Jabos* involved were from II/LG 2, a specialist unit, which approached from the south-east and accurately dive-bombed the aerodrome from 3,000ft, escorted by Major Adolf Galland's JG 26. As the first bombs fell, another twelve 109s attacked from the north.

Sergeant George 'Titch' Palliser's section of 249 Squadron was at thirty-minutes availability when, as another section of 249 was in the process of scrambling with 257 Squadron – too late – to intercept the raid:

> As the aircraft of both squadrons were preparing to take off, there was a mighty roar of engines, the clatter of machine-guns and the vicious crack of bombs exploding. Together with some of the others on stand-by, we ran like hell for our aircraft to join the action ... I swear I never did fasten my harness and simply sat on my parachute. The aircraft had been started by our ground staff, who had not run for shelter. I saw a clear run and went full throttle to get airborne as quickly as possible – the next second there was a mighty 'crack' from the direction of [Sergeant Alexander] 'Tubby' Girdwood of 257 Squadron, who was about a hundred yards on my starboard side, also about to be airborne.

Sergeant Alexander 'Tubby' Girdwood, Yellow 2, had just left the ground when a bomb exploded nearby, throwing his Hurricane into the air, which crashed in flames just outside the north-west perimeter of the aerodrome.

Palliser continued,

> At that instant I was airborne and felt a hell of a vibration which shook the aircraft – I thought that I was in trouble – and keeping in full throttle and staying low I executed a half turn of the airfield and landed. By this time the bombing was over and the 109s were being chased by those who had managed to take off satisfactorily.
> I managed to taxi back to the dispersal, noticing a Hurricane on fire a few hundred yards from the perimeter track – my immediate thought

was 'My God, "Tubby" Girdwood!' By this time many were running to the burning aircraft and I joined them, only to be prevented from getting too close as ammunition was exploding from the heat of the flames. We stood and watched so helplessly and witnessed the terrible sight of a friend burn to death – this was a shocking experience, considering we were talking and joking only fifteen minutes earlier with 'Tubby' and other sergeant-pilots before the scramble.

With regard to my own aircraft, it was found that a part of a propeller blade had been sliced off by fragments of the same bomb which had burst under 'Tubby' Girdwood. This type of attack was a great shock to us all.

Yellow Section of 249 Squadron was more fortunate, Flying Officer Keith Lofts, Pilot Officer William McConnell and Pilot Officer Antony Thompson taking-off over an exploding bomb – although Lofts's Hurricane was damaged by the blast, he returned safely to base.

No. 257 Squadron's Red 2, Pilot Officer Franciszek Surma,

saw the bombs falling as he was taxying [*sic*] over the aerodrome. A bomb exploded on his left-hand side as his aircraft was running up. The explosion jerked him, but he took off satisfactorily. He noticed four of the enemy aircraft flying over the hanger between 4,000 and 5,000 feet. He also saw many planes on his right, which he took to be Hurricanes.

When he had climbed to about 3,000 feet, he heard an explosion in his cockpit, which filled with white smoke. His plane went into a spiral dive, and he felt that he no longer had control of the steering gear. He opened the Perspex. After a moment the Hurricane appeared to come out of its dive and level out, however it soon began to dive again to starboard. After trying to bring it out of the dive for a second time, without result, he attempted to bale out. By this time he had lost height to 1,500 feet. After struggling to get out of the cockpit, he baled out at about 1,000 feet and made a successful parachute descent, landing in a tree top near an inn at Matching. After quickly convincing a Home Guard that he was a Pole and not a German, he was given two whiskies and driven back to the aerodrome. He had lost both of his flying boots on jumping out of the plane, received a black eye but was otherwise unharmed.

Pilot Officer Franciszek Surma had been shot down by an *Experte*, *Hauptmann* Gerhard Schöpfel, *Kommandeur* of III/JG 26, the Hurricane crashing into a sandpit on what is now the Bobbington Nature Reserve, south of the village of Moreton, near Matching in Essex.

Mrs Skepelhorn was landlady of the village's White Hart Inn, and together with her 16-year-old son, Joe, watched Surma's parachute descent, which ended with his silk canopy entangled in the elm tree adjacent to the pub.

Squadron Leader Tuck, commanding 257 Squadron, was not flying, and many years later recalled,

> Of course I knew 'Franek' Surma very well and there are many stories I could tell you of him. He was a wonderful little chap – but wild! He was also a loyal and thoroughly trusty wingman. Franek and myself were born on the same day – July 1st 1916. On the occasion he was shot down near North Weald, he was wearing a German leather flying jacket, which he had taken from a German bomber shot down in Poland. This did not assist positive identification!

As Joe ran to help the pilot, he and others noted with concern the Luftwaffe insignia, whilst Surma repeatedly shouted 'Me friend! Me friend!' – in his strong Polish accent. A local builder, Ernie Judd, arrived from his nearby yard with a ladder and climbed up to rescue the pilot, sawing through a substantial bough to reach him. Climbing down, Surma was entertained in the pub whilst Mrs Skepelhorn telephoned North Weald, which sent a car to collect him. According to Tuck's early biographer Larry Forrester in *Fly For Your Life*, a group of Free French soldiers present had decided that Surma was an enemy airman and prepared to lynch him on the spot. According to Tuck, writing to this author in 1987, 'Fortunately I arrived on the scene in time to stop this nonsense, the French then insisting that we have a drink with them.'

Meanwhile, in the skies above, 257 Squadron's Red 1, Canadian Flight Lieutenant Peter 'Cowboy' Blatchford, chased one of the *Jabos*: 'He got behind cloud, hoping to catch the enemy aircraft, but was there too soon. The Me 109 fired at him head on with cannon, making a big hole in the fuselage, piercing the oil tank and damaging the tail unit of his Hurricane.' Green 4, Sergeant Reg Nutter, went below the cloud and made a short beam attack on the same Me 109 but did not observe results. Blatchford continued the fight with the other Me 109s but made no claim.

North Weald was a shambles. According to the Station ORB,

> The Me 109s dived to about 3,000 feet and lower, and about forty-four bombs were dropped, about twenty-seven falling on the camp, mostly on the landing ground. The Guard Room, just re-built after a previous raid, was practically demolished, a Bellman hangar, already damaged, was virtually destroyed and a 30 Cwt lorry and a mechanical crane therein destroyed; several huts at dispersal point were destroyed or damaged and a Magister was destroyed. Despite damage to the landing ground it remained serviceable for day flying, and none of the telephone services, or gas or water, were affected. In all there were about six fatal casualties and about a dozen more injured. Two large bombs fell on open ground just near the Officers' Mess.

Flight Lieutenant Peter Brothers, 257 Squadron: 'I was having tea in the Officers' Mess when the raiders struck. We all dived under the table! My car, an open 3-litre Bentley, was parked outside and I was livid to find that a near-miss bomb had filled it with soil, which took forever to clean out!' It had been a successful attack by the enemy – but the raiders found squadrons of defending fighters awaiting their withdrawal.

Whilst North Weald was being attacked at low-level, 17 Squadron was overhead at 25,000ft, but at 16.50 hrs, Polish Pilot Officer Tadeusz Kumiega, Yellow 1, and Sergeant Robert Hogg, Yellow 2, saw a lone Me 109 below, at 19,000ft, 10 miles west of North Weald, which both pilots attacked. Kumiega described how the 109 climbed very fast, outpacing the Hurricanes until 'glycol smoke' poured from it. Just as the enemy fighter reached cloud, Hogg fired again, several times, and 'The E/A then turned over on his back and the pilot jumped while his aircraft was upside down at a height of 1,500–2,000 feet. We saw the machine crash and break up on Foulness Island; the pilot landed near the aircraft in a ploughed field.' This was 8/JG 26's *Oberfeldwebel* Konrad Jäckel, who was captured, his 109 crashing at Tillingham.

Flight Lieutenant Robert 'Butch' Barton DFC, commanding 'B' Flight, was leading 249 Squadron and engaged the retreating 109s, pursuing them from North Weald to Maldon. At 16.55 hrs, Barton attacked a 109, from which a small amount of white smoke emitted from the wing root before 'the petrol tank behind the pilot set on fire, pilot baled out OK'. This was a *Jabo* of 4/LG 2, which the badly burned *Feldwebel* Hans Rank baled out of, the aircraft crashing beside the 'Maldon – Goldhangar road'; Rank died of his wounds later the same day, in St Peter's Hospital. Polish Sergeant Michal Maciejowski had followed Barton into the attack on five Me 109s, firing at one which 'immediately burst into flames and fell to earth' – the being another 4/LG 2 *Jabo*, *Oberfeldwebel* J. Harmeling forced-landing at Langenhoe Wick where he was captured, slightly wounded. Sergeant George Stroud also hit a *Jabo*, of 5/LG 2, which 'belched black smoke and lost height over the River Blackwater' – *Oberleutnant* Hans-Benno von Schenk, the *Staffelkapitän*, crashed into the sea, 12 miles east of the Blackwater, and was killed. After a chase, Pilot Officer William Millington hit a 109, which 'disappeared, diving vertically down into the haze at about 500 feet, emitting large quantities of black smoke, and estimated that E/A crashed in sea in vicinity of Buxey Sands's' – very likely von Schenk and the same 109 claimed by Stroud. Sergeant Henry Davidson also claimed a probable, the squadron returning to North Weald without loss.

Further west, 92 Squadron was at 22,000ft over the Kenley and Gatwick areas when at 17.00 hrs the Spitfires intercepted twelve Me 110s of 2/*Erprobungsgruppe* 210 on a mission to attack London. Flight Lieutenant John Villa was 'Ganic Leader', patrolling with 74 and 222 Squadrons – and on sighting the Me 110s below, ordered 92 Squadron to attack:

> Me 110s jettisoned their bombs and attempted to get into a defensive circle. By this time I was on the tail of a rear one … fired two short bursts and broke away as glycol poured from the port engine. E/A broke away and dived vertically to ground level. I followed and continued to attack … E/A continued flying South and I followed it without any ammunition. E/A finally crashed into the sea about fifteen miles SSE of Rye.

This claim was shared with Pilot Officer Cecil Saunders, and 253 Squadron's Polish Pilot Officer Tadeusz Nowak, Blue 2, who had lost his leader when 253 Squadron also dived on the Me 109s, 'sighted a Do 17 at 200 feet with a Spitfire circling at 1,000 feet, apparently without ammunition'. Nowak also attacked and watched the enemy aircraft crash 'some fifteen miles out ... in sea.' No. 92 Squadron's Pilot Officer Trevor Wade and Sergeant Hugh Bowen-Morris claimed Me 110 probables, and Pilot Officer Thomas Sherrington one damaged – but, according to Luftwaffe records, the only Me 110 casualty was a 2/*Erprobungsgruppe* 210 machine, which crashed into a hillside near St Ingelvert with combat damage, killing the pilot, *Feldwebel* Siegfried Tröppl and his *Bordfunker*, *Unteroffizier* Otto Büttner – who would be the unit's last casualties of the Battle of Britain. There can be no doubt, though, that pilots from two squadrons, acting independently, namely Villa of 92 and Nowak of 253, definitely saw a twin-engined aircraft crash into the Channel 15 miles off Rye.

Flight Lieutenant John Mungo-Park DFC was Dysoe Leader again, leading 74 Squadron, and having joined up with 92 Squadron at 25,000ft over base, saw Ganic Squadron dive to attack the Me 109s at 17.00 hrs over East Grinstead. Dysoe Leader ordered 74 to do likewise, half-rolling and diving onto thirty Me 109s below. Mungo-Park then hit a 109, which 'burst into flames, the pilot did not get out', and another, which poured glycol and dived vertically; 'saw his hood fly completely off and part of his aileron but had to break off at 2,000 feet as I was going too fast. I came out at 800 feet and E/A was still going down very fast with black smoke pouring out and well over the vertical.' The 109 then disappeared into the thick ground haze. This is believed to have been *Oberleutnant* Egon Troha, *Staffelkapitän* of 9/JG 3, who was shot down and forced-landed at Shepherdswell, a few miles inland of Dover. When interrogated, Troha described having been about to attack a formation of Spitfires when, thinking his Rottenhund was protecting his tail, he was attacked from astern by a Spitfire which damaged his radiator and oil cooler (Squadron Leader Denys Felkin, Troha's interrogator at Cockfosters, the RAF Prisoner Interrogation Centre, described Troha as 'A good soldier with no pronounced political bias. Said as little as possible with the usual Austrian politeness').

Mungo-Park's Red 2, Sergeant Neil Morrison, followed his leader and, from his identical description of events, hit what was clearly the first Me 109 engaged by Mungo-Park, claiming a probable. Red 4, Pilot Officer Bob Spurdle followed Red Section into attack, hitting a circling Me 109 'which rolled onto its back and appeared to spin down, inverted' – this was also claimed as probably destroyed.

Flying Officer William Nelson was Dysoe Yellow Leader and during the first dive attacked a 109; as the enemy fighters scattered, Nelson

> was surprised and delighted to find my E/A climb to port and put up a
> fight. Whilst smoke was issuing from his engine, the performance of the
> E/A at 26,000 feet in turning was quite reasonable and I circled 1½ times
> before closing once more to point blank range with a three-second burst
> which caused him to half-roll down.

Nelson continued firing from 'point blank. He continued diving towards the ground, and to prevent him hedge-hopping away, in case he wasn't finished I gave him a further burst which sent him crashing into a field somewhere, I reckon, between East Grinstead and Tunbridge Wells.' *Leutnant* Heinz Tornow of 4/JG 51 was killed in the crash at Langton Green, immediately west of Tunbridge Wells.

Pilot Officer Edward 'Wally' Churches, a 19-year-old Aucklander, was Nelson's Yellow 2 and during the diving attack

> just caught a glimpse of a big twin-engined machine flying alone and heading SE at about 10,000 feet over Tunbridge Wells. I dived vertically ... identified it as a He 111K ... opened fire... saw my first burst entering the fuselage and wing roots. Passing the tail of the aircraft at nearly 350 mph and twenty yards astern I saw pieces flying off ... pulled out of dive ... blacked out completely.

The Heinkel was last seen 'in a gentle dive several miles ahead and making for the South coast. I gave chase but was unable to catch him, even after passing Dungeness.' This was also, optimistically, accredited as probably destroyed. No. 74 Squadron sustained no loss in the action, after which the 'Tigers' returned safely to Biggin Hill.

The Hurricanes of Kenley's 253 and 501 Squadrons were also in the same area, Sergeant Tony Pickering, Yellow 4 of 501 Squadron, reporting 'two waves of enemy aircraft at 23,000 feet' which were being 'engaged by Spitfires'. Peeling off after a Me 109, this 'easily out dived' the Hurricane pilot, who then orbited for ten minutes before seeing 'two Ju 88s at 12,000ft going east over Tonbridge. I climbed to attack but could not get within 800 yards and they were steadily drawing away from me' (years later, Pickering commented that 'A Spitfire would have caught those Ju 88s, the Hurricane was just too slow'). Pickering then attacked a Me 109 on his starboard side, from astern, which dived, turning and twisting, pursued by Pickering, constantly firing short bursts, and

> when he was at 500 feet, diving towards the ground, I gave him my last burst which set fire to his starboard petrol tank and he dived into the ground at the corner of a wood and immediately blew up. The pilot did not bale out. The aircraft crashed at Ham Street, approximately fifteen miles North of Dungeness.

This could only have been the 3/JG 51 Me 109, which exploded over the Gate Inn, west of Elham, although the pilot, *Feldwebel* Karl Bubenhofer, did bale out and was captured at Rhodes Minnis. Pilot Officer Kenneth MacKenzie, Blue 1, also attacked the 109s being engaged by Spitfires, following a 109 to Dungeness, at 17.15 hrs opening fire from 200 yards and below: 'he developed engine trouble and thick black and white smoke came from him. He went into a spin and I last saw him at 8,000 feet.' Just how chaotic and confusing such combats were, is emphasised by the following: 'Sergeant Machowski [*sic*], who followed me in this attack saw something diving with thick smoke in a wood just inland from Dungeness, shortly after the 109 developed the spin and went down to the ground.' Clearly, what Polish Sergeant Konrad Muchowski had seen was the 109 destroyed by Sergeant Tony Pickering. It is also possible that Sergeant Paul Farnes, Red 1, also attacked this aircraft, 'eight miles North of Dungeness' at

17.10 hrs, which 'was emitting dense volumes of blackish smoke and appeared to be on fire'.

Having found it 'impossible to engage either formation' of the Me 109s, 253 Squadron 'split into pairs to hunt isolated enemy aircraft'. Pilot Officer Guy Marsland, Green 1, 253 Squadron's weaver, was unable to catch the Me 109 he followed to 3,000ft, so waited over Gatwick and at 17.00 hrs sighted a 109 heading south. Climbing to 4,000ft, Marsland attacked from astern, the 109 half-rolled away and was last seen '300 feet from the ground in the vicinity of Horsham … Horsham Observer Corps report one Me 109 crashed at 1706 hrs.' This was another JG 51 machine, 4 *Staffel*'s *Unteroffizier* Alfred Lenz who had hit anti-invasion obstructions and crashed at Plummers Plain, Horsham, whilst attempting to forced-land; fatally wounded, Lenz died later the same day.

Having left the Duxford sector at 16.15 hrs, the Duxford Wing, 19, 266 (six Spitfires), 242 (Canadian) and 310 (Czech) Squadrons, were at 25,000ft over Hornchurch fifteen minutes later, heading towards Sheerness. When the North Weald raid was inbound, it was rightly suspected that the target was one of the sector stations north of the Thames, and 11 Group HQ required Hornchurch to communicate this information to the Duxford Wing – was unable to do so because of 'continuous R/T traffic between the Wing and Duxford' (this being a reference to the constant banter between Bader in the air and Woodhall at Duxford, which some found inspiring but clearly had negative practical implications). This claim by 11 Group, however, is at odds with evidence in 19 Squadron's ORB: 'No interceptions as the leader of the Wing had a U/S radio.'

On the ground, near Chelmsford, was 14-year-old Ivor Linsdell:

> I was in the garden of my home when I heard anti-aircraft fire and guessed that North Weald was getting hit. No air raid warning had sounded but that was not unusual. I watched the grey sky – 10/10ths cloud at about 3,000 feet – and hoped that some activity would later materialise. I reckoned that the German aircraft would retreat by the East coast rather than risk the Thames Estuary barrage and RAF fighters. Soon, a low-flying single-engined aircraft approached from the West. It was an Me 109 going very fast. As it passed only 200 feet over the field behind my house I could see that there was a plume of smoke streaming out from beneath it. I had by then heard no air firing, so assumed that the German had been hit by anti-aircraft fire. I could see the pilot quite clearly and he was gone before I could wave to him. We kids always waved at low-flying aircraft. Once, to our immense joy, a Hurricane pilot who had his cockpit canopy open had raised his hand in reply to our frantic waving. We were convinced that he was telling us that he had shot a German down; there had been a raid and he was certainly heading for North Weald.

After the raid, and with contact established, the Duxford Wing was requested to sweep over Kent and meet a raid incoming towards Biggin Hill – but Air Vice-Marshal

Trafford Leigh-Mallory recalled his squadrons owing to bad weather. Consequently, the opportunity to intercept this raid was lost. Not surprisingly, this result led to an unwelcome rebuke from Fighter Command HQ: Leigh-Mallory 'must not neglect his own responsibilities in future'.

Ivor Linsdell:

> Within a few seconds of the Me 109 passing overhead, I heard the sound of an engine under stress above the clouds and to the South. Then came the hammer of cannon-fire, which I thought must be from a German aircraft. I was looking towards Chelmsford and then I saw a Spitfire emerge from the cloud blanket diving vertically. I knew that he was never going to pull out in time. The engine note rose to a scream and continued for a second or two after the smoke arose – and then I heard the 'thud' of impact.
>
> It took me less than five minutes of furious pedalling to cycle to the crash site at Oak Lodge, London Road, Chelmsford. I reached the wreckage of house, brick garage and Spitfire just as two bodies were being loaded onto an ambulance – Chelmsford Hospital was only a few hundred yards down the road. What had been a tidy urban garden was now a chaos of bricks, twisted aluminium and oil-soaked, stinking, still warm mud. A piece of wing that fetched up in the next-door garden was the only recognisable part of the Spitfire. Some people poked around the ruins of the house whilst I scrabbled around in the filth, hoping to find some worthwhile souvenirs – instruments and bullets being highly prized, if I was lucky. I knew that time was running out, because if the adults saw me I would get hustled away. Then I found something I'd rather forget and lost interest in souvenir hunting.

The Spitfire and casualty young Ivor had seen belonged to 19 Squadron: Sub-Lieutenant Giles Arthur Blake, who was killed. Pilot Officer Richard Jones was also flying that day: 'Again, just as when I was shot down a month before, the "Admiral" was weaving behind the Squadron and got picked off by an unseen 109.'

Seven 109s had been seen, in fact, above 19 Squadron, but were not engaged. It was later considered 'probable that some of these attacked Sub-Lieutenant Blake who was doing a search behind the Squadron … It is a great loss to the Squadron as he was very well liked by all as well as being a pilot of exceptional ability.' [ORB].

In fact, Blake had most likely been shot down by *Leutnant* Herbert Huppertz of 6/JG 51, who claimed his fourth victory, a Spitfire, at 17.05 hrs (BST) 20–25km north-west of London.

No. 266 Squadron, flying at 25,000ft, also saw the Me 109s above, at 30,000ft, the six Spitfires orbiting in a single vic formation until the Germans attacked, according to Pilot Officer Richard Trousdale, a New Zealander, Red 2, at 16.45 hrs. No. 266 Squadron broke up, Trousdale firing at a 109 without visible effect. AA fire then attracted his attention to three other aircraft, which, having climbed into the sun, he identified as more Me 109s, flying in a wide vic and making for the east coast. Over Lympne, Trousdale attacked the rearmost machine from the rear, which

> started belching out black smoke from underneath the fuselage and port and starboard wing, and pieces fell away from the fuselage and wing. We were at 20,000 feet and the E/A dived vertically down, crashing into the ground and exploding in flames, ten–fifteen miles North of Lympne aerodrome … a one-track railway was in the vicinity of E/A's crash and people in field tending sheep and in a nearby house all saw combat and crash.

This was, of course, the same 3/JG 51 Me 109 also claimed by pilots of 501 Squadron, which crashed west of Elham.

With the action over, it was time to count the cost of what would prove to be the last major day of fighting before the Battle of Britain's official conclusion.

During the late afternoon's fighting, one Hurricane had been destroyed on the ground at North Weald, its pilot killed, another Hurricane had been destroyed in the air, and one damaged. The Spitfire squadrons suffered no loss. Both sides overclaimed, and yet again we have seen how one enemy loss was frequently multiplied many times over. The Germans, however, substantially overclaimed in this engagement, recording the destruction of eight Spitfires and two Hurricanes. Throughout the day, the Luftwaffe had lost fourteen Me 109s destroyed and one damaged; three pilots were killed, eight there captured, three of whom died of wounds, and a Me 110 had crashed in France with combat damage, killing the crew. It was, by any standards and despite overclaiming, a highly successful day for Fighter Command.

The day fighting, however, was not quite over. At 17.00 hrs, twelve Ju 88s of I/LG 1 dropped bombs on Portsmouth, causing damage to civilian and commercial properties; three people were killed.

An hour later, Blue Section of 1 Squadron's 'B' Flight was up from Wittering when a Do 17 was sighted below, at 3,500ft, flying slowly towards Feltwell. The enemy rear gunner was sharp eyed, however, and immediately spotted the three Hurricanes, opening up from 400 yards as his pilot turned to port. Blue Leader, Sergeant Wilf Page, returned fire, setting fire to the raider's port engine, but was hit himself, glycol fumes in his cockpit forcing him to retire. Blue 2, Pilot Officer James Robinson, also attacked, watching his incendiary bullets hit the Do 17, the nose of which 'was illuminated … there appeared to be something on fire inside the fuselage'; the bomber was then lost to Blue 2, and Blue 3, Czech Sergeant Venda Jicha, in cloud. Meanwhile, Sergeant Wilf Page was in difficulty:

> I requested Control for homing bearing and endeavoured to reach base. However, at a height of 2,000 feet over a large town I was forced to either bale out or land. Being over the town I considered it best to forced-land but failed to carry out a successful landing. I reported to Control and informed them of the damage, position and other details of the crash. When the police arrived I gave them details and then went to 264 Searchlight Battery at Yaxley and requested guard for aircraft. This was supplied and also transport for myself to Wittering.

Page came down at Orton, near Peterborough; no Do 17s appear damaged or lost in combat in German records, but a Ju 88 of 8/KG 4 failed to return from a mission over England, its crew reported missing.

With the day fighting finally over, 11 Group reported on the afternoon's action, providing essential information concerning both RDF and the Duxford Wing's deployment:

Area of Attack

1. About 200 E/A were engaged in the attack, which was made in three waves.

    In the first wave about 30 E/A crossed the North Foreland at 1624 hrs, followed by a second formation of 20 which flew across the Estuary to the river Crouch. Some of these reached North Weald, which was dive-bombed at about 1700 hrs.

    The second wave followed almost immediately in two formations of 30 and 20 E/A, but did not penetrate further than the Dover-Deal area.

    At 1646 hrs, the third wave of three formations crossed the coast and headed towards Biggin Hill. In this attack, several Italian aircraft were reported. This is the first occasion on which the Axis Partner's Air Force has been recorded as taking part in daylight raids on this country.

RDF Information

2. The first plot of Raid 50, 15+ at 6,000 feet, appeared over Cap Gris Nez at 1601 hrs. The raid reached North Weald about 1700 hrs.

    The first plot of Raid 4, 12+ (no height), appeared over Dunkerque at 1606 hrs. At 1617 hrs the strength was increased to 50+. This raid was in the Chelmsford area at 1648 hrs.

    The first plot of Raid 3 appeared 10 miles NE of Dunkerque as 12+ (no height), at 1607 hrs. This raid was lost over Margate at 1628 hrs.

    The first plot of Raid 9 (bombers), 20+ (no height), appeared near Arras at 1625 hrs and reached Dover area at 1633 hrs.

    The first plot of Raid 12 appeared as 4+ (no height), at Cap Gris Nez. No RDF warning was received of Raids 60, 61 and 62, which were picked up by the Observer Corps and plotted in the Tonbridge – Dungeness area.

Observer Corps Information

3. Observer Corps picked up the enemy formations and plotted them accurately. The tracks of Raids 4 and 50 were lost in the North Weald area.

    They reported two enemy formations which crossed the coast near Dungeness, and a third, Raid 60, which appeared inland in the same area. Those three raids totalled approximately 60 aircraft. Raid 61 appeared at 1646 hrs and Raid 62 at 1647 hrs.

Weather

4. Clouds 3/10ths at 3– 4,000 feet, thin layer at 27,000 feet. Visibility good below low cloud.

Action by Group Controller

5. At 1607 hrs, Nos 17 and 46 Squadrons were ordered to patrol North Weald at 15,000 feet and at 1619 hrs to proceed to Maidstone patrol line at 25,000 feet.

At 1615 hrs, Nos 501 and 253 Squadrons were ordered to patrol Brooklands at 15,000 feet and at 1630 hrs to patrol Biggin Hill patrol line on Readiness Patrol.

At 1621 hrs, Nos 222 and 92 Squadrons from Hornchurch and Biggin Hill respectively were ordered to patrol Hornchurch at 15,000 feet.

At 1626 hrs, No 74 Squadron was ordered to patrol Biggin Hill for aerodrome protection.

At 1711 hrs, Nos 41 and 603 Squadrons were ordered to patrol Rochford at 20,000 feet.

In addition, the 12 Group wing took off from Duxford at 1608 hrs. They originally were asked for by 11 Group to patrol Maidstone–Sheerness, then to intercept two raids that were crossing the Thames Estuary heading for Essex before attacking North Weald. Later, 12 Group wing was asked to make a sweep through North Kent.

Action by Fighter Squadrons

6. At 16.30 hrs, 12 Group wing was reported to be over Hornchurch at 25,000 feet, proceeding towards Sheerness. Immediately, two raids that had been approaching Sheerness turned northwards across the Thames Estuary; 12 Group was requested to intercept these raids between North Weald and the coast, as it was feared that the enemy was about to attack fighter aerodromes in Essex. As the Duxford Wing continued, however, to proceed towards Sheerness, Hornchurch was requested to try and inform it by R/T of the new patrol line, but was unable to communicate with the wing because of continuous R/T traffic between the wing and Duxford. Immediately it was evident that the Duxford Wing might fail to intercept the raids, a pair of 11 Group squadrons were ordered from East Kent to try and overtake, but unfortunately the enemy reached North Weald first and bombed the aerodrome, causing some casualties and damage. The enemy, however, was intercepted by 11 Group squadrons immediately after completing his bombing and heavy casualties were inflicted.

213

Immediately it was seen that the Duxford Wing was not going to intercept the raids, 12 Group was requested to make a sweep through North Kent to intercept two more raids heading towards Biggin Hill aerodrome, but the AOC 12 Group recalled the Duxford Wing because of a report that the weather was no longer fine at Duxford and he was afraid of difficulty in landing so many squadrons at one aerodrome. The Duxford Wing, therefore, missed an interception with these two raids, which fortunately did not proceed far inland, probably because they saw additional 11 Group squadrons climbing from Biggin Hill area.

The day's combat statistics were reported as follows:

Enemy casualties were 16 destroyed, 6 probably destroyed and 5 damaged, for the loss of 1 RAF pilot, who was killed.

Of this final phase of battle, Air Vice-Marshal Keith Park reported:

Use of Mass Formations – Big Wings and 'Balbos'
The Air Ministry held a conference … to examine a proposal that wings should be adopted as standard formation for air fighting, and that was whenever possible. 'Balbos' – mass formations of six squadrons – should be employed against enemy raids on this country. These proposals arose as a result of remarkable results against fighters as well as bombers.

As a result of the Air Ministry conference, the Duxford Wing was invited to operate in 11 Group area on every possible occasion during the last half of October. In view of the results obtained in 11 Group when employing mass formations, the operations of the Duxford Wing have been watched with close interest. The attached table of patrols by the Duxford Wing shows that in ten sorties, it effected one interception and destroyed one enemy aircraft. On only a few days was the weather considered fit for the Duxford Wing to operate. On several days that were unfit for these large formations, the squadrons in 11 Group were operating at high pressure, in pairs.

The intensity of the air fighting over 11 Group territory during the second half of October can be gauged by the fact that its squadrons accounted for 83 enemy aircraft destroyed, plus 62 probably destroyed, plus 66 damaged; a total of 211 aircraft accounted for in the period covered by the attached table, Appendix 'B' [author's note: see Fig. 1]. Moreover, during this short period, the squadrons in 11 Group, by successful interception, prevented scores of enemy raids from proceeding inland and bombing vital objectives. On numerous occasions the enemy turned about and retreated at speed before our fighters could come within effective range.

From watching the operations of the Duxford Wing of four squadrons during the second half of October, confirmation was obtained of the lessons previously learned in 11 Group in the employment of smaller wing formations. Other lessons appear to have been brought out as under:

1. Mass formations require the assistance of good sector controllers if they are to effect interceptions of enemy fighter formations;
2. Large wings of four or five squadrons suffer serious difficulties in R/T communications;
3. Increasing the number of squadrons in a wing does not appear to increase the chances of interceptions or the area of search effectively covered;
4. It is inadvisable to concentrate four or five squadrons on an aerodrome in the autumn, because all are likely to be weather-bound together.
5. The maximum size of a wing should be three squadrons, not four or five as previously practised in the North.

Returning to the actual aerial events of 29 October 1940, it had been a typical day for Coastal Command, Blenheims of which successfully attacked Brest power station. A Sunderland of 201 Squadron, based at Wick, crashed into high ground during an ASR search, four of the crew being killed, and another Sunderland, whilst searching for the lost 'Flying Porcupine', forced-landed on the sea in darkness; the crew were rescued but the aircraft sank and was lost when under tow. The PRU's sorties were substantially reduced by adverse weather, although 2 Group's Blenheims bombed Rotterdam, and various enemy airfields, including Antwerp, where a hangar was destroyed; a 144 Squadron Blenheim failed to return from Le Havre. At night, Bomber Command sent ninety-eight aircraft to hit industrial targets, marshalling yards, aerodromes and other military targets in Germany and the low countries. A 106 Squadron Hampden disappeared whilst mining the Baltic, and icing on their return trip caused a 50 Squadron Hampden crew to abandon their aircraft near Linton-on-Ouse. No. 99 Squadron, based at Newmarket, lost a Wellington which crashed into a Northumbrian hillside returning from Berlin, killing one of the crew, and similarly a 10 Squadron Whitley flew into a Cumbrian hillside whilst returning to Leeming, although the crew survived. When landing back at Dishforth in a cross-wind, a 51 Squadron Whitley also crashed, killing one of the crew.

Wednesday, 30 October 1940

The day awoke to a frosty start with light winds and cloud varying from 5/10ths to 8/10ths. Visibility, however, was good, and so *Jafü* 2's fighters prepared for *Jabo* operations. Perhaps indicative of the strain the *Jagdwaffe* was also under, only two of these raids would be mounted during the day.

At 11.15 hrs, the Spitfires of 41 and 222 Squadrons scrambled from Hornchurch to patrol base at 30,000ft, joining up over Tilbury, and five minutes later 249 Squadron's Hurricanes left North Weald to patrol their aerodrome at 20,000ft. At 11.30 hrs, the first raid, comprising 150 Me 109s in three waves, appeared, the first sixty fighters of which flew in over the North Foreland to Shoeburyness, leaving via Kent; the second wave also came in over the North Foreland, flying out over Hawkinge, and the third crossed the coast over Hastings, turning about over Ashford and withdrawing southwards.

Nos. 41 and 222 Squadrons were vectored south from the Hornchurch area to intercept, and at 11.45 hrs Flight Lieutenant Norman Ryder, Red 1 and leading 41, led the squadron into attack nine Me 109s south of Maidstone at 28,500ft, which were 'acting as rear-guard … I fired at enemy aircraft and saw smoke and light vapour. Followed E/A down and gave another long burst when E/A burst into flames and starboard wing broke in half. The pilot seemed not to abandon aircraft. I saw the 109 entering cloud in a spin burning furiously.' Clearly, this 109 was not getting home.

Pilot Officer Fred Aldridge, Yellow 2, dived after his leader to attack fifty Me 109s down-sun and 1,500ft below, but was attacked himself by two Me 109s. Evading his assailants through slow aileron turns, when one of the 109s dived away, Aldridge followed. After a one-second burst the 109 'started smoking before he entered cloud. I think the pilot tried to bale out but I am unable to confirm this. The 109 fell in a wood near a railway line, west of Ashford. I went down to investigate and saw the wreckage burning in the wood and the pilot lying in a field 600 yards away without any clothes on.' This was *Unteroffizier* Kurt Töpfer of 7/JG 26, who was killed at Brook Farm, Marden, this also being the same 109 hit by Flight Lieutenant Norman Ryder. No. 41 Squadron's intelligence officer considered that the 109 attacked between Ashford and Dungeness by the New Zealander Pilot Officer John MacKenzie, Blue 3, who saw bits flying off the 109, which skidded into cloud, pouring smoke, was the aircraft down at 'R2735' – also Töpfer's – although this seems scant evidence upon which to base that firm conclusion. Blue 1, Flight Lieutenant Tony Lovell, Pilot Officer Denis Adams and Sergeant Robert Angus all claimed damaged Me 109s. No. 41 Squadron suffered no loss.

As 41 Squadron went into the attack, Flying Officer Brian van Mentz of 222 Squadron sighted six Me 109s above, poised to engage the Spitfires. Van Mentz attacked the fifth of these fighters, which had gone into line astern: 'the enemy pilot jettisoned his hood, and dived away in the direction of France, emitting brown smoke' [ORB]. Pilot Officer John 'Chips' Carpenter also attacked on of these Me 109s, noticing 'bits falling off'. Attacked himself by two other 109s, Carpenter broke away, returning to Hornchurch with a damaged propeller and engine. Pilot Officer Hilary Edridge, however, was hit by a 109 and burst into flames, the pilot crashing at Ewhurst when attempting a forced-landing; rescued from the burning wreckage, the pilot died of his injuries. Pilot Officer Alfred Davies was also shot down and killed, his Spitfire 'seen to spin into the ground at a point near Battle, one of the mainplanes of his aircraft having parted at a great height' [ORB].

Patrolling over North Weald at 26,000ft, Pilot Officer Antony Thompson, Yellow 2, at 12.20 hrs saw twelve Me 109s flying west, towards North Weald at 28,000ft. The 109s turned upon seeing the Hurricanes, and Thompson climbed to 30,000ft, seeing a *Schwarm* of four Me 109s at 30,000ft, heading out to sea over Hawkinge. These then returned to the Kentish coast, one of the 109s attacking Thompson, who remained at 28,000ft whilst the 109s dived 500ft below. Diving after the Germans, Thompson hit the left-hand Me 109, which 'flicked over on his back and went down'. After a further burst the 109's 'rear tank caught fire and he crashed into the sea', this being a machine of 8/JG 26, the pilot of which was rescued unhurt by the *Seenotdienst*. Thompson was then shot-up by another 109, which he evaded and safely landed his damaged Hurricane at Hawkinge. Sergeant Michal Maciejowski was also shot down and forced-landed at

Herstmonceux: 'and was taken in charge by the local police who thought he was a German.' Pilot Officer William Millington, however, was shot down into the Channel and never seen again.

In this fight, 222 Squadron had lost two Spitfires destroyed, with a pilot killed and another who would die of his injuries, and another aircraft damaged. No. 249 Squadron had two Hurricanes shot down, with a pilot killed, and another damaged. Whilst *Feldwebel* Detlev Lüth of 1/JG 3 and *Feldwebel* Werner Bielfeldt of 7/JG 51 both claimed Hurricanes, *Major* Adolf Galland, *Kommodore* of JG 26, *Oberleutnant* Raithel and *Leutnant* Otto Grote, both of 4/JG 54, all claimed Spitfires destroyed.

After the Me 109s withdrew from Kent and the Channel, there was a short lull, during which the action briefly shifted to 12 Group. At 13.45 hrs, Blue Section of 1 Squadron, Pilot Officer Raymond Lewis, a Canadian, Pilot Officer George Goodman and Sergeant Venda Jicha, were scrambled to patrol base, shortly afterwards sighting a twin-engined aircraft Goodman mistook for a Blenheim. Lewis and Jicha, however, rightly identified the machine as a Ju 88, attacking the bomber at 14.18 hrs and shooting it down. This was a reconnaissance bomber of 8/LG 1 on a sortie to photograph the Metropolitan Vickers electrical factory at Salford, which crash-landed at Middle Fen, near Ely; two of the crew had already abandoned the machine and descended by parachute, being captured slightly injured, whilst the two remaining with their aircraft were taken into custody unharmed.

Since the first *Jabo* raid had retired, 11 Group's squadrons had maintained standing patrols at high altitude, in anticipation of another attack. At 14.45 hrs, 253 Squadron scrambled from Kenley to patrol Maidstone, being followed five minutes later by eight Hurricanes of 501 Squadron. No. 602 Squadron was off from Westhampnett at 15.05 hrs, to patrol Selsey Bill; 17 and 249 Squadrons left North Weald to patrol North Weald – Hornchurch – Dover, and at 16.15 hrs 41 Squadron took-off from Hornchurch to patrol Maidstone. The next attack, in fact, came in at 15.40 hrs, eighty Me 109s heading for Maidstone and reaching south-east London, dropping several bombs. Then, five smaller formations, totally fifty aircraft, crossed in between Beachy Head and Dover, twelve of which penetrated as far as Harwich.

Just after 16.00 hrs, 41 Squadron was patrolling over Ashford when bounced by *Major* Adolf Galland, *Kommodore* of JG 26, who shot down two Spitfires: Pilot Officer Gilbert Draper crashed at Postling and was admitted to Willesborough Hospital, slightly injured, but Sergeant Leonard Garvey was killed, crashing at Stanford. No. 41 Squadron made no response, the German ace's lightning attack being over in a matter of seconds; the unfortunate Garvey, however, has a place in history as the last of 'The Few' to be killed in action during the Battle of Britain.

No. 253 Squadron had climbed to 19,000ft, heading towards Maidstone, when the eight 501 Squadron Hurricanes joined them and the formation was ordered to increase height as there was a 'mill going on in France'. Climbing to 29,000ft, 253 Squadron opened up 'into attack formation' and vectored south-east, then north, sighting up to forty Me 109s 'flying in two clumps of no particular formation at 27,000 feet, from SE to NW. [Nos.] 253 and 501 Squadrons attacked simultaneously, 253 from three-quarters astern and port from sun side and general dogfight ensued.' [ORB].

Flying Officer Alan Eckford was 253 Squadron's weaver, Green 2, and over Biggin Hill at 27,000ft, at 16.00 hrs, dived on a *Schwarm* of four Me 109s, attacking the

Rottenhund of the leading *Rotte*, tracer hitting the enemy fighter which died away. Eckford then engaged the rearmost 109, pursuing it into a climbing left-hand turn and after a short burst white and black smoke, then flame, issued from the target, which 'dived vertically away into cloud'. This was possibly the same fighter attacked by 253 Squadron's Blue Leader, South African Pilot Officer Spencer Peacock-Edwards, who dived after a 109 heading for cloud, firing at it from 100 yards astern and watching 'a large piece of silvery white fabric come from the E/A.' At this point, the 109 was also attacked by Pilot Officer Bob Dafforn, Green 1 of 501 Squadron, who got on the 109's tail, firing two bursts of eight seconds: 'E/A eventually blew up mid-air, one wing (starboard) and part of tailplane flying off and many smaller pieces and undercarriage falling away'. Sergeant James Lacey, 501 Squadron's Red 3, was also diving after the same 109: 'I got in a burst from directly astern at 250 yards ... Almost immediately the starboard wing came off and I immediately pulled away to avoid the debris.' Eckford then 'came out of cloud at 3,000 feet and saw the wreckage burning in a field about four miles South of Meopham, near Gravesend. The pilot baled out and when I approached he held his hands up.'

For *Unteroffizier* A. Fahrian of 6/JG 3, whose machine lost a wing and crashed at Leylands, Meopham, the war was over – and, yet again, on the scorecard a single Me 109 destroyed had become three. No. 501 Squadron retired without loss, but 253 Squadron's Sergeant Peter Moore, an Australian and former Oxford scholar, was shot down, crash-landing at Southfleet, slightly injured. According to this pilot, 'his aircraft was damaged by a fixed gun on a Me 109, firing backwards' [ORB].

No. 17 Squadron had also sighted and attacked the Me 109s over Maidstone, Flying Officer Count Manfred Czernin diving to attack two aircraft below, one of which transpired to be a Hurricane; he attacked the other, a Me 109, which climbed at first before it 'finally dived down through cloud with black smoke pouring from it' [ORB], Czernin claiming a probable. This was possibly the same aircraft attacked by Sergeant Glyn Griffiths, Red 2, who chased and caught a Me 109 flying south-east, which, after three short bursts, 'became enveloped in black smoke and fell into a spin, and I thought I saw some pieces fall off the port mainplane. I last saw it in this condition when it spun from 19,000 feet into the clouds, which were at 5,000 feet.' This Me 109 ultimately crash-landed in a hop fiend at East Farleigh, Maidstone, where the wounded pilot, *Gefreiter* E. Schüller of 6/JG 3, was captured. All of 17 Squadron's pilots returned safely to base.

No. 249 Squadron suffered no losses, its only claim made by North Weald's station commander, Wing Commander Victor Beamish, who chased two Me 109s heading south-east, from a direction of London, and got within range near the coast. Out at sea, off Dover, Beamish fired all his ammunition at these retreating 109s; one dropped from 20,000ft to 8,000ft, streaming glycol, disappearing into the haze, 'the other one stood by it, swinging on its tail', but upon being attacked himself by other 109s, the Hurricane pilot made a quick exit; Beamish claimed a probable.

The final defending squadron to go in action, in what would be the last fighter combat of the Battle of Britain, was 602 Squadron, at 16.20 hrs over the Robertsbridge to Dungeness areas. Having initially patrolled Selsey Bill, the Spitfires had been vectored to Mayfield. Blue Section, however, became lost when Blue Leader's aircraft developed communication problems, and returned to base. The remainder of 602 Squadron were at 27,000ft, south of Mayfield and flying west when 'two clusters of Me 109s' were seen, flying north and 3,000ft above. The Spitfires went into line astern and the 109s dived to attack, after which the squadron split up and individual combats ensued, progressing seawards.

Sergeant Andrew McDowell, Blue 1, was flying north-east over Dungeness at 27,000ft when

> one E/A out of formation of approximately forty, heading north, 3,000 feet above us, dived down to make a head-on attack. I pulled up to make an answering attack but spun off before fire could be opened. I climbed up again to 23,000ft and was attacked by a Me 109 who half-rolled on top of me. I waited until E/A was in range, throttled back and jinked to the side. E/A was travelling too fast to follow and I got on his tail, giving a six-second burst. E/A caught fire and continued dive into sea. I endeavoured to make further attacks but each time was chased down by superior number of E/A.

Pilot Officer Osgood Hanbury, Yellow 2,

> [Made] a climbing beam attack on a Me 109 and accidentally went into a spin. I then climbed to the West up to 29[,000]–30,000 feet and came back into the fray and made a stern quarter attack on the last of three E/A who were trying to reach a defensive circle. E/A burst into flames, the pilot jumping out, and I was then forced to break away with Me 109s on my tail.

The only Me 109 pilot who baled out over Kent on this day was *Unteroffizier* Fahrian, at Meopham, so it is possible that Hanbury also attacked him. During the day, three Me 109s returned to France with combat damaged, but only the 8/JG 26 Me 109, which crashed during the previous raid appears in Luftwaffe records as having crashed into the sea. Both Hanbury and McDowell were credited with Me 109s destroyed. No. 602 Squadron's Pilot Officer Douglas Gage, however, was shot-up and forced-landed at Newchurch, unhurt. Sergeant William Smith crash-landed, wounded, on the foreshore at Lydd and Pilot Officer Archibald Lyall returned to base 'his aircraft slightly damaged' [ORB].

This final daylight skirmish had ended in the Germans' favour, who lost just two fighters. Two Spitfires had been destroyed and three more damaged, with one pilot being killed and two wounded, and a Hurricane had been damaged, its pilot wounded. The Germans slightly overclaimed, pilots of *Stab* JG 26, 5/JG 51, I/JG 77 and 4/JG 54 claiming nine 'Spitfires' destroyed.

Although Fighter Command had suffered its last combat fatality of the Battle of Britain, during the evening flying accidents claimed more young lives. At 20.10 hrs, one of the new Beaufighters, belonging to Redhill's 219 Squadron, crashed and exploded near Balcombe Park, Sussex, killing Pilot Officer Kenneth Worsdell, a Cranwellian, and his radar operator, Sergeant Eric Gardiner. The night fighter had been patrolling when the pilot descended through low cloud and crashed, the aircraft disintegrating. Finally, at 20.30 hrs, deteriorating weather caused the crash of a 23 Squadron Blenheim, up from Ford, Flying Officer John Woodward DFC, Pilot Officer Allan Atkinson and AC2 Tom Perry all being killed at South Bersted – the last Fighter Command aircrew to die in the Battle of Britain, by terrible coincidence Woodward's father had been killed in action at Passchendaele on 30 October 1917.

The worsening weather had much reduced Coastal Command's operations, although Ostend harbour was attacked by Blenheims. No. 2 Group's Blenheims successfully attacked E-boats off Cherbourg, where the docks were also bombed, and shipping off Barfleur. The bad weather led to most of Bomber Command's night operations being scrubbed, but Blenheims hit Duisburg port and marshalling yards at Ruhrorhafen, whilst Wellingtons went to Emden, Flushing and Antwerp. There was one casualty: a 101 Squadron Blenheim returning to West Rainham from Germany crashed near Scunthorpe. There were no survivors.

Thursday, 31 October 1940

October 1940, Churchill wrote, 'came in raw and rough' – but, owing to the weather, went out like a lamb.

At Kenley, 501 Squadron recorded: 'Weather very poor. Raining hard. The Squadron was brought to readiness at 13.00 hrs, and at 13.25 hrs two aircraft were ordered to investigate a single aircraft but pilots had to land owing to the weather. There was no further flying during the day.' [ORB].

No. 501 Squadron, in fact, had flown throughout the sixteen-week conflict without a rest period, mainly in 11 Group, and had lost the most pilots either killed or missing: nineteen.

No. 41 Squadron, another unit with a fine fighting record, reported at Hornchurch: 'Wind light westerly, increasing to gale, heavy rain, cloud 10/10ths.' [ORB]. There would be no flying whatsoever for the majority of fighters on both sides of the Channel.

On this historic day, the weather similarly curtailed Coastal Command's operations, although two 233 Squadron Hudsons bombed enemy shipping off Norway whilst the third Hudson was shot down by *Leutnant* Siegfried Freytag of 6/JG 77, its crew all missing. The majority of 2 Group Blenheims aborted their sorties due to the weather, just railway sidings at Soesterberg and E-boats off the Somme being attacked; there were no nocturnal operations by either Command.

General Adolf Galland:

> the weather over the Channel, especially in autumn, is predominantly westerly, i.e. developing from West to East, which, of course, is a grave disadvantage to an attacker from the East. The defender therefore knew the actual weather and what to expect in the battle zone sooner than the attacker. The British could nearly always forecast the weather early enough to make provisions for it. We were always surprised by it. More

and more frequently situations arose in which the assembling of bombers and fighters could be accomplished partially or not at all, and because of this the bombers sustained higher losses. With the seasonal deterioration of the weather it became increasingly difficult to carry out the biggest raids according to plan.

The German tactics of strong daylight fighter sweeps and high-altitude fighter-bomber attacks throughout October 1940, however, represented a sensible strategy. Although such indiscriminate light bombing could not bring about Britain's defeat, these raids were nonetheless inspired. Although the move to make one *Staffel* in every *Gruppe* a *Jabo* unit was unpopular with the German fighter pilots themselves, the fighter-bomber was an exceptionally dangerous weapon – as the Allies would later demonstrate to devastating effect during the second half of the war. Single-engined fighter-bombers were fast and could attack at any altitude, from 30,000 feet to ground-level, their presence within a single-engined formation being impossible for RDF or the Observer Corps to detect – and once bombs had been dropped the *Jabo* reverted to being a pure fighter. The high-altitude nature of these raids also meant that reacting to them several times a day, or more, was physically exhausting, especially in unpressurised cockpits. Moreover, the attacks by lone Ju 88s on days of bad weather ensured little rest for the aircrew of Fighter Command.

Equally, though, these were difficult missions for the *Jabo* pilots especially, owing to a lack of training and given that the Me 109 had no bomb-sighting apparatus, only lines on the side panels of the pilot's canopy, which if brought in line with the horizon indicated whether the aircraft was at an angle of 40, 50, 60 or 70°. The actual bombing, therefore, relied upon guesswork, and it was impossible to guarantee hitting a specific target from high-altitude. Little of any military value, therefore, was achieved during this final phase, and nor did the British economy unduly suffer – but these nuisance attacks got Fighter Command off the ground, to be engaged by German fighters. These raids, though, were incomparable to the sorties of Allied fighter-bombers later in the war, which were directly supporting the advancing army, usually at low-level, because of that and one other vital fact: the Allied fighters enjoyed total aerial supremacy, which the Luftwaffe never did over Britain in 1940. Certainly on particular days the tide of battle swung well in the enemy's favour – but the fact remains that, overall, Fighter Command never lost control of the air.

Flying Officer Frank Brinsden, a Spitfire pilot of 19 Squadron at Fowlmere in 12 Group commented that: 'I do not believe that many of us at squadron pilot level realized that we were engaged in a full-scale battle, nor how important the outcome would be if we lost. Again, in retrospect, intelligence briefing was sadly lacking in its scope.'

Flight Sergeant George C. 'Grumpy' Unwin DFM, the 'High Priest' of 19 Squadron added,

At the time I felt that we of Fighter Command had done nothing out of the ordinary. I had been trained for the job and luckily had a lot of experience. I was always most disappointed if the Squadron got into a scrap when I was off duty, and this applied to all the pilots I knew.

It was only after the event that I realised how serious defeat would have been, but then, without being big-headed, we never ever considered being beaten, it was just not possible in our eyes, this simply was our outlook. As we lost pilots and aircraft, replacements were forthcoming. We were never at much below full strength. Of course, the new pilots were inexperienced, but so were the German replacements.

Air Vice-Marshal Keith Park, the 'Defender of London', later reported on this final phase:

> I wish to pay high tribute to the fine offensive spirit of pilots in all squadrons during the past two months of difficult fighting. During the second phase of operations, the morale of our pilots has been severely tested, because the enemy has had a great advantage in superior performance at high altitude in the Fighter versus Fighter battle. When well-led, however, our pilots have out-fought the enemy at all heights. With few exceptions. Squadron commanders and flight commanders have quickly adapted themselves to the changing tactics of the enemy.
>
> The enemy's superior numbers enable him to throw our fighter forces on the defensive, resulting in the majority of the fighting in the past three months taking place either over British territory or close to our shores. Our constant aim, however, has been to intercept the enemy as far forward as possible and make him shed his bombs harmlessly in open country or in the sea. The aim of all squadrons in the Group now is to inflict such heavy punishment that the enemy will find it too hot to send his fighter patrols or daylight raids inland over home territory, and our pilots will not be satisfied until the air over the Homeland is again free of the German Air Force.

As the rain lashed down on Whitehall, the prime minister chaired a meeting of the Government Defence Committee deep underground in the Cabinet War Rooms. It was agreed that the invasion crisis had passed, the future threat of it 'remote', and that, therefore, with overseas military commitments in mind, Britain's defences should now be stood-down from their alerted state of 'Immediate Readiness'.

Officially, so far as the Air Ministry was concerned, the Battle of Britain was over.

Big Wing: A Bitter Postscript

So what did 'The Few' themselves think the 'Big Wing' and appended controversy?

Over the years I posed that question to a number of pilots and other personnel from both 11 and 12 Groups.

Wing Commander Douglas Blackwood, CO 310 (Czech) Squadron, Duxford Wing:

> I suppose I would not be speaking unreasonably by saying that the wing was eventually a failure in so much as there was never really time to get three or four squadrons off the ground and into some shape and form to attack the usual mass of enemy aircraft effectively. On one or two occasions I was detailed by Bader and the AOC to lead the formation, so I know something of the difficulty. But when we did attack a formation of enemy bombers, the wing was extremely successful. I would say that the main reason for any loss of effectiveness was primarily due to a sort of jealousy between the AOCs of both 11 and 12 Groups. [No.] 11 Group felt that it was their responsibility to protect London without 12 Group interfering.

Squadron Leader James Thomson, Hurricane pilot, 302 (Polish) Squadron, Duxford Wing:

> The Big Wing was a wonderful operation to take part in as we felt that we were answering numbers with numbers. However, subsequent study suggested that Air Vice-Marshal [Keith] Park's strategy may have been the sounder. He used smaller numbers to break up the attacking formations, so disrupting their concentration of force over the target area and the effectiveness of their attack. It also enabled him to retain some aircraft for the defence of their bases during that most vulnerable operation: refuelling and rearming. Furthermore, the Big Wing took some time to form up and reach the area under attack; occasionally it missed the boat.
>
> The relative merits of the two methods were argued openly by the circulation of correspondence on the subject between the two Groups. Many of us felt that this was a diversion of mental effort from the main aim of defeating the Luftwaffe and was not entirely becoming of the authorities concerned.

Squadron Leader Waclaw 'Vic' Bergman, Hurricane pilot, 310 (Czech) Squadron, Duxford Wing:

In those heady days I was a mere pilot officer who loved flying, loved the Hurricane, and was able to point my guns at a German target. But my English was limited. I have always had the impression that the initial interception of the enemy was left to No 11 Group. We were then to follow the raiders and damage or destroy as many as possible on their return journey. More than once, the wing was released for lunch when Douglas Bader pegged into the dining room and called 'Come on boys, we are wanted!' That was followed by the clautter of cutlery on the unfinished plates – rush for the door, transport to dispersals, and in fifteen–twenty minutes all twelve Hurricanes of 242 [Canadian] Squadron, took off in formation on the grass airfield, immediately followed by ours of 310, and 19 Squadron's Spitfires from Fowlmere soon appeared overhead, their job being to protect us from the enemy fighters while we Hurricanes went for the bombers. It did not always work out like that, though. In mid-September our squadron was meeting a formation of Do 17s when we were jumped by a swarm of Me 109s: I was shot down.

Warrant Officer Anton Markiewicz, Hurricane pilot, 302 (Polish) Squadron, Duxford Wing:

While flying with the Big Wing in 1940 I was in favour of it. Destroying German aircraft before they reached the target, or forcing them to drop their bombs just anywhere would be a great achievement. But to use a large force tlo do that, left the industrial Midlands without adequate protection. It was rather risky. No doubt Fighter Command knew that, and did not want to take any chances. One thing I do remember is that if we missed the Germans Bader was very displeased, and let us know in simple language!

Squadron Leader Sir Kenneth Stoddart, 611 Squadron, Spitfire pilot, Duxford Wing:

We of 611 Squadron were stationed at Digby and for a period of time flew down to Fowlmere on a daily basis, returning home at dusk. The only views I may have had about Big Wings or anything else in those days would have been made in ignorance; apart from Dunkirk, they were the first days that the squadron was truly involved in a big action.

Wing Commander George Unwin, 19 Squadron, Spitfire pilot, Duxford Wing:

It didn't take Douglas Bader long to realise that sending a squadron of fighters to take on huge bomber raids was not the answer, especially as these raids were usually escorted by fighters. As he put it – if only we had three times the number of fighters as a unit we could shoot down three times the number of enemy aircraft. In my opinion there was a further factor that was behind his argument for the Big Wing; for the first five months of his return to the RAF he had been flying Spitfires; with 242 [Canadian] Squadron, he was on Hurricanes, and no matter what the loyal Hurricane pilots may say, it was no match for the 109. Agreed, it could out-turn the Hun, but obviously this is far outweighed if the target is leaving you by 30 mph. On the other hand, the Hurricane had it over the Spitfire as a gun platform, both from the steadiness of that platform and concentration of fire. In my opinion the Hurricane was capable of shooting down bombers more effectively, provided it was not interfered with by the 109s. The Hurricane casualties at this time support this argument. Once we had the Big Wing operating it was very obviously the answer in that the Hurricane casualties dropped appreciably, whilst the number of German aircraft destroyed increased. The wing started operating in the first week of September 1940, and was in action until November. In my opinion it was an unqualified success.

As for the argument as to the value of flying sixty fighters together, there really was no basis for this disagreement between the two AOCs, for the simple reason that it would not have been feasible to assemble such a large number of fighters from the aerodromes in No 11 Group in time to intercept an incoming raid. We at Duxford and Fowlmere had a full fifteen minutes of flying to arrive at the battle area (north of the Thames) and with our two aerodromes only a couple of miles apart we could easily assemble the wing en route to London. I am convinced that the real trouble was caused by Keith Park steadfastly refusing to use the strength of Duxford to anywhere near its capabilities. Day after day we would sit at readiness without being called on to help out. When we were called out, quite often it was merely to patrol the No 11 Group aerodromes while their squadrons were rearming and refuelling. On other days we were too late on the scene. The most glaring example of this was when we were scrambled as a wing and vectored to London area. After about seven minutes our Controller, using plain language, said 'They are bombing North Weald, go there quickly!' This was the day that North Weald was very heavily damaged. When we arrived it was all over, we were too late, I suggest that sixty fighters could have considerably lessened that damage. The total flying time from Duxford to North Weald is six–seven minutes.

One other very important factor was the effect the Big Wing had on the German aircrews. They had been told that the RAF was just about finished and that all would soon be over. This was to boost their morale which by the time was pretty low – imagine their feelings when instead of being met by a depleted squadron, no less than sixty descended on them!

Flying Officer Ken Wilkinson, 19 Squadron, Spitfire pilot, Duxford Wing:

Fighter Command's strategy of aerodrome locations was successful in that there were very few attempts in daylight of mass bombing raids over the east coast of England and Scotland, but the possibility always remained. The squadrons resting at Wittering, Kirton, Newcastle, Drem, Montrose, etc maintained the defence of the east coast. Most critics seem to forget that we had a lot to defend – this aspect may have had some bearing on the infrequent calls upon the Duxford Wing. If one can be satisfied that there was little or no likelihood of a major bomber offensive from the east, then the Duxford Wing was right. Seeing these large numbers of bombers and fighter escorts, and realising that 11 Group was continually taking a pasting, there had to be some help we could give; if sixty additional RAF fighters arrived from the north in time, chances were that the Luftwaffe could have been deterred earlier. Being the lowest of the low (i.e. a brand new RAFVR sergeant pilot), I had no idea about the arguments that we are now told were taking place regarding tactics, but my personal experience tells me that Fighter Command was dedicated to protecting our country and so I am loathe to believe that **one** Group AOC was pursuing selfish interests contrary to the common objective of defeating (or negating) the Luftwaffe.

Flight Lieutenant Richard Jones, 19 Squadron, Spitfire pilot, Duxford Wing:

Early in September 1940 I was transferred from No 64 Squadron at Kenley in No 11 Group to No 19 Squadron at Fowlmere, a part of No 12 Group. By then, the latter was a part of Douglas Bader's Big Wing. My immediate impression was the experience of flying with a wing comprising five squadrons of both Spitfires and Hurricanes, instead of anything between 5–10 aircraft taking off from Kenley to intercept large numbers of enemy aircraft. To me this experience gave enormous confidence, looking around and seeing anything from fifty upwards of fighters keeping me company! The Big Wing must have had a great effect on the lowering of enemy morale, who, for the first time, encountered such a formidable opponent.

Wing Commander Frank Brinsden, 19 Squadron, Spitfire pilot, Duxford Wing:

The constraints of Bader's ponderous formation was a disaster in my opinion, a retrograde step. Nothing was achieved by arriving en masse because the wing disintegrated almost immediately battle was joined. In fact time, and therefore advantage, was lost during assembly and this compounded the effect of scramble orders. These observations on tactics are, of course, in retrospect, but I do recall at the time feeling some unease or dissatisfaction at No 19 Squadron's inability to do better.

Wing Commander David Cox, 19 Squadron, Spitfire pilot, Duxford Wing:

When the wing went into action, the Spitfire squadrons, or squadron, was left to their own devices to combat the 109 escorts.

I think five squadrons was too many. I remember going round and round for some fifteen to twenty minutes waiting for the wing to form up and get going. This resulted in the wing often arriving late at the patrol line given by the 11 Group Controller.

There is no doubt that some of the 11 Group squadrons blamed the Big Wing's late arrival for their airfields being bombed. This caused some bad feeling between the pilots. Even as late as the 1960s, an ex-pilot of 11 Group's 41 Squadron in a pub in Grimsby nearly gave me a punch on the nose, as during discussion on the war he found out I had been in 19 Squadron and part of the Big Wing!

I think a wing of three squadrons would have made better time. Why not the other two Spitfire squadrons operating as a further wing? They would have made the patrol line quicker and with the advantage of height. However, I do think that at times the wing could have been called for earlier by 11 Group.

Was the Big Wing a success? I doubt it. Its best effect was on the afternoon of 15 September 1940 when I remember the words of Bobby Oxspring, a flight commander in 66 Squadron, saying what a wonderful sight it was to see some sixty fighters suddenly appear. No doubt it was a bit of a shock to the Luftwaffe!

Regarding [Douglas] Bader, I was only a sergeant pilot and he was a snob, so wouldn't deign to converse with the likes of me at that time. He wasn't a man you could like, I would say, but he was an inspiration. His voice over the radio when we were in the air gave us confidence.

Some years after the war, I was on holiday somewhere in England and it turned out that the hotel was run by a former 11 Group Battle of Britain pilot. When he found out that I had been in 12 Group and flew with the Duxford Wing, he threatened to punch me on the nose!

Wing Commander Bernard 'Jimmy' Jennings, 19 Squadron, Spitfire pilot, Duxford Wing:

As I recall, the pilots had two views on the Big Wing. Firstly that it was rather cumbersome, even when led by Brian Lane, a wonderful pilot.

Secondly, if you were in one of the rear squadrons, those in front would get the first attack and we would have to go down and help them out at our best advantage. Or if we were the front squadron, then we had plenty of cover and help available.

Air Marshal Sir Denis Crowley-Milling, Hurricane pilot, 242 (Canadian) Squadron:

No leader has ever equalled Douglas Bader, in my experience, and I flew with him in both the Duxford and later Tangmere wings. He never ceased encouraging we young, inexperienced, pilots and helped us conquer our fears. We were captivated by his charisma and indomitable fighting spirit. In the air, over the radio, he kept up this constant flow of talk, cracked jokes and made us all feel ten times the men we were. I was lucky to have been under his guidance during the Battle of Britain. Naturally, Douglas wanted to get we of 242 [Canadian] Squadron into the action. He used to say 'Why don't they get us airborne when the Germans are building up over the Pas-de-Calais?' He felt that we could then proceed south and meet the enemy formation on the way in. We agreed, because it was impossible to accept sitting comparatively idle while our friends in the South were getting all the action.

Flight Lieutenant H.E. 'Teddy' Morton, Ops 'B' Controller, Duxford:

Squadron Leader [Douglas] Bader would frequently telephone Ops 'B' at Duxford to get the form. At mess parties he would discuss tactics, the 'Hun in the sun' and all that, demanding to know why the wing wasn't scrambled sooner by 11 Group. Alternatively he would insist on speaking to 'Woody' to get scrambles effected. It did seem that 11 Group were a law unto themselves.

Squadron Leader Peter Brown, 611 Squadron, Spitfire pilot, Duxford Wing:

I served in 12 Group for a year as a regular pilot with 611 Squadron. My experience included convoy patrols, Dunkirk, North Sea 'X' Raids and wing operations from Duxford. I flew several times with the five squadron Duxford Wing, including on 15 September 1940. We had all been aware in 611 Squadron that a tremendous battle was being fought by 10 and 11 Groups, and wanted to play our part in it. Nothing of any real significance, however, was happening in the 12 Group Sector. I did not, however, agree with the wing, and am convinced that the Controversy was why Dowding and Park – the real victors – were so badly treated afterwards. In October 1940, I was posted to 41 Squadron, at Hornchurch in 11 Group. By then I considered myself an experienced pilot – but the dramatic change in the tempo of operations and combat, owing to the presence of Me 109s, was traumatic.

Wing Commander H.R. 'Dizzy' Allen, 66 Squadron, Spitfire pilot, 11 Group:

Had [Douglas] Bader served in 11 Group he might have realised that his 'Big Wing' idea was balderdash, for the frontline anyway – and that was the line that mattered.

Group Captain Tom Gleave, 253 Squadron, Hurricane pilot, 11 Group:

> Douglas Bader was completely wrong about tactics. He had been out of the service for ten years and lagged far behind on modern concepts. All he was thinking of was the old First World War 'flying circuses' – which were irrelevant to the Battle of Britain, which was fought by modern aircraft and technology.

Group Captain Thomas Long, 11 Group controller:

> All very well for LM and his 'yes' men to say that the Balbo would have won the Battle of Britain, I think he would have lost it with his policy had he been (which thank heaven he was not!) AOC during August and September 1940.

Air Commodore Peter Brothers, Hurricane pilot, 32 and 257 Squadrons, 11 Group:

> I was surprised by Peter Townsend's suggestion in *Duel of Eagles* that Air Vice-Marshal [Keith] Park formed an 11 Group wing to avoid criticism. He was far too strong a character to do that, and in fact exercised flexible tactics, alternating to whichever was appropriate at the time. My log book shows that the most operational sorties I flew in 257 Squadron between 28 September and 8 October 1940 were in a wing with 73 and 17 Squadrons from Castle Camps, we being based at Martlesham Heath, all in the Debden Sector and so nearly as far North of the Thames as Duxford. We then moved to North Weald and between 9–27 October, operated together with 46 and 249 Squadrons. All sorties are recorded as 'Defensive Wing Patrols', a total of sixteen.
>
> Apart from one occasion which I have not recorded but vividly remember, our wings saw little action. We were just below cloud when two Me 109s swept past to the left and below us, shooting down two Hurricanes of 17 Squadron, which was leading, then pulled up and vanished into cloud. All far too quick for our great lumbering formation to react.
>
> By October 1940, the period of intensive activity was drawing to a close and so we could afford wasteful standing patrols – the 'Maidstone Line at 20,000 feet' being the usual one. We were far enough inland to form up into a wing when enemy activity was brewing. All this was so different to my days at Biggin Hill, Manston or Hawkinge, when we were scrambled late to ensure that the raid was the real thing and not a 'spoof' to get us airborne, then catch us on the ground refuelling.
>
> Douglas Bader, a close and dear friend, based further North at Duxford, allowed his fretful anxiety to be in the forefront of the activity to cloud his judgement. Dowding's SASO, Air Vice-Marshal Douglas Evill, was right when he said, 'It was quite useless to argue whether

wing formations are or are not desirable, both statements are equally true under different conditions.' Those conditions were to come later to us in 11 Group.

[Trafford] Leigh-Mallory, unlike [Keith] Park, lacked experience in the fighter world and was also very ambitious. You have, correctly in my view, indicated that because Douglas Bader was a pushy, newsworthy, character, 'LM' used him and his operational experience to draw attention to himself and conceal his ignorance.

In the confusion of battle, it was inevitable that claims made later proved to be duplicated or worse. Apart from the few would-be aces, one of whom fired and claimed me as an Me 109 destroyed without even hitting me, I believe everyone reported what they honestly thought had happened. Douglas Bader put the whole thing into context after the war, though, when he said 'What does it matter? We won, didn't we?'

The truth of it, though, is that it did matter – and still does – because of how and why the architects of victory, namely Air Chief Marshal Hugh Dowding and Air Vice-Marshal Keith Park, were consequently treated, and, indeed, because of the disastrous effect Air Vice-Marshal Sholto Douglas and Air Vice-Marshal Trafford Leigh-Mallory's obsession with mass fighter formations, in both defence and offence, would have on Fighter Command strategy and operations going forward. As we have seen, there was really no argument to be had, in fact: this was an unprecedented aerial conflict with no blueprint – and Park's tactics evolved accordingly. At first the tactical situation required a flexible response, and a critical need to preserve resources, hence the use of carefully shepherded small formations. The crisis over and the German battle plan ever-changing, Park used both two and three squadron wings to meet the enemy fighter sweeps and high-flying, heavily escorted, fighter-bomber raids. The man, quite simply, was a tactical genius – and should have been beyond criticism, especially from officers of incomparable operational experience.

On 3 November 1940, Air Vice-Marshal Sholto Douglas wrote to Air Chief Marshal Hugh Dowding, enclosing Harold Balfour's 'Duxford Memorandum', in which the Under Secretary stated that there was 'a conflict of operational views between 12 Group and 11 Group', which had 'passed from being confined to operational questions and has, in the minds of those concerned, become a personal issue with the pilots, who feel resentful against 11 Group and its AOC, as well as the Air Ministry'. Balfour clearly sympathised with 12 Group's perspective, writing that this was because they were at 11 Group's 'disposal' but were 'never called to function, according to their new practised tactics of wing formation, until too late', denying Duxford's pilots 'opportunities to shoot down Germans'. Balfour alleged that 11 Group objected to 12 Group 'poaching' over its area and 'are jealous of the wing formation being likely to shoot down 11 Group Germans'. Balfour went on to criticise the system, when he clearly misunderstood its technical limitations and modus operandi, and alleged that the morale of 11 Group pilots was 'unnecessarily shaken' owing to 'having to meet enemy forces in superior numbers', and were 'not succeeding in repelling the enemy in a way that a large formation can do'.

The DCAS's covering letter included a postscript: 'The US of S asks me to say that he hopes Bader will not get into trouble for having been so outspoken.'

Hugh Dowding was shocked:

> The only natural conclusion that I could come to was that the political branch of the Air Ministry was now concerning itself with the details of the running of my Command … It was becoming a political issue … No matter how strongly I might feel about the Parliamentary Under-Secretary making enquiries in the way he did, and my disagreement with the facts provided, it was still my duty to reply to the Air Ministry letter … It was my job, even if it was such a waste of everybody's time, to set them right.

Having tasked Air Vice-Marshal Douglas Evill with assembling the required facts and data, Dowding replied on 6 November 1940:

> I agree that this operation is causing so much friction and ill-feeling that I must withdraw the control of combined operations between numbers 11 and 12 Groups from the Group Commanders themselves and issue the orders through my own Operations Room.

This step overturned the intended system and Dowding's policy of entrusting his group commanders with tactical control. That it was necessary can only be considered, whichever way the matter is approached, as a failure in Command, which Dowding himself later acknowledged. Regarding Balfour, Dowding wrote that 'the story which Balfour has collected by his direct methods is wrong in its conclusions and in the facts on which these conclusions are based.'

Harold Balfour's 'Duxford Memorandum' had also claimed that 12 Group was not being provided all available RDF information. Dowding contested this, confirming that in reality 12 Group received all RDF information covering southern Kent and Cap-Gris-Nez direct from Bentley Priory. Balfour also alleged that 12 Group was denied Observer Corps reports, which Dowding similarly quashed; the problem was 12 Group's use of a locally arranged but unauthorised system which had been stopped by the Southern Area Observer Corps commandant. Regarding the charge that 12 Group was being called too late, he wrote that 'My criticism is that the recent conference and al the fuss that has been made has resulted in 11 Group calling for assistance from 12 Group too early, but without the slightest excuse.' Dowding also emphasised that the continual use of certain squadrons in the Duxford Wing,

> diverts them from the normal tasks of 12 Group, which are the defence of its own area, including some highly important industrial districts … I am inclined to the conclusion that for the moment in this present phase, the use of the Duxford Wing is a misemployment of a valuable element of very limited strength … [Trafford] Leigh-Mallory has many commitments of his own … and should 'keep his eye on the boat.

With regarding to politicians and officials from outside Fighter Command being provided critical information regarding internal matters, Dowding considered that 'improper', adding,

> There remains the question of the Under-Secretary of State listening to the accusations of a junior officer against the Air Officer Commanding Group, and putting them on paper with the pious hope that that officer will not get into trouble ... Balfour has been in the service and ought to know better.

Indeed, Hugh Dowding blamed Squadron Leader Douglas Bader for much of the trouble: 'a good deal of the ill-feeling which has been engendered in this controversy has been directly due to young Bader, who, whatever his other merits, suffers from an over development of the critical faculty.' Dowding added that while he had enormous regard for Bader's courage, that had nothing to do with the matter in hand: 'This might give an opportunity of moving young Bader to another station where he would be kept in better control. His amazing gallantry will protect him from disciplinary action if it can possibly be avoided.' Clearly, too late, Dowding realised that the Leigh-Mallory-Woodhall-Bader alliance needed breaking.

In Dowding's response, made on 6 November 1940, his acute displeasure was plain, provoking the wrath of the Air Staff and politicians alike. Having sent his letter, however, Dowding got on with the job in hand; the night Blitz, of course, was a much more important battle to fight.

The day fighting at this time, however, was a sideshow to the main event: the night Blitz on British cities. Britain's nocturnal defences, however, remained inadequate – a huge concern for Dowding. Airborne interception radar remained in its infancy and the Bristol Beaufighter – which had greater speed and firepower than the Bristol Blenheim Mk IF currently pressed into service as a night fighter – was only just becoming operational. Consequently, both Spitfires and Hurricanes were used as night fighters – although neither had been designed as such. With two rows of exhausts glowing either side of their Merlin engines, situated in front the pilot, and small canopies, visibility was not good. Moreover, with a narrow track undercarriage, the Spitfire could be tricky to land at night – as Douglas Bader had already discovered. Nonetheless desperate measures were called for. 'Fighter Nights' were therefore launched that dreadful winter, during which Spitfires and Hurricanes patrolled above British cities. Guided by searchlights and anti-aircraft fire, the fighters sought out German bombers – but more often than not landed without having espied a raider. On the night of 14/15 November 1940, the Luftwaffe, guided by radio beams, decimated the heart of Coventry. That night, Squadron Leader Douglas Bader and two other 242 (Canadian) Squadron Hurricane pilots patrolled above the burning city but saw not one German bomber.

The Coventry attack and apparent lack of progress in combating the night raiders has been suggested as a factor in the Air Ministry's attitude towards Dowding towards the end of the Battle of Britain and immediately afterwards, and contributed to what happened next; Dowding wrote that on 16 November 1940 he received a telephone call from Sinclair, of whom he had been critical in his robust response to the DCAS ten days earlier, as Robert Wright related in *Dowding and the Battle of Britain*:

> He told me that I was to relinquish my command immediately. I asked what was meant by 'immediately' and was told that it would take effect within the next day or so. Since that was tantamount to being given 24 hours' notice, and verbally at that, I pointed out that it was perfectly absurd that I should be relieved of my Command in this way unless it was thought that I had committed some major crime or whatever. But all I could get in reply was that the decision had been reached, and that was that, with no explanation for such a precipitate step being taken.

Sinclair also told Dowding that he was to take no disciplinary action over Bader, and advised him that his successor was to be ... Air Vice-Marshal Sholto Douglas.

In his memoir *Wings Over Westminster*, however, Balfour argues that Wright:

> portrays Dowding in retirement as an embittered, disillusioned, double-crossed, intrigued against and betrayed by his Air Ministry associates and political masters. The truth is that Dowding was shamefully served by successive Chiefs of the Air Staff over his personal career. Promised the future appointment as CAS in 1937, this was repudiated. Between this and his final retirement his service was extended for short terms no less than four times and the requests conveyed in cold, discourteous, terms. He was never, as he should have been, promoted to Marshal of the RAF. In all this, Dowding had grounds for complaint.

Balfour is absolutely right when mentioning Dowding's 'one great failure in the Battle of Britain', that being not having intervened in the dispute between 11 and 12 Group early on, which 'contributed to the regrettable circumstances of his departure'. Balfour is wrong, though, when continuing, 'But for this failure no one can tell what the effect might be upon the duration of the battle and the cost in lives.' Clearly, Balfour is implying that had Big Wing tactics been adopted throughout, the Battle could well have been shortened and lives saved. The evidence and facts presented in this book conclusively proves otherwise: the Duxford Wing was nowhere near as effective as certain influential men were so keen to believe at the time, and lives were, in fact, lost because of it.

Balfour also claimed that 'there was no political intrigue against Dowding', and that he himself had done his 'duty in a proper manner in accordance with the wishes of the Secretary of State', contesting Dowding's description of how his Command was so abruptly terminated:

> It just doesn't stand up. Of course, his relinquishment had been discussed with the Secretary of State, and A.J.P. Taylor endorses this in his letter to *The Times*, dated 22 January 1970, when he reveals notes of a conversation between the Secretary of State and Dowding at the Air

Ministry on 17 November 1940. Sinclair's notes of this discussion show clearly that arrangements for a change in command had already been under discussion and had been decided upon. I can confirm this meeting was held. Each morning I received a copy of the Secretary of State's engagements for that day and he received a similar slip giving mine. On Sinclair's slip was marked 'Meeting with Dowding'. Any subsequent telephone conversation was not to convey notification of a decision but to agree a date and details for implementation of a decision already known to both parties. One final comment: Dowding says that Churchill told him that he had known nothing of the change in command until he read it in the papers. This is pure nonsense and someone's memory must seriously be at fault. Churchill was Prime Minister and also Minister of Defence. Any Service Secretary of State would not have made a vital change in command without reference to, and prior agreement with, the Minister of Defence ... Whether Dowding's memory was at fault or Churchill's accuracy of statement, I shall never know, but I would wager any sum that Churchill knew and had approved the change, and also the name of Dowding's successor.

By the time Harold Balfour's book was published in 1973, though, Lord Dowding was dead and unable to respond, having passed away in 1970, aged 87. Wright's book was published in 1969, but whether Dowding's memory was affected by the passage of time, as Balfour argued it was, is impossible to say.

Some argue that Dowding's dismissal was more a matter of natural retirement, having just fought and won a demanding, critical, battle. In August 1940, however, the Air Ministry had extended Dowding's period of service 'indefinitely', so with the daylight battle won, 'Stuffy' had turned his technical mind to resolving the night bombing. Others argue that his failure to address this sooner was actually Dowding's downfall, especially as his old enemy Viscount Trenchard was consequently calling for his dismissal. There can be absolutely no doubt, though, that Dowding's 'one great failure' in the Battle of Britain, and the 'Big Wing Controversy' arising, was a primary factor in his dismissal. As Dowding himself acknowledged, he should have known what was going on, because 'it is the Commander's job to know', and acted decisively. Had his SASO, Air Vice-Marshal Douglas Evill, brought before him Park's letter of complaint dated 27 August 1940, however, the C-in-C would have known. But Evill did not – and does appear to be 'the one that got away', apparently escaping criticism and responsibility for so failing Air Chief Marshal Hugh Dowding.

On 17 November 1940, Dowding received a letter from the CAS:

With reference to your recent correspondences with Douglas (DCAS) about a report made by Balfour after conversation with Woodhall and Bader, the Secretary of State has directed that no reproof should be offered to either of the two officers on account of the conversations referred to.

On the same day, Leigh-Mallory reported to Bentley Priory regarding the Duxford Wing's operations, therein refuting 11 Group's allegations that the Duxford Wing only intercepted bomber formations after 11 Group squadrons had broken up the escorting fighters. Although the AOC 12 Group claimed that the Wing had actually intercepted raids before 11 Group on all but one occasion, the evidence presented in this book proves otherwise.

On 25 November 1940, Dowding was replaced as C-in-C by Air Marshal Sholto Douglas. Before leaving his office at Bentley Priory for the last time, 'Stuffy' Dowding sent one last signal to Fighter Command:

> In sending you this, my last message, I wish I could say all this is in my heart.
>
> I cannot hope to surpass the simple eloquence of the Prime Minister's words 'Never before has so much been owed by so many to so Few.' That debt remains and will increase.
>
> In saying goodbye to you I want you to know how continually you have been in my thoughts, and that, though our direct connection may be severed, I may yet be able to help you in your gallant fight.
>
> Goodbye to you and God bless you all.

A month later, when the church bells rang out across England to celebrate Christmas Day, the primary architect of victory in the Battle of Britain, Air Chief Marshal Hugh Dowding, was well out of earshot, having been packed off out of the way to America, on a public relations trip to which he was completely unsuited.

Inevitably, Park was also replaced. On 27 December 1940, the victor of the Battle for London left 11 Group to take over 23 Group, Flying Training Command, at South Cerney, Gloucestershire. His successor was none other than Trafford Leigh-Mallory.

An eyewitness to Leigh-Mallory's take-over at 11 Group HQ was one of Park's former group controllers, Group Captain Thomas Long:

> I will remember [Trafford] Leigh-Mallory and his 12 Group 'followers' dashing in and out of the Ops Room shortly after they arrived and discussing the type of weather boards which should be displayed for the Controller and adjacent staff to note. Time and again they had to change the deep blue to 'duck egg' blue etc etc until we thought that they would never finish their caperings. All the staff on the Floor looked on with supressed amusement.
>
> I remember that after LM assumed command of 11 Group he issued several directives on the policy of his Balbos. In this paper, he said that the Wing Leader was fully responsible for **all** enemy formations in the sky. The Wing Leader had to intercept each formation with adequate resources etc. History does not relate would have happened, as for our good fortune the Luftwaffe never attempted a raid on England again during my time at Group. I ask you: how on earth could a wing leader

see a picture spread out over miles in each direction, and possibly a depth of activity of 10,000ft?

Shortly after LM became AOC, he said he would like to try a 'real battle' as we fought them in 1940. So one was selected at random, and on 29 January 1941, he said that he would take it on. He asked me to be the Umpire, as I had been in the Group at the time of this raid, which was made against Kenley and Biggin Hill on 6 September 1940 (in fact I was the last of the 'Old Brigade' left, the others having 'seen the light' and left as hurriedly as they could...) Now, we were in the depths of winter so the actual readiness state at each station was one squadron at Readiness, one at fifteen minutes available, and the third or more at thirty minutes Available. That was the state as displayed for this exercise. Before we started the plotting, I asked LM if he was satisfied with this state, and he replied that he was 'Ready to go!' – so we went!

Now this actual raid was a very rapid one in that the main attack came in without much weaving around over the Pas-de-Calais, in fact within ten minutes it was on its way over the coast of [Cap] Gris Nez and flying fast towards London over the Kent and Sussex counties.

LM's first order shook the entire Floor – as the WAAF and RAF plotters knew what we had to cope with during the actual battles. His order was, as far as I can remember, to either Biggin Hill or Hornchurch, 'Wing patrol Maidstone at 30,000ft' (you will recall the readiness state as not exactly being on alert at any station). I sent up a message to the Ops Officer adjacent to LM to say that it would take fifteen minutes or more for that wing to get airborne (stations 'played' this battle on the ground but did not take-off as it was thick fog everywhere that day. But for the exercise we had a perfect summer's day)! Believe it or not, the same wing order went out to Kenley and North Weald, and finally Northolt! So we on the Floor, where I had taken up my perch on a plotting desk, watched the outcome, as NO squadron had time to take-off except the first wing from Biggin Hill or Hornchurch. By this time the raids had crossed into Kent and were heading for the airfields around London, to the South. The plots eventually showed Kenley and Biggin Hill 'bombed' with their fighters still not airborne!

Naturally that ended the 'battle', so I went upstairs to the Controller's Room, and LM asked me how it had gone. I had to reply that Kenley and Biggin Hill had both been bombed with aircraft still grounded etc. Having heard me patiently, he said that next time he would do better! BUT the impression left with the WAAF and RAF plotters was one of amazement that he made so many errors with his 'abominable wings'. One plotter said to me, 'Thank God you never did that when controlling', which sums up the feeling.

It was hardly an auspicious start for the new AOC 11 Group.

In March 1941, the official Air Ministry account of the Battle of Britain was published, failing to mention the names of either Dowding or Park; even Winston

Churchill was surprised, complaining strongly to Sir Archibald Sinclair on 12 April 1941, likening the scenario to Nelson's name being omitted from a pamphlet on Trafalgar, adding that 'This is not a good story ... The jealousies and cliquism which have led to the committing of this offence are a discredit to the Air Ministry.'

Consequently, in June 1941, Dowding was invited by the Air Ministry to provide a despatch on the Battle of Britain which, he considered in a private letter to his friend Lord Beaverbrook on 1 July 1941, to be 'an odd request, after this lapse of time, and after they have already issued an official account, but I will do my best to provide a document of some historical interest.' Dowding's Despatch was published in the *London Gazette* on 20 August 1941. Two years later, in recognition of his great service, Dowding received a hereditary peerage and became the first Baron of Bentley Priory.

Park remained embittered to his dying day at how Dowding and himself had been treated and remained very clear as to why. In private correspondence, on 18 May 1960, he wrote,

> The reason why Dowding was cast aside was because he had strenuously fought the Air Ministry, and there were one or two air marshals who were ambitious to get his job. Dowding was too friendly with Churchill for a frontal attack, and so Air Staff attacked him through his principal tactical commander of 11 Group, and fostered a controversy about the tactics of AOC 11 Group, and Leigh-Mallory of 12 Group.
>
> The tasks and locations of the above two groups were quite dissimilar, so that comparison of their tactics – after the Battle was well and truly won – were quite specious. For example, 11 Group was charged with the defence of London, munitions factories, Portsmouth, and other vital points; whereas 12 Group was responsible for the defence of a northern area. Moreover, 11 Group aerodromes were in the frontline and under heavy bombing attacks, which frequently put some temporarily out of action. In order to continue the Battle, it was therefore vital for 11 Group to intercept and disrupt bombing attacks before they reached their aerodromes, otherwise they would have lost the Battle of Britain.
>
> [No.] 12 Group was outside the Battle area and its aerodromes were not under attack, so, if it chose, it could devote additional time to scramble and assemble massive wings of 4/5 squadrons. On numerous occasions, when 11 Group had called for 12 Group for a pair of squadrons to cover a vital aerodrome quickly, it delayed to form up its Big Wing which arrived too late to prevent Hornchurch, and another time North Weald, from being severely damaged by enemy bombing. I reported this verbally and in writing to Dowding, but as far as I know he took no action against Leigh-Mallory, who was a personal friend of the Air Secretary and the DCAS.
>
> [No.] 10 Group, on my right rear, never delayed when asked to send one or two squadrons to reinforce and cover Portsmouth, Southampton etc, when all my squadrons were fully engaged elsewhere. Incidentally, AOC 10 Group used exactly the same tactics as 11 Group by employing

pairs of squadrons, as opposed to Big Wings favoured by 12 Group, and yet Brand (AOC 10 Group) was not arraigned before the assembled Air Council as I was in October 1940, to explain why I did not copy 12 Group's tactics which were supported by the DCAS, who later displaced Dowding at Fighter Command.

To show how personal was this attack on me at Air Ministry, I was given no warning of the Air Council meeting, nor was I told beforehand even the object of the meeting, whereas AOC 12 Group had prepared his brief and was permitted to bring along the principal protagonist of the Big Wing (Bader), who made extravagant claims of his successes to the full Air Council.

During October and November, 11 Group kept accurate records of the times they called on 12 Group for reinforcement, and on the majority of occasions the Big Wing led by [Douglas] Bader arrived too late to intercept raids on London, even after they had dropped their bombs. This was reported in writing to [Hugh] Dowding and to Air Ministry – who no doubt mislaid the document.

On several occasions, when the 12 Group wing had claimed abnormally big victories in the south-east of England, I told my staff to check with the ground defences in the area for confirmation of enemy shot down. To our surprise and disgust, I remember two occasions in late August when we could get no confirmation of 12 Group claims from Observer Corps, Searchlights or Gun Stations. It may possibly be that 12 Group squadrons shot the enemy down over the English Channel and not over land as reported, but my staff were unconvinced!

... If I were not so busy earning my living, I would write a book and disclose the intrigue that caused [Hugh] Dowding and myself to be cast aside after defeating the Luftwaffe in 1940, and so making easy the task of air commanders from then onwards.

After his exile to Training Command, Keith Park was appointed AOC Egypt, and on 14 July 1942, took over as AOC Malta – arriving on the besieged Mediterranean island during an air raid. This certainly concerned the enemy, an intelligence report stating that Park's arrival was likely to 'make the air forces in the eastern Mediterranean more active'. Again, in private correspondence, in 1960 Park recalled that when he took command of Malta – where he would encounter Wing Commander Alfred Woodhall once more:

my airfields were being bombed three or four times daily with consequent loss of aircraft and personnel on the ground. The tactics in vogue were to despatch our fighters to the rear of Malta while they assembled and climbed in big formation, and then to come in and attack after the bombs had been dropped and the enemy was diving away in full retreat under the cover of its fighter escort. These tactics were being employed by the Commander of the Fighters, who had been the Station Commander at

Duxford in 12 Group which had originated the Big Wings led by Bader in 1940. I immediately sent this officer back to England, and changed the tactics to what I called a forward interception plan used in 11 Group. I sent the fighter squadrons forward, climbing to meet the enemy bombers head on, and to intercept them well before they reached Malta, when the bombers were in tight formation, heavily laden and unable to take evading action. The result was that within two weeks, with exactly the same number of squadrons, I stopped the daylight raids on Malta, and our casualties to our fighters were no greater than previously. Incidentally, this enabled the Navy, Army and civil authorities to clear up the bomb damage and bring back our submarines to operate against enemy convoys that were feeding [Erwin] Rommel in North Africa. According to German accounts ... Rommel was defeated through lack of petrol and other supplies, due to the losses caused by aircraft and submarines from Malta.

Yet again, Park's tactical skill saved the day – and lives.

In January 1944, Park became AOC-in-C Middle East, and a year later Allied Air C-in-C of the South East Asia Command (SEAC). In 1946, (now) Air Chief Marshal Keith Park retired from the service and returned home to Auckland. There, in 1968, the victor of the battles of London and Malta became most anxious regarding the making of the film *Battle of Britain*, concerned about how Hugh Dowding and himself would be portrayed. According to Reuter's, the ageing Park charged the film makers with covering up 'a dirty little wartime intrigue, which led to the sacking of Lord Dowding, Chief of the RAF Fighter Command then'. It had, coincidentally, been arranged for Lord Dowding to visit Pinewood Studios, near London, to meet the actor playing him – Laurence Olivier. Trevor Howard was to play Park, to whom Dowding also spoke, sharing with him Park's concerns. Dowding watched the scene being filmed showing a meeting between 'Park', 'Leigh-Mallory', played by Patrick Wymark, and Olivier as 'Dowding', at Bentley Priory, in which the two AOCs' differences in opinion over the Big Wing were briefly discussed. In reality, this is the meeting that never happened but should have – Dowding's one, fatal, 'failure of command'. Afterwards, Dowding said nothing – but was sufficiently satisfied to write to Park the following day, 8 July 1968, reassuring him that the treatment of them both would be 'actively sympathetic'. Ultimately, Park thought the film 'entertaining', although pointing out that the meeting as described never took place, and that the confrontation in the air council room, which was infinitely more dramatic, was not mentioned, presumably, he opined, to save the face of certain RAF officers and politicians. To be fair, Trevor Howard played a good part in the film, which was most certainly 'actively sympathetic', so, for once, Park really had nothing to complain about.

Beyond doubt, Park was a primary architect of victory in the Battle of Britain and later Malta air battles, and it is fitting that as a direct result of research for this unprecedented narrative, evidence was discovered confirming that when AOC 11 Group, on 10 and 12 July 1940, he actually made two operational flights in his personal Hurricane, OK-1. This led to the MOD Air Historical Branch (RAF) accepting in 2023 that Park was a legitimate recipient of the Battle of Britain Clasp – so eighty-three years after the event, the New Zealander officially became not just a leader of 'The Few' – but one of 'The Few' himself. That the great man should be recognised in this way, all these years later, is entirely appropriate and as time goes on, it seems his contribution may consequently become better known and appreciated.

On 15 February 1970, Lord Dowding died, aged 87. When visiting Pinewood, it was none other than Group Captain Sir Douglas Bader who insisted on pushing the 'old man' around in his wheelchair, and now said,

> Lord Dowding is probably unknown to most of the younger generations. Yet it was because of him as much as any other man that they have been brought up in the English way of life, speaking the English language. They might have been speaking German. Without his vision, his planning, his singleness of purpose, and his complete disregard for personal aggrandisement, Fighter Command might have been unable to win the Battle of Britain in the summer of 1940. What rankled most with the fighter pilots of 1940 was that he was never made a Marshal of the RAF. Seldom in our history has a man deserved so much of his fellow countrymen but wanted and received so little. He surely earned his place alongside Nelson and Wellington and other great military names in our history.

Lord Dowding's ashes were buried in Westminster Abbey, where a tablet commemorates that 'He Led The Few in the Battle of Britain'. None of this, however, makes up for the fact that Dowding was never made MRAF – a matter which even puzzled King George VI. Indeed, on 17 July 1942, the king formally suggested to Sir Archibald Sinclair that Dowding should be promoted to MRAF. His Majesty's suggestion was never acted upon. The greatest tribute of all, perhaps, came on 30 October 1988, when Her Majesty the Queen Mother – Patron of the Battle of Britain Fighter Association – unveiled Faith Winter's statue of the great man outside the 'RAF Church' of St Clement Danes, in the Strand. Her Majesty, in fact, was aware of her late husband's feelings that 'Dowding performed really wonderful service to this country in creating and putting into practice the defence system which proved so effective in the Battle of Britain' and that the king's suggestion was never implemented. The statue project had been initiated and overseen by Air Chief Marshal Christopher Sir Foxley-Norris, one of 'The Few' and chairman of the Battle of Britain Fighter Association. That his 'chicks' still held him in such high esteem and affection so many years later would have doubtless deeply moved his Lordship. Appropriately, the base of this magnificent tribute bears these words: 'To him the people of Britain and the free world owe largely the way of life and the liberties they enjoy today.' Equally, those words arguably apply to Air Chief Marshal Keith Park.

Keith Park died on 12 September 1975. A memorial service was subsequently held at St Clement Danes, in which the Lesson was read by Air Commodore A.R.D. MacDonell, the Laird of Glengarry, chairman of the Battle of Britain Fighter

Association and who commanded 64 Squadron during the Battle of Britain. Somewhat surprisingly, the address was read by Group Captain Douglas Bader, at the association's unanimous invitation:

> The awesome responsibility for this country's survival rested squarely on Keith Park's shoulders. Had he failed, Stuffy Dowding's foresight, determination and achievement would have counted for nought. This is no sad occasion. Rather it is a time during which we can let our memories drift back to those halcyon days of 1940 when we fought together in English skies under the determined leadership of that great New Zealander we are remembering now. Keith Park was one of us. We all shared the great experience. That is what we remember today. British military history of this country has been enriched with the names of great fighting men from New Zealand, of all ranks and in every one of our services. Keith Park's name is carved into that history alongside those of his peers.

Whether the legless group captain's words at the passing of both architects of victory in the Battle of Britain healed any rifts from beyond the grave, we will never know.

Reflections

For Adolf Hitler, the supreme war lord, the invasion of southern England had proved intractable. The *Führer*'s brinkmanship, his 'air fleet diplomacy', and *Reichsmarschall* Hermann Göring's air offensive had both failed to effect an early victory over and occupation of Great Britain. This was Germany's first reversal of the Second World War and evidence that the Nazi juggernaut was not invincible – sending out a clear message to the world. Had Britain not been an island, though, the country would undoubtedly have been overrun in June 1940 by Germany's overwhelming superiority on land, with unimaginably appalling consequences. But Britain is an island – and in 1940 had the best aerial defence system in the world at that time.

According to the Air Ministry, this unprecedented aerial conflict began on 10 July 1940, lasting sixteen bloodstained weeks, until 31 October 1940. This epic defence of Britain was fought, essentially, by nearly 3,000 Allied aircrew of Fighter Command, 'The Few', supported by 'The Many' – including Britain's other defences and, of course, the RN, which represented a substantial deterrent to any would-be invader. RAF Coastal Command had shepherded convoys delivering crucial supplies to Britain's shores, and undertaken reconnaissance work, as did the PRU, and together with Bomber Command took the war across the Channel to the Germans in north-west France, bombing the invasion preparations and airfields, whilst Bomber Command's night-bombers even attacked Berlin itself – making a mockery of Hermann Göring's infamous boast that 'No enemy plane would ever fly over the *Reich* territory'. The Battle of Britain, as fought by Fighter Command, is a comparatively well-known and epic story, the contribution of Coastal Command and Bomber Command, however, remains a largely forgotten battle. This narrative, however, provides an insight into those operations, and these brave aircrews must also, surely, share the credit for Britain remaining free.

The RAF aircrew involved were, in fact, immortalised by British Prime Minister Winston Churchill in his speech of 20 August 1940:

> The gratitude of every home in our Island, in our Empire, and indeed throughout the world, except in the abodes of the guilty, goes out to the British airmen who, undaunted by odds, unwearied in their constant challenge and mortal danger, are turning the tide of the world war by their prowess and by their devotion. Never in the field of human conflict was so much owed by so many to so few.

Although the popular narrative has interpreted Churchill's comments as having referred exclusively to Fighter Command's aircrew, the prime minister was arguably paying tribute to all RAF aircrew involved. Nonetheless, Churchill's reference to the 'few' immortalised the aircrew of Fighter Command, those of which who fought the Battle of Britain forever after remembered as 'The Few'. During the Battle of Britain, 544 of these men lost their lives; 795 more would not survive the Second World War. Sadly, the last of 'The Few', Group Captain John 'Paddy' Hemingway DFC, an Irishman who flew Hurricanes with 85 Squadron, died in March 2025, aged 105.

After the war, it was acknowledged that so significant was victory in the Battle of Britain that 'The Few' must be officially recognised. An Air Ministry Order (AMO) on 24 May 1945 announced that a Clasp to the 1939–1945 Star would be issued for aircrew who had flown in fighters during the Battle of Britain between the official dates. A further AMO followed on 23 July 1945 confirming this, adding that 'Issues are to be confined to those who operated with the undermentioned squadrons' – and went on to list sixty-three RAF fighter squadrons with which a recipient must have served. Over time, up to and including 1960, several more AMOs were issued concerning the units involved, which currently stands at seventy-two. There would be no such recognition, however, for either Fighter Command's support staff or either Coastal Command or Bomber Command.

Contrary to Churchill's reference to 'British airmen', though, these brave men actually represented a multi-national – albeit exclusively white – force: men from the Commonwealth: Canadians, New Zealanders, Australians, South Africans, and even volunteers from still neutral America, and, of course, free airmen from the occupied lands: Poles, Czechs, Belgians, French and Dutchmen. The most numerous of the foreign airmen were the Poles, of whom Lord Dowding said, 'Had it not been for the magnificent material contributed by the Polish squadrons and their unsurpassed gallantry, I hesitate to say the outcome of the Battle of Britain would have been the same.' There could be no higher praise than this.

In this new narrative, the pilots themselves have spoken to us via their personal combat reports, written after each engagement, describing the often-visceral fighting in which neither side asked for quarter, and none was given. There were countless acts of gallantry in the air – but although many decorations were awarded for gallantry and leadership, only one Victoria Cross was awarded to a fighter pilot, Flight Lieutenant James Brindley Nicolson. Howsoever many other Fighter Command aircrew deserved this high honour is anyone's guess. It might also have been a foregone conclusion that the C-in-C of Fighter Command prevailing in this crucial conflict would be made MRAF – but, for complex reasons already discussed, this never happened. Whether Fighter Command, therefore, really did receive due recognition for its achievement is perhaps, therefore, a moot point.

This investigation, which has forensically deconstructed every squadron action throughout the entire sixteen weeks involved, has repeatedly highlighted multiple victory claims being made and confirmed for the same enemy aircraft, meaning that a single aircraft could be – and often was – multiplied many times on the balance sheet. What this irrefutably proves, therefore, is the infinite gulf of difference between a combat claim and an actual aerial victory. Although the Air Ministry issued instructions for awarding claims as 'destroyed' 'probably destroyed' or 'damaged', there was demonstrably no consistency whatsoever between squadrons in practical terms and application of this criterion. Indeed, the same squadrons repeatedly appear to destroy every aircraft apparently fired at, the law of averages alone confirming the implausibility of this, and to say hundreds of such claims were 'optimistic' but nonetheless confirmed is an understatement.

What all this really means is that the list of top-scoring RAF squadrons is more than just questionable, because this is based upon the claims of the time, not rigorous post-war analysis with the benefit of more information being available. Indeed, it would be superfluous to say, therefore, that the accepted list of top-scoring pilots, compiled from identical questionable data, could also be re-drawn. That said, the nature of aerial combat coupled with the frequently confusing and contradictory records concerned, make definitively accurate assessments impossible. Overclaiming, in the confusion of battle, is perfectly understandable and applied to both sides. What is unforgivable, however, is that Major Helmut Wick, *Kommodore* of JG 2, apparently fabricated the kills necessary to be awarded the Oak Leaves to his Knight's Cross.

It is often argued that there was no victory in the Battle of Britain, because neither air force was destroyed. This is patent nonsense. The Battle of Britain was not a case of the RAF and Luftwaffe fighting each other to a standstill – it was fought with a specific enemy objective in mind, which was achieving the aerial supremacy required for the launch of Operation *Seelöwe*, the proposed seaborne invasion of southern England. This intention was announced by the OKW on 2 July 1940, postponed indefinitely by Hitler on 17 September 1940, and cancelled completely on 12 October 1940. Why? Because aerial supremacy had not been achieved, owing the Britain's stiff defences, meaning that *Seelöwe* could not set sail. That being so, there is absolutely no question: the Luftwaffe lost the Battle of Britain, the actual dates of which, contrary to the Air Ministry's official dates, were arguably 2 July 1940–12 October 1940.

Indeed, not even the Germans, who initiated the Battle of Britain, are sure of the dates. Former Luftwaffe bomber pilot Gerhard Baeker, for example, said that 'For me, the battle lasted from August 1940 until July 1941. What they call the Battle of Britain in England was just August and September.' The facts, however, do not support this, or the assertion by JG 2 Me 109 ace Julius Meimberg that the Battle of Britain has been 'exaggerated' by the British. Meimberg, a Knight's Cross holder, argued that 'When you look at how we fought the Americans later, the Battle of Britain was very little in comparison.' That may indeed be so, in terms of the numbers of aircraft involved and the incomparably heavy fighting – but nonetheless the stakes in 1940's summer skies were infinite for the Western democracies: had Germany achieved aerial supremacy, Britain would have been invaded. Had that happened, simply put, there would have been no other battles. No Battle of the Atlantic, no D-Day, no American daylight strategic bombing campaign. Nothing. Just a Nazi dominated Europe – and ultimately, quite possibly, one day the world, including the United States. Given Imperialism and the age of Empire, the Western democracies may not have been perfect – but Nazism represented an untold evil based around crackpot racial theories. After the war, Imperialism and Empire was dismantled – but that could not have happened, either, without the RAF's victory in the Battle of Britain. So much, in fact, has arisen from Britain remaining free and in the war that it is almost incomprehensible.

It has often been argued that the Germans lost the Battle of Britain because of repeatedly changing tack, especially when Göring turned away from pulverising 11 Group's airfields and instead attacked London, and because the Luftwaffe was ill-equipped for a strategic aerial campaign. The latter is certainly true, as is the inescapable fact that the *Reichsmarschall* ignored von Clausewitz and his 'Principles of War', forgetting that maximum effort should be concentrated on one thing and that plan adhered to until the objective is achieved. The long-established popular narrative tells us that Air Vice-Marshal Keith Park's airfields were on their knees when Hermann Göring attacked London, this reprieve saving them. This, though, is an exaggeration: all of Park's airfields sector stations remained operational, and if rendered non-operational this was only for short periods. The truth of the matter is not one of such a dramatic reprieve, but it is fair to say that had the principles of war been applied and the airfield attacks continued, the outcome may have been quite different. *Generalfeldmarschall* Albert Kesselring, however, commander of *Luftflotte* 2 throughout the Battle of Britain, justified this frequent changing of strategy as 'tactical mobility'.

Albert Kesselring also said,

> I gladly agree with Churchill's words of praise when he says that the RAF, 'far from being destroyed, was triumphant'. The British airmen undoubtedly deserved this praise for their pluck and skill, as did the whole defence for its exemplary reaction to the new technical methods.

In this, Kesselring was surely referring to RDF, the early warning provided by which constantly exasperated the Luftwaffe.

By the war's end, Adolf Galland had succeeded his friend Mölders, who had been killed in a flying accident, as *General der Jagdflieger*, and had this to say: 'Britain had passed victoriously through one of the most serious ordeals in her history. She never lost her courage of self-confidence. Staggering and bleeding, but with clenched fists, she stood fast during the period.' And few men will ever know as much about aerial combat as the now late General Adolf Galland.

The German night Blitz, of course, continued unabated throughout the winter of 1940/1941, an aerial offensive Galland considered 'the fifth and last phase of the Battle of Britain'. It was certainly a development and another phase of the war against Britain – but, there can be no doubt, with *Seelöwe* abandoned, the Battle of Britain was over. The terrifying night raids continued, in fact, until May 1941, when Hitler's war machine turned eastwards, ready to invade Russia – and, surprisingly, a little-known fact is that the invasion of Russia on 22 June 1941, Operation Barbarossa, was also part of Hitler's revised strategy in the ongoing war against Britain.

With the air offensive having failed, in the autumn of 1940 Hitler had no choice but to reconsider how to quickly end the war with Britain in a German victory. In September 1940, the still officially neutral United States had supplied Britain destroyers under the Lend-Lease arrangement, this being a clear indication to Hitler of where President Franklin D. Roosevelt's sympathies lay. The *Führer*'s pressing need, therefore, was to defeat Britain before the Americans entered the war – against Germany. In July 1940, Hitler had first discussed with his high commanders the possibility of invading Russia, and on 18 December 1940 this became a formal entity through War Directive 21: a 'war of annihilation' against Joseph Stalin's Soviet Union.

This time, there would be no moat to protect Hitler's unsuspecting victim – the Nazi-Soviet Non-Aggression Pact still being in place – and the OKW looked forward to another lightning land victory against an unprepared foe armed with obsolete weapons. Britain's other hope, Hitler knew, lay in Russia reneging on its unholy alliance with Hitler and joining with Britain. All signposts now, therefore, pointed to Moscow: with Russia defeated and out of the war, there would be no chance of Stalin supporting Churchill, and this would substantially increase Japanese influence in the Far East – that being of much greater concern to Americans, Hitler believed, than the war in Europe, thereby preoccupying Roosevelt and ensuring that the United States remained out of the war against Germany. Isolated and without hope of support from resource-rich potential Allies, Britain would then have no choice but to accept terms – or, like Russia, be annihilated.

For Frank Kamp, serving in *Infantrie Pioneer Ersatz Kompanie* 211, remembered that

> On 22 June 1941, a *Sondermeldung* (special announcement) was broadcast over the radio, making Operation Barbarossa public knowledge. I simply could not believe it, although I understood to some extent Hitler's thinking. Now we had war on two fronts … a development quite incredible and to our great disadvantage. Gone were any hopes of an early end to the war, replaced now by the prospect of a long and drawn-out fight to the death.

Kamp was right – and arguably the devasting war between Germany and Russia, matched only in barbarity by the subsequent conflict between the Americans and Japanese – was another consequence of the RAF's victory in the Battle of Britain. Indeed, it would be impossible to over emphasis the ultimate effect of Barbarossa on Germany and, indeed, the Second World War.

That event, and ultimately the total defeat and unconditional surrender of Germany, however, were still a way off when the Battle of Britain officially ended on 31 October 1940. The weather had prevented air operations that day, but on 1 November 1940, the fighting continued. Indeed, on that day, some fine RAF pilots were killed in action, all five of whom had fought valiantly during the Battle of Britain – foremost amongst them the gallant Squadron Leader Archie McKellar, commander of 605 Squadron. Indeed, the fighter forces of both sides would continue fighting, their operations only reduced by the weather, unabated into 1941, and many more fine young men would perish in the defence of Britain. That spring, with the appointment of the first wing leaders and Fighter Command re-organised so that every sector station accommodated a three-squadron strong fighter wing, the so-called 'Non-Stop Offensive' began, 'reaching out', taking the war across the Channel to the enemy. All of that, though, as they say, is another story. In conclusion, let us, finally, hear from some of 'The Few'.

Group Captain 'Sailor' Malan, commanding 74 Squadron: 'Taking a Spitfire into the sky in September 1940 often corresponded to entering a dark room with a madman weaving a knife behind your back. We could see behind us and the Hun was everywhere, ready to spit his guns ...'

Pilot Officer Harry Whelford, 607 Squadron:

> We hadn't long refuelled when we were scrambled that evening. There was no interception, but the following morning we lost six out of twelve Hurricanes. Three sergeants were wounded and three officers killed. One of the latter was my best friend, Stuart Parnall, and the others, 'Scotty' and the young South African George Drake, were all lovely people, people like Alex Oblenski and 'Ching' MacKenzie, with whom I would have flown to hell in glorious comradeship. Somehow we could not believe it. No-one talked about it. Of course we all hoped that news would come through from some remote pub or hospital. When no news came, we hardened ourselves for the worst: 'Killed in Action'. We bit back our tears and sorrow. It was 'You heard about Stuart and Scotty – rotten luck, wasn't it?' Someone would add 'And young George, bloody good blokes'. After that epitaph the matter would apparently be dismissed with the ordering of another round of drinks, to avoid any further trace of sentiment.

Squadron Leader Harry Hogan, commanding 501 Squadron:

> Some of our Hurricane squadron's replacement pilots were straight from OTU, and these we tried to get into the air as quickly as possible, to provide a little extra experience. We were just too tired, though, to give any dogfight practice at all. They were all very 'green', youngsters who were bewildered and lost in action.

Squadron Leader John Hill, commanding 222 Squadron, in a letter to Mrs Whitbread, the mother of Pilot Officer Laurie Whitbread, killed in action on 20 September 1940:

> It is with deep regret that I have to write to you from 222 Squadron and offer our sympathy on the very sad loss of your son. He was killed instantly by a bullet from an enemy aircraft when doing his bit in the defence of his country. His passing is a great loss to us; he had been in the squadron since its formation and was always most popular, having a quiet and efficient disposition and charming manner.

Pilot Officer Roger Boulding, 74 Squadron: 'It is astonishing, upon reflection, how many young pilots failed to return from their first sortie; to see was to live, but your "eyes" only grew with experience.'

Squadron Leader Gerry Edge DFC, commanding 253 Squadron:

They didn't like that head-on attack, you know, but you had to judge the break-away point just right. If you left it to the last 100 yards then you were in trouble, due to the fast closing speeds, but once you got the hang of it a head on attack was a piece of cake. When you opened fire, you'd kill or badly wound the pilot and second pilot. Then you'd rake the whole line as you broke away. On one attack, the first He 111 I hit crashed into the next.

Flying Officer James Coward, 19 Squadron:

Flight Lieutenant Clouston led us into a copybook Fighter Command No 1 Attack from dead ahead, turning in three sections, line astern, to come up in sections echelon port, behind the enemy, who were in sections of three, in vic line astern. Our fourth section, led by Flying Officer Frank Brinsden, was detailed to climb and intercept the fighters. I got a cannon shell through the cockpit, which shattered my left leg below the knee, also severing the elevator controls, and I had to bale out. I put a tourniquet around my thigh, using my helmet radio lead, and landed by parachute about 4 miles north of Duxford on the Royston to Newmarket Road. I was admitted to Addenbroke's Hospital in Cambridge and obviously out of the battle from then on.

Pilot Officer John Bisdee, 609 Squadron:

My most vivid memory of the entire Battle of Britain is coming right down to see that Ju 88 burning on the Downs, with a crowd of yokels waving pitchforks and dancing around it! I did a victory roll over them, then went back 'upstairs' to see what was happening.

Pilot Officer Michael Appleby, 609 Squadron: 'I must not forget the time when the invasion was supposed to be imminent, church bells ringing, and we were all sitting in our aircraft awaiting a massed attack. Nothing happened.'

Squadron Leader Duncan MacDonald DSO DFC, commanding 213 Squadron:

Jackie Sing was shot down over the sea and rescued by an American oil tanker. You can imagine his feelings when informed by the Captain that the cargo consisted of 100 octane aviation fuel for Fighter Command! The tanker made landfall at Shoreham, Sussex, and I motored down from Tangmere in the early evening to recover this valuable member of my squadron, who was a bit shaken but fortunately uninjured. He was in the air again the next day, none the worse for this most frightening experience.

REFLECTIONS

Pilot Officer Roger Hall, 152 Squadron:

We saw our own fighters, the 11 Group squadrons, and some from 12 Group in the Midlands, climbing up from the north. There seemed to be quite a number of us. They too were black dots, climbing up in groups of twelve, or thirty-six in wing formation. Most of them were Hurricanes. I recalled for an instant Mr Baldwin's prophecy, not a sanguine one, made to the House of Commons some five years before, when he said that the bomber would 'always get through'. Now it was doing just that.

Pilot Officer William Walker, 616 Squadron:

After I was shot down and baled out over the Goodwin Sands on 26 August 1940, I was picked up by a passing fishing boat before transferring to an RAF launch, which took me into Ramsgate harbour. With a bullet in my foot, I was carried up the steps to a waiting ambulance, by which time quite a crowd had gathered and gave me a loud cheer. A kind old lady handed me a packet of cigarettes, so I decided that being shot down was perhaps not such a bad thing after all!

Later, after surgery, I was convalescing at the Palace Hotel in Torquay with Flight Lieutenant James Brindley Nicolson when a telegram arrived for him. 'Nick's' response was simply 'Well, what do you make of that?' It was, of course, notification that he had been awarded the Victoria Cross for his 'signal act of valour' over Southampton on 16 August 1940. He was genuinely puzzled and not a little embarrassed, that of hundreds of brave deeds performed by RAF fighter pilots that summer, his had been singled out for this very great honour. His was, in fact, the only VC awarded to an RAF fighter pilot during the entire war, because due to the speed and height of fighter combat, witnesses are hard to find, supporting evidence being a prerequisite. At first Nick got into trouble for being improperly dressed, because he refused to stitch the maroon ribbon onto his tunic. In the end I think he adopted the attitude that he was accepting the medal on behalf of us all. He was a good sport, in fact, and we enjoyed playing together in the four-piece band that we formed with other wounded pilots down at Torquay.

Sergeant David Cox, 19 Squadron:

Now you must admit that when we were following Bader on 15 September 1940, all of us arriving together over the capital was pretty inspiring! I well remember the words of Bobby Oxspring, then a flying officer in an 11 Group Spitfire squadron, 66, exclaiming what a wonderful sight it was to see us appear. We must have given the German aircrews, who had been told that we were down to our last handful of fighters, one hell of a shock!

Squadron Leader Harry Fenton, commanding 238 Squadron:

Our routine was to rise before first light, about 0330 hours, have a coffee and then then go to dispersal. We then spent the day there, being scrambled at intervals in either squadron or section strength. We shared Middle Wallop with 609 Squadron and so took it turns to spend every third day down at Warmwell, undertaking convoy protection patrols. That was during the early days, but I was shot down and wounded on 8 August, returning to the squadron on 12 September. By that time, 238 Squadron had been back to Middle Wallop for two days, but we already had two pilots missing from action over 11 Group: David Hughes, an able flight commander, and a Polish pilot, Duszinski, whom I had not met. The tempo of combat had totally changed.

Pilot Officer John Greenwood, 238 Squadron:

I remember being with Sergeant [Ernest] Kee and diving for our lives into cloud. As I recall he copped a little enemy fire and we landed together shortly afterwards, having made no effort to locate the rest of the squadron. Kee's Hurricane had a little fabric missing and a few holes. I had stopped an armour-piercing bullet through my head-armour, the point of which bullet lodged in my neck. It had only just penetrated and was as sharp as a needle. I kept it for many years afterwards as a souvenir.

Sergeant Reg Nutter, 257 Squadron:

For me personally, the Battle of Britain remains a vivid kaleidoscope of memories. I recall trying to warn Pilot Officer [Pilot Officer Cardale] Capon that he was about to be attacked by a 109, but my radio was unserviceable; I remember The Hon[ourable] David Coke returning from a battle over Portsmouth during which a German bullet had nicked him in the little finger of the throttle hand. Once I chased a lone Do 17 reconnaissance bomber in and out of the clouds along the south coast, whilst listening to American jazz music coming over the squadron frequency. Vivid memories all.

Pilot Officer Jerzy Poplawski of 229 Squadron:

The Battle of Britain was the most exciting time of my entire war, although later stages, including the Dieppe landings and D-Day period provide me with unforgettable memories. Although I did not shoot anything down in the Battle of Britain, I did fire at several enemy aircraft. I think I was so excited that I trembled too much, and as a result my aim was not good!

Pilot Officer Valclav Bergman, a Czech, of 310 (Czech) Squadron:

In those heady days I was a mere pilot officer who loved flying, loved the Hurricane and was happy to point my guns at any German target. But my English was limited. I have always had the impression that the initial interception was to be by 11 Group, whilst we of 12 Group were to follow the raiders and destroy as many as possible on their return journey. More than once the Duxford Wing was released for lunch when Douglas Bader 'pegged' into the dining room and shouted 'Come on boys, we are wanted!' That was followed by the clatter of cutlery on the unfinished plates – rush for the door, transport to dispersals, and in fifteen to twenty minutes all twelve Hurricanes of Bader's 242 [Canadian] Squadron took off in formation from the grass airfield, followed by ours of 310; 19 Squadron's Spitfires, based at nearby Fowlmere, would soon appear overhead. Their job was to protect us from enemy fighters whilst our Hurricanes went for the bombers (not that it always worked out like that, though). In mid-September our squadron was engaging a formation of Do 17s when we were jumped by a swarm of Me 109s: I was shot down.

Pilot Officer Richard Jones, 64 Squadron:

When we returned from a sortie, anyone who had been successful in shooting down an enemy aircraft might do a victory roll over the airfield, but these were not encouraged, because you didn't know whether your aircraft had some unseen damage to the flying controls. Immediately we landed, the Intelligence Officer took full details from each pilot regarding what had happened, whilst the groundcrew, who were absolutely marvellous, did a fantastic job of rapidly preparing the aircraft for another immediate take-off.

Squadron Leader George Denholm commanding 603 Squadron:

We had to learn quickly and rapidly determined not to allow ourselves to be bounced. I therefore decided to fly on a reciprocal of the course provided by the ground controller, until at 15,000 feet, when the squadron would turn about, climbing all the time. Flying in this way meant that we usually saw the enemy striking inland beneath us, and were therefore better positioned to attack. We also ensured that pilots always flew in pairs, for mutual protection. After an action, though, the squadron would come home individually, in ones and twos, at intervals of about two minutes. In addition to leading the squadron in the air, my duties also included checking who was missing after each action, which I generally did an hour after the end of the patrol. In that time, a call would often come in from a pilot who had baled out or landed elsewhere.

Pilot Officer Lionel 'Buck' Casson, 616 Squadron:

We were a confident lot. Up north we had chased about after reconnaissance jobs and enjoyed great success during the '*Junkers Party*' off Flamborough Head. We thought air-fighting was pretty straight forward, I suppose. When we were posted to Kenley, the squadron went off, and I just said 'Cheerio, see you later', as I was to follow with a replacement Spitfire we were awaiting. How naïve. Very few of us were to survive the next fortnight.'

Flight Lieutenant Wallace 'Jock' Cunningham DFC, 19 Squadron:

Lord Dowding's is the big success story here – a strong man who had resisted political pressure to throw away a lot more fighters in France for a battle already lost. He was preserving Fighter Command for the battle to come. Again, a success story in the Battle of Britain. Clearly, his was the credit for the strategy. He listened, said little but acted decisively. I had direct experience of his quick and clear thinking when our 20 mm cannons were performing badly; he visited the Squadron, heard what we had to say, and within hours we were re-equipping with machine-gun Spitfires. So, treasure the memory of 'Stuffy' Dowding – do not sell him short. His was the victory in directing and sustaining his 'Twelve Legions of Angels'.

The last word goes to Squadron Leader Geoffrey Wellum DFC, 92 Squadron:

People say to me 'How do you remember these things?' How do you expect me to forget? You can't. I can remember it vividly, see things, see people, see aeroplanes. The experiences of being a Spitfire fighter pilot in the Battle of Britain stay with you forever. You can't do anything about it. 'I asked myself 'Was it worth it?' All those young men I fought and flew with, all those chaps no longer with us. I asked myself that question and I can't answer it. I suppose it must have been. I am still struggling.

Appendix

The Hawker Hurricane
and Supermarine Spitfire
in the Battle of Britain

During the Battle of Britain, Fighter Command was equipped with two thirds more Hawker Hurricanes than Supermarine Spitfires. The reason for this was that the Hurricane had flown and entered production first, and Supermarine was too small a concern to mass produce the Spitfire in the numbers now required – this subsequently being addressed by the huge Castle Bromwich Aeroplane Factory. The popular narrative of the Battle of Britain tells us that the Hurricane destroyed more enemy aircraft than all the other defences combined, and states the case that the more charismatic Spitfire achieved less – but walked off with the glory.

But is this true? What does the actual evidence tell us? As this investigation has emphasised, there is a gulf of difference between a combat claim and an actual aerial victory, sometimes the ratio being as much as, or more than, seven to one. Considering that there were so many more Hurricanes than Spitfires, that being so, it would naturally be the case that the Hurricane squadrons would submit more claims than the less numerous Spitfire force.

Officially, according to the Air Ministry, one of the main reasons for the Luftwaffe's defeat in the Battle of Britain was its

> failure to take sufficient account of the fighting qualities of the Spitfire and Hurricane, which had first become evident in France and over Dunkirk. The single and twin-engined fighter force employed in the Battle of Britain – which was thought to be ample in strength – was consequently outclassed by those very fighting qualities in combination with the British system of plotting and fighter control.

Indeed, the German bomber and fighter crews morale was 'badly shaken by the superiority of the Spitfire', so there is no doubt regarding which of the British machines was feared most. Nonetheless, to Battle of Britain Hurricane pilot and squadron commander Group Captain Peter Townsend it rankled that the Me 109 pilots treated Hurricanes with 'contempt'. He countered,

> We thought they were great and we would prove it by shooting down around 1,000 Luftwaffe aircraft in the Battle. The Luftwaffe airmen often

mistook Hurricanes for Spitfires. There was the crew of their famous *Heinkel* which 'landed in the sea' on Wick airfield, who swore a Spitfire had downed them. During the Battle of France, Theo Osterkamp seemed to see Spitfires everywhere. There were no Spitfires in France, only Hurricanes. Even *General* Kesselring said, 'Only the Spitfires bothered us'. The Luftwaffe seemed to be suffering from Spitfire snobbery.

Be that as it may, the following statement by *Leutnant* Heinz Knocke of 1/JG 52 is telling: 'We consider shooting down a Spitfire to be an outstanding achievement, which it most certainly is.' There was clearly more prestige attached to destroying a Spitfire than a Hurricane. This is clear when analysing German combat claims: an impossibly high proportion of Spitfires claimed destroyed when the actual size of the Spitfire force in action over southern England is considered.

Primary sources are obviously of crucial importance in any attempt to cross-reference combat claims against losses. In the case of Fighter Command, historians have access to many such records preserved at The National Archives. These include group, squadron and pilots' personal combat reports, ORBs, details of losses and intelligence reports. German records, however, are inevitably incomplete. The principal source concerning losses is the Luftwaffe quartermaster general's loss returns, or more accurately *Oberbefehlsaber der Luftwaffe Genst. Gen. Qu./6 Abteilung/40.g.Kdos.I.C.*, which is available to researchers at the Imperial War Museum. These records are not for propaganda purposes but internal audit and as such they are considered reasonably accurate. German fighter combat claims can be found in the OKL records of the *Chef für Ausz. und Dizsiplin Luftwaffen-Personalamt L.P. (A) V*, preserved in Germany. The information contained, however, comprises basic details regarding the victory claimant's identity, unit, time, date and place of the combat concerned, and the type of enemy aircraft involved. Unfortunately German pilots' individual combat reports – comparable to Fighter Command's 'Form "F"', have not survived.

The compilation of accurate statistics concerning the losses and *claims* of both sides during the Battle of Britain is relatively straightforward, however. My own research with German combat claims, for example, reveals the following:

TABLE ONE
German Claims for Hurricanes and Spitfires Destroyed 10 July 1940–31 October 1940

10 July 1940–31 July 1940
Hurricanes destroyed by 109s: 33
Hurricanes destroyed by 110s: 9
Total Hurricanes destroyed: 42

Spitfires destroyed by 109s: 68
Spitfires destroyed by 110s: 13
Total Spitfires destroyed: 81

1 August 1940–31 August 1940
Hurricanes destroyed by 109s: 262
Hurricanes destroyed by 110s: 30
Total Hurricanes destroyed: 292

Spitfires destroyed by 109s: 362
Spitfires destroyed by 110s: 88
Total Spitfires destroyed: 450

1 September 1940–30 September 1940
Hurricanes destroyed by 109s: 238
Hurricanes destroyed by 110s: 11
Total Hurricanes destroyed: 249

Spitfires destroyed by 109s: 458
Spitfires destroyed by 110s: 104
Total Spitfires destroyed: 562

1 October 1940–31 October 1940
Hurricanes destroyed by 109s: 127
Hurricanes destroyed by 110s: 1
Total Hurricanes destroyed: 128

Spitfires destroyed by 109s: 129
Spitfires destroyed by 110s: 7
Total Spitfires destroyed: 136

Overall total of Hurricanes destroyed by Me 109s: 660
Overall total of Hurricanes destroyed by Me 110s: 51
Total Hurricanes destroyed: 711

Overall total of Spitfires destroyed by Me 109s: 1,017
Overall total of Spitfires destroyed by Me 110s: 212

Total Spitfires destroyed: 1,229

Total number of Spitfires and Hurricanes destroyed: 1,940

Table One is illuminating. Firstly, we know that there were more Hurricanes than Spitfires. Taking the usually quoted figure of 33 Hurricane squadrons and given an operational number of 12 aircraft per unit, we arrive at the figure of 396 Hurricanes. Using the accepted number of 19 Spitfire squadrons, applying the same calculation arrives at 228 Spitfires. This, however, relates to all of Fighter Command, not just 11 Group, which area concerns the majority of German claims for single-engined RAF fighters. On the 8 August 1940, for example, the Fighter Command Order of Battle indicates fifteen Spitfire squadrons and twenty-one of Hurricanes in 10, 11 and 12 Groups. This represents a total (again assuming an operational strength of 12 aircraft per unit) of 180 Spitfires and 252 Hurricanes: a ratio of one to four in the Hurricanes favour. The German claims, though, confirm that their Me 109 and Me 110 crews were seven times more likely to claim a Spitfire destroyed than a Hurricane. Given the Spitfire's technical superiority over the Hurricane, and evidence provided by following tables, this is impossible. It does, however, confirm Peter Townsend's suggestion of 'Spitfire Snobbery' and the fact that greater prestige was attributed to the destruction of a Spitfire. The Order of Battle referred to is also of interest, confirming as it does that all but two of Dowding's Spitfire squadrons were in 10, 11 and 12 Groups, whilst 13 Group was also equipped with eight Hurricane squadrons. This also confirms the fact that, because of their superior performance, it was Spitfires that Air Chief Marshal Hugh Dowding needed in the front line – not Hurricanes.

Next, actual Hurricane losses are examined.

TABLE TWO
Hurricane losses 10 July 1940–31 October 1940
NB: Number of German combat claims shown in brackets.

10 July 1940–31 July 1940
Total destroyed in combat: 25 (German claims = 42)
Total damaged in combat: 24
Total destroyed by Me 109s: 14 (33)
Total damaged by Me 109s: 10
Total destroyed by Me 110s: NIL (9)
Total damaged by Me 110s: 4
Total destroyed by bombers: 9
Total damaged by bombers: 9
Total destroyed by friendly fire: nil
Total damaged by friendly fire: 1
Misc: 1 destroyed in collision with an Me 109 and 1 destroyed by He 115

1 August 1940–31 August 1940
Total destroyed in combat: 124 (292)
Total damaged in combat: 100
Total destroyed by Me 109s: 77 (262)
Total damaged by Me 109s: 38
Total destroyed by Me 110s: 24 (30)
Total damaged by Me 110s: 18
Total destroyed by bombers: 20
Total damaged by bombers: 42

Total destroyed by friendly fire: 3
Total damaged by friendly fire: 2

1 September 1940–30 September 1940
Total destroyed in combat: 200 (249)
Total damaged in combat: 149
Total destroyed by Me 109s: 113 (238)
Total damaged by Me 109s: 63
Total destroyed by Me 110s: 21 (11)
Total damaged by Me 110s: 22
Total destroyed by bombers: 35
Total damaged by bombers: 28
Total Destroyed by friendly fire: 2
Total Damaged by friendly fire: 5
Misc: 29 destroyed in combat but unable to account for loss by enemy aircraft
    type and 31 as above

1 October 1940–31 October 1940
Total destroyed in combat: 57 (128)
Total damaged in combat: 24
Total destroyed by Me 109s: 45 (127)
Total damaged by Me 109s: 23
Total destroyed by Me 110s: 5 (7)
Total damaged by Me 110s: 0
Total destroyed by bombers: 3
Total damaged by bombers: 1
Total destroyed by friendly fire: 0
Total damaged by friendly fire: 0
Misc: 4 destroyed in combat but unable to account for loss by enemy aircraft
    type
Total number of Hurricanes lost 10 July 1940–31 October 1940: 406
Total number of Hurricanes claimed by the Luftwaffe: 711
Table Two indicates an over-claiming factor of 1.75 in the case of Hurricanes.

TABLE THREE
Spitfire Losses 10 July 1940–31 October 1940
NB: Number of German Combat Claims shown in brackets.

10 July 1940–31 July 1940
Total destroyed in combat: 20 (81)
Total damaged in combat: 39
Total destroyed by Me 109s: 19 (68)
Total damaged by Me 109s: 16
Total destroyed by Me 110s: nil (13)
Total damaged by Me 110s: nil

Total destroyed by bombers: 1
Total damaged by bombers: 22
Damaged by unknown enemy aircraft type: 1

1 August 1940–31 August 1940
Total destroyed in combat: 108 (450)
Total damaged in combat: 86
Total destroyed by Me 109s: 78 (362)
Total damaged by Me 109s: 52
Total destroyed by Me 110s: 6 (88)
Total damaged by Me 110s: 7
Total destroyed by bombers: 12
Total damaged by bombers: 21
Destroyed by unknown enemy aircraft type: 8
Damaged by unknown enemy aircraft type: 6
Total destroyed by friendly fire: 2
Total destroyed by seaplanes: 2

1 September 1940–30 September 1940
Total destroyed in combat: 111 (562)
Total damaged in combat: 100
Total destroyed by Me 109s: 86 (458)
Total damaged by Me 109s: 60
Total destroyed by Me 110s: 6 (104)
Total damaged by Me 110s: 11
Total destroyed by bombers: 10
Total damaged by bombers: 22
Destroyed by unknown enemy aircraft type: 9
Damaged by unknown enemy aircraft type: 17
Misc: 1 destroyed in collision with Me 110

1 October 1940–31 October 1940
Total destroyed in combat: 37 (136)
Total damaged in combat: 38
Total destroyed by Me 109s: 33 (129)
Total damaged by Me 109s: 26
Total destroyed by Me 110s: nil (7)
Total damaged by Me 110s: 3
Total destroyed by bombers: 7
Total damaged by bombers: 2
Total destroyed by friendly fire: 1
Destroyed by unknown enemy aircraft type: 2
Damaged by unknown enemy aircraft type: 2

Total Spitfires lost 10 July 1940–31 October 1940: 276

Total Spitfires claimed by Luftwaffe: 1,229

Table Three indicates an over-claim of 4.45 in respect of Spitfires. Given the actual losses and size of the Spitfire force, the number of Spitfires claimed destroyed by the Germans are impossible. The combined number of Spitfires and Hurricanes lost, ironically given the year involved, was 1, 940, indicating an actual *Luftwaffe* over-claiming factor of 2.84. This figure concerns the claims of both German fighters and bombers, however. The 109 pilots claimed a total of 1, 017 Spitfires destroyed, whereas 216 were actually destroyed by them: an over-claim of 4.7. The 109s claimed 660 Hurricanes but actually destroyed 249 – an over-claim of only 2.6. The predominance of Spitfire claims is again immediately apparent – even though there were thirty-three less Spitfires actually destroyed. In total, the 109 pilots claimed to have destroyed a combined total of 1,667 Spitfires and Hurricanes. Only 465 of both types were actually destroyed by 109 pilots, representing an overall over-claiming factor of 3.58. This, though, is more accurate than Fighter Command's overall average of five to one. It could be argued, of course, that the Big Wing disproportionately increased Fighter Command's claims, but that formation only went into action, in fact, on a handful of occasions. Moreover, the German fighters frequently operated in similarly sized *Gruppe* formations, and we know that the more aircraft are involved, the greater the overclaiming factor generally is. In sum, although this study of German claims against RAF losses indicates an inaccurate and disproportionate inclination towards claiming Spitfires, the information is of no use in trying to confirm which of the two British fighter types was more effective during the Battle of Britain.

It is next necessary to reverse the foregoing process and consider RAF combat claims against German losses.

TABLE FOUR
German Combat Losses July–October 1940
NB: The nil return on *Stukas* in September and October is because this type was withdrawn from operations after the heavy losses suffered in August.

July 1940
Bombers: 76
Me 110s: 19
Me 109s: 34
Stukas: 12

August 1940
Bombers: 183
Me 110s: 114

Me 109s: 177
Stukas: 47

September 1940
Bombers: 165
Me 110s: 81
Me 109s: 187
Stukas: nil

October 1940
Bombers: 64
Me 110s: 10
Me 109s: 104
Stukas: nil

Totals
Bombers: 488
Me 110s: 224
Me 109s: 502
Stukas: 59

Grand total: 1,273
Total claimed by Spitfires and Hurricanes: 2,051

The overall over-claim represented by Table Four is 1.6. The actual losses of 1,273 did not arise simply from combat with Spitfires and Hurricanes, however. Other RAF aircraft types, such as the Defiant and Blenheim also contributed to this figure, as indeed did *General* Pile's anti-aircraft defences. Much more research is therefore required before a definitive figure can be provided regarding the over-claiming factor applied to Spitfire and Hurricane pilots overall. Moreover, it is impossible to say from the information available exactly how many of each enemy type was lost to Spitfires or Hurricanes. It will never, therefore, be known how many enemy aircraft, and of which type, Spitfires and Hurricanes actually destroyed – not claimed. Nonetheless, it is interesting to review the claims of Hurricane and Spitfire pilots.

TABLE FIVE
Hurricane Combat Claims: 10 July 1940–31 October 1940

10 July 1940–31 July 1940
Bombers: 34
Me 110s: 15
Me 109s: 29
Stukas: 13

1 August 1940–31 August 1940
Bombers: 94
Me 110s: 132
Me 109s: 148
Stukas: 77

1 September 1940–30 September 1940
Bombers: 156
Me 110s: 140
Me 109s: 188
Stukas: nil

1 October 1940–31 October 1940
Bombers: 23
Me 110s: 10
Me 109s: 65
Stukas: nil

Totals
Bombers: 297
Me 110s: 292
Me 109s: 430
Stukas: 90
Grand total: 1,109

TABLE SIX
Spitfire Combat Claims: 10 July 1940–31 October 1940

10 July 1940–31 July 1940
Bombers: 17
Me 110s: 5
Me 109s: 36
Stukas:6

1 August 1940–31 August 1940
Bombers: 99
Me 110s: 68
Me 109s: 174
Stukas:33

1 September 1940–30 September 1940
Bombers: 152
Me 110s: 65
Me 109s: 193
Stukas: nil

1 October 1940–31 October 1940
Bombers: 13
Me 110s: 6
Me 109s: 85
Stukas: nil

Totals
Bombers: 271
Me 110s: 144
Me 109s: 488
Stukas: 39

Grand total: 942

Although the foregoing are claims, as opposed to actual victories, there are some interesting facts arising. Firstly, if the old myth was true regarding the more numerous Hurricanes having destroyed more enemy aircraft than all other British defences combined, it could reasonably be expected that the pilots of that type would have claimed substantially more victories than the less numerous Spitfire pilots. They did not. The total number of enemy aircraft claimed by Hurricane pilots was 1,109 – only 167 more than the Spitfire pilots. This statistic alone suggests that the Hurricane did not, in fact, destroy more enemy machines than the other combined defences. In fact the Spitfire's record, considering that on 8 August 1940 there were 62 more Hurricanes and 168 more of that type in Fighter Command overall, is beginning to look distinctly impressive – even allowing for an over-claiming factor of 5:1. Applying that formula to the Hurricane claims reduces the number of claims to a more realistic 221, the Spitfire 188 – just 33 less than the more numerous Hurricanes. If the generally accepted Fighter Command totals are used, of nineteen Spitfire squadrons and thirty-three of Hurricanes, 228 and 396 aircraft, the respective figures are 0.87 and 0.55–0.32 in the Spitfire's favour. Although these figures are essentially hypothetical, arguably they are likely to be fairly accurate. The less numerous Spitfire, therefore, emerges in the lead – firmly challenging the established narrative.

Statistics, however, must always be treated with great caution. In 1996, the American researcher John Alcorn published his 'statistical study of the Battle of Britain' in the former *Aeroplane Monthly* magazine, which, he believed, 'sheds new light on that epic action'. Alcorn claimed that 'By collating information regarding times, locations and targets, it was possible to link German losses and R.A.F. claims'. Whilst it is certainly possible to cross-reference certain claims with actual losses, as has been explained this does not relate to the majority of combat claims. Given the great difficulties already outlined concerning research of this nature, and given the quantity of claims by Spitfire and Hurricane pilots (2,051 combined, see Tables Five and Six), it can only be considered astonishing that Alcorn claimed to have cross-referenced all but thirty combat claims to actual German losses. Of interest is that his analysis of enemy losses to fighter action arrived at a figure of 1,218, which is more likely than not a reasonably accurate figure. Of great concern, however, is that Alcorn established an over-claiming factor of 'almost exactly two-to-one'. This figure is contrary to British historian John Foreman's assessment of it being on average nearer five to one, with which I concur from my own researches. Nonetheless, Dr Alfred Price commented on Alcorn's article, highlighting that 'Of the ten top-scoring units, six flew Spitfires. In the top 26 units, Spitfires and Hurricanes feature in exactly equal numbers.' Writing of his own findings whilst researching the events of 18 August 1940, Price wrote that 'the two fighter types were roughly equal in their ability to shoot down enemy aircraft. However, compared with the Spitfire, in combat, the Hurricane with its lower performance stood nearly twice the risk of being shot down.'

The New Zealand ace Air Commodore Alan Deere flew Spitfires with 54 Squadron during the Battle of Britain, achieving twenty-two kills – all made in Spitfires – by the war's end. He wrote,

> There can be no doubt that victory in the Battle of Britain was made possible by the Spitfire. Although there were more Hurricanes than Spitfires in the Battle, the Spitfire was the R.A.F.'s primary weapon because of its better all-round capability. The Hurricane alone could not have won this great air battle, but the Spitfire could have done so.

There is no question that this extremely experienced Spitfire pilot and fighter leader was absolutely right. As has been explained, the Spitfire performed well at all altitudes, even as high as 30,000ft, whereas the Hurricane could not. Had Fighter Command only been equipped with Hurricanes, therefore, it would have been decimated by the high-flying 109s, which would always have enjoyed the height advantage. In practice, the Hurricane was able to attack bombers because the Spitfire provided a protective high-altitude fighter screen – but the Spitfire could do both. To put the late Air Commodore Deere's comment into context, he did not mean that in 1940 Fighter Command did not need the Hurricane. Dowding made it clear that he required a minimum of fifty-two squadrons with which to defend the British Isles. Nineteen of Spitfires and thirty-three of Hurricanes gave him exactly the required fifty-two. Nineteen Spitfire squadrons alone, regardless of the aircraft's performance, were not enough, therefore, so the Hurricane was desperately needed in the absence of more Spitfires. So, whilst the claim that the Hurricane executed greater damage upon the enemy is a demonstrable myth, the fact is that in 1940 the Hurricane was equally essential to the defence of this country.

Acknowledgements

This unique series of books has arisen from over forty years of research and study of the subject, throughout which time I enjoyed a privileged relationship with survivors and the relatives of casualties – too many to thank individually, but all have my appreciation.

In relation to this special project, I must thank Charles Hewitt, Martin Mace and Matthew Potts of Pen & Sword, and the production and marketing teams, who are always a pleasure to work with and collectively do a first-class job. Martin, of course, deserves a special mention for his sterling work on my behalf at The National Archives, and for being a very good friend and kindred spirit, always helpful and sharing my passion for making history both accessible and inclusive.

Suffice it to say, it has been an absolute privilege to produce this work for the Battle of Britain Memorial Trust and National Memorial to 'The Few', and I must thank our Chairman, Richard Hunting CBE, Honorary Secretary, Group Captain Patrick Tootal OBE DL RAF, Trustee Wing Commander Andrew Simpson RAFVR(T), Major (Ret'd) Jules Gomez, Site Manager, National Memorial to 'The Few', and both Malcolm Triggs and Becca Collier-Cook for their help in promoting the work. I would also acknowledge kind assistance from Edward McManus of the Battle of Britain London Monument.

All of the pilots, other survivors and eyewitnesses mentioned in this book are all now sadly deceased – but all have my enduring gratitude for so kindly supporting my work many years ago, and helping me reconstruct the dramatic past.

As always, my old friend Andy Long was ever-helpful, as, in relation to this particular volume, were Peter Taghon, the sadly now late Allan White, Georgia Stone and Sarah Halil.

Finally, I must reserve a special thanks to my wife, Sue. This particular eight-volume project is an unprecedent investigation into the Battle of Britain, from many angles, and the process is intense. The forbearance of my family, especially Sue, and friends, therefore, is essential, and I am also grateful for the interest and support reflected by my Facebook and other social media followings.

Bibliography

The National Archives

The National Archives at Kew is the main repository for primary source documents; the following documents were consulted during the course of research for this book.

Operations Record Books

AIR25/219: HQ No 12 Group
AIR27/2018: 'A' Flight, Photographic Reconnaissance Unit
AIR27/2015: 'B' Flight, Photographic Reconnaissance Unit
AIR27/589: 1 Squadron
AIR27/528: 1 (RCAF) Squadron (Listed as 401 Squadron by TNA)
AIR27/32: 3 Squadron
AIR27/164: 12 Squadron
AIR27/202: 15 Squadron
AIR27/252: 19 Squadron
AIR27/287: 23 Squadron
AIR27: 305: 25 Squadron
AIR27/317: 26 Squadron
AIR27/341: 29 Squadron
AIR27/360: 32 Squadron
AIR27/435: 42 Squadron
AIR27/441: 43 Squadron
AIR27/447: 44 Squadron
AIR27/460: 46 Squadron
AIR27/554: 50 Squadron
AIR27/503: 53 Squadron
AIR27/511: 54 Squadron
AIR27/528: 56 Squadron
AIR27/554: 59 Squadron
AIR27/598: 66 Squadron
AIR27/624: 72 Squadron
AIR27/629: 73 Squadron
AIR27/640: 74 Squadron
AIR27/655: 77 Squadron
AIR27/664: 79 Squadron
AIR27/681: 82 Squadron

AIR27/712: 87 Squadron
AIR27/783: 91 Squadron (421 Flight)
AIR27/764: 96 Squadron (422 Flight)
AIR27/776: 97 Squadron
AIR27/801: 101 Squadron
AIR27/807: 102 Squadron
AIR27/813: 103 Squadron
AIR27/826: 105 Squadron
AIR27/841: 107 Squadron
AIR27/857: 110 Squadron
AIR27/866: 111 Squadron
AIR27/882: 114 Squadron
AIR27/969: 141 Squadron
AIR27/984: 145 Squadron
AIR27/1008: 150 Squadron
AIR27/1025: 152 Squadron
AIR27/1298: 210 Squadron
AIR27/1315: 213 Squadron
AIR27/1340: 217 Squadron
AIR27/1360: 219 Squadron
AIR27/1365: 220 Squadron
AIR27/1371: 222 Squadron
AIR27/1385: 224 Squadron
AIR27/1428: 232 Squadron
AIR27/1442: 235 Squadron
AIR27/1445: 236 Squadron
AIR27/1453: 238 Squadron
AIR27/1471: 242 (Canadian) Squadron
AIR27/1481: 245 Squadron
AIR27/1495: 248 Squadron
AIR27/1498: 249 Squadron
AIR27/1511: 253 Squadron
AIR27/1526: 257 Squadron
AIR27/1553: 264 Squadron
AIR27/1558: 266 Squadron
AIR27/1661: 302 (Polish) Squadron
AIR27/1663: 303 (Polish) Squadron
AIR27/1680: 310 (Czech) Squadron
AIR27/1691: 312 Squadron
AIR27/1941: 500 Squadron
AIR27/1949: 501 Squadron
AIR27/1964: 504 Squadron
AIR27/2059: 600 Squadron
AIR27/2068: 601 Squadron
AIR27/2028: 604 Squadron
AIR27/2088: 605 Squadron
AIR27/2093: 607 Squadron
AIR27/2102: 609 Squadron
AIR27/2106: 610 Squadron

AIR27/2112: 612 Squadron
AIR27/2123: 615 Squadron
AIR27/2126: 616 Squadron
AIR27/2263: 928 Squadron

Pilots' Combat Reports

AIR50/1: 1 Squadron
AIR50/4: 3 Squadron
AIR50/9: 17 Squadron
AIR50/10: 19 Squadron
AIR50: 29 Squadron
AIR50/16: 32 Squadron
AIR50/18: 41 Squadron
AIR50/19: 43 Squadron
AIR50/20: 46 Squadron
AIR50/21: 54 Squadron
AIR50/22: 56 Squadron
AIR50/24: 64 Squadron
AIR50/25: 65 Squadron
AIR50/26: 66 Squadron
AIR50/31: 73 Squadron
AIR50/32: 74 Squadron
AIR50/33: 79 Squadron
AIR50/36: 85 Squadron
AIR50/37: 87 Squadron
AIR50/40: 92 Squadron
AIR50/43: 111 Squadron
AIR50/62: 145 Squadron
AIR50/63: 151 Squadron
AIR50/64: 152 Squadron
AIR50/83: 213 Squadron
AIR50/84: 219 Squadron
AIR50/85: 222 Squadron
AIR50/88: 232 Squadron
AIR50/89: 234 Squadron
AIR50/91: 238 Squadron
AIR50/92: 242 (Canadian) Squadron
AIR50/96: 249 Squadron
AIR50/100: 257 Squadron
AIR50/104: 264 Squadron
AIR50/105: 266 Squadron
AIR50/116: 302 (Polish) Squadron
AIR50/177: 303 (Polish) Squadron
AIR50/122: 310 (Czech) Squadron
AIR50/123: 312 Squadron
AIR50/163: 504 Squadron
AIR50/165: 601 Squadron

AIR50/166: 602 Squadron
AIR50/167: 603 Squadron
AIR50/171: 609 Squadron
AIR50/173: 611 Squadron
AIR50/172: 610 Squadron
AIR50/175: 615 Squadron
AIR50/176: 616 Squadron
AIR50/473: 7 Operational Training Unit

Casualty Files

AIR81/3642: LAC A. Mackley
AIR81/3656: Sergeant J.M. Strawson
AIR81/3660: Pilot Officer A.R. Covington

Miscellaneous Documents

AIR22/296: Personnel: Casualties, Strength and Establishment of the RAF
AIR22/14: War Room Daily Summaries, October 1940
AIR16/300: German bomber tactics
CAB66/12/38: Loss of Time Due to Air Raid Warnings

RAF Station Operations Record Books

AIR28/64: RAF Biggin Hill
AIR28/178: RAF Croydon
AIR28/345: RAF Hawkinge
AIR28/384: RAF Hornchurch
AIR28/512: RAF Manston
AIR28/526: RAF Martlesham Heath
AIR28/419: RAF Kenley
AIR28/509: RAF Lympne
AIR28/601: RAF Northolt
AIR28/815: RAF Tangmere
AIR28/907: RAF West Malling
AIR28/603: RAF North Weald

Ministry of Home Security Daily Intelligence Reports

HO203/4: 24/06/40–29/09/40
HO203/5: 29/09/40–31/12/40

Magazines

Aeroplane Monthly
American Life
Der Adler

Newspapers

London Gazette, 20 August 1941
Rushden Echo & Argus, 4 October 1940
Worcester News & Times, 4 October 1940

Pilots' Flying Log Books (ranks as at time consulted)

Air Vice-Marshal Sir Keith Park (courtesy RNZAF Museum)
Wing Commander H. Broadhurst
Squadron Leader D.R.S. Bader, 242 (Canadian) Squadron (courtesy RAF Museum)
Squadron Leader R.G. Kellett, 303 (Polish) Squadron
Squadron Leader H.C. Burton, 66 and 616 Squadrons
Squadron Leader B.J.E. Lane DFC, 19 Squadron (AIR4/58)
Squadron Leader W.J. Lawson (TNA, AIR4/6)
Flight Lieutenant G.C. Matheson, 222 Squadron
Flight Lieutenant E. Thomas, 222 Squadron
Flight Lieutenant F.M. Thomas, 56 Squadron
Flying Officer I.M. Hallam, 222 Squadron
Pilot Officer R.J.E. Boulding, 74 Squadron
Pilot Officer D. Crowley-Milling, 242 (Canadian) Squadron
Pilot Officer H.S.L. Dundas, 616 Squadron
Pilot Officer D.M.C. Crook DFC, 609 Squadron (AIR4/21)
Pilot Officer F.W. Higginson DFM, 56 Squadron
Pilot Officer J.E. Johnson, 616 Squadron
Pilot Officer R.L. Jones, 19 and 64 Squadron
Pilot Officer A.G. Osmand, 213 Squadron
Pilot Officer A.F. Vokes, 19 Squadron
Flight Sergeant G.C. Unwin DFM, 19 Squadron
Sergeant B.J. Jennings, 19 Squadron

German Documents

OKW Directives for Invasion of the UK, Operation *Seelöwe*, summer and autumn 1940, Bundesarchiv
Luftflotte 2 and 3 records, available via Digital History Archive (see website detailed below)
German fighter combat claims can be found in the OKL records of the Chef für Ausz. und Dizsiplin Luftwaffe-Personalamt LP(A)V (available via various online sources)
German loss records can be found in the Oberfehlsaber der Luftwaffe Genst. Gen. Qu/6 Abteilung/40.g. Kdos.I.C, records, preserved by the Imperial War Museum.

Miscellaneous Sources

Interview of Air Chief Marshal Sir Keith Park: BBC Archive / British Library 01 January 1961 http://www.bbc.co.uk/archive/battleofbritain/11422.shtml
The Bader Papers, The Douglas Bader Foundation

Taped interview of Group Captain Sir Douglas Bader by Dr Alfred Price (undated)
Air Vice-Marshal J.E. Johnson Papers
Air Marshal Sir Denis Crowley-Milling Papers
Sayer Archive
Woodhall, Group Captain A.B., *Soldier, Sailor, Airman Too*, unpublished memoir
Correspondence, papers and interviews, Dilip Sarkar Archive
Original and uncensored manuscript of Spitfire Pilot, Flight Lieutenant D.M. Crook DFC
Unpublished memoir of Group Captain R.G. Kellett

Published Sources

Ackroyd, P., *London: The Biography*, Chatto & Windus, London, 2000

Adams, P., *Hurricane Squadron: 87 Squadron at War 1939–1941*, Air Research Publications, New Malden, 1988

Aders, G. and Held, W., *Chronik: Jagdgeschwader 51 'Mölders'*, Motor Buch Verlag, Stuttgart, 2009

Addison, P., and Crang, J.A. (eds.), *The Burning Blue: A New History of the Battle of Britain*, Pimlico, London, 2000

Addison, P., and Crang, J.A. (eds.), *Listening to Britain: Home Intelligence Reports on Britain's Finest Hour – May to September 1940*, Vintage Books, London, 2011

Addison, P. and Crang, J., *The Spirit of the Blitz: Home Intelligence and British Morale, September 1940–June 1941*, Oxford University Press, Oxford, 2020

Alexander, K., *Australia's Few and the Battle of Britain*, Pen & Sword Books Limited, Barnsley, 2015

Allen, Wing Commander H.R., *Fighter Squadron: A Memoir 1940–42*, Granada, London, 1982

Anon., *The Battle of Britain: August–October 1940*, Ministry of Information on behalf of the Air Ministry, London, 1941

Anon., *The Battle of Britain*, Air Ministry Pamphlet 156, Issued by the Department of the Air Member for Training, August 1943

Anon., (MoI), *Roof Over Britain: The Official Story of The AA Defences 1939–1942*, HMSO, London, 1943

Anon., *Air/Sea Rescue: The Second World War 1939–1945*, Royal Air Force, Air Publication 3232, Air Ministry (AHB), London, 1952

Anon., *The Rise & Fall of the German Air Force 1939–45*, Air Ministry Pamphlet 248, Public Record Office, London, 2001

Ashworth, C., *RAF Coastal Command: 1936–1969*, PSL, Sparkford, 1992

Balss, M., *Deutsche Luftwaffe Loses & Claims, Part 4-1: 1 September–15 October 1940*, self-published, Tugos, Philipines, no publication date recorded.

Bekker, C., *The Luftwaffe War Diaries*, Corgi Books, London, 1972

Bekker, C., *Hitler's Naval War*, Corgi, London, 1976

Bialer, U., *The Shadow of the Bomber: The Fear of Air Attack and British Politics 1932–39*, Royal Historical Society, London, 1980

Bishop, E., *The Battle of Britain*, George Allen & Unwin Ltd, London, 1960

Boot, H. and Sturtivant, R., *Gifts of War: Spitfires and Other Presentation Aircraft in Two World Wars*, Air Britain (Historians) Limited, Tonbridge, 2005

Bowman, G., *Jump For It! Stories of the Caterpillar Club*, Evans Brothers Limited, London, 1955

Bowyer, M.J.F., *2 Group RAF: A Complete History, 1936–1945*, Faber & Faber, London, 1974

Calder, A., *The People's War: Britain 1939–45*, Pimlico, London, 2008

Caldwell, D., *JG 26: Top Guns of the Luftwaffe*, Orion Books, New York, 1991

Caldwell, D., *The JG 26 War Diary: 1939–42*, Volume 1, Grub Street, London, 1996

Campion, G., *The Good Fight: Battle of Britain Propaganda and The Few*, Palgrave-Macmillan, London, 2010

Cannandine, D. (ed.), *The Speeches of Winston Churchill*, Penguin, London, 1990

Churchill, W.S., *The Second World War, Vol. II, Their Finest Hour*, Cassell & Co., London, 1949

Clapson, M., *Britain in the Twentieth Century*, Routledge, Abingdon, 2009

Collier, B., *The Defence of the United Kingdom*, HMSO, London, 1957

Cox, S. and Probert, H., (eds.), *The Battle Re-Thought: A Symposium on the Battle of Britain*, Airlife, Shrewsbury, 1991

Cox, S., 'RAF & Luftwaffe Intelligence Compared' in Handel, MI (ed.), *Intelligence & Military Operations*, Frank Cass, Abingdon, 1990

Crang, J.A., *Sisters in Arms: Women in the British Armed Forces During the Second World War*, Cambridge University Press, Cambridge, 2020

Dean, Sir M., *The Royal Air Force in Two World Wars*, Cassell, London, 1979

Deere, Air Commodore A.C., *Nine Lives*, Hodder Paperback Limited, London, 1959

Deighton, L., *Fighter: The True Story of the Battle of Britain*, Triad/Panther Books, St Albans, 1979

Dierich, W., *Kampfgeschwader 'Edelweiss': The History of a German Bomber Unit, 1939–45*, Purnell Book Services Ltd, London, 1975

Dierich, W., Chronik: *Kampfgeschwader 55 'Greif'*, Motorbuch Verlag, Stuttgart, 2012

Devon, S., *'Glorious': The Life-story of Stanley Devon, Twice 'British News Photographer of the Year'*, George G. Harrop & Co. Limited, London, 1957

Dimbleby, J., *The Battle of the Atlantic: How The Allies Won The War*, Penguin Books, London, 2016

Donnelly, M., *Britain in the Second World War*, Routledge, London, 1999

Donnelly, L., *The Other Few: The Contribution Made by Bomber and Coastal Aircrew to the Winning of the Battle of Britain*, Red Kite, Walton-on-Thames, 2004

Douglas, S., MRAF Lord Douglas of Kirtleside, with Wright, R., *Years of Command: A Personal Story of the Second World War in the Air*, Collins, London, 1966

Dowding, ACM Lord H.C.T., *Dispatch: The Battle of Britain*, London Gazette, London, 1946

Ellan, Squadron Leader B.J., *Spitfire! The Experiences of a Fighter Pilot*, John Murray, London, 1942

Filton Parish Church, *Remembering Filton: The Air Raid Targeting the Bristol Aeroplane Company (BAC) Factory at Filton, 25th September 1940*, Filton Parish Church with Filton Community History, Filton, 2010

Fleming, P., *Invasion 1940*, Rupert Hard-Davis, London, 1957

Flint, P., *RAF Kenley: The Story of the Royal Air Force Station 1917–1974*, Terence Dalton, Limited, Lavenham, 1985

Forbes, A. and Allen, H.R. (eds.), *Ten Fighter Boys*, Collins, London, 1942

Foreman, J., *RAF Fighter Command Victory Claims of World War Two*, Volume 1, Air Research Publications, Red Kite, Walton-on-Thames, 2003

Forrester, L., *Fly For Your Life: The Story of R.R. Stanford Tuck DSO, DFC and Two Bars*, The Companion Book Club, London, 1956

Francis, M., *The Flyer: British Culture and the Royal Air Force 1939–1945*,Oxford University Press, Oxford, 2011

Galland, A., *The First and the Last: Germany's Fighter Force in the Second World War*, Fontana, London, 1954

Gleave, Group Captain T.P. (writing as 'RAF Casualty'), *I Had a Row with a German*, MacMillan & Co., London, 1941

Gleed, Wing Commander I.R., *Arise to Conquer*, Victor Gollanz Limited, London, 1942

Green, W., *Aircraft of the Battle of Britain*, MacDonald & Co. (Publishers) Limited and Pan Books Limited, London, 1969

Haining, P., *The Chianti Raiders: The Extraordinary Story of the Italian Air Force in the Battle of Britain*, Robson Books, London, 2005

Hallam, I.N., *One of The Few: Ian Lewis McGregor Hallam*, privately published, 2020

Handel, M.I. (ed.), *Intelligence and Military Operations*, Frank Cass, Abingdon, 1990

Honeysett, J., *Death in the Afternoon: The Bombing of Vickers-Supermarine Works, Southampton, September 15th, 24th and 26th 1940*, privately published, Southampton, 2000

Hough, R. and Richards, D., *The Battle of Britain: The Jubilee History*, Hodder & Stoughton Limited, London, 1990

Howes, R.M. and Harley, F.H., *History of the Mining Engineering Company Limited 1909–1959*, MECO, Worcester, 1959

Humphreys, R., *Target Folkestone*, Meresborough Books, Rainham, 1990

Humphreys, R., *Dover at War 1939–1945*, Alan Sutton, Stroud, 1993

James, T.C.G., *The Battle of Britain*, Frank Cass, London, 1990

Jenkins, R., *Churchill*, MacMillan, London 2001

Johnson, AVM J.E., *Wing Leader*, Chatto & Windus Limited, London, 1956

Johnson, AVM J.E., *The Story of Air Fighting*, Hutchinson, London, 1985

Johnstone, AVM A.V.R., *Spitfire into War*, William Kimber & Co. Limited, London, 1986

Jones, Wing Commander I., *Tiger Squadron*, Award Books, New York, United States, 1966

Kesselring, Field-Marshal A., *The Memoirs of Field-Marshal Kesselring*, Greenhill Books, London, 1997

Kershaw, I., *Hitler: 1936–1945, Nemesis*, Penguin Books, London, 2001

King, R., *303 Squadron: Battle of Britain Diary*, Red Kite, Walton-on-Thames, 2010

Kingcome, Group Captain B.F., *A Willingness to Die: Memories From Fighter Command*, Tempus Publishing, Stroud, 1996

Knight, D., *A Harvest of Messerschmitts: The Chronicle of a Village at War, 1940*, Frederick Warne (Publishers) Limited, London, 1981

Legg, R., *Battle of Britain Dorset*, Dorset Publishing Company, Wincanton, 1995

Lisiewicz, Squadron Leader M. (ed.), *Destiny Can Wait: The Polish Air Force in the Second World War*, William Heinemann Ltd, London, 1949

MacDonell, Air Commodore A.R.D. (MacDonell L. and MacKay A, eds.), *From Dogfight to Diplomacy: A Spitfire Pilot's Log 1932–1958*, Pen & Sword Books Limited, Barnsley, 2005

Mason, F.K., *Battle Over Britain*, Aston Publications, Bourne End, 1990

Middlebrook, M. and Everitt, C., *The Bomber Command War Diaries: An Operational Reference Book 1939–1945,* Midland Counties Publications, Hinckley, 1996 (republished by Pen & Sword Books Limited, Barnsley, 2014)

Morgan, E. and Shacklady, E., *Spitfire: The History*, Key Publishing, Stamford, 1987

Moyes, P.J.R., *Bomber Squadrons of the RAF and Their Aircraft*, MacDonald, London, 1964

Muggeridge, M (ed.), *Ciano's Diary 1939–1943*, William Heinemann Limited, London, 1947

Nash, P., *Beachy Head! Angels 20: The Battle of Britain Around Eastbourne Over the Summer of 1940*, privately published, Eastbourne, 2008

Orange, V., *Park: The Biography of Air Chief Marshal Sir Keith Park*, Grub Street, London, 2001

Orange, V., *Dowding of Fighter Command: Victor of the Battle of Britain*, Grubb Street, London, 2008

Overy, R., *The Air War 1939–1945*, first edition, Europa Publications Limited, London, 1980

Overy, R., *The Battle of Britain*, Penguin, London, 2004

Overy, R., *Goering: The Iron Man*, Bloomsbury Revelations, London, 2021

Penny, J., *Bristol at War*, The Derby Books Publishing Company, Derby, 2010

Pilsen, I., *More Memories of Bitterne: Patchwork of People and Places We Loved,* Bitterne Local History Society, Southampton, 1984

Pope, R., *War & Society in Britain 1899–1948*, Longman, Harlow, 1991

Price, A., *Battle of Britain Day: 15 September 1940*, Sidgwick & Jackson, London, 1990

Prien, J., *Jagdgeschwader 53: A History of the 'Pik As' Geschwader*, March 1937–May 1942, Schiffer Publishing Ltd, Sedona, Arizona, United States, 1997

Priestley, J.B., *Postscripts*, William Heinemann Limited, London, 1940

Quill, J.K., *Spitfire*, Arrow Books, London 1985

Ramsay, W. (ed.), *The Battle of Britain: Then & Now*, Mk V Edition, Battle of Britain Prints International Limited, London, 1986

Ramsay, W. (ed.), *The Blitz Then & Now*, Volume I, Battle of Britain Prints International Limited, London, 1989

Rayner, G.H., *One Hurricane: One Raid*, Airlife Publishing Limited, Shrewsbury, 1990

Richards, D., *RAF Bomber Command in the Second World War: The Hardest Victory*, Penguin, London, 2001

RAFHS, *Air Intelligence: A Symposium*, RAFHS, London, 1997

Rootes, A., *Front Line County: Kent at War, 1939–45*, Robert Hale Limited, London, 1980

Roskill, Captain S.W., *The War at Sea 1939–45*, Volume 1, HMSO, London, 1954

Rohwer, J. and Hunnelchen, G., *Chronology of the War at Sea*, Ian Allen Limited, London, 1972

Russell, B., *Which Way to Peace?*, M Joseph Limited, London, 1936

Russell, C.R., *Spitfire Odyssey: My Life at Supermarines 1936–1957*, Kingfisher Railway Productions, Southampton SO2 4BE

Sarkar, D., *Battle of Britain 1940: The Finest Hour's Human Cost*, Pen & Sword Ltd, Barnsley, 2020

Sarkar, D., *Forgotten Heroes of the Battle of Britain*, Pen & Sword Books Limited, Barnsley, 2022

Sarkar, D., *Letters From The Few: Unique Memories From the Battle of Britain*, Pen & Sword Books Limited, Barnsley, 2020

Sarkar, D., *Missing in Action: Resting in Peace?*, Ramrod Publications, Worcester, 1998

Sarkar, D., *Sailor Malan: Freedom Fighter*, Pen & Sword Books Limited, Barnsley, 2021

Sarkar, D., *The Final Few*, Amberley Publishing, Stroud, 2015

Sawyer, Group Captain T., *Only Owls and Bloody Fools Fly at Night*, Crecy Publishing, Manchester, 2000

Schenk, P., *Operation Sealion: The Invasion of England*, Greenhill Books, Barnsley, 2019

Shirer, W.L., *The Rise and Fall of the Third Reich*, Simon & Schuster, New York, United States, 1960

Shores, C. and Williams, C., *Aces High: A Tribute to the Most Notable Fighter Pilots of the British & Commonwealth Forces in WWII*, Grub Street, London, 1994

Shores, C., Cull, B. and Maliza, N., *Malta: The Spitfire Year, 1942*, Grub Street, London, 1991

Smith, M., The RAF. In Addison, J., & Crang, J.A. (eds.), *The Burning Blue: A New History of the Battle of Britain*, Pimlico, London, 2000

Spurdle, B., *The Blue Arena*, William Kimber & Co., London, 1986

Steinhilper, U. and Osborne, P., *Spitfire on My Tail: A View From the Other Side*, Independent Books, Bromley, 1989

Taylor, A.J.P., *English History 1914–1945*, Oxford University Press, Oxford, 1965

Titmuss, Professor R.M., *Problems of Social Policy*, HMSO, London, 1950

Thompson, Wing Commander H.L., *New Zealanders With the RAF*, Volume 1, NZ Electronic Text Collection, Victoria University of Wellington, New Zealand, 2016

Toliver, Colonel R.F., & Constable, TJ, *Fighter Aces of the Luftwaffe*, Schiffer Publishing Ltd, Atglen, PA, United States,1996

Townsend, Group Captain P., *Duel of Eagles: The Classic Account of the Battle of Britain*, Weidenfeld & Nicolson, London, 1990

Townsend, Group Captain P., *Time & Chance: An Autobiography*, Collins, London, 1978

Trevor-Roper, H.R. (ed.), *Hitler's War Directives 1939–45*, Pan Books, London, 1966

Vasco, J.J. and Cornwell, P.D., *Zerstörer: The Messerschmitt 110 and Its Units in 1940*, JAC Publications, Norwich, 1995

Vasco, J., *Bombsights Over England: The History of Erprobungsgruppe 210 Luftwaffe Fighter-Bomber Unit in the Battle of Britain*, JAC Publications, Norwich, 1990

von Below, N. (translated by Brooks, G.), *At Hitler's Side: The Memoirs of Hitler's Luftwaffe Adjutant 1937–1945*, Greenhill Books, London 2001

von Clausewitz, Carl, *Principles of War*, Dover Publications Inc, New York, United States, 2003

Wakefield, K., *Luftwaffe Encore*, William Kimber & Co. Ltd, London, 1979

Wakefield, K., *The First Pathfinders: The Operational History of Kampfgruppe 100*, 1939–1941, Crécy Books, Somerton, 1992

Wallington, N., *Firemen at War: The Work of London's Fire-fighters in the Second World War*, David & Charles, London, 1981

Warner, G., *RAF Biggin Hill: The Immortal Story of One of the Battle of Britain's Most Famous Fighter Stations*, Putnam & Co. Limited, London, 1969

Wellum, Squadron Leader G.H.A., *First Light*, Penguin, London, 2003

Wicks, B., *Waiting For the All Clear: True Stories From Survivors of The Blitz*, Bloombury, London, 1990

Willis, J., *Churchill's Few: The Battle of Britain Remembered*, Guild Publishing, London, 1985

Wheatley, R., *Operation Sealion*, Oxford University Press, Oxford, 1958

Wright, R., *Dowding and the Battle of Britain*, Corgi, London, 1970

Ziegler, F.H., *The Story of 609 Squadron: Under the White Rose*, MacDonald, London, 1971

Ziegler, P., *London at War 1939–1945*, Pimlico, London, 1995

Websites

The National Archives:	www.nationalarchives.gov.uk
Commonwealth War Graves Commission:	www.cwgc.org
Battle of Britain Memorial Trust:	www.battleofbritainmemorial.org
Battle of Britain: The People's Project:	www.battleofbritainthepeoplesproject.com

Dilip Sarkar: www.dilipsarkarauthor.com
Digital History Archive: www.digitalhistoryarchive.com
Kenley Revival Project: www.kenleyrevival.org
Battle of Britain London Monument: www.bbm.org.uk

Films

Battle of Britain, directed by Guy Hamilton (Spitfire Productions, 1969)

Television

The World at War, directed by David Elstein (ITV, 1973)
Churchill's Few, Directed by John Willis (Yorkshire TV, 1985)
First Light, directed by Matthew Whiteman (Lion Television, 2010)

Other Books by Dilip Sarkar

Spitfire Squadron: No. 19 Squadron at War, 1939–41
The Invisible Thread: A Spitfire's Tale
Through Peril to the Stars: RAF Fighter Pilots Who Failed to Return, 1939–45
Angriff Westland: Three Battle of Britain Air Raids Through the Looking Glass
A Few of the Many: Air War 1939-45, A Kaleidoscope of Memories
Bader's Tangmere Spitfires: The Untold Story, 1941
Bader's Duxford Fighters: The Big Wing Controversy
Missing in Action: Resting in Peace?
Guards VC: Blitzkrieg 1940
Battle of Britain: The Photographic Kaleidoscope, Volumes I-IV
Fighter Pilot: The Photographic Kaleidoscope
Group Captain Sir Douglas Bader: An Inspiration in Photographs
Johnnie Johnson: Spitfire Top Gun, Part I
Johnnie Johnson: Spitfire Top Gun, Part II
Battle of Britain: Last Look Back
Spitfire! Courage & Sacrifice
Spitfire Voices: Heroes Remember
The Battle of Powick Bridge: Ambush a Fore-thought
Duxford 1940: A Battle of Britain Base at War
The Few: The Battle of Britain in the Words of the Pilots
Spitfire Manual 1940
The Sinking of HMS Royal Oak *in the Words of the Survivors* (re-print of Hearts of Oak)
The Last of the Few: Eighteen Battle of Britain Pilots Tell Their Extraordinary Stories
Hearts of Oak: The Human Tragedy of HMS Royal Oak
Spitfire Voices: Life as a Spitfire Pilot in the Words of the Veterans
How the Spitfire Won the Battle of Britain
Spitfire Ace of Aces: The True Wartime Story of Johnnie Johnson
Douglas Bader Fighter Ace: The Extraordinary Life of Douglas Bader, Battle of Britain Hero (re-print of above)
Spitfire: The Photographic Biography
Hurricane Manual 1940
River Pike
The Final Few: The Last Surviving Pilots of the Battle of Britain Tell Their Stories
Arnhem 1944: The Human Tragedy of the Bridge Too Far
Spitfire! The Full Story of a Unique Battle of Britain Fighter Squadron
Battle of Britain 1940: The Finest Hour's Human Cost
Letters From The Few: Unique Memories of the Battle of Britain
Johnnie Johnson's 1942 Diary: The War Diary of the Spitfire Ace of Aces

OTHER BOOKS BY DILIP SARKAR

Johnnie Johnson's Great Adventure: The Spitfire Ace of Ace's Last Look Back
Sailor Malan – Freedom Fighter: The Inspirational Story of a Spitfire Ace
Spitfire Ace of Aces – The Album: The Photographs of Johnnie Johnson
The Real Spitfire Pilot, being the previously unpublished original manuscript of Spitfire
    Pilot, by Flight Lieutenant David Crook, with introduction, commentary and photographs
    by Dilip Sarkar
Bader's Big Wing Controversy: Duxford 1940
Bader's Spitfire Wing: Tangmere 1941
Spitfire Down: Fighter Boys Who Failed to Return
Forgotten Heroes of The Battle of Britain
Faces of The Few
Spitfire Faces
Arise to Conquer: The Real Hurricane Pilot by Wing Commander Ian Gleed, introduction,
    commentary and photographs by Dilip Sarkar *Free French Spitfire Hero: The Diaries of*
    and Search for René Mouchotte (with Jan Leeming)
I Had A Row with a German by Group Captain Tom Gleave, introduction by Dilip Sarkar
Battle of Britain: The Finest Hour in Cinema
Battle of Britain: The Movie (contributor to and publisher of the now late Robert Rudhall's
    original edition (2000), and editor and substantial contributor to 2022 revised edition)
Faces of HMS Royal Oak: The 'Mighty Oak' Disaster at Scapa Flow
Battle of Britain, Volume 1: The Gathering Storm – Prelude to the Spitfire Summer of 1940
Battle of Britain, Volume 2: The Breaking Storm – 10 July 1940–12 August 1940
Battle of Britain, Volume 3: Attack of the Eagles – 13 August 1940–18 August 1940
Battle of Britain, Volume 4: Airfields Under Attack – 19 August 1940–6 September 1940
Battle of Volume, 5: Target London – 7 September 1940–17 September 1940
Battle of Britain Volume, 6: Daylight Defeat – 18 September 1940–30 September 1940

Index

INDEX